P9-CEG-973

TEACHER EDUCATION
IN AMERICA

TEACHER EDUCATION IN AMERICA

Reform Agendas for the Twenty-First Century

Christopher J. Lucas

St. Martin's Press
New York

ISBN 0-312-16444-0   **LB
1715
.L73**

Library of Congress Cataloging-in-Publication Data   **1997**

Lucas, Christopher J.
    Teacher education in America : reform agendas for the 21st century / Christopher J. Lucas.
        p. cm.
    Includes bibliographical references and index.
    ISBN 0-312-16444-0
    1. Teachers—Training of—United States. 2. Educational change--United States. I. Title.
LB1715.L73 1997
370.71'0973—dc20   96-35421
                         CIP

Book design by Acme Art, Inc.

First Edition: March 1997
10 9 8 7 6 5 4 3 2 1

CONTENTS

Major / The Professional Component in Teacher Education: Methods Courses / The Teacher Effectiveness Question / Alternative Views / Student Teaching and School Culture / Changing the Teacher Workplace / Teaching as a Profession

PART III.
FUTURE POSSIBILITIES

ACKNOWLEDGMENTS

Special thanks are owed to Karen Stauffacher, Phillip Besonen, and Teresa Bevis, who kindly consented to review and critique preliminary manuscript drafts; to Amy Charland and Diane Damicone, for their invaluable help with source materials; to Bart Cohen and Gary Shepard, for technical support; to Leanne Hoofnagle, Tommy Van Asten, and Sonja Bennett, for essential clerical assistance; to Sean Mulvenon, Eric Stricker, Debbie Alberth, Fred Bonner, Brenda Hall, Donna Goodwin, and Beverly Reed of the Arkansas Leadership Academy, for help in conducting the teacher study; to Clyde Iglinsky, John Murry, Gerald Siegrist, Barbara Gartin, George Denny, James Bolding, David Hart, James Swartz, Martin Schoppmeyer, Jack Helfeldt, and Charles Stegman, for their several provocative suggestions, documents, and ideas; and to the hundreds of public school administrators and teachers who lent their cooperation in the survey portion of this project.

Without their help, this study could not have been completed. Opinions and suggestions within the narrative (except as otherwise noted), of course, are the author's sole responsibility.

PREFACE

In 1988, the Carnegie Foundation for the Advancement of Teaching released a profoundly disquieting study of American teachers. Entitled *Report Card on School Reform: The Teachers Speak,* it found public-school teachers across the nation feeling deeply "dispirited."[1] In the aftermath of successive waves of reform, working conditions in schools had changed, but not necessarily for the better; and teachers reportedly felt "more responsible but less empowered" in their jobs. "Loss of status, bureaucratic pressures, negative public image, and lack of recognition and rewards" for teaching had all allegedly contributed to a precipitous decline in morale. Despite the many high-profile initiatives launched to improve public schooling in the 1980s, the study concluded, almost half of all teachers polled claimed morale had actually gone down. Less than one-fourth claimed it had gotten better.[2]

Writing four years later, Benjamin R. Barber, Whitman Professor of Political Science at Rutgers, judged that teachers still ranked "among the least respected and least remunerated of American professionals." Directly contradicting the rhetoric of teacher empowerment, Barber's estimation was that the standing of American schoolteachers had changed little if at all and that teachers as an occupational class generally enjoyed neither the respect of their students nor that of the public at large. Per-capita spending on public schooling in the United States, he further noted, was high compared with that of many other developed societies. But teachers' wages and monies for educational programs remained low.[3]

Barber's assessment of low teacher status was probably on target, although perhaps it did not fully take into account trends already beginning to affect teachers' salaries. Figures released by the U.S. Department of Education in 1994, for example, indicated that over the previous seven years, the average annual salary of the country's esti-mated 3 million teachers actually had registered a significant increase, marking a substantial gain over levels prevailing throughout the decade or so preceding. Actually, between 1980 and 1993, mean compensation for elementary and secondary teachers, adjusted for inflation, had risen no less than 21 percent on average, or by more than one-fifth—equaling and in some cases exceeding the rate of increase in average compensation during the same period for other comparable occupational groups.[4]

Improvement in teacher compensation notwithstanding, between 1988 and 1991 an important change had occurred in sources of teacher supply. Increasingly, schools were compelled to hire a much higher percentage of first-time teachers and proportionately fewer reentrants than had previously been customary.[5] Attrition among experienced teachers, it was suggested, helped account for most of the shift in supply. Whether low morale and job disillusionment figured directly in so many seasoned classroom veterans leaving remained an open question. Whatever the factors responsible, it was clear the nation's school systems were now more dependent than ever on recent college graduates to fill vacant teaching positions.

Questions about the characteristics and quality of new entrants to the field came to dominate discussion in education circles from the early 1980s up through the mid-1990s and beyond. It was clear, for instance, that beginning teachers generally were no more representative of the nation's population as a whole than were their predecessors. Over 71 percent of all teachers in 1987-88 were female, and the subsequent influx of novice teachers into the field thereafter had done practically nothing to change the gender imbalance. Fully 87 percent of all female teachers and 90 percent of male instructors were white non-Hispanics—this at a time when minority students already constituted a majority in 23 of the 25 largest city school systems in the country. It was projected that by the end of the century, one-third or more of the nation's total student population would be members of minority groups. Yet expectations were that majority-culture teachers as a proportion of the total pool would continue to predominate well into the twenty-first century.[6]

Doubts about the academic ability of entering teachers and the adequacy of their training assumed renewed urgency amid charges of widespread incompetence and underpreparedness. According to a national public opinion commissioned in the early 1990s by the National Council for Accreditation of Teacher Education (NCATE), less than one in every five respondents (18 percent) surveyed believed that teachers were sufficiently trained to meet the challenge of improving students' academic performance in schools. Three-quarters of those polled indicated they believed teachers were only partially trained or were not adequately trained to fulfill the task. Also, two of every three respondents (68 percent) claimed that if teachers were required to meet higher professional training standards, student performance would improve. More than seven in ten (72 percent) reportedly affirmed that teachers needed more specialized training.[7]

Debate over teacher education continued unabated throughout the 1990s, with fierce battles waged over what a teacher needed to know and how teachers' preparatory programs should be organized to best effect. In the face of unrelenting public criticism, education schools and colleges, of course, could hardly stand by idly—nor in fact had they done so. Since the mid-1980s, if not before, many were already tackling the challenge of upgrading teacher education standards and strengthening the subject-matter preparation of teaching candidates. Admission standards were ratcheted up, even as higher minimum grade point averages required for graduation were imposed. In many teacher-training institutions, preservice curricula underwent extensive revisions on a scale rarely before attempted in recent memory. Clinical experiences often were expanded or revamped as well. Indicative perhaps of the continuing disrepute of so-called Mickey Mouse education courses, however, some states were taking steps to abolish all minimum credit-hour requirements in pedagogy, imposing instead a lower ceiling on the *maximum* number of pedagogical courses education majors might be required to complete.[8]

Mainstream thinking in teacher education today, still beset on all sides by continuing allegations of laxity and anemic standards, calls for even tighter quality control, ever more protracted training programs at the post-baccalaureate level, more stringent licensing mechanisms, national advanced certification standards, and "career ladders" for teachers. One widely touted model, for example, would take a novice from "instructor" to "professional" teacher, based on the amount of advanced training he or she had completed, and would culminate finally with standing as a nationally certified "master" teacher. Some proposed innovations, of course, upon closer inspection turn out to be simply recommendations for more of the same. But by the same token, a few seem genuinely novel.

Interestingly, the 1990s also have witnessed growing political support for reforms headed off in exactly the opposite direction: toward briefer, simpler "alternative" teacher preparation programs conferring temporary licensure or, in some states, leading to renewable certification. Some states have mandated postbachelor's course work for teachers; two or three have proscribed the undergraduate education major entirely, substituting instead a requirement that every teacher candidate complete an undergraduate major in a teaching field or in some academic discipline other than education. Some states are promoting training programs offered exclusively in and through school districts. Elsewhere the talk is about creating quasi-independent and autonomous teacher centers or pedagogical centers as training agencies, separate and distinct from traditional schools or colleges of education. In short, judging by the number of incommensurable policy directions currently being pursued or under active consideration, there appears to be scant agreement on the most desirable thrust or future direction for reform in teacher education.

Skeptics attribute the growing trend toward lengthier and more complex postbaccalaureate teacher training programs more than anything else to the status needs of teacher educators within academe.[9] Leaders within the education establishment, on the other hand, typically invoking lofty appeals to professionalism, have sought to justify longer preparatory programs as a response to popular demands for more rigor and higher quality and to society's changing needs. "We are still operating under an outdated certification system," declared NCATE president Arthur Wise in 1994. "For many years teachers taught students the basic skills needed on farms or in factories, and this arrangement served the public well. Our society thrived as an industrial nation even though many people in the work force were trained in only basic skills." But today's teachers, Wise emphasized, need to be far better trained to help prepare learners to survive in tomorrow's complex postindustrial society. He added pointedly, "We have been teaching today's students to meet yesterday's needs."[10]

Alluded to by Wise and made more explicitly by others has been a salient point worth reiterating—taking the longer historical view, it is helpful as background to bear in mind that provision for *any* sort of adequate teacher preparation is a relatively recent undertaking. Prior to the 1870s or thereabouts, most teachers usually had completed little more than elementary schooling themselves and rarely were afforded much pedagogical training of any substance. Nor, traditionally, have teachers ever enjoyed much prestige and status in American society. "Teachers have not fared well in the United States," notes historian Jurgen Herbst. Elementary teachers since time immemorial have been looked upon as little more than hired hands who would discharge their homely tasks for a short interval only, perhaps until an offer of marriage was forthcoming.

As for secondary-level teachers, according to Herbst's account, "only the college-educated masters of the colonial Latin grammar schools, of private boarding schools, and of public preparatory schools enjoyed public recognition and rewards." Most nineteenth-century and early twentieth-century high-school teachers were seen to differ but little from their counterparts in the elementary schools. "Their education in normal schools and teacher colleges and their conditions of employment did not differentiate them sufficiently to justify a claim to separate consideration."[11]

Yet it is worth recalling that however meager their preparation might have been, most secondary and many elementary teachers were not wholly untrained either, at least not from the middle of the nineteenth century, except in remote rural areas. Many of them—although perhaps not even a majority—did receive some rudimentary preparation in a teaching institute, a pedagogical academy or seminary, a normal school or department, or, later, in a fledgling teachers' college of one sort or another. Much practical experimentation occurred. So, too, did long and intense discussion of basic issues surrounding questions of how to prepare teachers for their classroom tasks.

A great deal of contemporary literature on teacher education, nevertheless, seems curiously uninformed and unencumbered by any awareness of past precedent. This cheerful historical amnesia helps explain perhaps why every minor innovation nowadays tends to be hailed as wholly "new" and "original," why so many reform measures are "revolutionary," and why any given proposal for change is likely to be represented—in that most overworked of phrases—as a "paradigm shift" in thinking. Education reform in America tends to be carried forward in the "evangelical" mode, with a hyperbolic fervor and intensity more typically reserved for political campaigns and other less secular concerns. Perhaps the rhetoric has to be overblown (sometimes to the point of fatuity) simply to be heard amid a chorus of voices competing for public attention. But the argument also could be made that its self-assured stridency owes just as much to lack of historical perspective.

Accordingly, it seems helpful to open this modest contribution to the debate over teacher preparation with a historical overview. Part I begins by tracing the outlines of the development of teacher education in America. Chapter 1 looks to teacher recruitment and licensure from the colonial period onward, the feminization of the teaching workforce in the antebellum era, and the emergence of formal training institutions for teachers from just before the middle of the nineteenth century up to its close. Chapter 2 extends the story of how so-called "normal" schools evolved into state teachers' colleges in the early twentieth century, the shape of the campaign to enshrine preparatory programs within universities, and the often-harsh and strident criticisms to which academic teacher education was subjected in the postwar period—and, it might be added, the attacks it has endured ever since.

Part II focuses on contemporary developments marking the course of the last two decades or so, continuing up to the present. Selected for reconsideration in chapter 3 are just some of the most enduring and recurrent issues faced by today's teacher educators. They range from admissions criteria and the role of liberal learning in educating teachers, to the role and scope of specialized technical training as a component element of preparatory programs. The question of a "science of pedagogy" or a "knowledge base" for teacher education and the dilemmas of teacher professionalism also are briefly considered.

Chapter 4 affords an abbreviated look at various alternatives for organizing teacher training, from "extended" graduate level programs in universities to site-based apprenticeships conducted under public school auspices. Chapter 5 rounds off the analysis with an examination and assessment of state and national program accreditation and teacher certification criteria, including current trends toward national advanced licensure procedures and standards.

Part III casts an eye toward the multiple possible futures of teacher education in the United States. Because classroom teachers themselves (as distinct from their national representatives) are so rarely asked for their opinions, chapter 6 is devoted to reporting the results of an informal survey conducted to ascertain how experienced elementary and secondary teachers feel about preservice training for initial certification or licensure. The results have proven both illuminating and provocative. They offer much material for would-be reformers of teacher education to ponder. Chapter 7 concludes with a retrospective assessment of arguments and issues previously taken up for consideration, to which is appended a specific proposal for a direction formal teacher education might explore in years to come.

Hostile treatises unreservedly critical toward teacher education are practically guaranteed to attract a wide public readership, especially if they serve to confirm the more lurid charges levied by education's harshest critics. Panegyrics written to praise rather than bury teacher education are less common, but they too are bound to attract attention and support from stakeholders within professional education circles.

More problematic by far is the genre to which this current work aspires, representing as it does simply a modest effort to understand and assess the condition of American teacher education today. Its intent is neither to condemn uncritically formal teacher education programs in their present forms, nor is it to buttress or endorse the conventional wisdom that undergirds them. Throughout, little attention has been paid to inservice and graduate education for teachers, and practically none to the specifics of preparatory curricula and instruction. Nor are the details of clinical training and experience much discussed. The global focus, rather, is on a single important question: *What is needed in the way of basic preparation for a beginning teacher seeking initial licensure?* Exploring this seemingly simple and straightforward query, and doing so in some thoughtful and reflective way, as it turns out, poses a challenge of formidable proportions.

PART I

A HISTORICAL PERSPECTIVE

1

ORIGINS AND DEVELOPMENT OF TEACHER EDUCATION IN AMERICA

COLONIAL SCHOOLMASTERS

Until approximately the first third of the nineteenth century, the notion that prospective schoolteachers needed formal preparatory training for their work, apart from whatever regular academic studies they might have pursued, would have attracted scant attention and even less popular support. Even after the mid-1800s, the overwhelming majority of people would have found anything much resembling the modern idea of teacher education wholly unnecessary and likely incomprehensible. It is helpful to recall, perhaps, that throughout the colonial and early republican periods, only a minuscule proportion of the population attended any school whatsoever. Among those who did, attendance was apt to be both brief and irregular; and formal learning beyond the most rudimentary level was rarely deemed important to success in the trades and agrarian occupations most people were destined to pursue. Hence, the thought or expectation that a classroom pedagogue might require formal preparation for the lowly task of instructing schoolchildren would have been quite unthinkable.

Colonial schooling varied considerably in terms of its availability, formality, and quality.[1] In the seventeenth century especially, primary education was mostly a private undertaking, conducted at hearthside by widows and spinsters who relied on whatever scant income their charges' tuition afforded. More widespread in later years were village and district elementary schools offering instruction in the common essentials of learning—reading, writing, arithmetic, and religion. The towns of Massachusetts, for example, had committed themselves to maintaining publicly supported schools since the early 1640s. In the middle colonies and throughout the South, by way of contrast, the English tradition of private tutelage and philanthropic schools sponsored by charitable or religious bodies persisted much longer. In South Carolina and Virginia, so-called "old field" schools were private ventures sponsored by plantation owners to serve the needs of their children and sometimes those of other local youngsters. More common still was the itinerant tutor who kept a seasonal round of visits and offered abbreviated courses of instruction in selected venues.

Meanwhile, private secondary Latin "grammar schools," whose chief function was collegiate preparation for young men, and, later in the eighteenth century, private academies supplying shorter and more utilitarian curricula offered courses of study beyond the elementary level. Finally, there existed a handful of colleges, all of them imbued with the tradition of classical literary training for a narrow range of professional occupations, the ministry in particular.

Seventeenth- and eighteenth-century teachers were as diverse a lot as the schools they inhabited. Many in the 1600s were housewives and widows, barely literate themselves, who organized what were colloquially called "dame schools." Working out of their kitchens, they taught simple literacy skills to a handful of neighborhood children for a small fee. Others were much better-prepared, well-educated collegiate graduates who found employment in the leading secondary grammar schools of the day.[2] Hence, at one extreme might be found schoolteachers who themselves had scarcely mastered the ability to read and write. At the other were teachers who could claim a college degree. Qualifications aside, in almost all cases teaching was looked on as a part-time occupation to augment one's income—neither the school day nor the school year was lengthy—or as a strictly temporary occupation.[3] Acquaintance with the common subjects imparted to children was considered sufficient qualification for practically anyone to teach.

Young divinity students, for example, frequently taught school for short intervals to support their studies while in seminary. Further, it was commonplace for a ministerial graduate to accept a short-term position as village schoolmaster while awaiting a call to his first pastorate. (More than a fourth of Harvard's graduates between 1642 and 1689 reportedly spent some period of time teaching school before continuing their studies or seeking other professional employment.) Otherwise, itinerant adventurers, drifters, young men seeking to avoid physical labor, chronic malcontents, and perhaps misfits who had failed at other enterprises most typically were claimants on teaching posts.

For many, schoolkeeping was little more than a last attempt to keep body and soul together. Others applied for teaching positions chiefly in hopes it would serve as a stepping-stone to something better. Whatever their individual circumstances, lower-school instructors were not looked upon as professionals, and the common presumption would have been that teaching hardly qualified as an occupation requiring special training or lengthy preparation.[4]

Despite abysmal working conditions and the lack of prestige attached to teaching at the lower levels, a certain number of schoolmasters in the colonies did enjoy some measure of distinction and repute. In Dorchester, Massachusetts, for example, the tradition was well established of hiring only college graduates as schoolmasters, usually from nearby Harvard. The same high standard was maintained in many other towns. The ranks of well-respected teachers in this early period included the Reverend John Bertrand, who supervised a highly regarded school in Rappahannock County, Virginia, throughout the 1680s and 1690s; Elijah Corlet, who maintained a well-known grammar school in Cambridge, Massachusetts; Evert Pieterson, a pedagogue of some renown at the New Amsterdam school in New Netherland; and Benjamin Tompson, a schoolmaster-physician who taught at Quincy, Boston, and then at Charleston.

Perhaps best known of all was Ezekiel Cheever of the Boston Free School, later to be immortalized as "a learned master of the languages" in Cotton Mather's panegyric *Corderius Americanus,* published in 1701. Unfortunately, for every Ezekiel Cheever presiding in a classroom, there were scores of others who more nearly exemplified the semicomical archetype dramatized by Washington Irving's Ichabod Crane—an object of ridicule, the earnest but simple-minded fool and buffoon.

Not surprisingly, considering the lack of social standing accorded teachers and the inadequate salaries they commanded, the tenure of the colonial schoolmaster was almost always brief. Turnover was high in almost every community. Much was made of the need to attract men of good moral character—though even in this respect townsfolk had to settle for what they could get. In Virginia, evidence of "good life and conversation" and basic competence in reading and writing represented virtually the sole qualifications demanded.[5] So too in rural Pennsylvania, the schoolmaster was expected only to "read, write and cipher."[6] Elsewhere, apart from a knowledge of the subject matter to be taught, the main prerequisite for a candidate's consideration appears to have been his professed willingness to wield the rod and maintain stern discipline in the classroom. In Springfield, Massachusetts, as late as 1800, it was stipulated by the town fathers that the local teacher needed only "the knack to continue in the schoolroom the discipline of the kitchen" and to be "a good mender of quill pens."[7]

Attempting to recruit qualified instructors of the young, some communities offered prospective candidates emoluments such as exemption from taxation and military conscription. Or the inducement could be a gift of land, a rent-free house, or a constantly replenished supply of firewood. Sometimes it happened that a town was fortunate enough to attract a teacher who was sober, upright, virtuous, and God-fearing, someone willing to render years of service to the community at minimal cost. Rural enclaves unable—or possibly unwilling—to offer special inducements, on the other hand, could expect at best a succession of transient "ne'er-do-wells, rogues, knaves and scoundrels," men of dubious ability and still more questionable character. Either way, because salaries were exceedingly modest, anyone holding the schoolmaster's position would have to augment the miserly pittance paid with supplementary employment, More than a few labored on the side as town crier, meetinghouse custodian, church bell ringer, Sunday choir leader, town gravedigger, and so on. More than a few schoolmasters worked as tailors, brewers, or innkeepers—whatever supplemental positions were available during the several months of the year the local school was not in session.

Judging from how often complaints were heard, hopes of attracting an acceptable teaching candidate at minimum expense were rarely fulfilled. Among the early Dutch settlers, to cite a case in point, a certain Master Van Marken of Flatbush, Long Island, was reputed to pay "more attention to the tavern than to the school." Jan Tibout of Flatbush was publicly criticized for being "too intoxicated at times to know what he was doing or saying."[8] John Sullivan of Thomaston, Maine, was judged to suffer "habitual intervals of intemperance." Again, it was said of the first schoolmaster at Francestown, New Hampshire, that he made "rather free use of cider and rum."[9]

Oftentimes teachers were targets for accusations of slander, crimes of violence, gross immorality, gambling, and public profanity. Straight-laced communities of the 1600s and 1700s were not in the least hesitant about holding the local schoolmaster to the same strict standards as their clergymen.[10] In the former case at least, accusations of impropriety seem to have been more than amply justified. Noah Webster was only one of many who complained about how frequently teachers' ranks were filled with former convicts, drunkards, and coarse "low-bred clowns."[11] Benjamin Franklin noted with considerable understatement in 1750 that the colonies were "suffering at present very much for want of good schoolmasters."[12]

EARLY TEACHER LICENSURE

Whereas formal qualifications to teach were woefully low in colonial America, throughout the seventeenth century (and to a somewhat lesser degree in the century following) religious orthodoxy figured as a major consideration in the hiring of schoolmasters in all of the colonies except Rhode Island and Maryland. In Massachusetts, the general court in 1654 commended "to the serious consideration and special care of the . . . selectmen in the several towns, not to admit or suffer such to be continued in the office or place of teaching, educating, or instructing of youth or child, in the college [that is, Harvard] or schools, [those] that have manifested themselves unsound in the faith, or scandalous in their lives, and not giving due satisfaction according to the rules of Christ."

In New Netherland, prospective schoolmasters seeking employment were subject to review by officials of the Dutch West India Company. They were further required to gain approval by the local consistory and court. Following the English conquest of New Amsterdam in 1664, the prerogative of licensing teachers passed to the colonial governor, who retained the privilege until the year 1686, when King James II ordered that "no schoolmaster be henceforth permitted to come from England and to keep school within our province . . . without the license of the . . . archbishop of Canterbury."[13] Three years later, in 1689, responsibility for teacher licensing was given over to the bishop of London. In Virginia, teacher licensing was inaugurated in 1683 when Governor Lord Howard of Effingham was instructed by King Charles II to guarantee that every schoolmaster teaching in the colony held a license issued by the bishop of London (if the candidate had migrated from England) or from the colonial governor himself.

In New Hampshire and New Jersey, schoolmasters were licensed either by the governor or by ecclesiastical representatives of the bishop of London. By the end of the century, official efforts to ensure doctrinal conformity to the established church began to slacken and were rarely enforced with any stringency thereafter. In Massachusetts after 1701, every grammar-school master still required approval by the local clergyman in the town where the teacher sought employment. In Connecticut, it was decided the assembly would serve as a licensing authority for all teachers in the colony.

Subsequently, and throughout the remainder of the eighteenth century, the trend was toward delegating hiring and firing powers to local town officials, those in whose hands responsibility had devolved for establishing, supervising, and funding schools (most often through a combination of local taxes and modest tuition charges). By the mid-1700s, it had become customary to authorize town selectmen to negotiate on their own for the teaching services of whomever they wished. Sometimes the schoolmaster was elected by the townsfolk in an open town meeting. More often, an appointed or elected school committee did the hiring and firing.

A rather broad and crude burlesque on the custom of allowing local officials unrestricted authority to judge the qualifications of candidates, published in 1807 by Caleb Bingham, is suggestive of the problems that attended the business of recruiting a teacher for the local school. A certain "Master Ignoramus" is depicted presenting himself for a job interview before the village school committee. By his own admission, he is innocent of much "book larnin' " and can claim to have finished only a single year of formal schooling. The prospect is a self-confessed militia deserter and a drunkard. (He proudly announces to a local school committee member on the day of his job interview that he has not had a single drink since six o'clock that same morning.) When interrogated, he cannot answer the simplest questions about the primary-school curriculum he proposes to impart. He cannot explain the difference between the diameter and the circumference of a sphere, he is totally lacking even a basic knowledge of geography, and so on.

His evident incompetence notwithstanding, the candidate promptly wins approval on the strength of his willingness to work for a fraction of the wages paid his predecessor. Only the local minister dissents from the committee's decision to hire the applicant on the spot. "It has always been surprising to me," the parson complains, "that people in general are more willing to pay their money for anything else, than for 'the one thing needful,' that is, for the education of their children. Their tailor must be a workman, their carpenter, a workman, their hairdresser, a workman, their hostler, a workman; but the instructor of their children must—work cheap!"[14]

ANTEBELLUM TEACHERS

In spite of its obvious disadvantages, the grass-roots practice of leaving the certification and hiring of teachers to the discretion of local school committees or to private school trustees was to survive basically unchanged throughout the waning years of the eighteenth century and on into the nineteenth. Qualifications for teaching continued to range from the arbitrary to the nonexistent. Many candidates acquired positions through family connections or simply for lack of competition. Cynics observed more than once that a guaranteed way to obtain a job was to be in debt to a school board member.

Sometimes a candidate's political orientation or his sectarian orthodoxy loomed as the paramount consideration in the selection process. Just as often, as in Bingham's satire, the most acceptable applicant was the person willing to take the post at the lowest salary. Typically, school committees sought pro forma reassurances of good moral character. Equally important was the teacher's promise to act as a strict classroom disciplinarian, not to mention his readiness to keep the school building swept clean, chop wood for the stove, watch over the younger siblings of the pupils attending, and otherwise perform all necessary chores demanded of him.[15] As Samuel Hall rightly observed in 1829, the job of schoolmaster conferred no more respectability than the lowest "manual labor."[16] If a prospective teacher's academic qualifications were considered at all, most rural communities relied on some type of informal oral interrogation. By the late 1830s, some towns were experimenting with locally devised written examinations intended to ensure that an applicant had himself mastered the curriculum to be taught. Even basic academic competency could not be taken for granted.

Over the course of the republic's first half century or so, teachers wages and working conditions improved only slowly, if at all. Salaries had increased slightly by the 1820s and 1830s, although as a rule they remained well below the level paid common day laborers and artisans, blacksmiths, bricklayers, and scrubwomen. Meanwhile, a teacher's ability to maintain classroom order was as important as ever—in 1837 in Massachusetts alone, it was reported, over 300 schools were closed because unruly students had ejected their hapless teachers.

Predictably enough, early nineteenth-century schoolmasters who worked in insular rural communities tended to find village life isolating and confining in the extreme. The local teacher was under constant scrutiny at all times. He was expected to be a model of decorum and propriety, to refrain from the use of alcohol and tobacco, to forswear the use of profanity, and not to consort unsupervised with members of the opposite sex. The frequent practice of "boarding around"—residing on a rotating basis in the homes of the children he taught—denied him even the basic privacy of his own living quarters.[17] By any measure or standard, the attractions and satisfactions of the village schoolmaster's life were thus far and few between.

Almost no one, it seemed, was satisfied with the caliber of candidates drawn to teaching. Yet few had specific remedies to offer. Complaints continued unabated, as in the case of a state superintendent in Vermont who observed, "In some of our larger towns, I have been informed that men have been employed for years as the instructors of youth who tarry long at the wine press . . . and are not infrequently incapacitated in the after part of the day to proceed even with the ceremonies of the school."[18] Yet sobriety alone could hardly have compensated for the lack of academic qualifications common among school instructors. President Humphrey of Amherst College spoke for many early in the century when he declared "It is impossible to have good schools for want of good teachers. Many who offer themselves are deficient in everything: in spelling, in reading, in penmanship, in geography, in grammar, and in common arithmetic. The majority would be dismissed and advised to go back to their domestic and rural employments, if competent instructors could be had."[19]

THE COMMON-SCHOOL CRUSADE

If qualified teachers were in short supply in the early 1800s, the situation could only worsen with each passing decade as schools and the numbers of students enrolled multiplied. Some of the increase was accounted for by population expansion. More important still was a popular drive to extend the advantages of learning to all children. The campaign for universal free schooling in the United States was a long and complex development, taking many unexpected twists and turns as the century progressed. In its origins it was a crusade inspired more than anything else by an emerging conviction often expressed in the 1820s that if every citizen of the fledgling republic was to participate intelligently in affairs of state, it was imperative for all persons, regardless of social class or position in society, to have received at least some rudimentary education. Proponents such as Horace Mann, first secretary of the Massachusetts Board of Education, and Henry Barnard, who held the same post in neighboring Connecticut, ranked foremost among those who advanced extravagant if well-intentioned claims on behalf of common schools.

A universal system of free public schools open to all, they promised, would reduce dangerous class tensions between rich and poor, forestall civil disorder, help assimilate immigrants, instill middle-class morality, inculcate the Protestant work ethic among the masses, and in general conduce to greater economic prosperity. Respect for private property would be strengthened by the raising up of a literate, obedient citizenry. The sheer power of popular learning would hold dissension and anarchy at bay. Public schools where the children of citizens of every station in life could mingle freely, they further assured their audiences, would promote decency and gentility, buttress democratic social values, and otherwise serve to unite the people in the service of common civic ends.

In 1827, the Commonwealth of Massachusetts became the first state to make elementary instruction free to everyone. Two years later, in October 1829, the *New York Free Inquirer* reported that a delegation of the Working Men of Philadelphia had made education its top reform priority, having called for "an equal and general system of education" based on provision for "an open school and competent teachers for every child in the state, from the lowest branches of an infant school to the lecture rooms of practical science. . . ." The year following, the Boston Working Men's Party, resolving to oppose "all attempts to degrade the working classes," announced that "the establishment of a liberal system of education, attainable by all, should be among the first efforts of every lawgiver." Josiah Holbrook, writing in 1826, launched the idea of a public drive "to establish on a uniform plan, in every town and village, a society for mutual improvement and the improvement of schools." The idea caught on, and by the mid 1830s literally thousands of counties, towns, and villages had taken up the cause.[20]

Despite strong opposition from those who argued that schools should be left to private initiative, the idea of compulsory, secular, tuition-free schools open to everyone at state expense gained steadily in popularity. It seemed to be—to invoke a hackneyed phrase—an idea whose time had come. Governor Edward Everett of Massachusetts won broad support in 1837 for his declaration, "Provision ought to be made for affording the advantages of education, throughout the whole year, to all of a proper age to receive it."[21] By the 1850s, close to 81,000 public elementary schools were flourishing—approximately one school for every 370 persons. Of leading states such as Ohio, it could be judged that most had established schools within walking distance of virtually every child. It was by any measure a truly impressive expansion. By midcentury or shortly thereafter, the public school systems of almost all the eastern states were enrolling over three-quarters of all children of school age.[22] Left unanswered was the question as to where teachers were to come from in numbers sufficient to meet the needs of the hundreds of thousands of new pupils crowding into those same common schools.

FEMINIZATION OF THE TEACHING FORCE

Part of the answer to the problem of a nascent teacher shortage in the early 1800s, as it turned out, was to admit more females to the teaching ranks. Older women had long been involved in instructing the young under private auspices. Up until the early 1830s, however, females had accounted for only a small fraction of those engaged in public schoolkeeping. One practical consequence of the establishment and proliferation of primary-level common schools was that villages and towns came to rely increasingly on the more talented graduates of their own local schools to serve as teachers. In time an informal division of labor evolved. Young men would teach part time in the winter months when conditions precluded productive farmwork. Then during the interval between planting and harvesting, young women would be called on to take up the slack.

It was soon apparent, however, that in an era of burgeoning school enrollments, male teachers would be unavailable in anything approaching the numbers needed. By tradition, boys and young men were expected to work in the fields or enter the various trades. With the first stirrings of industrialism, fewer and fewer still were inclined to enter the classroom. Many also were being siphoned off from teaching by the allure of adventure and economic opportunities beckoning from the western frontier. Hence, the custom arose of selecting a young female teenager who had proven herself adept at academic subjects in the lower grades of the common school and to appoint her to supervise the same classroom she had just left. A traditional presumption holding since time immemorial that women should preoccupy themselves with domestic pursuits and the care of children was now extended to take new circumstances into account. In the absence of qualified male candidates for teaching positions, it was suggested, women should be called on to provide the same nurturing child care in school they had traditionally afforded children within the home.

Practical necessity was converted into a moral imperative. The rationale offered for encouraging more women to become teachers stressed both economic and pedagogical advantages. Utilizing women in classroom roles helped alleviate the teacher shortage problem. More important, or so it was claimed, women possessed innate abilities and dispositions best suited to the care and upbringing of the young. As Catherine Beecher wrote in 1829, "It is to mothers, and to teachers, that the world is to look for the character which is to be enstamped on each succeeding generation."[23] Women, she claimed, had a critical responsibility to inculcate within the young the elevated morality needed by civilized society. By their very nature, she argued, women were divinely ordained and equipped to fulfill this sacred responsibility. Seeking to disarm critics, Beecher reassured her readers in 1841 that "in civil and political affairs" women had little "interest or concern." But "in matters pertaining to the education of their children . . . in all benevolent enterprises, and in all questions relating to morals or manners, they have a superior influence."[24]

Whether women possessed the temperament, disposition, and purity of morals claimed for them by Beecher and others remained an open question. But it did not long escape notice that there was another important advantage to encouraging women to teach—namely, that their services could be secured for half or even a third of the pay commanded by men. Susan B. Anthony, for one, inverted earlier arguments advanced on behalf of female teachers. In a speech delivered before a conference of mostly male educators at Rochester, New York, in 1853 she explained why teaching remained in such low esteem. It was because it was a job increasingly dominated by females. Her reasoning was that because single women were viewed as unsuited for any other occupation except for laboring in the sweatshops and mills, men who elected to pursue teaching as a career were tacitly conceding they had "no more brains than a woman." Furthermore, male teachers would continue to receive poor salaries precisely because they competed "with the cheap labor of women."[25]

Calvin E. Stowe, who later married Harriet Beecher, worried that bringing women into teaching might serve to deflect feminist impulses to hold elective office and to participate actively in civic life. If a practical consequence of the feminization of the teaching workforce was to defuse women's efforts to be accepted as full-fledged participants in public affairs, he opined, any enlargement of the numbers of female teachers in the nation's schools could hardly be welcomed as an unmitigated blessing.[26] Left unexplored was a further implication. Teachers henceforth would carry the double burden of contending not only with a social bias against women generally but one against their chosen profession as well.[27]

Stowe's apprehension seemed more and more justified with each passing year. By the early 1840s, female teachers were beginning to outnumber their male colleagues in the common and private day schools of several states, most notably in Massachusetts. By the 1860s, female teachers had become far more numerous than their male counterparts in Vermont, New Jersey, and Ohio, and possibly also in Pennsylvania.[28] For either sex, teaching was still a poorly paid occupation. And as always, it was strictly a part-time job, since the common schools of the day remained in session for no more than seven or eight months at a time, as in New York or Massachusetts, and for no more than four months out of the year, as in Kansas and in some other midwestern states.

Nor by the 1850s and 1860s had the status of teachers improved to any marked degree. The ideological justification for utilizing so many ill-prepared female common-school graduates as primary-level teachers was that they were fulfilling a sacred "calling" second only to the ministry in its importance. Wages therefore ought not to figure importantly as a consideration. In returning to the classrooms they had so recently departed as graduates, it was said, young unmarried women were simply anticipating the domestic happiness and personal fulfillment that matrimony would later confer. For widows and spinsters, the rewards of teaching would serve in part to compensate them for their unhappy fate. But for males, on the other hand, teaching was more likely to be regarded as a "career" in the fullest sense of the term, albeit one still lacking adequate salary or social recognition. Thus, a duality within teachers' ranks began to open up that would persist throughout the remainder of the 1800s and endure basically unchanged throughout most of the twentieth century as well.

Women were considered best fitted to teach young children in the lower grades. At higher levels, where obstreperous youngsters posed more challenging discipline problems and where the intellectual demands made on the teacher were presumably greater, male teachers would find their own place. Women who taught little more than the rudiments of literacy were considered to have little need for advanced education beyond whatever they had themselves received while enrolled as common school students. Men, however, were advised to prepare themselves for a teaching career in a secondary-level academy, of which, according to the survey contained in the 1855 edition of Henry Barnard's *American Journal of Education,* there were then some 6,000 in existence.

Private academies, which had historical roots in the courtly academies of the Renaissance and in the dissenters' academies of the English Puritans, offered the earliest extension of the common-school program, and in some states at least later on would be publicly subsidized as "terminal" elements of the common school system. Eventually, in the latter half of the 1800s, some academies were to evolve into independent college preparatory schools. Others were converted into public secondary schools of the sort that ultimately became high schools in the modern sense of the term.[29] The pattern prevailing was for female elementary teachers to assume their duties directly upon completing the lower common school course of studies or, at best, after attending a secondary-level institution for a brief interval. Young men intending to teach in the upper primary grades, unlike their female counterparts, more typically pursued a complete secondary-level course of study in one or another of the academies, consistent with the belief that it was more important for them to have finished schooling at the level next highest to the one at which they would teach.

The gender division among elementary teachers was, if anything, even more pronounced at the secondary level. Whereas some few womens' colleges were beginning to provide secondary and postsecondary education for women—among them, the Troy Seminary, Mount Holyoke, Rockford College, Elmira College, Vassar and Georgia Wesleyan—prior to the Civil War far fewer women than men elected to attend college and embark on a teaching career at the high-school level. Nineteenth-century male college graduates, for their part, might start out as postelementary teachers. But in disproportionate numbers they tended rather quickly to gravitate toward positions as school principals or superintendents. The result was an almost exclusive monopoly of educational leadership roles by men. Hence continuing male control over an increasingly female occupation was practically a foregone conclusion.[30]

ADVOCACY FOR FORMAL TEACHER PREPARATION

As early as 1789, an editorialist in the *Massachusetts Magazine* had offered a suggestion that every county in the state found a school "to fit young gentlemen for college and school keeping."[31] The writer's recommendation was not acted on immediately, any more than had been Benjamin Franklin's proposal almost 40 years earlier to found an academy where "a number of the poorer sort will be . . . qualified to act as schoolmasters."[32] Similar demands had begun to appear with increasing frequency over the course of the next few decades and were given renewed impetus by the expansion of common schools in the early 1800s. Among the first private academies and colleges attempting to offer some specific preparatory course for teachers were Zion Parnassus Academy, near Salisbury, North Carolina (founded in 1785); the Westtown Boarding School (founded in 1799); Nazareth Hall (founded in 1807); and Washington College (founded in 1831), all in Pennsylvania.

Reasons why there was so little initial enthusiasm for the idea of teacher training are not difficult to discern. As contemporary historian Jurgen Herbst aptly notes, the opinion of the majority held that "teachers were cheap, easily and quickly replaced when necessary, and not expected to possess extraordinary capabilities or devotion. In the view of the ordinary school committee member, anyone could teach in a pinch. . . . School reformers thus had to persuade a doubting people that teachers needed to be trained and that such training would indeed pay for itself in the benefits communities could derive from their common schools."[33]

A further consideration in the minds of many, it may be supposed, was the widespread perception that the practice of teaching itself was neither sufficiently complex nor intellectually challenging enough to justify any sort of special preparation. And in point of fact some such view seemed fully warranted. Throughout most of the nineteenth century, teachers in rural and urban schools alike customarily resorted to a highly ritualized pedagogy—rigid and inflexible—aimed at little more than fostering rote learning. With few important exceptions classroom usage rarely made use of anything more imaginative or creative than the simple student recitation.[34]

Proposals to institutionalize and make professional training a requirement failed to attract much support from would-be teachers either. All things considered, the prospect of expending time, money, and energy preparing for a part-time or temporary teaching position, one that promised few benefits and even less pay, could hardly have seemed attractive or compelling. Hence calls for institutions in which the special preparatory needs of future teachers would receive attention generally failed to attract the popular support so ardently sought by their advocates.

Finally, a fundamental ambiguity resided in the call for preparatory training itself. It was by no means always plain what reformers had in mind or what they hoped to achieve. Some clearly wanted formal courses of instruction in what would later be dubbed "the science and art" of teaching—in other words, training in pedagogy and classroom management. But just as often the notion of preparatory training for teachers meant little more than additional study of the subjects a teacher was expected to teach. Had it not been for the indefatigable efforts of a relatively small handful of innovators, the idea of teacher training as a discrete enterprise in its own right might have languished much longer than it did.

In this respect, older accounts of the history of teacher education in the United States have tended to imply a sort of linear evolutionary development, an inexorable and somehow irresistible march of progress toward some roseate future. The appearance on the scene of institutions devoted to teacher training toward the midpoint of the nineteenth century, for example, is hailed as a triumphal milestone en route to the almost inevitable maturation of teaching as a bona fide profession in the century following.[35] Yet the historical reality, on later reading, seems far more complex and ambiguous than anything suggested in its traditional rendering. When agitation for teachers' pedagogical seminaries and "normal" schools occurred in the 1820s, for example, it did not bear immediate fruit. And when those urgings did eventually yield results, the consequences were by no means those anticipated by those who had pressed hardest for the founding of publicly supported teachers' institutions. Nor, as events would show, was it the case that what the public wanted from these new types of schools, once established, would necessarily coincide with the lofty intentions of their founders.

An early appeal for public "seminaries" designed for future teachers came in a spirited commencement address delivered by Denison Olmstead at Yale in 1816. James T. Kingsley, also of Yale, authored a 1823 article for the *North American Review* in which he issued a similar call. The Reverend Thomas H. Gallaudet, principal of a well-known school for the deaf in Hartford, Connecticut, writing in the *Connecticut*

Observer for January 4, 1825, offered a "Plan of a Seminary for the Education of Instructors of Youth" that was subsequently reprinted and circulated widely. "Let an institution be established in every state for the express purpose of training up young men for the profession of the instructors of youth," he urged.[36]

In the same year Kingsley's article appeared, a Congregational clergyman by the name of Samuel R. Hall established a private seminary devoted to preparing teachers in Concord, Vermont. An ambitious three-year course of studies for prospective classroom instructors was projected. (Hall later authored a work entitled *Lectures on Schoolkeeping* that found extensive use as a pedagogical text throughout the 1840s and 1850s.) Seven years later, Hall accepted a teaching post at the Phillips Academy in Andover, Massachusetts. There he directed a similar experiment until the dissolution of his position in 1842. His original school, meanwhile, had failed for lack of funds some five years after he resigned the principalship. Fewer than 100 young men had completed the course of study during the school's brief existence of a dozen or so years.

Henry E. Dwight was one of several in the late 1820s who had traveled extensively in northern Germany and returned home to champion the merits of the Prussian system of teacher education. Similarly active in supporting teachers' schools drawn along the same lines was yet another Congregational minister, William Channing Woodbridge, who in 1831, two years after Dwight's first reports appeared in print, published his own commentary on Prussian teacher seminaries in the *American Annals of Education and Instruction*. In his report, Woodbridge lent vigorous support to the idea that the United States should emulate the institutional models supplied by the Prussian state.

Late in the year 1835, a 40-year-old Unitarian clergyman from Massachusetts, Charles Brooks, launched a series of addresses and speeches urging American adoption of the Prussian example. For months on end he sought out audiences wherever a forum was available: lecturing state legislatures in New Hampshire, New Jersey, Pennsylvania, and Connecticut; addressing professional and political conventions; and otherwise laboring to drum up support for the idea of teachers' schools. There was, Brooks avowed, "one provision preparatory to a full instruction of our youth, which I deem of vast moment: I mean a seminary for preparing teachers. After this is established all other improvements may be easily carried forward; and until it is done we shall, I fear, advance but in very slow and broken steps." Indicative perhaps of the reaction of a bemused public, an editorial newspaper cartoonist of the day represented "Captain Brooks," as he was known, holding a ferule in hand and leading a troop of determined-looking schoolmasters and schoolmistresses as they marched upward toward a teachers' seminary floating atop a cloud in the sky overhead.[37]

Walter Johnson, principal of the Germantown Academy in Philadelphia, published a pamphlet in 1825 in which he recommended the creation of special schools dedicated to teacher preparation. "We have theological seminaries, law schools, medical colleges, military academies, institutes for mechanics, and colleges of pharmacy for apothecaries," he pointed out, "but no shadow of an appropriate institution to qualify persons for discharging with ability and success the duties of instruction." Echoing the sentiments of other like-minded campaigners, Johnson concluded, "Men have been apparently presumed to be qualified to teach from the moment they passed the period of ordinarily pupilage—a supposition which with few exceptions must of course lead only to disappointment and mortification."[38]

Identical in tone were the speeches and writings of James G. Carter, who, according to his contemporary Henry Barnard, did more than any other single person in Massachusetts to draw the connection between school reform and teacher education. "Our ancestors ventured," Carter argued in 1824, "to do what the world has never done before, in so perfect a manner, when they established the free schools. Let us do what they have never so well done yet, and establish an institution for the exclusive purpose of preparing instructors." This proposal, he insisted, would represent simply "a development or consummation of the plan of our fathers."[39]

Writing in the *Boston Patriot* between 1824 and 1825, Carter sketched out in his *Essays Upon Popular Education* the essential outlines of the type of school he felt was needed. It much resembled the institution he and a handful of supporters would later found as a private venture in Lancaster, Massachusetts, in 1827. The aim, he insisted, should be a school designed specifically to meet the preparatory needs of those planning to teach in the public common schools. It would give attention both to the subject matter to be taught and to methods of teaching. Ideally, also, there would be a practice school attached where pedagogical principles could be demonstrated and applied in "real-life" settings.

Since it was manifestly impossible for local districts and townships to bear the expense of the sort of teacher-training school he envisioned, Carter felt that the state would need to assume responsibility for its establishment. Like Brooks, Carter believed further improvements in the state and nation's lower schools awaited the appearance of higher schools, agencies capable of developing a more advanced and rigorous system of teacher training and licensing than anything heretofore contemplated. Typical of the overheated rhetoric of the day was Horace Mann's confident declaration that everything depended on the creation of public teacher-training schools. "Coiled up in [the idea of] this institution, as in a spring," he avowed, "there is a vigor whose uncoiling may wheel the spheres."[40]

Confronted with a flood of demands for publicly assisted teacher-training institutions from the likes of Horace Mann, James Carter, Alexander D. Bache, Calvin Stowe, and several others, opponents were more than willing to concede the inadequacies of the prevailing system of teacher recruitment. Sentiment was growing that alternatives were needed to the customary practice of hiring some selectman's daughter to serve as teacher in the local school, or of enlisting the help of some other unmarried female relative of a school committee member. What skeptics denied was the alleged need for the state to bear the cost of operating teachers' seminaries or pedagogical institutes of the sort demanded. New York State's Board of Regents in 1832 proclaimed its unwillingness to contemplate the expenditure. What it recommended instead was that private academies such as the St. Lawrence Academy at Potsdam and the Canandaigua Academy be called on to offer a few teacher-training courses supplemental to their regular curricular offerings. Two years later the state's legislature went so far as to provide modest state subsidies to those private secondary-level academies within its jurisdiction willing to incorporate some type of pedagogical lecture series into their programs. Not long afterward Pennsylvania, Indiana, and Wisconsin cautiously followed suit, each authorizing limited financial aid to private schools in support of teacher training.

Throughout, general opinion held that if it was to be extended at all, state aid should be modest in scope and limited to supporting nothing more elaborate than secondary-level instruction for schoolteachers. To it would be added some special pedagogical instruction as deemed necessary. As the Committee on Education for the Massachusetts Legislature declared in March of 1840, "Academies and high schools cost the Commonwealth nothing; and they are fully adequate to furnish a competent supply of teachers. . . . Considering that our district schools are kept, on an average, for only three or four months in the year, it is obviously impossible, and perhaps it is not desirable, that the business of keeping these schools should become a distinct and separate profession, which the establishment of [teachers'] schools seems to anticipate."[41] What was needed was a simpler, lower-cost alternative for teacher training. Short courses, or teachers' institutes, offered one possibility that at the time seemed worth exploring.

TEACHERS' INSTITUTES

The most widespread form of teacher training in the antebellum period and beyond was that provided by teachers' institutes. The original idea, it appears, was developed jointly by Emma Willard, founder of the Troy Seminary for women, and by Henry Barnard, Connecticut's first education secretary. In the autumn of 1839 in Hartford, Connecticut, Barnard launched a six-week course of instruction in "pedagogics" for 26 young men. Assisted by Charles Davis and Thomas Gallaudet, Barnard promised a thorough review of all the subjects taught in common schools. In addition, practical counsel in teaching methodology would be offered, not to mention site visits to Hartford's local schools.

The apparent success of this first institute, and of those that followed, quickly gained attention elsewhere. In New York State, Samuel N. Sweet organized his own institute for prospective teachers. A "pedagogical convention" for 28 teachers was held in Ithaca, New York, in the spring of 1843 by the Tompkins County superintendent of schools. Reportedly it, too, was well received. Other districts followed the Ithaca example. Within the next two years similar institutes were convened in 39 different New York counties, collectively attracting over 1,000 participants. Massachusetts hosted an institute for teachers in Pittsfield in the fall of 1845; and over the next five years a dozen or so other states had made similar arrangements. New Hampshire, Maine, Ohio, Michigan, and Illinois all sponsored a considerable number of assemblies for teachers throughout the 1840s.

Attendance at institutes was purely voluntary at first, and participants were required to bear the expenses involved themselves. Beginning in Massachusetts in 1846 public funds were budgeted to provide stipends and scholarships to help defray the cost of compulsory participation by instructors already employed in schools. Over time, both private and public aid was forthcoming in amounts sufficient to allow prospective teachers to attend institutes as well. Much the same arrangement was worked out in other states.

Teachers' assemblies generally were held once or twice yearly, usually at a district school facility. Summer convocations lasted from two to eight weeks. The standard bill of fare was a short course in the theory and practice of teaching, leavened by inspirational talks from prominent guest lecturers. The common pattern at most institutes was to occupy each day with formal lectures, followed in the evening by campfire meetings, songfests, and informal open discussion on topics of general interest. At the Chautauqua County Institute held at Maysville, New York, in 1847, for example, two urgent questions preoccupied participants' attention. The first dealt with recommended procedures for preventing whispering among schoolchildren. The second had to do with effective techniques for the teaching of morality.[42]

The atmosphere of an institute oftentimes seems to have resembled nothing so much as that of an old-time religious revival, a camp meeting complete with didactic sermonizing and liberal doses of motivational rhetoric. Extended attention was given over to such questions as how teachers should use their leisure time, the "true philosophy" of school management, what incentives should be appealed to in striving to maintain classroom order and discipline, and the relation between intelligence and public morality. Prominent as a theme at many convocations was the lofty responsibility borne by the teacher as a shaper and molder of childrens character.[43]

Few observers could have supposed that teachers' institutes afforded an adequate or complete response to the problem of teacher preparation. But in the great majority of cases throughout most of the nineteenth century, institutes supplied the only type of training available to teachers, either before or during their tenure working in schools. Their limitations aside, the fact that teachers' institutes generally were popular with novices and experienced pedagogues alike assured their flourishing throughout the 1800s. Many were still being convened in the early years of the twentieth century. Eventually most gave way to the summer courses, workshops, and special district conferences on which teachers came to rely for their continuing education and inservice development.

NORMAL SCHOOLS

Dependence on "home-grown" common-school graduates as primary instructors within the local community was the time-honored method for recruiting classroom teachers at the elementary level. Long-standing also was the custom of hiring teachers directly on graduation from a secondary-level academy for the upper primary levels or grades. Institutes and short courses had evolved into yet another form of teacher preparation and development, particularly once public funds were made available for their support. State subsidies encouraging private academies and high schools to offer a limited array of classes in pedagogy ancillary to their standard courses of academic study—the practice followed early on in Pennsylvania, New York, Wisconsin, and Indiana—offered still another approach. Private pedagogical seminaries yielded yet another partial solution to the problem of preparing teachers, although it must be said that their financial viability was too precarious and their numbers too few for them to have much of an impact.

All fell short of what some reformers had long been arguing was essential: a system of publicly supported normal schools. Piecemeal measures were insufficient, critics claimed. Now was the time for state legislatures to step in and fulfill their responsibility for helping to ensure a supply of well-trained teachers for the nation's common schools. Public normal schools, or so it was claimed, offered the best hope of accomplishing that end. (The term "normal" as an appellation for teacher-training institutions derived via the French from the Latin *norma,* meaning conforming to a "rule, pattern, or model." Hence the intended connotation was a place imparting the "norms" or "rules" for exemplary teaching practice.)

Early in 1838, Edmund Dwight, a Boston industrialist and member of the Massachusetts Board of Education, offered the sum of $10,000 toward the establishment of a state normal school for the purpose of "qualifying teachers of the common schools." His bequest was extended on condition that the state legislature appropriate an equal amount on the school's behalf. On April 19, Governor Edward Everett signed a bill authorizing the assignment of the requisite funds to the Massachusetts State Board of Education. The board was charged, as it turned out, with opening not just one but three state normal schools; and the legislative appropriation it received was made contingent on the board's success in obtaining suitable facilities and furnishings from private sources for each institution. The first school was established in Lexington, in the northeastern part of the state. The second was located in the central portion, at Barre. The third was placed in the southeastern part of the state, at Bridgewater.[44] All were intended to operate on a trial basis for a three-year period.

Chosen to head the first of the three at Lexington was the Reverend Cyrus Peirce, a 49-year-old Harvard graduate and former Unitarian pastor who had served as a school principal on Nantucket. On July 3, 1839, three apprehensive young ladies presented themselves on the occasion of the school's opening to take the entrance examinations. Peirce later wrote to Horace Mann of his disappointment that so few students had showed up despite extensive advance publicity accompanying the school's debut. Even by September no more than 12 students were enrolled. Notwithstanding, he was determined to make a success of the fledgling institution—he reportedly confided to his wife that he would rather die than fail in the undertaking.

Peirce at first was the school's sole staff member. To him fell the burden of shoveling snow, carrying water, keeping the fires supplied, performing all janitorial chores, preparing each of the lessons, and hearing students' recitations. Managing on four hours of sleep nightly, Peirce was responsible for teaching no fewer than 17 different subjects.[45] In October of 1839 a model school was opened, further adding to his supervisory responsibilities. In September of 1844 the school was relocated in West Newton, where it remained until December of 1853. Thereafter it moved to a more permanent site in Framingham.

Meanwhile, a coeducational state normal school had opened its doors on September 4, 1839, at Barre under the direction of the Reverend Samuel P. Newman, formerly a professor of rhetoric and acting president at Bowdoin College. Twelve young women and eight men attended. In September 1841 the school closed temporarily, reopening once again in September of 1844 at Westfield under the interim leadership of Emerson Davis, a local clergyman. The third school opened as planned at Bridgewater on September 9, 1840, under the directorship of a former West Point graduate by the name of Nicholas Tillinghast. It too was open to both young men and women. During the first few years, enrollments remained low at all three schools, rarely exceeding 30 or 40 at a time.

A fourth state normal school was added in Salem in September of 1854. During its first three years of operation, it was directed by Richard Edwards, who later assumed the principalship of the City Normal and High School in St. Louis. The Salem school, like its prototype at Lexington, admitted only female students. In 1856, the four schools were reporting a total combined enrollment of no more than 332 students, of whom 290 were young women.

At both Lexington and Salem, candidates for admission had to be at least 16 years of age; the minimum age for male applicants at Barre and Bridgewater was set at 17. Those admitted were required to declare their intention to teach; to pass an entrance examination over primary-school subjects; and to document their good moral character. The minimum course of study, as at Lexington, was no more than one year in length. Not until 1860 was it feasible for any of the state's normal schools to keep a longer, two-year course of instruction afloat. With allowance for minor variations among the several institutions, the standard one-year curriculum encompassed a thorough review of the "common branches" of learning taught in primary schools—spelling, reading, writing, geography, and arithmetic; a limited number of secondary-level academic subjects—geometry, algebra, natural and moral philosophy (that is, elementary physical science and ethics); studies devoted to the physical, mental, and psychological development of children; one or more methods courses; a course in classroom management; and a period of practice teaching in a model school.

Candidates who completed the entire one-year course were awarded a formal certificate to teach in the state's district elementary schools. Considering the chronic teacher shortage in Massachusetts, those who failed to win a certificate were still more or less assured a teaching post somewhere within the state. Predictably, few students remained to complete the course. Commenting on the problem in 1846, a member of the Board of Education admitted, "Many have remained but a single term, but few have given themselves time for the whole course, and the normal schools have been held answerable for their deficiencies. This is unreasonable, as nobody ever pretended that the new system could work miracles—that coming in one door and going out the other would make good teachers."[46]

Other states gradually followed Massachusetts' lead.[47] In New York State, the legislature acted to fund a normal school in 1844 for "the instruction and practice of teachers of common schools in the science of education and in the art of teaching." The old Mohawk and Hudson railroad station in Albany was refurbished to house the school; and some 25 students were enrolled on opening day. David Perkins Page of Newburyport, Massachusetts, who in future years would gain prominence as the author of a well-known text, *Theory and Practice of Teaching,* was drafted to direct the new school. Page was assisted in this venture by another highly-respected educator of the day, William F. Phelps (who later was chosen to head the New Jersey State Normal and Model School at Trenton when it first opened in October 1855).

In New York State in 1853, Edward Austin Sheldon was elected secretary of the Oswego Board of Education. During his tenure as superintendent of schools, a well-organized model school was first developed. Subsequently, a full-fledged normal school also was begun. Teacher-training methodologies developed at Oswego soon gained national attention and were widely emulated elsewhere for a number of years. Between 1866 and 1867, New York founded several other normal schools: at Brockport, Cortland, Fredonia, and Potsdam, followed by two more, at Geneseo and Buffalo, respectively.

In Connecticut, a public normal school was organized at New Britain in May 1850. About 30 or so students comprised its first class. Henry Barnard himself was enlisted to serve as principal. Unlike normal institutions elsewhere, from its inception the New Britain school had no difficulty retaining students for a full three-year course of studies. (More than anything else, its success was due to the fact that under state law, teachers' salaries were tied directly to completion of the curriculum in its entirety.) In May of 1854, the General Assembly of Rhode Island assumed support for Rhode Island State Normal, successor to a former private normal school founded two years previously in Providence in the fall of 1852. In Pennsylvania, the Lancaster County Normal Institute opened for business in April of 1855. Otherwise, no other public normal schools were established in the Commonwealth until the early 1900s.

Michigan initiated its first teachers' school in 1849 and subsequently followed up with the creation of four others, including Michigan State Normal at Ypsilanti. The assignment of a location for the latter institution was decided on through what turned out to be a spirited competition among several communities vying for the honor of supplying its site. (The tiny town of Gull Prairie reportedly went so far during the bidding war as to claim that "Nature or the God of Nature has planned and arranged the place for the special purpose of accommodating the State Normal School of Michigan." Unimpressed even by this revelation of theological predestination, state officials passed over Gull Prairie in favor of Ypsilanti when the latter turned out to be the highest bidder.) The new school first admitted students in March of 1853.

Minnesota founded a state normal school at Winona between 1858 and 1860, following up with another at St. Cloud in 1869. North Carolina's first entry in the field came in 1853 with funding for Union Institute, later renamed the Normal College. Wisconsin's Board of Regents embarked on an abortive attempt to earmark funds for normal training from the proceeds of the sale of public swamplands but without marked success. Only after 1866 was formal teacher preparation established under state appropriation.

Otherwise, with the exception of the founding of the Illinois Normal University in 1857 and of the Oswego Normal School in New York State, which was begun in 1861 and placed under state auspices in 1866, the movement to found normal schools did not gain momentum quickly. By 1865, there were still no more than 15 such state institutions in existence throughout the country. As events were to show, a broader, albeit desultory, expansion of the normal school movement was more of a post–Civil War phenomenon.[48]

Those attending municipal teacher-training institutions augmented enrollment at the earliest state normal schools. Boston had its own normal school by 1852. A city normal school separate and apart from the high school was opened in 1872; formerly it had been combined with a girls' high school. Worcester sponsored its own separate municipal normal school by 1868. In 1856, New York City's Board of Education organized a Normal School for Females; and within a few short years, Baltimore, San Francisco, and St. Louis (not to mention several smaller municipalities) had moved to create their own teacher-training institutions. Philadelphia opened a normal school for girls as early as 1848. In Chicago, to cite yet another example, a normal department was attached to a high school in 1856. St. Louis launched a normal school in 1857; Cincinnati, in 1868; and Cleveland, in 1874.[49] Not all municipal normal schools offered specific pedagogical instruction after the fashion of the state model. Many of them, although intended primarily for prospective teachers, offered little, if anything, besides a standard secondary-level course of instruction.

New Hampshire did not establish a state normal institution until 1871. Vermont launched a teachers' seminary in 1866, followed the next year by Nebraska. California established its first in 1862; Indiana, in 1865; Virginia and Louisiana, in 1884; North Carolina, in 1889; and Georgia, in 1890. Arizona and Florida both founded preparatory institutions in 1887. By 1875, there were state normals in 25 states, with a total combined enrollment of some 23,000 students. Added to the roster after 1864 was a state normal school in Emporia, Kansas; in Florence, Alabama, in 1873; at Cedar Falls, Iowa, in 1875; at Kirksville and Warrensburg, both in Missouri, in 1870 and 1871; and at Athens and Shepherdstown, West Virginia, in 1872.

By 1880, Maine, Minnesota and Vermont each had three state normal schools operating; Wisconsin had four; Missouri, five; Massachusetts and West Virginia, a half dozen or so each; and New York, eight. By 1885, state normal schools were scattered from Maine to

California and from Louisiana to Minnesota. Fifteen years later, there were almost 130 in existence, together with about an equal number of private normal schools.

Even with due allowance made for the increase in numbers, it is worth noting that the expansion and spread of normal schools took over half a century. Depending on the state in question, at the century's close normal-school graduates accounted for no more than about 10 to 40 percent of the total number of teachers entering schools each year. By 1898, the combined number of normal-school graduates in all states was still estimated to be less than a quarter of all teachers then employed nationwide. Thus, overall, the founding of normal schools occurred only by fits and starts; and it was obvious to nearly everyone at the end of the century that the degree of influence they exercised had fallen far short of the ambitious hopes nurtured on their behalf by the likes of James Carter and Horace Mann.

While normal schools were being founded in the mid-1800s, other educational agencies that traditionally had been relied on to supply teachers remained in operation. Private academies, some Latin grammar schools, and an expanding number of public secondary high schools all continued to turn out graduates intending to teach in the lower schools. Many observers felt the academic training these institutions afforded their students was infinitely preferable to anything the new normal schools were likely to develop. More often than not, in fact, economy-minded taxpayers and state officials looked at separate teacher-training institutions as a wholly unnecessary expense, believing that, at best, they could only hope to duplicate the work of the better-established schools with which they would inevitably begin to compete.

Unlike most students who completed a normal-school course of studies, those who matriculated as teachers from colleges or multipurpose secondary-level institutions (more than a few were virtually indistinguishable from one another in terms of their level of instruction) did so without benefit of any particular pedagogical training. This supposed deficiency in no way troubled those who had been skeptical about the advisability of creating normal schools all along and who resented the demands they placed on the public purse. At best, it was sometimes said, the value of self-styled teacher-training schools was the prospect that they too would evolve into serviceable secondary schools, fulfilling the needs of students in rural areas where academic high schools did not yet exist in any appreciable numbers. And therein lay the crux of a dilemma—one of "blurred identity" and disputed purpose—that was to plague normal schools ever after.

CONTROVERSY AND CONFLICT

From the outset, normal schools were controversial. They remained so over the span of their operations in the nineteenth century and on into the twentieth, when most were absorbed within or evolved into four-year colleges and universities. No small part of the problem they faced was popular skepticism about their utility. The question was whether normal preparatory training satisfied any genuine need whatsoever. All things considered, it was observed, instruction of the young had been managed successfully down through the ages, and without benefit of prior training for those who conducted the process. Why, then, it was asked, was it now thought necessary to establish special schools in which to prepare today's teachers for this time-honored undertaking? Was it not presumptuous for normal schools to claim that they alone could teach teachers to do what had been done without special training all along? Mastery of a body of subject matter, acquired through the example afforded by rigorous and systematic instruction, many declared emphatically, was sufficient, as always, to confer the ability to impart that same knowledge to others.

The rejoinder from normal schoolmen assumed a familiar form. Teaching subject matter to young children, they argued, was neither an easy nor an uncomplicated task, especially now when more and more students were attending school and for longer periods of time than ever before. Success in the classroom, it was held, required, first, that a teacher command knowledge of sound techniques for teaching, and, second, that he or she have acquired a high degree of proficiency in their use. Familiarity with what was to be taught was not enough by itself. Learning how to make good use of teaching methodologies, ran the argument, was not necessarily an intuitively obvious process at all; and it could not be assumed that acquiring the skills necessary on a hit-or-miss basis was assured. Hence prospective teachers needed to be *taught* appropriate pedagogical principles and rules, using a combination of didactic instruction and guided practice.

Cyrus Peirce, headmaster of the first normal school at Lexington, was only one of many to give the theme expression. "I do not now . . . assent," he wrote, "to the doctrine so often expressed in one form or another, that there are no general principles to be recognized in education; no general methods to be followed in the art of teaching; that all depends on the individual teacher; that every principle, motive and method, must owe its power to the skill with which it is applied . . . and that every man must invent his own methods of teaching and governing, it being impossible successfully to adopt those of another."[50] Novice teachers, he observed, might learn the necessary skills by trial and error and thereby attain a minimal level of proficiency—but often only at the expense of their students. Pierce entertained no doubt that the preferable alternative by far was to impart the basic rules for teaching and the underlying principles from which they were derived through direct instruction.

Whether any such principles and norms actually existed or needed to be taught explicitly was often disputed, as was the question as to whether normal schools were sufficient to the purpose. In any event, given their lack of broad support, it was perhaps inevitable that pedagogical academies and seminaries should remain objects of suspicion, derision, and distrust. Teachers' schools of any sort, public or private, it seemed, forever faced an uphill struggle in their quest for legitimacy and public acceptance.

One factor in particular further contributed to undermining their credibility and respectability, namely, the custom of admitting students directly from primary schools. However necessary or appropriate may have been the practice, it did serve to weaken claims that the normal school was destined to become not just a glorified high school or academy but a special type of postsecondary institution in its own right.

Second, for all their pretensions to model exemplary classroom practice, the quality of instruction in many normal schools was widely perceived to be inferior to that available in the better public high schools and academies of the day. The irony of teachers' institutions themselves plagued with a reputation for poor teaching seems not to have occasioned much public comment. But the perception of "normal" schools failing to live up to their name did not entirely escape notice either, even among schoolmen who themselves were sometimes their own severest critics.

Third, the level of instruction normal schools supplied was seen to fall well below that found in academic secondary schools. What normal students received in all but a very few institutions, depending on whether they finished a given course of study, amounted to little more than a brief review of the subjects they were expected to teach when they returned to primary classrooms, plus some didactic instruction in pedagogy and a smattering of advice on school discipline and classroom management. Otherwise, even for the minority who completed the abbreviated course of studies, only later into the century was additional work offered at anything approximating a secondary level.

Finally, lacking any sort of articulation or transfer arrangements with institutions of higher learning, normal schools tended to be consigned second-class status as so-called "terminal" institutions. Precisely because most secondary normals neither aspired to nor were acknowledged as providing an education equivalent to that supplied by a college preparatory academy or high school, those who graduated from them—with very few exceptions—were ineligible to apply for admission to a four-year college or university.

Naturally, over time admission standards gradually were tightened; and the clear trend toward the end of the century was one of requiring the high school diploma as a prerequisite for admission to the normal school course of studies. Nevertheless, as late as the 1890s, teacher educators had to concede that the typical normal curriculum in many institutions was still tied closely to that of the elementary school and that students who had not attended a secondary school were still admitted.

Normal educators themselves were deeply divided over the question of institutional mission and focus. Speaking in support of the idea that normal schools should emphasize the subjects future elementary teachers would teach, a speaker addressing the first meeting of the American Normal School Convention in 1859 declared, "A normal school is a professional institution aiming to impart to its pupils a thorough preparation for their future profession, and this preparation must include an ample and complete knowledge of the branches of learning properly belonging to that profession." The speaker added, "Any other theory of the normal school seems to me far too rigid, narrow, partial, pinched, and chilling."[51]

The unique mission of the normal school on this view was first and foremost providing "remedial" instruction for common-school graduates and, on that basis, preparing elementary schoolteachers. No other consideration, it was argued, should be allowed to divert normal schools from their central task. As Horace Mann himself had insisted almost 20 years earlier, "The first intellectual qualification of a teacher is a critical thoroughness, both in rules and principles, in regard to all the branches required . . . to be taught in the common schools; and a power of recalling them in any of their parts with a promptitude and certainty hardly inferior to that with which [the teacher] could tell his own name."[52]

By the same token, the general trend throughout the 1870s and 1880s was to expand and lengthen the normal-school course of study, adding on academic subjects resembling those taught in the old-time academies or the newer high schools. Normal school leaders defended the upward expansion of their curricula on the grounds that as professional standards were raised, it was increasingly expected that primary-school teachers should have completed something approaching a secondary education. Instruction at that level could only broaden and enrich a future teacher's preparation.

Critics were unconvinced, perceiving a self-interested effort to turn the normal school into an imitation academy or public high school. It was enough that a few schools should be supported at public expense, offering some modicum of training for the work of elementary schoolkeeping. But the notion that normal seminaries should be allowed to compete directly with secondary schools for enrollments, offering many of the same subjects of instruction, struck many as extremely ill-advised. Protestations on the part of normal schoolmen that their postelementary curricula were in fact different, that the subject matter was "professionalized" by emphasizing how the content could best be imparted by students to younger children, were not found persuasive.

An illustration of the argument was encapsulated in an address delivered as early as 1865 by Richard Edwards, who later served as president of Illinois Normal University. A normal school, he claimed, differed fundamentally in its aim from all other types of educational institutions. "Using, to a great extent, the same instruments as other schools, namely, treatises upon science and language, it nevertheless uses them for purposes very diverse," he explained.

> In an ordinary school, the treatise on arithmetic is put into the hands of the student in order that he may *learn arithmetic;* in the Normal School, the same book is used to enable him to learn *how to teach* arithmetic. In the ordinary school, the youth reads his Cicero with the purpose of learning the structure, vocabulary, and power of the Latin language; the normal student pores over the same author that he may adjust in his mind a method by which he may most successfully teach others these things. Both use the same materials, acquire, to some extent, the same knowledge, but aiming all the while at different ends.

In normal schools, Edwards stressed, "the whole animus of both teacher and pupil is this idea of future teaching. Every plan is made to conform to it. Every measure proposed is tried by this as a test. There is no other aim or purpose to claim any share of the mental energy of either. It is the Alpha and Omega of schemes of study and modes of thought."[53] Confirming the same point was a declaration delivered by S. S. Parr, president of the Department of Normal Schools of the National Education Association, in 1888, when he spoke at some length about the "teaching knowledge of subjects" that normal students should receive. "An analysis of the process of teaching," he claimed, "shows that there is a special knowledge in each subject that belongs to instruction. This is quite distinct from academic knowledge. It differs from it in purpose, in its relation to the facts in things, and in the mode by which it is obtained."[54]

For a time, the idea that subject-matter content could be adapted in a way specially fitted to suit the needs of those planning to teach the same material enjoyed great popularity among normal educators. Nevertheless, the details of the argument for pedagogic intent were difficult to elucidate clearly. Nor was it easy to defend with enough precision to make it persuasive; and the theme appears not to have attracted much support outside of normal school circles.

As it happened, for quite different reasons, support for normal schools as full-fledged secondary institutions came indirectly from a position enunciated by Chancellor Henry Tappan of the University of Michigan. In his annual report for 1856, Tappan argued that teachers at any level within the school system ought to be graduates of the unit just higher. Elementary teachers should be graduates of secondary schools, including normal schools. Secondary teachers, including normal school instructors, should be college graduates. College professors should have completed postbaccalaureate training, up to and including the doctoral level.[55] A variation on the theme urged simply that every prospective teacher ought to have completed a minimum of four years of formal education beyond the level at which the candidate was preparing to teach.

Some normals aimed at having students complete their high-school studies elsewhere before enrolling for a short course in pedagogy at a normal school. The Salem Normal School, for example, in 1858 advised prospective applicants, "When you have thoroughly completed [a secondary course of study] and acquired maturity and discipline of mind, if you wish to become teachers, come to us, and engage for our brief term, with the aid and company of others having the same end in view or already in the work, in the special study of the philosophy and art of teaching, and in the practical exercises tending to an immediate preparation for this noble work."[56]

Yet another complication facing normal schools as they struggled to define themselves was the high percentage of those enrolled who had no intention of becoming teachers. Many who sought admission to the normal school, it was apparent, did so only in hope of securing a secondary education for themselves at minimal cost. A substantial number were attending normal schools simply as a way of escaping agrarian life and as a means of qualifying for urban white-collar employment. Even among those young girls who did intend to enter classrooms, it was obvious that preparing to teach was at best a short-term expedient, an easily attained occupation to engage in before marrying and starting a family.

Nor was the academic caliber of students drawn to normal schools especially high—admission standards were extremely lax, particularly in the early years. Practically anyone who sought entrance, in other words, was admitted. In 1849, a former teacher wrote of so-called normalites that it seemed as if "at their birth, God Almighty stamped D-U-N-C-E in capital letters upon their foreheads." At a time when tuition charges for secondary education in a private high school were markedly higher and the tuition-free public high school was still something of a novelty, most students enrolled in a normal school allegedly had been sent for no other reason than "to save the expense of getting the rudiments of an education elsewhere."[57]

More than a few normal educators chafed at the restrictions students who did not intend to enter teaching placed on their ambitions to concentrate on teacher preparation. Furnishing a program of general academic instruction required so much time and energy, frustrated normal-school heads complained, that few opportunities existed to devote to professional teacher training—the very *raison d'être* of normal schools in the first place.[58] But sometimes it seemed normal educators were destined to come under harsh criticism no matter what. Once again, detractors felt that normal schools had no business offering any so-called professional studies whatever and that in so doing they were simply seeking the greater status and prestige more typically associated with academic colleges and universities.

As if offering confirmation, around the turn of the century skeptics could point to the example of Illinois Normal, Michigan State Normal at Ypsilanti, the teachers' institution in Albany, and a handful of others, all of them busily engaged in transforming themselves into full-fledged multipurpose colleges and universities. Several were already four-year schools preparing to confer bachelor of pedagogy degrees, and there was talk of two or three planning in addition to offer some graduate work. The same tendencies were at work at Kansas State Normal, at Southern Illinois Normal University at Carbondale, and elsewhere across the country.

Thomas J. Morgan of Rhode Island State Normal, writing in 1885, argued strongly that advanced normal schools, whatever their eventual destiny, should concentrate on pedagogical matters to the virtual exclusion of all else. They should refuse on principle, he held, to engage the task of offering secondary-level academic instruction. Neither should they seek to provide a review of elementary subject matter, as was still customary in a majority of teachers' institutions. "A large part of the strength of normal schools is spent in giving their pupils the rudiments of the common-school studies," he observed.

> They do academic instead of professional work. Against this policy it may be argued that it is a waste of resources. The normal school faculties are required to do what the faculties in the high school should do. It creates rivalry and jealousy between the normal and high schools. It degrades the normal from a professional to a secondary school, thus helping it to defeat its own ends—the creating of a professional spirit. It fatally lowers the standard of attainment that should be required of every teacher. It overcrowds the course of study, and by attempting to teach both matter and method, does nothing with thoroughness. It attempts the impossible.[59]

Even while debate continued, the context of the discussions was beginning to shift perceptibly. American education had been undergoing a major transformation, and the pace of change itself was accelerating. Elementary schooling in the post–Civil War era continued to expand as it had since the 1830s, but now at a rate markedly disproportional to the growth of the nation's population as a whole. By the century's end there would be an estimated 16 million or more children enrolled in the lower grades, a number fast approaching the entire school-age population for that level, those between the ages of five and 13. Gains in secondary education were even more phenomenal. Prior to 1860, the percentage of children age 14 or older who attended private secondary academies had been relatively small. In the 1870s and beyond, as tuition-free, publicly supported secondary education won acceptance and the numbers of free public high schools continued to expand, enrollments soared. In New England, in the mid-Atlantic states, and then in the Middle Western states as well, secondary enrollments had doubled almost every decade. They would attain the 1 million mark around the year 1900.

Needless to say, enrollment increases intensified the need for well-trained elementary and secondary teachers. Yet public opinion on how best to achieve the goal remained as divided as ever in the closing years of the century. The precedent was well established, of course, of allowing normal schools a role in preparing common-school teachers at the primary level. Whether it was possible or even desirable for normal institutions to assume the task of training secondary teachers was another matter entirely. Many believed that normal schools that were themselves basically still secondary-level institutions were, in the nature of things, unequal to the job.

Normal schoolmen responded by proposing an array of "lower" normal institutions for training elementary teachers and, superimposed upon it, a system of "advanced" or "higher" normal schools dedicated to preparing secondary teachers. Rebuffed in their efforts to persuade the public to look on teaching as a true profession, normal educators thus reacted or compensated, so to speak, by projecting the vision of an elaborate, graduated hierarchy of preparatory institutions. (Contemporary proposals late in the twentieth century to create a "career ladder" for teachers, beginning with interns or apprentice teachers and culminating with "master" teachers, appear to be motivated in part by the same desire to achieve full professional status for teachers, the elusive goal sought with so little success by nineteenth-century teacher educators.)

One blueprint envisioned a system of county training centers that would continue to prepare young women for a few years' service in the classrooms of the common schools. Lower normals in particular would focus on training elementary or primary teachers to work on a short-term basis in outlying rural areas. Higher normal schools, for their part, would train secondary teachers and normal instructors. Their central mission, in contrast with that of county schools, would be to address the long-term needs of future education professionals, those entering the field with an ambition to make teaching a full-fledged career. The intended beneficiaries would be mostly males, and they would be equipped to become not just high-school teachers but high-ranking school administrators and normal faculty members.[60]

Another suggestion was to turn some of the better normal schools into multi-tiered, multipurpose institutions capable of sponsoring parallel courses of study at several different levels simultaneously. A basic curriculum would service the needs of normal students admitted with only a rudimentary knowledge of the common branches of knowledge taught in elementary schools—those who would need to complete a full four years of study. Two- or three-year courses of study would take students through the equivalent of high school and fit them to become secondary teachers. A briefer course would be taught for students who had already completed secondary education and were now seeking specialized training as future high-school teachers.[61] The normal school would offer special courses for college graduates needing brief instruction in the art of teaching. Finally, it was proposed, for those who had come up through the ranks, as it were, and now were planning to prepare themselves to assume positions as normal faculty instructors, specialized training would be made available. In short, given the chance, normal schools would do it all.

UNIVERSITY TEACHER TRAINING

An obvious alternative was to look to the nation's colleges and fledgling universities to help prepare teachers. Lower normal schools, it was suggested, should be encouraged to continue in their work of preparing qualified elementary teachers from an ever-growing pool of secondary graduates. But high-school teachers, not to mention future school administrators and other specialists, it was said, needed to complete a full baccalaureate program of study. Hence the logical place to append whatever specialized preparation might be required was at the college level, not in a normal school. In sum, if there were to be "higher" normal courses of study established, they should be organized as collegiate curricula. Many normal schoolmen themselves actively supported the idea of locating teacher education within universities.

William H. Payne of the University of Michigan reversed the thrust of the argument. Speaking of the preparatory needs of the great majority of teacher candidates, he remarked, "The most that can be expected, with any show of reason, is that this preponderant body of teachers receive a good secondary education, and, in close connection with it, instruction in the most approved methods of doing school work. This, I repeat, is the utmost that can be expected of the transient members of the teacher's profession. Here lies, as it seems to me, the function of the normal school."[62] Similarly, as early as 1871 William F. Phelps, then serving as principal of a Minnesota normal school, noted that "the true office of a normal or training school for teachers is to impart professional, rather than general instruction; to make good teachers rather than profound scholars."[63] The implication, of course, was that if more advanced or higher academic learning was considered essential for teachers, its provision would necessarily fall within the purview of colleges and universities rather than traditional normal schools.

Part of the problem, however, was that up until the early 1880s, institutions of higher learning had been exceedingly slow to evince much interest in the training of teachers. To the extent that academicians in the various established disciplines troubled themselves to consider the matter at all, the common presumption was that a sound liberal education, perhaps combined with some greater in-depth exploration of the subject or subjects to be taught, would enable a person to teach effectively—and presumably at any level. Only infrequently was it conceded that a limited number of pedagogical courses also might be helpful to those planning to teach in elementary or secondary schools. And even if some special training were needed, it was by no means clear in the minds of many faculty members that a college or university was the proper place to offer it.

In 1827, the faculty of Amherst College, for example, initially endorsed a proposal to sponsor a course in the "science of education" but subsequently reversed itself and rejected the idea. In 1831, a department of education was opened at Washington College, Pennsylvania. A year later, New York University founded a chair in education to instruct "teachers of common schools." (There is some question as to whether the proposed pedagogical lectures were ever actually delivered.) In 1850, Brown University inaugurated a normal department headed by the city school superintendent in Providence, who held the post of "Professor of Didactics." The arrangement was suspended five years later when the Rhode Island Normal School began accepting students. By 1860, a lecture series open to seniors entitled "Philosophy of Education, School Economy, and the Teaching Art" was under way on the campus of the University of Michigan.

The first permanent chair of education seems to have been that established at the University of Iowa in 1873, building on a normal department created in 1855. The announced intention was to educate teachers "for advanced schools." This initiative was followed five years later on the same campus by the creation of a College of Normal Instruction. During the academic year 1879-80, the University of Michigan inaugurated a Department of the Science and Art of Teaching. In 1881, Wisconsin authorized the establishment of its own Department of Pedagogy. By 1884, there were similar pedagogical departments in operation at the University of North Carolina and at Johns Hopkins University. Indiana University and Cornell followed with their own teacher-training units in 1886. One year later, in 1887, the forerunner of Teachers College at Columbia University was open for business.[64]

Some college trustees and presidents steadfastly resisted pressures to assume responsibility for training teachers. Others acceded but only reluctantly, fearing perhaps they might otherwise be left behind. Still others welcomed the challenge, either as a matter of principled conviction or, it may be supposed, because they foresaw a low-cost opportunity to augment student enrollments. Whatever the reasons, despite an earlier lack of enthusiasm, from the early 1880s college-based teacher training grew at an unprecedented rate. Before century's end there were at least 114 colleges and universities out of a total of approximately 400 sponsoring teachers' courses or programs of study in one form or another. In 1900, an estimated one-fourth of all private liberal colleges had begun offering pedagogical sequences or were making plans to do so within the very near future.

In 1890, over 3,400 students were enrolled in teacher preparatory courses, approaching nearly 9 percent of the student total enrolled in all American collegiate institutions combined. By 1892, at least 31 major universities had authorized chairs of pedagogical didactics, and many more had linked chairs of pedagogy with appointments in philosophy, rhetoric, or some other field or discipline. From the mid-1800s to the beginning of the new century, the number of colleges and universities sponsoring departments or chairs of pedagogics had practically doubled, climbing to a total of close to 250 before 1910.[65]

Partly concealed by impressive enrollment increases in the 1890s and early 1900s was the precarious and somewhat problematic nature of the toehold teacher training had gained in academe. Around the middle third of the 1800s, it was true, a number of state universities (particularly in the Midwest) had begun establishing so-called normal departments, many of them having done so practically at their inception.[66] Yet despite occasional pretensions to the contrary, normal units of the late nineteenth century were by no means organizational entities comparable in stature or standing to the discipline-based academic departments then beginning to coalesce within the nation's leading universities. Most teacher-training programs, such as they were, were still little more than ancillary operations, mere institutional appendages in no way fully coordinate with other academic components of the institution. Quite the contrary, what they offered more often than not was an entirely separate course of instruction, pitched not much above the secondary level, and for students who might not otherwise have qualified for regular admission. Nor were those enrolled in normal departments necessarily eligible to receive the same baccalaureate degrees their peers in other fields were awarded upon completing their studies.

Almost no one, it seemed, was satisfied with what increasingly looked like a halfway measure. College and university faculties, for their part, did not necessarily welcome the advent of normal schools and departments of any sort in their midst, regarding them as a kind of secondary-level encroachment on collegiate education. That preparatory training for future teachers was being conducted at the possible expense of a regular college education inspired even champions of teacher training to issue complaints. "The attempt to teach professional studies to callow minds," declared Walter L. Hervey of the New York College for the Training of Teachers (later Teachers College, Columbia University), "disgusts the mind and discredits the studies." He added, "There exists no more fruitful source of complaint against professional training than this unfortunate blunder."[67]

Anticipating an argument heard with more and more frequency in the years to follow—and as regularly ignored—Burke Hinsdale of the University of Michigan, speaking at the National Education Association's National Convention in 1890, avowed, "Neither special methods nor general methods can be taught successfully until the pupil has a good academic education. The *what* must come before the *how*."[68] Hinsdale himself was a strong supporter of collegiate-level teacher education, both because he believed it was a legitimate function of postsecondary education and because he felt that if high standards were maintained, the full incorporation of teacher training within academe would confer upon it the prestige and respectability it sorely needed and deserved. "It is a function of the university to furnish society with teachers," he insisted. "Research, teaching, and the preparation of teachers, are the three great duties that it owes society."

Hinsdale still foresaw a continuing role for normal schools: "The preparation of teachers for primary and grammar schools, and possibly for the lower classes of high schools, may be left to normal and training schools." But high schools and other secondary schools, he emphasized, "must receive their character from teachers of a higher grade of scholarship." He concluded, "The chair of pedagogy and the teaching profession need the strength and dignity that university recognition will give them. Such recognition will be the strongest testimony that the university can bear to the public of the estimate in which it holds the art that it exists to practice."[69]

Similarly, in 1888, President Charles Kendall Adams of Cornell told conference participants attending a meeting of the New England Association of Colleges and Preparatory Schools that institutions of higher learning in America had a special responsibility to provide professional teacher training and to carry it forward to a higher level of development.[70] Adams entertained no doubt that the "systematic teaching of pedagogy" was both possible and necessary. In his address he took issue with those who argued that good teachers were born, not made; that it was inherently impossible to instruct someone in the art of teaching; and that, in the nature of the case, learning to teach was simply a matter of imitation or trial and error. "At best," he responded, "observation can teach only the mere method of imparting instruction; whereas no small part of the vocation consists of knowing what to teach and what to leave untaught. . . . The untrained teacher is obliged to pick up at haphazard and by dint of observation, and perhaps long and painful experience, a knowledge of a very large part of the means and conditions of success."

Adams did not deny that "the great and rare art of most successfully imparting instruction is a gift that seems often to have been bestowed by nature herself." And yet, he asked, "Who has not observed that sometimes the most successful teachers have grown slowly into their exceptional efficiency by a painstaking experience leading them gradually away from a most unpromising beginning?" He concluded, "It would be flying in the face of all observation and experience to deny that many of the best teachers have come up to their present condition with no other helps than the gifts of nature and opportunity; but this important fact no more proves the inutility of training than the successes of Washington and Franklin and Lincoln prove the inutility of a collegiate education."[71]

Many remained unconvinced. The question hotly debated was whether trying to take in pedagogical training was not "liable to infringe upon and diminish" the true work of a college or university.[72] Academic traditionalists for the most part remained unpersuaded that pedagogy, a subject formerly taught only at the secondary level, would ever deserve to be elevated to the status demanded of a true college discipline. The feeling was that not only did Education lack any coherent or well-defined body of content, it was unlikely to acquire one any time soon. Attempting to transform it by mere administrative fiat into a legitimate subject of scholarly inquiry and formal instruction at the university level, they alleged, was both quixotic and something of an imposture.

President Charles W. Eliot of Harvard gave voice to the sentiments of many skeptics who were inclined to look with ill-concealed derision and scorn on newly established chairs of pedagogy and education departments. "The faculty, I feel," he commented, "has but slight interest or confidence in what is ordinarily called pedagogy."[73]

If college faculties steeped in the liberal arts tradition were dubious over prospects for making pedagogy a bona fide discipline, they harbored even greater reservations about the academic abilities and qualifications—or rather, the seeming lack thereof—of those recruited to accomplish the task. The truth of the matter was, scholars experienced in organizing genuine college-level courses of pedagogical study simply did not yet exist. The trend that aroused the most criticism was assigning responsibility for the development of preparatory programs to faculty members who were ill-equipped to meet the challenge. A typical complaint about the cavalier way appointments were being handled came in 1903 from one professor who observed, "In some cases it seems that the call has been the result of an effort to find a place for a man who is thought to be able to do less harm in a department of education than elsewhere."[74]

Lacking qualified professors, universities sometimes turned to former public school officials—to school superintendents, principals, and normal-school functionaries—to help build up academic teacher-training programs. In some cases at least, the outcome was reasonably successful, judged by prevailing standards of the day. More often the results were nothing short of disastrous, consisting of courses treating the minutiae of classroom practice in the most mechanical fashion imaginable. Lacking much in the way of intellectual content or substance, most differed but little from offerings commonly found in lower-level normal schools.

Explaining why so many prospective teachers sought to avoid the courses being devised, one professor conceded frankly it was because "the pedagogical work is so namby-pamby and stupid that an active brain gets too weary to stand it." Partly for this reason, more acceptable by far was the practice of combining academic appointments—that is, of commandeering someone already holding an accredited position as a philosopher, rhetorician, sociologist, historian, or psychologist, and appointing him to a post as professor of pedagogical didactics. He would then be given a mandate to offer one or two special courses expressly for teacher candidates. Among the early pioneers whose interests turned to pedagogy and held joint appointments were William James and G. Stanley Hall, Edward L. Thorndike, John Dewey, Albion Small, Thorstein Veblen, and Herbert Baxter Adams, among others.

Pedagogy as a college-level subject of instruction, it must be said, tended to be quite abstract and theoretical in character when academics from the traditional disciplines were placed in charge. Not much was made at first of the now-familiar distinction between general education and separate specialized "professional" training for teachers. Opinion held, rather, that if there was to be teacher training at all, subject matter of special relevance and interest to teachers should be incorporated with only some slight shift in emphasis or focus as an element within a solid liberal-arts education.

The notion that professional teacher education had virtually no separate identity apart from liberal learning prevailed, of course, at a time when pedagogical studies were still in their embryonic form and were as yet poorly defined. Very little in the way of a separate or systematic body of knowledge, in other words, had yet grown up around teaching as an activity. Inevitably, it was to the established humanities and fledgling social science disciplines that most teacher educators looked for inspiration and guidance. The aim essentially was to draw on established academic subject fields for whatever relevant insights they might afford relative to the work of the lower classroom. Certainly at first, in the search for a substantive content for pedagogical studies, no better alternatives suggested themselves.

Philosophy, law, psychology, political economy, and sociology were the undergirding studies most commonly called upon. The expectation or hope was they might contribute, for example, to a better understanding of schools as social institutions, of learning in its cultural contexts, the nature of instructional goals, formative processes of child development, ethical considerations in instruction, and so on. The result was the emergence of such disciplinary hybrids as history of education, philosophy of education, sociology of education, comparative education, and educational psychology—specialized studies derived from their respective parent disciplines—which were then deployed to furnish the staples of the early teacher preparation curriculum. What prospective teachers needed to acquire, it was assumed, was a sense for the critical and interpretive context of teaching and learning, a broad intellectual perspective on their future work.

Only later on did the notion of pedagogy as *teknikós*—as almost exclusively a matter of acquiring and applying specific instructional techniques—begin to win acceptance in higher education. In the twentieth century it eventually came to exercise a controlling influence in teacher-training circles, assuming for a time something akin to the status of unquestioned dogma. Needless to add, as specialized methods courses began to crowd in and dominate the preparatory curriculum, older "foundational" studies in education—educational psychology being the sole exception—tended to lose their central role within preparatory curricula. Increasingly, instead, the trend was to assign them a purely "ceremonial" role or to consign them more and more to the periphery of teacher education. The fact that history and philosophy of education courses acquired a certain notoriety for being poorly taught and irrelevant to the practical concerns of classroom practitioners probably only hastened the process.

As it turned out, looking to former classroom teachers, school administrators, and normal officials as well as university scholars to build up an education faculty tended to produce what can only be characterized as highly eclectic curricula. A typical course of studies, such as that offered at Michigan in 1889-90, included four hours of mandatory course work in the first semester, including lectures on "the art of teaching and governing," instruction in methods of instruction and general classroom practice, school hygiene, and school law. In the second academic term, students enrolled for three hours of courses devoted to the history of ancient and medieval education, school supervision, general school management, and "the art of grading and arranging courses of study." Subsequent terms were given over to a study of "the theoretical and critical principles underlying the art of teaching and governing," the historical development of modern education, comparative study of educational systems, and seminars ("seminaries") on special topics in the history and philosophy of education.[75]

Even within larger institutions, it was not until after the opening of the twentieth century that colleges and universities went much beyond the appointment of a single individual to handle all responsibilities pertaining to teacher training. Charles DeGarmo, writing in 1892, deplored the fact that a genuine institutional commitment to the preparation of teachers for the lower schools was so frequently lacking. "Our chairs of pedagogy in American universities," he alleged, "are fatally defective, in that they are component but not organic units of university life. They are mechanically but not organically connected with their own allied subjects. . . . The professor of pedagogy is neatly glued on the university as a whole, but he has no group of men with whom he can organize an education department."[76]

On the other side, even when full departments or schools of education were assembled, doubts persisted across campus about their academic rigor and integrity, doubts that extended to the scholarly abilities of those recruited to staff them. A decidedly uncomplimentary portrait of the education professor dating from the early 1900s foreshadowed unkind epithets heard frequently throughout the rest of the century. The erstwhile expert in pedagogics, it was remarked, was "gentle, unintellectual, saccharine, and well-meaning . . . a bumbling doctor of undiagnosable ills, harmless if morosely defensive," someone apt to be "either a mechanic" or a "flatulent promoter of irrelevant trivia."[77] Nothing else perhaps so vividly illustrates how schoolmen-turned-professors at the turn of the century had failed to win the confidence of their academic peers and colleagues. Nor, more fundamentally, had the teacher preparation over which they presided yet gained acceptance as a sound and legitimate academic undertaking. (The aspiration to make it so, it could be argued almost a full century later, has still to be realized.)

All the while, the problem of how best to mount baccalaureate teaching-training programs loomed large. By the end of the nineteenth century, most of the basic organizational or structural issues had already surfaced and were fast becoming subjects of lively debate. Much depended on how the work of teacher preparation was conceived. Was teacher training something to be *grafted onto* liberal learning? Could the former somehow be *infused* or *integrated within* the latter? Or were the two *indistinguishable* from one another?

Unresolved questions abounded. Was it appropriate, it was asked, to introduce professional and methodological courses to teacher candidates while they were still in the midst of pursuing their own general academic studies, possibly even in their first or second year of college? Within a four-year program of studies, what sort of balance should be struck between the professional or technical components of a future teacher's preparation and the liberal elements of the student's undergraduate education? Could the two be intertwined somehow, or run parallel to one another? Or ought they to be sequenced apart, in entirely separate courses? Finally, who should decide all such issues—should responsibility for teacher training be assigned exclusively to an education faculty, or should it be an undertaking shared by the institution as a whole? If the latter, what would be required to enlist the cooperation and support needed from professors in the various liberal arts and sciences?

Other questions followed. Should future secondary teachers be required to have an academic "major" or field of concentration based on the subjects they intended to teach eventually? And should the teaching of pedagogical courses be delayed until late in a baccalaureate degree program? Or was it preferable to postpone specialized teacher training until even later, after candidates had completed their bachelor's degrees? Again, were the preparatory needs of elementary teachers significantly different from those of prospective high-school teachers? When should practice teaching occur? Did student teaching need to be preceded by guided observation and prior internship experiences in elementary or secondary classrooms? These and other considerations continued to challenge teacher educators throughout the course of the twentieth century—and it might be said that in a very real sense they have never admitted of any authoritative resolution or consensus.

Overshadowing all other issues late in the nineteenth century and early in the twentieth was the still-unresolved question of the intellectual and academic legitimacy of teacher education itself as a professional enterprise. *Was* there in fact an accredited and reliable body of knowledge underlying preparatory programs, regardless of how they were organized? Or at least were there grounds for believing that a body of knowledge capable of providing their intellectual and empirical underpinnings was in process of development? Had the study of "education" begun to construct its own unique conceptual apparatus, an organizing framework of ideas, its own modes of inquiry and investigation? Or was pedagogy inherently derivative from other more basic disciplines, possessing no special identity of its own?

The tendency among early nineteenth-century educators had been always to assume or flatly assert that a true "science" of education already existed. Alternatively, confidence was expressed that an authentic discipline could be expected to emerge within the near future. As James Carter told the American Institute of Instruction in 1830, although it was true to say of pedagogy that it was still in its infancy as a field of inquiry, further progress in its development as a valid science was destined to advance "with a motion as steady and irresistible as that of the spheres."[78] Lending support to the theme, Richard Edwards weighed in with much the same judgment years later. Speaking before a meeting of the National Education Association in 1865, he responded to critics, observing "It has been sometimes intimated that this pretended science of education is a myth—that the talk of it is of little account. It has been charged, perhaps not altogether generously, that its advocates and professors are more enthusiastic than wise—that they are either intentional deceivers of the public, or unwitting deceivers of themselves—that, in short, the whole matter is a sort of well-intentioned imposture."

Edwards expressed confidence that the basic principles of teaching were already known and that, much as was happening in the field of medicine, their implications and applications would be further drawn out and added to over time. "There is here," he avowed, "as noble a science as ever engaged the thought of men. There are immutable principles here, that ought to be studied and comprehended by every young person entering on the work of teaching. There is, in the nature of things, a foundation for a profession of teaching."[79]

By the end of the century, with so little seeming progress registered, growing skepticism about the alleged inevitability of a discipline of education emerging might have been understandable. The task of making a case for a true "science" of education by now had acquired a certain intellectual urgency about it; and with so few solid advances in evidence, the attempt to carry it forward tended to place proponents on the defensive. Showing that preparatory programs for classroom teachers rested on a solid foundation of knowledge, that they could be made more academically defensible, was a challenge that would occupy the attention and energy of teacher educators for decades to come.

2

TEACHER PREPARATION IN THE TWENTIETH CENTURY

TEACHER CERTIFICATION

Accompanying dramatic increases in the numbers of students attending school at the turn of the century and beyond was an enduring, always troublesome, teacher shortage. In the year 1890, according to official estimates, some 14.1 million youngsters were enrolled in American schools; of these, more than half a million were attending secondary institutions (including 357,800 or so in public high schools and the remainder—about 142,000—in private schools). In 1930, four decades later, school enrollments had reached 23.5 million, including an estimated 4.5 to 4.7 million in public and private high schools. By 1940, the secondary enrollment total alone exceeded 7.1 million. Elementary enrollments between 1900 and 1930, meanwhile, had increased on average nearly 14 percent each decade.

Finding enough teachers to meet expanding needs of this magnitude, especially at the secondary level, posed a major challenge. Some 364,000 full-time teachers were employed in the nation's public schools as of 1890, of which only slightly over 9,000 were secondary teachers. Together with those teaching in private elementary and secondary schools, the total amounted to 403,000. In the school year 1896-97, the tally stood at 404,300, much of it still accounted for by primary-grade teachers. The number of secondary teachers thereafter increased by about 6,000 yearly, representing a disproportionately greater rate of increase than that registered for elementary teachers. Yet even this rise in the numbers of high-school teachers entering the field failed to keep pace with the upward trend of secondary enrollments. By 1900, the total number of elementary and secondary teachers combined had jumped to 423,062, including over 20,300 employed in public high schools. In 1930, the combined total exceeded 640,000.[1]

The most charitable thing to be said of teachers' academic credentials from the 1890s into the early 1900s, possibly, is that they still left much to be desired. Formal qualifications for entry into teaching—reflective perhaps of the dynamics of supply and demand—were to improve only incrementally as the new century wore on. The typical elementary teacher employed in 1895, for example, had less than the equivalent of a high-school education. By 1922, the same was still true of approximately one-fourth of all teachers working in the primary grades. Perhaps 50 percent or less had completed two or fewer years of college. Ten years later, it was estimated, upward of 40 percent of all secondary teachers had not completed a full four years of college.

As late as the 1920s, one in every 20 elementary teachers in the United States still had no schooling beyond the high-school level. One-fifth of all elementary teachers who had completed high school reported having attended college for one year or less; and more than one-fourth of that same group had finished less than two years of college. In 1931, only about 10 to 12 percent of all elementary teachers held a bachelor's degree. As for senior high–school teachers, in 1930-31 fully 25 percent had not completed four years of college. Even as late as 1952, not even a majority of elementary teachers had graduated from college, although by then the percentage of teachers with fewer than two years of college had fallen overall from 25 percent in 1931 to around 8 percent.[2]

State control over teacher certification standards and licensing was slow to develop over the course of the first third of the twentieth century. In 1898, only three states had assumed exclusive authority for establishing minimum qualifications and issuing teaching licenses. Responsibility for teacher licensure in virtually all other states was divided between state and county authorities. The common pattern was for the state to prescribe general guidelines only, leaving it to school district officials in the various counties to decide how regulations were applied. Usually it was the county superintendent of schools or a local district examiner who drew up written examinations required of all teacher applicants. For all practical purposes, test results served as the sole basis for certification and employment.

As might be expected, standards varied greatly from state to state. In more than half the states in 1900, a prospective teacher was given a license to teach in the elementary grades simply by passing an examination on the primary-level subjects taught. The same was true in half the states in 1921, when an applicant could obtain a provisional license without having satisfied any other academic requirements whatsoever. In 1907, Indiana was the first state to require graduation from high school as a minimal teaching qualification. By 1921, 14 states had imposed the same prerequisite, and 4 others required additional schooling beyond the secondary level. In 1926, 27 states required more than high-school graduation. By 1937, a year or more of college training was required in 32 states; only 8 still did not stipulate any postsecondary schooling requirement.[3]

Undifferentiated or "blanket" teaching licenses were the norm in the early 1900s. Certificates specific to teaching levels were a later innovation, as were licenses tied to a particular teaching field at the secondary level. Some states experimented with a graduated system of licenses based on the number of years of formal schooling an applicant had completed. By 1930, practically all states issued certificates specifically for teaching in the elementary grades; 26 states issued licenses for junior high–school teachers; and 31 states issued them for high-school teachers.[4]

In 1910, 30 states issued special certificates or licenses for those who had graduated from college, nineteen of which required a specified amount of professional training added in. In 1906, approximately three-fourths of all the states were requiring completion of at least one general course in the theory and art of teaching as a minimal condition for licensure. By 1925, at least 21 states had added provisions requiring an applicant for a teaching license to have completed multiple professional preparatory courses. Most frequently cited were courses in educational psychology, history of education, and school law.

Indicative both of progress registered and of how much further improvement was needed, at the century's halfway point 37 states required more than four years of college; and only six states allowed less. Two years later it was reported that only 17 states required a college degree for elementary-school teachers; five required two and one-half or three years of college work; 18 required one and one-half years or two years of college training; and one state required no college work preparatory to working in an elementary classroom. In that same year, 1952, fully half the nation's 600,000 public elementary-school teachers did not hold college degrees.[5]

How teacher licensure was managed or administered was the subject of frequent complaints. State officials in the early years especially were notorious for imposing extraneous or questionable requirements at will. The most egregious example perhaps was that of an Arkansas law in 1893 denying eligibility to atheists—examiners were "not to license any person to teach who is given to profanity, drunkenness, gambling, licentiousness, or other demoralizing vices, or who does not believe in the existence of a Supreme Being."[6] Ideological considerations and partisan interests similarly affected the content of certification examinations administered at the local level. Tests tended to be perfunctory or amounted to little more than exercises in triviality or irrelevance. A standard "gate-keeping" question in one instance queried candidates about the effects of alcohol on the human circulatory system. Anyone who did not concur that consumption of alcoholic beverages led inevitably and fatally to arteriosclerosis was assured of failure.[7]

Efforts to introduce reforms in teacher licensure in the early 1900s more or less converged with attempts to transform the governmental civil service system. In place of the patronage typical in many urban school districts (where job candidates were subject to the capricious, often corrupt machinations of political machines and often lived in fear for their positions once they had attained them), the movement was to create more rational standards for eligibility to teach. Uniform, impartial procedures governing teacher hiring and retention were a high priority. Exemplifying the reform impulse were initiatives seeking to consolidate teacher licensure functions within state departments of education, to require applicants to have completed four years of college, and to replace locally administered examinations with required college-level courses in pedagogical theory and classroom methodology. Most frequently cited as obligatory subjects were educational psychology, general teaching methods, history and philosophy of education, and practice teaching.

Teacher educators from university departments of pedagogy, not surprisingly, were in the forefront of the campaign to inaugurate state-mandated course requirements for teacher licensure. Active too in the work of recommending criteria and lobbying for standards were the American Association of Teachers' Colleges, the National Education Association, the Society for the Study of Education, the National Society of College Teachers of Education, and a number of other associations and professional interest groups. Inevitably, as soon as state standards were drawn up and approved, so-called educationists moved with alacrity to adjust preparatory programs within their respective institutions to conform to the new regulations—requirements that they themselves or their professional advocates had helped enshrine in state statutes.

So long as prospective teachers were not required to submit credits from pedagogical courses to support their applications for certification, it has been said, most colleges and universities remained indifferent to teacher preparation. But once the completion of specified education courses was made prerequisite to licensure, institutions of higher learning awoke from their lethargy and hastened to adjust their offerings accordingly.[8] The need to accommodate the large numbers of their own students planning upon graduation to teach in the lower schools now assumed an urgency it had heretofore lacked. Needless to add, pedagogy departments were the major beneficiaries of the new system. With the full weight of the state's authority behind them, a market for their curricular offerings was now virtually assured. If students wanted to become teachers, in most states they had no choice but to complete a required battery of courses under the control of the fledgling education professorate.

In the opening years of the century no great prescience was needed to foresee the direction in which public policy was moving. The wave of the future was teacher certification tied to possession of the baccalaureate degree (or something approaching the better part of four years of college) and completion of a stipulated number of state-mandated education courses. Established four-year colleges and universities were poised to ride the wave's crest. Threatened by engulfment and much less well positioned to respond were lower-level normal schools of the old-fashioned variety. They would need to evolve quickly or die.

FROM NORMAL SCHOOLS
TO STATE TEACHERS' COLLEGES

In 1890, there were approximately 135 public normal schools of varying types and sizes still in existence. Their combined student enrollment stood at 27,000, representing only a fraction of the total number of students preparing to become teachers. Additionally, there existed 40 or so private normal schools, the majority of which were strictly regional or local institutions that specialized in providing some type of general education beyond the eighth grade. Ten years later, the total number of normal schools had shrunk to 127 (although a few of them had grown larger and their combined student enrollments had risen to a total of

47,000). By 1920, the number had fallen to sixty-nine; and by 1933 there were no more than 50 public normal institutions still flourishing. The trend in the early 1930s if not before was unmistakable: Single-purpose normal schools of the traditional sort were fast disappearing.

Few mourned their impending demise. Public or private, normal schools had long suffered a reputation for inferior academic quality and lax standards. In the opening decades of the twentieth century, it was widely acknowledged that admission standards had remained low despite repeated overtures to make them more stringent. In 1895, for example, only 14 percent of a sample of 51 normal schools required a high-school diploma. By 1905, ten years later, the percentage had increased to no more than 22 percent. In 1908, the Department of Normal Schools of the National Education Association passed a resolution in favor of requiring a high-school diploma for admission to normal schools. Not until the 1930s was it required by the majority of the few schools then remaining.[9]

Meanwhile, criticism of normal schools for reasons unrelated to entrance standards had been mounting steadily since the 1880s. It reached a crescendo of sorts just after the turn of the century, when practically no one—or so it seemed—had good things to say about them. Homer H. Seerly, president of Iowa State Normal, offered a representative judgment in 1902 when he remarked, "The normal schools have made and still make too much of theory, dogma, and philosophy and too little of the real, the practical, and the essential."[10] Charles A. McMurry spoke to the same point a few years later, emphasizing that his remarks were intended to encompass teacher education generally. "Our teachers," he declared, "have had an overdose of theory not well related to practice."[11]

Normal schools were increasingly looked upon with something akin to professional embarrassment. More and more they were seen as an anachronism, as a vestigial atavism of the past, steeped in outmoded lore and no longer well connected with present needs. Through no fault of their own, it was suggested, normal schools had never fully succeeded in providing a reliable supply of high-quality classroom teachers for the nation's public elementary schools. Still less had it proven possible to enlist them for training high-school teachers. Perhaps now they had outlived their usefulness altogether.

Whatever the reasons for the negative perception of normal schools, something had to be done. Indicative of the direction events were moving, in 1908 the Department of Normal Schools of the National

Education Association drew up a policy statement recommending that "Good as the word 'normal' is, it should be dropped from the name of these schools and they should be called Teachers [*sic*] Colleges."[12] Scarcely appreciated at the time was that in most cases something more than a simple name change would be needed to turn these schools into authentic collegiate institutions.

Sorting out the details as to which normal schools went out of business and which successfully transformed themselves into four-year colleges is no easy task.[13] Some private normal schools simply sank into oblivion, their passing unnoticed and unlamented. Here and there, a few public normals likewise folded quietly for lack of support. More often, however, the better public normal schools were able to manage the transition, undergoing metamorphosis into full-fledged state teachers' colleges or universities. (In still other cases, state normal colleges were built from the ground up, having no lineage tracing back to some antecedent institution.) Serving to confirm the change from normal school to college was the gradual elimination of the abbreviated one- or two-year courses of study in which old-time normals had once specialized, and their replacement by four-year sequences leading to the baccalaureate degree. Some colleges, seemingly reluctant to divest themselves entirely of their normal school identity, did preserve for a time two- and three-year courses of study for elementary teachers. Simultaneously, they began introducing four-year courses of study for future secondary teachers.

Whereas in the year 1913 there were less than a dozen teachers' colleges in existence, and in 1915, about 18 such colleges, by 1920 or soon thereafter, almost 50 institutions had sprung up to claim the title. By 1928, their numbers had mushroomed to 137. Two years later, by 1930, at least 88 former normal schools had transformed themselves into four-year, degree-granting institutions. It was estimated overall that publicly supported teachers' colleges were preparing 21 percent of all junior high –school teachers and 17 percent of all senior high school teachers. (The rest were trained in universities or normal institutions.) By 1933, the total number of state teachers' colleges had risen to 146. An alternate estimate placed the number in 1931 at 156.[14] In 1939, something on the order of 180,000 students were enrolled in teachers colleges. The institutions these candidates were attending furnished close to 60 percent of all the public school teachers entering the field. By the early 1950s, no fewer than 200 state teachers' colleges were in full operation.[15]

Not all teachers' college graduates necessarily completed a full four years of postsecondary education, however. As late as 1930, of the

60,300 graduates of teachers' colleges and the small handful of normal schools remaining combined, approximately one in every five had completed nothing more extensive than a one-year course of studies. About half had finished a two-year curriculum. Fifteen percent or so had gone through a three-year course sequence; and only 18 percent had actually graduated from a four-year program.[16]

Especially influential in the field of teacher preparation in the last years of the 1800s and into the early twentieth century was a small group of institutions founded prior to 1900 as normal colleges or universities. Unlike former normal secondary schools now engaged in turning themselves into four-year collegiate institutions, the former were ostensibly postsecondary institutions from their very inception. Oftentimes they afforded the model or example to which newer colleges looked for guidance in their own development. The former included Kansas State Normal in Emporia (founded in 1865), Southern Illinois State Normal University at Carbondale (founded in 1873), Iowa State Normal (founded in 1876), and the Illinois State Normal University. Among them, Michigan State Normal at Ypsilanti was actually the first (1897) authorized to operate as a public, state-supported teachers' college. It conferred its first bachelor's degree in 1905.

Even when the conversion of a normal institution into a state teachers' college meant little more than a change in nomenclature, the promotion of once-lowly teacher-training agencies into free-standing state colleges or public universities did not go unopposed, any more than did the elevation of normal units within universities into coordinate schools or departments. What helped bolster the cause of state teachers' colleges and university-based normal departments alike was their evident willingness to leave the preparation of elementary teachers to lower normal schools. Although almost all institutions of higher learning engaged in teacher education certainly were predisposed to assume this duty as well, the initial focus was upon the preparation of high-school teachers. Kansas State Normal and Illinois Normal, for example, had been operating extensive preparatory programs for secondary teachers since the 1880s, including courses in school law, school methods and management, educational psychology, and history and philosophy of education. Included at Kansas State were courses in music, elocution, art, gymnastics, French and German, drawing, science, and manual training—practically all of the subjects taught at the high-school level. Much the same held true at Illinois Normal.

Taking into account the swelling numbers of secondary enroll-ments and a continuing shortage of teachers, the argument that true postsecondary institutions were needed to fulfill the role of preparing people as teachers at the high-school level—that lower-level schools were inadequate to the challenge—proved difficult to resist. James E. Russell was only one of many who took the position early in the 1900s that the work of training secondary teachers should be assigned to colleges and universities. Unless standards were raised drastically among normal schools, he averred, they could not possibly undertake the job with much hope for success. In any event, as he pointed out, they were too few in number to be relied on. Russell's judgment that the latter option was no longer a real possibility won widespread agreement.[17]

By the 1920s, public teachers' colleges were common throughout the country, and their numbers were growing yearly. Quite unlike the normal schools from which so many were descended, all required a high-school diploma for admission. Each had at least one four-year course sequence in place leading to a bachelor's degree (typically in secondary education). And almost from their inception, as if seeking to reinforce their identity as true collegiate institutions, the tendency of most teachers' colleges was to diversify their academic curricula and to become as much as possible like liberal arts colleges. Adding on liberal arts faculty members was essential, both to support teacher preparation and to allow colleges to build up programs in other fields and disciplines.[18]

Many years later a common allegation from critics of teacher education was that at the time normal schools were being converted into state teachers' colleges, educationists seized upon the opportunity to ensure their pedagogical interests would dominate a disproportionate share of the undergraduate curriculum, doing so at the direct expense of liberal arts courses. As historian Arthur Bestor phrased it in a 1952 critique, the "pedagogical locusts ate up the harvest" of added time when the teacher preparatory course of studies was lengthened to four years.[19] Otherwise eager to emulate the norms, standards, and practices of academic institutions of higher learning, Bestor alleged, teachers of teachers were resolved to retain as much control as possible over the destiny of the new colleges emerging.

In point of fact, the evidence lent only partial support to any such charge. In the early 1920s, the median number of credits in education courses required of secondary-education majors in most teachers' colleges, including credits awarded for practice teaching, was not much more than 20 hours out of a total of 120 needed for graduation, or 16 percent of the total hours demanded.[20] In 1934, the median number of credits in education courses at most colleges ranged from 17 to 23. Admittedly, many students elected to *exceed* the required minimum (ranging to as high as 94 credit hours in some cases); and few colleges appear to have troubled themselves to set an *upper* limit on the number of pedagogical courses a student might apply to satisfy requirements for the baccalaureate degree. Moreover, it was probably the case that elementary-education majors often were encouraged—or required—to complete a somewhat higher total of credit hours in preparatory classes than that mandated for secondary majors. But as a rule, it simply was not true even from the beginning that general learning was necessarily sacrificed in favor of a preponderance of courses in teaching methodology and the like.

The further evolution of four-year normal institutions and teachers' colleges into multipurpose regional state colleges and universities of a more general character was essentially a post–World War II phenomenon.[21] The arrival on campuses in the late 1940s of hundreds of thousands of returning veterans, for example, had a powerful impact, mainly because many so-called nontraditional students were entering college with no intention of readying themselves for teaching. In a replay somewhat reminiscent of the predicament in which nineteenth-century normal schools had found themselves, colleges whose long-standing focus had been on preparing teachers were compelled now to shift resources to support programs and courses of study having nothing whatever to do with teacher training. Within a remarkably brief period of time, the appellation "teachers' college" no longer adequately reflected the broadened mission and interests of regional state institutions.

Subsequent expansion in the late 1960s and early 1970s, when postwar "baby boomers" hit campuses and enrollments skyrocketed, served mainly to accentuate and further expand the multipurpose nature of most of the nation's state colleges. Ironically, in their scramble to take on the accouterments of research and scholarship associated with more prestigious universities, the faculties of schools and colleges of education within regional state institutions themselves typically did not oppose suggestions to delete references to "teachers" in the names of their respective institutions. Quite the contrary, some vigorously championed the change, particularly when it was coupled with a proposal to elevate the "college" more or less by legislative fiat and have it declared a "university." Teacher educators were joined by the rest of their faculty colleagues who had no direct investment in teacher education, who preferred not to be associated with it, and who welcomed whatever terminological change might serve to detach their institution's identity from its origins as a teachers' college. The progression was much the same in practically every state: from "normal college" or "teachers' college" to "state college" to "state university."

TEACHER PREPARATION IN THE UNIVERSITIES

While colleges and universities were slow to introduce pedagogy into their programs of study, the trend in this direction was clearly apparent by 1910.[22] Some few years previously, A. Ross Hill, dean of a recently founded Teachers College at the University of Missouri, speaking before an audience at the annual meeting of the National Education Association, advanced what was still held in some quarters to be a bold idea: that preparatory normal departments, traditionally the poor stepchildren of academe, should be made fully coordinate with colleges of law, engineering, and medicine. "Courses in the philosophy of education, the history of education, and in genetic and educational psychology," he insisted, "have the same right to place in a scheme of liberal education that have general philosophy, ethics, sociology," and other subjects. Classes in "the theory and practice of teaching, in school management and the like," Hill declared, should be placed on the same level as "technical courses in law, engineering, or medicine."[23]

The question Hill was raising in 1905 essentially was whether normal preparatory departments should be abolished—as some still argued for vociferously—or whether, as he strongly recommended, they should be elevated instead to full status as schools or colleges within universities. As it turned out, within a relatively short time those who shared Hill's views had won the day. The University of Texas already had a Teachers' College resembling that opened previously at the University of Missouri. So too did Columbia University and the University of Chicago. Minnesota was in the process of establishing its first College of Education in the same year Hill delivered his address.

In 1906, at least 9 universities had education colleges. In 18 or so others education was already organized as a department more or less coordinate with other academic departments. At Ohio State a College of Education was formed in 1907. That same year the State University of Iowa founded its own School of Education (placed at first within the College of Liberal Arts). Similarly, at the University of Michigan teacher preparation remained a department within the College of Literature, Science and the Arts until 1921, when a separate School of Education was created.[24]

In 1890, teacher preparation courses were being offered in approximately 114 colleges and universities out of a total of just over 400 institutions (including a number of normal schools). In 1897, the number of schools offering courses in pedagogy had jumped to 220, including those sponsored by separate secondary-level preparatory departments. In 1900, three years later, at least a dozen or so normal departments had been converted into regular academic units within four-year institutions.[25] Their numbers included Johns Hopkins, Stanford, Clark, New York University, Harvard, and the University of Pennsylvania, among others. Less than five years after Hill's address, there were 156 full-scale teacher preparation programs to be found in American higher education. By 1932, toward the end of the first third of the century, almost 600 institutions of higher learning were offering teacher preparatory courses of study.[26] In 1948, a total of 196 of these institutions offered fully accredited or officially approved programs of teacher training. By 1950, the total number of schools with preparatory programs had gone up to 1,200; and in the last third of the century, the total would climb to almost 1,400.

Making teacher education an integral feature of the academic landscape of higher education was no small accomplishment. Yet even from the outset there were those who argued that schools of education should be positioned not at the undergraduate but at the graduate level, similar to colleges of law or medicine, where courses of study were open only to those who had already completed a bachelor's degree.[27] Among those persuaded that professional education should be offered primarily or even exclusively at the postbaccalaureate level were such luminaries of the day as Elwood P. Cubberley, William H. Burnham, Frederick E. Bolton, Charles F. Thwing, and Frank McMurry.

Education units at Harvard, Columbia, and California at Los Angeles had the best chance of transforming themselves into graduate schools of education. Preservice preparation of elementary and secondary teachers would retain its importance in some of these and in most other leading universities. But the main interest of their faculties had ascended rather quickly to graduate education, with the emphasis placed on advanced training for ranking administrators, curriculum specialists, and other upper-echelon leaders and school managers. Many of the larger state institutions soon followed suit, building up consultancies, instituting research and development centers, expanding graduate degree programs, and in countless other ways distancing themselves as much as possible from the less prestigious work of educating prospective classroom teachers at the undergraduate level.[28]

Speculation about the motives of those early in the century who pressed hardest for graduate-level professional education must remain just that—a matter of conjecture. Unquestionably, some did believe strongly and sincerely that the preparation of educational leaders needed to proceed from a foundation built on undergraduate education. By the same token, it would be naive to assume that issues of prestige and status had nothing whatever to do with the positions they took and fought for so vigorously. Undergraduate preservice teacher training involving large numbers of students was destined to remain an important enterprise at most schools—it was a "cash cow" generating far too much in the way of tuition revenues to be dispensed with entirely. But in the meantime efforts would continue throughout the century to elevate education to the standing of a discipline resembling law or medicine, a field most appropriately pursued at the postbachelor's level.

The first step was to argue that school administrators and other *leaders* needed advanced training at the postbaccalaureate level. Then, second, the argument was expanded to advance the notion that *all* prospective classroom teachers should receive their training at the graduate level. The former won acceptance in teacher-training circles rather quickly. The latter was slower to win support, although well before the end of the century the case for "extended" programs was attracting vigorous support from many educationists in larger universities. Nevertheless, in order to lend academic or intellectual credibility to either proposal, an age-old challenge remained: that of pressing the case for professional education as a legitimate field of inquiry and instruction.

THE CONTINUING QUEST FOR ACADEMIC LEGITIMACY

The ongoing search in the twentieth century for ways of making teaching a true profession, one capable of conferring the same status and respectability accorded practitioners in other recognized professions, had roots extending far back into the century preceding. In the formative period of the normal school movement, for example, much discussion had been given over to the question about whether there could be a true "science" of education capable of furnishing a reliable foundation for classroom practice. Conventional wisdom among educators held that an authentic "discipline" of education was fast emerging. Jerome Allen, for one, delivering a presidential address before the National Education Association in the early 1880s, cautioned that "The vocation of teaching will never become a profession until it is believed that the laws of mental growth are as fixed as the laws of physical growth and that they must be known by those who guide the developing power of the mind."[29]

Better understanding of the laws of human development, he and others felt, offered the best hope of yielding an authentic science upon which classroom usage henceforth might rely. Armed with a solid corpus of scientific knowledge to guide them in their work, teachers would no longer be left to their own devices as they had in the past, forced to improvise on the basis of their own subjective predilections and fallible personal experience. Informal rules of thumb, many of them of dubious reliability but handed down since time immemorial, would be supplanted by a true pedagogical technology. Confusion over instructional aims would be dispelled and the efficacy of sound teaching methods, properly employed, would be virtually assured.[30]

Among normal educators, there had been much talk for a time about "eternal laws" or "immutable" principles drawn a priori from some broader philosophic context or system of thought. Writers of the 1800s expressed the idea in varying ways. But the recurrent theme was one of absolute laws and axioms capable of being deduced and laid out systematically. Basically, what educationists seemed to have in mind when they spoke of a "science" of pedagogy, in other words, was some orderly arrangement of things yielding up deductive laws and rules to guide practice.[31] Alpheus Crosby, speaking at one of the earliest normal school conventions, sought to distinguish between such basic principles and their contingent applications. "It seems obvious," he declared confidently, "that any course of professional training *which is not merely mechanical or empirical* [italics added], must have for its basis a thorough consideration of the principles of the profession, of its philosophy, and that this should underlie and give form to all the attention which may be paid to practical methods [which] must be constantly changing accordingly as circumstances change. . . . But principles are in their nature eternal . . . [and] for the training of educators, the prime subject of study should be the principles of education."[32]

Opinion divided over the source from which enduring pedagogical principles might be derived. Some were convinced that certain exemplary usages of the past offered a rich repository of wisdom to be mined by educators. Thomas J. Morgan, writing in 1886, observed, "Much is to be learned as to both the philosophy of education and methods of teaching by studying the systems of education that have been formulated, the theories that have been promulgated, and the methods recommended and followed by those who have wrought on this great question in past ages." He went on to declare, "Nothing, perhaps, so liberalizes the mind of the teacher as the intelligent study of the words and ways of such men as Locke, Ascham, Rousseau, Comenius, Pestalozzi, Froebel, and Spencer."[33] In a similar vein, F. A. P. Barnard, writing in 1881, observed, "If we can once get the teacher thoroughly interested in the thoughts of the greatest thinkers about education . . . we have done both him, and his pupils, the greatest possible service."[34]

The so-called Oswego plan of "object" teaching in the post–Civil War period, inspired by the teachings of the Swiss educator Johann Heinrich Pestalozzi (1746-1827) and popularized by Edward A. Sheldon in the 1870s, represented one early effort to build up a systematic pedagogy based on a specific set of philosophic principles. Experimentation by pioneers in the kindergarten movement, rooted in the teachings of the German innovator Friedrich Wilhelm August Froebel (1782-1852), was another. Still another infusion of German thought came late in the nineteenth century with the introduction of Herbartianism, deriving from a teaching methodology inspired by the writings of Johann Friedrich Herbart (1776-1841). First popularized at Illinois Normal and then elsewhere by Charles DeGarmo, Frank McMurry, and Charles McMurry, Herbartian pedagogy, much like the Pestalozzian method before it, offered an instructional scheme readily if often mechanically applied by classroom teachers.[35]

Growing numbers of skeptics were unconvinced that purely introspective and rationalistic deductions inspired by speculative philosophy would ever prove of much help to classroom practitioners.[36] Emerson D. White's comment was typical: "It is feared that even the more thoughtful teachers are confused, rather than helped, by the mass of subtle facts and speculations, which are sometimes given . . . and the author confesses his inability to see of the practical bearing of much of the so-called philosophy now so often presented as the basis of educational methods."[37]

Suggestive of the change in thinking that was beginning to occur as the nineteenth century drew to a close, William T. Harris, the well-known school superintendent in St. Louis, called attention to the dependence of pedagogy on a wide range of disciplines, not just philosophy. "The science of education is not a complete, independent science by itself," he declared. "It borrows the results of other sciences, e.g., it presupposes psychology, physiology, aesthetics, and the science of rights; it presupposes also the science of anthropology.... It presupposes all the sciences named, and will be defective if it ignores nature or mind, or any stage or process of either, especially anthropology, phenomenology, psychology, ethics, rights, aesthetics, religion, or philosophy."[38]

Articulating much the same view was a speaker at the 1894 meeting of the National Education Association. "It is not enough that pedagogy be rooted in psychology," observed Richard G. Boone. "It sustains, of necessity, vital relations with ethics, physiology, anthropology and logic, in addition to the almost equally helpful ones of sociology and philosophy. Indeed, the one thing that most distinguishes the current study of educational questions is, perhaps, this vitalizing of our notions and our interpretations of them, through a better insight into and employment of these collateral relations."[39]

Josiah Royce was one of the earliest to deny that the "vitalizing" of pedagogy could be made to depend on rules drawn directly from other disciplines. "There is no universally valid science of pedagogy that is capable of any complete formulation, and of direct application to individual pupils and teachers," he stated flatly. "Teaching is an art. Therefore there is indeed no science of education. But what there is," he added pointedly, "is the world of science furnishing material for the educator to study. If [the teacher] seeks in that world for exact and universally valid direction, he will fail to get it, and deservedly fail, because science is not there . . . to furnish short and easy roads to even the noblest callings."[40]

Psychologist William James was even more emphatic in denying that knowledge taken from the various discipline afforded simple rules for classroom practice. In his *Talks to Teachers,* an 1899 revision of lectures delivered to Harvard students in 1892, James insisted, "I say . . . that you make a great, a very great mistake, if you think that psychology, being the science of the mind's laws, is something from which you can deduce definite programmes and schemes and methods of instruction for immediate classroom use."[41]

"The tendency of educational development to proceed by reaction from one thing to another, to adopt for one year, or for a term of seven years, this or that new study or method of teaching, and then as abruptly to swing over to some new educational gospel," John Dewey commented in 1904, "is a result which would be impossible if teachers were adequately moved by their own independent intelligence."[42] More to the point, Dewey was convinced that proposals to found a supposed science of education on a priori principles and deductive logic were fundamentally misconceived. The shift in thinking needed, he argued, would be from rationalism to empiricism, from armchair theorizing to controlled empirical investigation. "We may carry on," he insisted, ". . . with the object of giving teachers in training working command of the necessary tools of their profession; control of the technique of class instruction and management; skill and proficiency in the work of teaching."[43] But ultimately the knowledge teachers required, he emphasized, would come through practical experimentation and a testing in social experience of whatever ideas and innovations seemed most promising.

Calls in the early 1900s for a more "scientific" approach to the study of education elicited a robust response. Edward L. Thorndike, writing in 1910, aptly captured the spirit of the movement toward quantification and controlled inquiry. "Experts in education," he noted, "are becoming experimentalists and quantitative thinkers, and are seeking to verify or refute the established beliefs concerning the effects of educational forces upon human nature . . . [and] the shares of the various physical and social forces in making individual men differ in politics, crime, wealth, service, idealism or whatever trait concerns man's welfare."[44] Inspired in no small measure by the pioneering work of such psychologists as Thorndike himself, of Francis Galton, William James, J. McKeen Cattell, and many others, educators embarked upon the effort to subject educational problems and questions to experimental and quantitative analysis. "Science" in education was now construed not as the deductive derivation of overarching principles but as a matter of building up a body of validated truths based on controlled observation and the empirical testing of hypotheses.[45]

Coupled with increasing reliance on quantitative studies in education was the growing popularity of proposals to adapt managerial concepts and principles from business and industry for use in school settings. Hence from both sides—instructional development and school management—the pronounced and ever-increasing tendency among schoolmen was to look on or at least to represent education as a purely technical enterprise, and the business of teacher education as a technical design task aimed at turning out skilled craftsmen.[46]

Underlying the "child study" movement much in vogue throughout the early 1900s, for example, was a pervasive assumption that any desired traits or attributes could be developed within learners by means of a simple conditioning or shaping process. Similarly, or so it was often argued, virtually any problem involving teacher education could be resolved by analyzing in detail the traits considered essential to a good teacher, or the specific demands of the teacher's task, and then, in a process almost akin to manufacturing, produce teachers possessing just those proper traits and skills.[47] As a theme in the burgeoning literature on teacher education and the development of scientific pedagogy, nowhere else perhaps did it find clearer application than in a well-known three-year national survey known as the Commonwealth Teacher-Training Study, released in 1928.[48]

The vogue for quantitative surveys, polls, and studies typical of the 1920s was to continue undiminished in vigor throughout the 1930s and beyond.[49] Foremost among them was a multivolume compendium of data about teacher education sponsored by the U.S. Office of Education, one of the most comprehensive surveys of its type ever attempted.[50] Others followed, including numerous reports prepared under the auspices of the Progressive Education Association, the Commission on Teacher Education of the American Council on Education, and the Rockefeller Foundation.[51] All told, if the appurtenances of statistical compilation and tabulation in exhaustive detail had been sufficient to confer the status of "science" upon education, by the eve of World War II, it might have seemed that long-sought goal had finally been achieved.

Progressivist educator and radical social critic George S. Counts spoke for those who remained unimpressed by the mania for quantification. "From state to state over the entire land," he avowed, "the curricula of the public normal schools and teachers colleges are as like as peas in a pod. So-called reforms there have been; they pass in waves from region to region—patchwork tinkerings with the familiar curricular pattern." Troubled by the essential sameness of preparatory courses of study for teachers and skeptical about prospects for change, Counts continued, "No matter how much science in the way of statistical summaries, surveys by experts, and correlational studies is applied to this type of curriculum, the best result obtainable can be only a minor refinement added to something fundamentally inadequate. It is necessary to get completely outside the present teacher-training picture and from a new vantage point to consider modern educational needs and modern teaching opportunities."

Counts spoke of the various "standardizing" agencies at work ironing out the few remaining sectional variations in policy and technique among professional schools of education. In the main, he believed, "the familiar curricular pattern of orientation courses, subject matter courses, theory courses, observation courses, and practice-teaching assignments" amounted to little more than "a conglomeration of precepts and practices inherited from the more limited environment of a former day."

Foreshadowing a common criticism levied against teacher education a decade or so later, Counts took aim at the tendency to lengthen preparatory programs: "It was easily assumed that the main fault with the traditional teacher-training program was its briefness. Thus the cause for the reported poor quality of teaching was shifted from the *nature* of the training which candidates received to the *shortness* of the training program." He added, "An examination of the recently revised courses of study in the state teachers colleges shows quite clearly that the new ones are mere padded versions of the old."[52] This charge, that teacher-training programs were overblown and overextended, would return to haunt teacher educators with a vengeance in the decades following World War II.

POSTWAR CRITICS

Debates over school policies and teacher education, rather obviously, were overshadowed, then eclipsed, as America prepared for war. For the duration, quite understandably, public attention was riveted elsewhere. But with the restoration of peace in 1945, popular discussion returned to the question (among other things) of what direction American schooling should assume in the postwar period. At home the country was beset by unforeseen challenges: inflation, a baby boom, the conversion of industrial output to peacetime uses, uncontrolled urban and suburban sprawl. Abroad, the picture appeared equally unsettling. In the euphoria accompanying the end of the war, a weary public had looked forward to what was assumed at the time to be the irresistible advance of freedom, democracy, and prosperity around the globe. But events had rather rapidly revealed those hopes would not be realized any time soon. Although military victory had put an end to the most destructive conflagration in all history, the United States still found itself embroiled in a succession of conflicts in distant lands. Worse yet, as the Cold War deepened and the world's two major superpowers moved toward armed confrontation, the possibility of a still more terrifying atomic holocaust loomed large.

Looking back on the ensuing school debates of the late 1940s and the first half of the decade following, two distinct if overlapping phases are easily recognizable. The first thrust of criticism alleged that public education was failing to safeguard the values of "Americanism" and to conserve the nation's unique cultural heritage. In the face of suspected domestic subversion, near-hysterical alarms were sounded. Super-patriots set to work to rebuild the schools as bastions of anti-communism. Religionists, fearful that creeping secularism was eroding public virtue, urged renewed emphasis on school prayer and direct instruction in religion. Cost-cutters for their part extolled the values of belt tightening and sharp reductions in expenditures for education.

Simultaneously, a second wave of school reform advanced amid charges that school curricula had grown vapid, that standards everywhere were anemic, that education generally had lost its moorings and was now adrift. Commenting on the escalation of controversy over school policies and goals, Mary Anne Raywid aptly summed up the situation as it appeared in the early 1960s: "Since World War II," she observed, "there is virtually no aspect of public education that has gone unquestioned by one source or another. . . . Not only is American education under fire; the practice of criticizing our schools is well on its way to becoming a national pastime." She added, "For some it is already a favorite armchair sport. For others, it has become a full time career."[53]

Accompanying charges that public education was failing to promote the virtues of loyalty, patriotism, and love of country were allegations that the schools had grown soft, that they lacked discipline and rigor. Conservative critics announced the time was long overdue for adopting a no-nonsense approach to education. Frills had to be jettisoned. Curricula should be overhauled and replaced by a stress on "hard-core" learning. Singled out for special criticism was progressive education and a convenient new target, a *bête noir* called "life-adjustment" education that rather quickly came to symbolize for conservatives everything fundamentally wrong with modern public education.

Nurtured originally in the Vocational Education Division of the U.S. Office of Education, life adjustment had been acclaimed by proponents as a fresh, innovative response to the "real-life" needs of students allegedly ill-served by traditional academic curricula. What was advocated essentially was a course of study through which high-school students could acquire basic survival skills needed in daily life: that is, tools for "adjustment" to society and the rudiments of vocational training. Opponents, on the other hand, saw in this nascent initiative merely an attempt to perpetuate in new guise the worst errors of progressive education.

In retrospect, the term "life adjustment" was ill-advised, if only because it lent itself to so much ridicule. It is doubtful too whether the abortive movement launched under its banner ever exerted even a fraction of the influence its detractors imputed to it. Still, hostile critics never tired of castigating professional educators for having allegedly succumbed to its influence; and they spared no effort in trying to discredit it. To a very great extent, as events were to reveal, teacher education caught the spillover of criticism directed against progressivism and life-adjustment education.

A caustic diatribe typical of many to follow in the years thereafter was supplied with the publication in 1949 of Mortimer Smith's *And Madly Teach*. Educationists, he alleged, were chiefly responsible for the anti-intellectualism and moral myopia rampant in public education; and he urged an end to the stranglehold they exerted on the schools. "If anyone will take the trouble to investigate," he charged, "it will be found that those who make up the staffs of the schools and colleges of education, and the administrators and teachers whom they train to run the system, have a truly amazing uniformity of opinion regarding the aims, the content, and the methods of education." On this point Smith was adamant: "They constitute a cohesive body of believers with a clearly formulated set of dogmas and doctrines, and they are perpetuating the faith by seeing to it, through state laws and rules of state departments of education, that only those teachers and administrators are certified who have been trained in correct dogma."[54]

The "dogma" to which Smith referred, of course, was progressivism and its later incarnation, life adjustment. However implausible was the allegation that educators collectively shared allegiance to any monolithic doctrine, the same charge was to be repeated over and over again in the writings of school critics, including Paul Woodring's *Let's Talk Sense About Our Schools* (published in 1953), in Albert Lynd's *Quackery in the Public Schools* (appearing in 1953) and again in Mortimer Smith's *The Diminished Mind* (1954).[55] John Keats, writing in a 1957 issue of the *Saturday Evening Post,* summed up the common complaint. "Most of this nation's public schools," he claimed, "now offer America's children an education that is anticultural, anti-intellectual, narrowly utilitarian at best and utterly vapid at worst."[56] And lest there be any doubt, critics were quick to point a finger at the culprit allegedly responsible: an education "establishment" dominated by professors of education ensconced in the nation's colleges and universities.

Arthur E. Bestor's *Educational Wastelands,* first published in 1953 and later expanded and reissued in 1955 as *The Restoration of Learning,* made the charge explicit.[57] A clique or "interlocking directorate" of state education officials, school administrators, and professors of education, virtually all of them uniformly hostile to scholarly and academic values, he alleged, had conspired to gain control over the preparation and employment of teachers everywhere. "As a prospective teacher looks out over his future career," Bestor wrote, "one hard, inescapable fact stares him in the face. He must acquire a certain number of hours in 'education.' State certification requirements demand it. Regional accrediting agencies check up on the matter. Local school authorities cannot waive the requirement. . . . In the university itself the department of education will constantly remind of the fact that there is no way to get a teaching certificate except by entering the classroom of a professor of education. . . . "[58] Previous teaching experience would not satisfy the requirement. Nor was it asked whether the candidate was a good teacher. The sole issue, as Bestor put it, was whether an applicant had piled up the right number and type of course credits in pedagogy.

Requiring future teachers to complete preparatory courses would be unobjectionable, claimed Albert Lynd, were it not for the fact that the study of educational methodology itself tended to be, as he phrased it, "90 percent mixed humbug and wind." One of the troubles with modern teacher training, he wrote, was that it left almost nothing to the "good common sense, intelligence, or imagination of the teacher." Methods were presented "ready-made to cover every contingency; courses are devised for every subject, no matter how trivial, and every subdivision of a subject."[59] Given the monopoly over entry into teaching exercised by an inflexible and self-protecting pedagogic cabal, Bestor complained, anyone seeking to teach had no choice but to undergo the humiliation of amassing credits in vacuous and superfluous pedagogy courses, classes distinguished only by their triviality. Agnes Snyder, commenting on much the same theme in 1952, summed up what many other critics had been claiming for years: "As to techniques of teaching, these can be learned effectively only in the classroom. Courses of method divorced from practice are notoriously ineffective."[60]

Harold L. Clapp of Grinnell College, writing in 1949, observed that the attitude of many university professors toward educationists varied from indifference to contempt and that the entire situation was often a subject of faculty club humor. But he too conceded it was no laughing matter. "Some years ago, in some way or other," Clapp observed, "these theorists sold to an unsuspecting public and a drowsy academic world a strange bill of goods: the notion that there is a special branch of learning, a *science,* called 'Education,' . . . a subject to be studied." In actuality, he judged, it was mostly "mumbo jumbo," a "pseudo-scientific shibboleth," an aggregate of "drivel" awash in "oceans of piffle."[61]

Bestor believed it was time "to open the valves and let some of the gas out of the over-inflated educational balloon." American intellectual life was threatened because the schools had fallen prey to "a new breed of educator who has no real place in—who does not respect and who is not respected by—the world of scientists, scholars, and professional men." Bestor placed a good share of the blame on faculties of liberal arts and sciences, who, he claimed, had failed to take seriously the problem of devising "sound and appropriate" curricula for the education of teachers. Their failure to act, he avowed, had left a vacuum into which the professional educationists moved: "The latter set up programs and devoted time and effort to the task when others were too proud or too lazy to do so."[62]

Bestor claimed it was "self evident" that at the undergraduate level, the education of future teachers should be one in the liberal arts and sciences. The university, he asserted, "should commence an orderly process of devolution with respect to many of the activities hitherto associated with departments and colleges of education." He felt that opportunities to satisfy minimum pedagogical requirements should be provided through electives that would be a normal complement of a college program of liberal studies. But, he added, "under no circumstances should the department of pedagogy be permitted to exercise any sort of control over the undergraduate programs of prospective teachers."[63]

"A new curriculum for the education of teachers, based firmly upon the liberal arts and sciences, rather than upon the mere vocational skills of pedagogy, will do more to restore the repute of the public schools than any other step that can be taken," Bestor promised. "Not only will teachers be adequately trained in the disciplines they undertake to teach, they will also be imbued with respect for those disciplines and will be prepared to resist the anti-intellectualism that currently threatens the schools." He concluded, "And when the tide begins to turn, young men and women of genuine intellectual interest and capacity will be attracted in increasing numbers into the profession of public school teaching. They will not be repelled at the outset by being asked to lay aside their intellectual interests and fritter away their time in the courses of the pedagogues. Under a well-ordered plan, the gateway to teaching will be the gateway of learning itself."[64]

THE MISEDUCATION
OF AMERICAN TEACHERS

The launching of *Sputnik I* by the Soviet Union in October of 1957 sent shock waves reverberating throughout American society, including its system of public education. Almost inevitably a search for scapegoats was mounted in short order. Why, it was asked, had the Soviets, not the Americans, been the first to succeed in placing the world's first artificial satellite in orbit? What had become of America's much-vaunted technological excellence, its commanding lead in all branches of science and technology? Was American technical know-how somehow inferior to that of the Soviets? Did their triumph presage the eclipse of American power, and had the United States lost its ability to compete successfully in the international arena? Who was responsible?

    Within a matter of months, if not weeks, it had become fashionable in some quarters to assign a good share of the blame for the nation's traumatic humiliation to the public schools. In a desperate race to regain lost time, conferences were hastily convened, reports issued, and prescriptions drafted to correct all the ills—real and imagined—plaguing the nation's educational system. Predictably, teacher education came in for harsh criticism as well; and the internecine struggles between liberal arts scholars and educationists seemed to take on new vigor and new venom in the aftermath of *Sputnik*. Accompanying attacks on the education establishment were renewed calls for innovation and change.

    The newly founded Fund for the Advancement of Education of the Ford Foundation, to cite but one case in point, acted quickly in redoubling its reform efforts, achieving considerable notoriety in the state of Arkansas, for example, where vast sums were expended on programs designed to bypass traditional teacher certification requirements and create "alternative" licensing routes. (Cynical observers referred to the initiative as the "Arkansas Purchase.") Monies were allocated on an unprecedented scale to help universities across the country set up fifth-year teacher preparation programs, most of which culminated in the awarding of a Master of Arts in Teaching degree. The National Education Association under its then-active professional division, the National Commission on Teacher Education and Professional Standards (NCTEPS), weighed in with initiatives of its own, all aimed at transforming and improving the ways in which classroom teachers were prepared to work in public schools.[65]

Speaking at one of a series of joint conferences of liberal arts scholars and professors of education held between 1958 and 1960, John Goodlad, then director of the Center for Teacher Education at the University of Chicago, was unusually frank in expressing his views on teacher education. "I have long been embarrassed," he admitted, "by the proliferation of courses in this most barren of educational wastelands. I readily concede the point so often made to justify the addition of still another three-hour impoverishment of the undergraduate's education: Teachers need to know something about safety education, about how to use a movie projector, and about rhythmic games for rainy days." But, he continued, "not all of these things need to be done before the teacher begins to teach; nor do they require a three-hour course for the learning. Furthermore, most of them can be learned best on the job. Any proposed addition to the curriculum, at all levels of education, should first stand the rigorous test of whether it is more valuable than what it must necessarily replace."[66]

Harold L. Clapp, head of the division of language and literature at Grinnell, was a vocal participant at another 1959 national conference on teacher education, one of many convened in the aftermath of the controversy surrounding what pundits had by now dubbed the superpower "space race." His judgment on the typical elementary-education curriculum was especially acerbic: "a dismal array of one-, two-, and three-hour courses in art for the artless, biology for babes, chemistry for kiddies, math and music for moppets, along with such academic fantasies as 'Creative Experiences with Materials'—which is to say, cutting and pasting for college credit."[67] Another conference participant, perhaps seeking to soften the tone of the debate, declared, "One of the cherished fringe benefits of any faculty of a college of liberal arts . . . is that of freely casting unwarranted, uninformed, and nonsensical aspersions upon the ancestors, the progeny, the intent, and the capabilities of the faculties and programs of the professional schools."[68] The question at issue, however, was whether educationists for their part truly deserved the calumny heaped on them by their academic colleagues.

Defenders of traditional teacher preparation programs, naturally enough, were unwilling to concede that pedagogical training programs were entirely without utility. "People can and do learn how to be good teachers, when they obviously were not 'born' to it, in the same fashion as they learn to do other things," insisted Donald Cottrell, dean of the College of Education at Ohio State University.[69] Yet as a conference report from 1958 had admitted a year earlier, teacher training still rested on a precarious empirical foundation. "We are virtually devoid of research evidence as to the relationship between the kind of preparation taken during one's four-year career as a college student and his performance later on the job as a teacher," it was conceded.[70]

The so-called laws of learning upon which teacher educators hoped to erect training programs, as William Chandler Bagley had earlier commented, have always had an irritating habit of collapsing as evidence accumulated.[71] Isaac L. Kandel accordingly urged greater caution in making claims for teacher education programs, because, as he wrote, "The search for incontrovertible laws on which education and instruction could be based has not been and probably will never be successful and the hope of developing a science of 'human engineering' is fortunately unrealizable."[72]

Among the more thoughtful contributors to public discussion about teacher education in the early 1960s was James D. Koerner, author of a widely read volume entitled *The Miseducation of American Teachers*. He agreed with those like Kandel who felt that in the absence of hard data to support any particular position, arguments over how best to train teachers rested ultimately on suasive grounds. "An examination of the evidence available on the effectiveness of preparing teachers one way as against another leaves one is a familiar cul-de-sac, the only way out of which is through one's reasoned convictions," he observed. Considered as an academic discipline, in his opinion, education had poor credentials to offer. It had not yet developed a body of knowledge and technique of sufficient scope and power to warrant being given full academic status, he judged, and it lacked data its graduates could use with confidence and that could "form the basis for intellectual advancement in the field."[73]

Tracing the long history of efforts to build a theoretical and empirical foundation for pedagogy as an authentic discipline, Koerner felt educationists had been lured "into the trap of scientism—trying to quantify the field, search for the laws and irrefrangible principles they supposed governed the ways in which learning took place." The "old-time religion," as he phrased it, was still very much alive, though there was much less talk about a "science" of education as such. "Only partly is this preoccupation a reflection of the educationist's belief in the ubiquitous usefulness of the scientific method," he commented. "Partly it is the old problem of concern for status and professionalism; and partly it is a refuge from the necessarily imprecise, intuitional, frustrating means that must be used in any effort to solve the really important problems of education." Not only did scientism in education produce little of value relative to the time and energy invested in it, Koerner declared, but it encouraged "the pernicious belief that . . . teaching can be based on some kind of exact or scientific foundation."[74]

Summing up, Koerner characterized the academic enterprise of education as "one of the intellectually weakest, most nebulous, and generally unsatisfactory" fields in higher education, a far-flung endeavor still lacking a viable definition of its own purposes and a foundation to give form to its multifarious programs and activities. "It is," he wrote, "no closer now than it was 25 or 50 years ago to basing itself on scientifically derived principles, though it continues to pursue the scientific will-o'-the-wisp as ardently as ever; meanwhile it gives short shrift to the non-quantitative and unscientific parts of education that are, in all probability, the most important for the training of teachers."[75]

Koerner felt educationists should abandon the "manifestly absurd" claim that people could become competent teachers only by passing through orthodox training programs, and its corollary, that "all teachers, before the advent of professional Education, must have been blithering idiots who knew nothing about their job." Greater caution was called for, he believed, as well as a wider recognition of the tenuous nature of all claims about teacher preparation.

As for typical courses offered by teacher educators, Koerner felt they more than deserved their bad reputation. They were, he alleged, unfailingly puerile, repetitious, dull, and ambiguous; their substance "remorselessly fragmented, sub-divided, and inflated." Most, he insisted, were "vague, insipid, time-wasting adumbrations of the obvious, and probably irrelevant to academic teaching." Wrapped up in a "pernicious patois" he called "Educanto"—a compound of empty slogans and pretentious-sounding incantations—courses in pedagogy could not help but repel any educated mind forced to endure them. "When one considers the thin and elusive substance of these courses . . . and the failure to relate this professional training to the quality of teaching actually done by graduates, the educationist asks a great deal," he alleged.[76]

In common with Bestor, Koerner felt that teacher training had expanded beyond all reasonable limits. It needed to be curtailed drastically. Reporting the results of one national survey, Koerner found that secondary-teacher candidates were being required to take an average of 27 semester hours in education, close to a full year's work. This, he concluded, was "clearly excessive." Elementary-education majors were completing an average of 49 semester hours, or about 40 percent of their total undergraduate work—a pattern he likewise felt was "wholly indefensible."[77]

Koerner reported that in 1961, state requirements for prospective teachers mandated, on average, 23.4 hours for elementary-education majors and 18.7 hours for secondary majors. But preparatory program requirements in colleges and universities consistently exceeded those state norms, calling for an average of 34.8 hours for elementary majors and 23.6 hours for secondary-education students, representing 28 and 19 percent respectively of a total college course of studies. In elementary education an average of 36 percent of all credits earned in the four undergraduate years was given over to preparatory courses in education; in secondary-education programs the average was 17 percent. Upon analyzing 435 elementary-education student transcripts and another 446 for secondary-education majors from 32 different institutions, Koerner discovered that elementary-education majors were actually devoting almost half of their studies to professional education courses, while methodology accounted for about a fourth of the studies of secondary majors.[78]

His considered judgment was that if the "fat" were rendered out and needless duplication of content eliminated, the number of courses teacher candidates completed could be reduced by at least half, while still accomplishing everything pedagogical theorists claimed was essential.[79] Koerner's summary recommendations were to shut down all teachers' colleges, to eliminate "majors" in education within the universities, and to require all prospective teachers to specialize in academic subjects. For secondary-education teachers, 48 semester hours should be devoted to a teaching specialty, leaving 54 hours for general education and 18 hours for professional education courses. For future elementary teachers, a 36-hour major could be required, leaving 60 hours for general education and 24 for professional education.

The goal, he emphasized, was to cap education courses at an absolute maximum of 18 hours for secondary-teacher candidates and 24 for future elementary-classroom teachers. Taking into account how poorly educated most teacher educators themselves allegedly were, Koerner felt it was important that education courses derived directly from academic disciplines be taught henceforth only by persons qualified to teach in the appropriate academic department of the same institution. Methods courses should be incorporated into practice teaching and managed only by persons who held advanced degrees in some academic subject.

Koerner judged that, in the final analysis, most of the ailments of teacher education were the natural result of a narrow concentration of power protecting accumulated professional orthodoxies. An Establishment obviously exists, he reiterated; and he claimed it suffered from all of the customary disabilities of large and monopolistic bureaucracies. State departments of education, accrediting associations, professional interest groups, the education professorate—"All of these agencies, in complementing and reinforcing one another, compose, I submit, a monolithic Establishment in which academicians and noneducationist organizations have very little voice, though they have the largest stake in the education of American teachers."[80]

Koerner closed his critique with the assertion that a regular four-year undergraduate program should remain the standard for preparing new teachers. While he approved of the new Master of Arts in Teaching programs then coming into vogue, he felt the accelerating movement toward making five years of preparation mandatory for all new teachers was ill-advised. "If successful," he wrote presciently, "this movement will inflict an enormous and unnecessary burden on graduate schools; it will remove whatever incentives now exist for tightening up the undergraduate programs in teacher education; and it will aggravate a number of the vices presently found in the undergraduate programs."

Furthermore, he continued, "the fifth-year programs are frequently overrated, involving nothing more than the piling up of further Education courses with two or three academic ones that might well be at the undergraduate level. . . . " What was needed now, Koerner announced, was "a tough-minded attack on the waste and weakness of the standard undergraduate program in teacher education."[81]

THE CONANT REPORT

Something resembling the far-reaching assessment Koerner had in mind, as it happened, was forthcoming the same year *The Miseducation of American Teachers* made its appearance. Less inflammatory and considerably more moderate in tone than critiques adduced by the likes of Bestor, Clapp, Lynd, or Koerner himself, it took the form of a Carnegie Corporation-funded study of teacher education authored by former Harvard President James B. Conant. Published in 1963 as *The Education of American Teachers,* it too was widely discussed, rather quickly coming to be known simply as the Conant Report.[82]

Conant opened his discussion by taking note of the "considerable gap" that existed between "two hostile camps"—professors of education allied with public school teachers and administrators, on the one hand, and professors of arts, sciences, and humanities, on the other. Traditional academicians, he observed, had always tended to dismiss the course offerings of educationists as worthless and degrees in pedagogy as of little value. That schools and colleges of education had long been beneficiaries of a high protective tariff—state teacher certification requirements—and hence exercised a monopoly on entry into teaching, Conant judged, was the single aspect of the present-day education of teachers "most maddening" to the academic professorate.

Were it not for state-mandated instruction in pedagogy, colleges and universities would never have been obliged to offer positions to professors of education in the first place. Yet academic professors had never shown much interest in public schools. Nor had they evidenced any willingness to share responsibility for the preparation of public school teachers. All told, Conant reported, "I have found much to criticize strongly on both sides of the fence that separates faculties of education from those of arts and sciences."[83]

Conant agreed with critics before him that the "science" of education was largely chimerical. There were, he concurred, few reliable guidelines or hard scientific data to bolster arguments for one way of preparing teachers against another. Hence, paradoxically perhaps, state-mandated requirements for licensure had assumed exaggerated political importance. As Conant saw it, teacher educators believed that classroom teachers would never be regarded as true professionals unless they were perceived by the public to possess some esoteric body of knowledge. They needed to command an expertise setting them apart from laymen whose general learning was otherwise equivalent to their own or, in some cases, more extensive still. But the only body of knowledge available to distinguish teachers from other well-educated people was that provided in professional education courses. Hence the education establishment had fought vigorously to retain specific courses required by the state or as components in state-approved preparatory programs.

In fact, Conant claimed, there was no empirical warrant for, nor agreement on, a specific body of principles that could be taught and that assured a person would become a better teacher. Accordingly, Conant urged that all state-mandated course requirements be eliminated. The competence of teacher candidates, he believed, could be tested for by practice teaching under conditions set by the state and subject to state supervision. "Except for practice teaching and the special methods work combined with it," Conant proclaimed, "I see no rational basis for a state prescription of the time to be devoted to education courses, whether or not an attempt is made to specify the content. I see even less excuse for prescription by a voluntary accrediting agency whose decisions become in one way or another assimilated by a state authority." The time had not yet come, he claimed, when educational science could play the same role in training teachers as, for example, the medical sciences in training doctors. "The one indisputably essential element in professional education is practice teaching."[84]

On the other side, Conant acknowledged that few thoughtful people had denied that the art of teaching could be developed by practice, under suitable conditions. He quoted without disagreement from the Massachusetts Board of Education's declaration of 1838 that "No one can entertain a doubt that there is a mastery in teaching as in every other art. Nor is it less obvious that within reasonable limits this skill and this mastery may themselves be made the subject of instruction and be communicated to others." Conant was prepared to spell out in some detail exactly what those "reasonable limits" might be in terms of a modern undergraduate course of studies. Much of his study, in fact, consisted of detailed prescriptions for various course sequences.

For prospective secondary teachers, Conant suggested a 60-hour pattern of general education: English language and composition (six hours); Western world literature (six hours); history, half of which should be non-Western (nine hours); art and music appreciation (six hours); mathematics (six hours); biological and physical sciences, studied consecutively (twelve hours); psychology (three hours); sociology or anthropology (three hours); philosophy (three hours); economics (three hours); and political science (three hours). Additionally, future high-school teachers under his proposed scheme would complete 16 courses or a total of 48 hours in a single teaching field, such as mathematics, physical science, biological science, English, social science, and so on. For elementary teachers, Conant envisioned a similar course concentration of 36 hours.[85]

The ideal "professional sequence" for preparing elementary teachers, according to Conant, would consist of a three-hour course in child growth and development; a three-hour course in the history, philosophy, or sociology of education; three to six hours of courses in the teaching of reading, depending on the grade levels to be taught; a series of intensive workshops in the content and methods of teaching elementary-school subjects (a maximum of ten to thirteen hours); and eight hours of year-long laboratory experiences, including at least eight weeks of practice teaching.[86] The professional sequence for secondary teachers would be more modest, consisting of 12 to 18 hours of course work, including practice teaching and special methods (nine hours); philosophy, history, or sociology of education (three hours); educational psychology (three hours); and one or two others.[87]

Conant went on to lay out in extensive detail virtually all the appropriate course patterns for concentrations, by subject-matter specialization and grade level, he felt prospective teachers should complete. Nevertheless, he was insistent on the point that courses were not ends in themselves. They were only means to the larger end of promoting teaching competence, the promotion of which should be accepted as the responsibility of the institution as a whole, not just its education faculty. So far as he was concerned, a policy of certification based on completion of state-specified courses was utterly bankrupt. The ultimate test, he stressed, should be how the teacher actually performed in a classroom, as judged by experienced teachers.[88]

Attempting to be as judicious and fair-minded as possible, Conant had staked out a middle ground between two sharply opposed positions. Inevitably, few were pleased. Hard-core academic traditionalists criticized Conant's report for the allowance it made in retaining pedagogical courses within the undergraduate curriculum. Teacher educators, for their part, were outraged by Conant's denial that their work rested on a sound empirical foundation. They likewise took offense at his insistence that the number of courses in professional education be severely circumscribed. Disgust greeted his claim that state certification requirements should be dispensed with in favor of a "performance-based" assessment of each candidate during student teaching. Not surprisingly, in spite of the fact that it was often invoked or referred to in the literature of teacher preparation throughout the 1960s, there was little to indicate that the Conant Report could win acceptance as a blueprint for future reform.

FADS AND FASHIONS: THE RHETORIC
OF TEACHER-EDUCATION REFORM

Much of the literature on teacher preparation from the mid-1960s into the late 1970s and early 1980s was written against the backdrop of an unprecedented growth in school enrollments. That expansion was coupled—as had been the case earlier in the century—with a severe shortage of teachers. In the decade from 1950 to 1960, for example, the number of children enrolled in the nation's elementary and secondary schools had grown more than in the entire preceding half century—some 13.3 million in 10 years as compared with some 11.7 million in 50 years. This rapid increase, amounting to nearly a third of the 42 million children in school in 1960, reflected both a sharp rise in the national birth rate following World War II and a growing trend toward more schooling for all children.

Between 1950 and 1965, the number of teachers virtually doubled, from slightly more than a million to nearly 2 million. In the same period, however, teacher turnover, rising standards of preparation, and new mandated educational services combined to keep demand consistently in excess of the supply of qualified teachers. The annual average increase in numbers of teachers had run around 57,000; yet in 1955, the estimated shortfall was fully 140,000. In 1960, estimates of the shortage of teachers placed the total around 135,000; and in 1965, that figure had grown to 148,000.[89]

Multiple factors were responsible for the teacher shortage plaguing the nation's school systems toward the end of the 1960s. Part of the reason lay with increased competition from business and industry seeking college-trained people to exploit the new knowledge and technologies on which postwar growth was based. It was, by any standard, a competition in which schools almost invariably turned out to be the losers. Relatively poor pay, low status for teachers, and a high incidence of less than optimal working conditions also did much to discourage talented young people from entering teaching. But so too did the process through which candidates had to pass to gain entry, with its array of reputedly dull courses, the minutiae of certification, and so forth. With good reason it was often lamented that the best and brightest among those attending college intended to pursue careers in other, more prestigious, remunerative, and intellectually stimulating fields.[90]

Nevertheless, by any yardstick teacher preparation had assumed gargantuan proportions. In the mid-1960s, fully three-quarters of the nation's colleges and universities were engaged in the business of preparing teachers; and it was estimated that fully 90 percent of all those who planned to teach attended multipurpose institutions—municipal, private, and state colleges or universities—each of them preparing more than 100 teachers a year.[91] By 1967, colleges and universities were turning out nearly 207,000 students eligible for initial certification. About 192,000 of them were recipients of baccalaureate degrees, the rest receiving Master of Arts in Teaching degrees or their equivalent. The combined total represented 35 percent of all bachelor's and first professional degrees conferred. By 1969, the number of graduates certified for teaching rose to nearly 260,000; and it was expected to exceed 300,000 by 1975.[92] According to an American Council on Education study of freshmen entering college in the fall of 1967, 22.4 percent of the freshmen at all institutions, but 42.2 percent of those at public four-year colleges, were in fact planning to go into elementary or secondary teaching.[93]

With 190,000 beginning teachers entering the schools in the 1970-71 school year, and the number expected to increase by about 10,000 a year over the next five years thereafter, it was clearly impossible to rely upon native talent alone as the means of improving teaching, as Charles Silberman, author of *Crisis in the Classroom* (1970), observed. Many "average" people needed to be educated to teach well. The question, then, was not whether teachers should receive special preparation for teaching, but, rather, what kind of preparation they should receive. That the training should be substantially different from what prospective teachers were receiving or had received in the past seemed to Silberman hardly open to debate.

"There is probably no aspect of contemporary education on which there is greater unanimity of opinion than that teacher education needs a vast overhaul," he observed. "Virtually everyone is dissatisfied with the current state of teacher education: the students being educated, the teachers in the field, the principals, superintendents, and school board members who hire them, the liberal arts faculties, and the lay critics of education."[94]

The basic question, as always, was what specific form teacher preparation should assume. Most often cited (though not well defined) as components of the types of preparatory programs needed were a broad pattern of liberal, general education; in-depth study of at least one academic field; solid preparation in professional education; and an internship or extended period of practice teaching.[95] Otherwise, disunity and chaos appeared to reign supreme throughout the 1960s and 1970s, as one study followed another in bewildering succession.[96]

A 1961 report entitled *New Horizons for the Teaching Profession,* commissioned by the National Education Association's National Commission on Teacher Education and Professional Standards, offered one comprehensive set of proposals. *Teachers for the Real World,* edited by B. O. Smith, a 1969 manifesto sponsored by the National Institute for Advanced Study in Teaching Disadvantaged Youth and the American Association of Colleges for Teacher Education, supplied quite another.

Charles Silberman's 1970 Carnegie-sponsored study of American education devoted a great deal of space to the challenge of designing more effective teacher education programs. Yet another major study was that undertaken by the California Commission for Teacher Preparation and Licensing in cooperation with the National Institute of Education, a multimillion-dollar, six-year effort culminating in a report entitled *Time to Learn* that had much to say about teacher education.[97] The American Association of Colleges for Teacher Education, meanwhile, was issuing recommendations and proposals for teacher education reform almost on a yearly basis. So too were several other national educational organizations.[98]

Promising innovations in teacher education, it seemed, were taken up and as quickly discarded in rapid succession. In the late 1960s and early 1970s, for example, "microteaching" appeared to offer a worthwhile approach to the reform of teacher education, with much research being reported out of the Far West Laboratory for Educational Research and Development, among other places.[99] Almost as soon as it had surfaced and become a subject of national attention in professional circles, however, interest in the microanalytical approach to instilling a limited array of pedagogical skills seemed to subside. It had virtually disappeared by the late 1970s or early 1980s.

Reflecting back on what had been learned, Walter Borg argued in 1975 that in order to be effective, a student teaching program should have at least three characteristics. First, he claimed, it should focus the student teacher very sharply on specific behaviors or skills to be employed in teaching. Second, the student teacher should have a competent model, that is, a supervising teacher who could effectively demonstrate the skill being learned by the student. Third, the student teacher should practice and receive specific feedback on his or her use of those skills. It was exceedingly difficult, he warned, far more difficult in fact than anyone had previously imagined, to equip prospective teachers with the specific skills they would need in order to succeed in "real-life" classroom settings.

In practically every respect, Borg reported, his exhaustive review of the literature had turned up virtually no evidence that any other aspect of a conventional teacher education program made the slightest difference in affecting a student's subsequent teaching behavior. "With regard to college courses in teaching methods," he insisted, "the literature provides virtually no evidence that conventional courses in this area have any measurable effect on either subsequent teaching performance or pupil outcomes." There were no significant correlations to be found between pupil outcomes and either the amount of teacher training, the grades that teachers had earned in their teacher education courses, or their overall professional knowledge.[100]

Spawning an enormous amount of literature in the 1970s was a related movement to conceptualize teachers' roles and functions in terms of particular skills or "competencies" and, through a detailed analysis of levels of mastery, to derive objectives for competency-based training programs. Owing much to the behavioral objectives movement then in vogue in the public school arena and anticipating the "outcomes-based" accountability movement that would later gain in favor, performance-based teacher education, or PBTE, was hailed by many as the next wave of the future. Rather than defining the task as one of specifying courses a teacher in training ought to complete, proponents alleged, it was far more meaningful to require a candidate to demonstrate mastery of the competencies or "performances" a successful classroom teacher needed to possess.[101] This approach, like others before it, excited much attention for a number of years but then virtually dropped out of sight for the next two decades.

Passage of the Education Professions Development Act in 1967 and the creation shortly thereafter of a new Bureau of Educational Personnel Development within the U.S. Office of Education served to underscore the importance of at least two other major themes in the literature surrounding teacher education. More insistent than ever were renewed calls for training programs designed to prepare teachers to work with special populations, including children of the poor, members of ethnic minorities, and handicapped youngsters. At the same time recommendations were made to provide more on-site instruction in schools for teachers and to cultivate "partnerships" between departments or colleges of education and the public schools.[102] Working together, it was said, public school teachers and academic teacher educators could design, conduct, and evaluate more functional training programs.

Whether colleges of education were prepared to relinquish any significant portion of their authority over teacher education and to share their responsibility with classroom practitioners in the public schools remained an unanswered question. Extending the same theme of partnership and of relocating parts of teacher training off campus, the 1970s witnessed strong if short-lived interest in the idea of teaching centers, both as places for teachers' inservice development and, in some proposed versions, as preservice teacher-training agencies linked more closely with school districts than with institutions of higher learning.[103]

In the early 1980s, it once again had become fashionable to extol the virtues of a liberal arts education for teachers.[104] Peter F. Carbone, Jr., of Duke University was only one of many who endorsed the idea that a strong liberal arts background was indispensable for prospective teachers. Liberal learning, he argued, was one that develops students' rational abilities, their cognitive skills, and the quality of mind they bring to their work. It can free the mind from error and illusion. It has the potential to loosen the intellectual constraints imposed by dogmatism and prejudice. Liberal learning fosters in its recipients a disposition to act on the basis of reflection rather than impulse. The ability to think effectively, to communicate thought with clarity and precision, to make relevant judgments, and to discriminate among values—these have been the contributions liberal education traditionally has been thought to offer.[105]

It was one thing to recommend that liberal education be considered an integral element in the preparation of teachers, Carbone observed. It was quite another to specify what should be studied, how it should be approached, and what criteria or standards were appropriate in making those choices. "The notorious failure of college and university faculties to arrive at anything approaching a consensus regarding the courses to be included, or a convincing rationale for the selection process itself in the new liberal education programs that are springing up everywhere," he commented, "is eloquent testimony to the difficulty of the problem." Because contemporary culture lacks an underlying system of values to serve as a foundation, and there is no longer the same sort of consensus of attitudes, ideals, and convictions that once lent support to liberal learning, there has been little basis for agreement as to what subject matter is essential to a liberal arts program. As a result, it has become extremely difficult to develop a modern program of liberal studies. Colleges still committed to the ideal have tended to waver between open-ended elective systems and somewhat arbitrary distribution requirements, Carbone noted. Neither had proven satisfactory in bringing coherence or integration to courses of study.[106]

Skeptics were inclined to believe that no matter how importantly general or liberal learning might figure in the education of teachers, disarray and confusion over purposes evident among those responsible for general learning in academe were sufficient to give teacher educators pause for thought. "The faculties responsible for [general or liberal learning] in the preparation of teachers," observed Paul Shaker and Walter Ullrich of Mount Union College, "are, arguably, among the least accountable on campus. They appear to endure through force of convention rather than demonstrated service to student or society. . . . This is not to say that the *possibility* of benefit does not exist; it is, rather, a call to demonstrate such liberating outcomes."[107] Fragmented curricula taught by narrow specialists, lack of intellectual integration, poor pedagogy, as illustrated by excessive reliance on the lecture method of teaching—these all-too-common tendencies within colleges of arts and sciences, it was judged, threatened to vitiate the potential contribution liberal learning could make to the education of tomorrow's teachers.

What was especially galling to many professors of education throughout the latter third of the century was that whenever teacher education was attacked for its alleged shortcomings, few of their liberal arts colleagues seemed willing to share culpability—despite repeated findings that in most teacher preparation programs, up to three-quarters or more of a prospective teacher's time was already being spent in arts and sciences courses.[108] The more characteristic response by far from academicians in the various liberal disciplines was the issuance of condescending and sanctimonious broadsides against teacher education. Contrary to what was often alleged by proponents of the liberal arts, most education professors, as Christopher Jencks and David Riesman pointed out, had always been more eager to expose their students to liberal learning than most of their peers in other professional schools or colleges.

Educationists, they claimed, characteristically display none of the same self-confident contempt for the humanities and social sciences that engineering professors, for example, have always tended to exhibit.[109] Yet liberal arts professors forever seemed unwilling to subject to the same scrutiny they demanded of educationists and their programs their own common prescription for reform: the elimination or reduction of pedagogical courses in favor of more course work in liberal arts courses.

And the question fair-minded critics were raising, basically, was what "more of the same" in terms of arts and sciences courses really had to offer for the education of entry-level classroom teachers.

Throughout the 1980s, unrelenting antagonism and mutual distrust appeared to mark the relations between educationists and professors in the liberal disciplines, as they had in previous decades. Nor was the cause of rapprochement helped by the shrill bombast released in Richard Mitchell's 1981 diatribe, *The Graves of Academe.* It was Mitchell, for instance, who first spoke derisively about "educational pygmies," an intellectually diminutive species of academic pretenders allegedly inhabiting the stale cloisters of departments, schools, and colleges of education. Purportedly given to the interminable belaboring of the obvious, rendered in a "formalized pastiche" of ungrammatical jargon and meaningless stock phrases, pygmies, Mitchell insisted, were the great frauds of American academe.

His vitriolic attack upon American educationism, what Mitchell called a "brooding monstrosity," an "immense, mindless brute" of "awesome dimensions and seemingly endless tentacular complexities," understandably did little to bring protagonists on both sides closer together.[110] Echoing criticisms directed against educationists from within the halls of ivy in the 1980s was a widely reported complaint of Colorado governor Richard Lamm: "List the ten most somnolent courses in a university, and nine of them will be teacher courses."[111]

Suggestive of prevailing attitudes in American academe was one reported instance among many where, speaking of a colleague who had accepted an appointment in a college of education, a professor in the humanities exploded, "[He] is now a professor in the foundations of education, whatever the hell they do over there, and that mishmash that goes in all directions, people without disciplines, six characters in search of an author, twelve characters in search of a discipline!"[112] Thus, no less than in the 1940s or 1950s, in the 1980s and 1990s criticism against teacher education both on campus and beyond was to continue with undiminished vigor.

Typical in terms of the contours of the argument it presented was a 1991 study entitled *Ed School Follies* authored by Rita Kramer, an investigative journalist who had spent a year visiting schools and colleges of education throughout the nation. Very much in the tradition of Bestor and Koerner, Kramer concluded that much was wrong with the nation's schools, and she traced the problem back to the ways in which teachers were trained. We will never improve schooling, no matter how many reports by commissions, panels, and committees prescribe reforms, she insisted, until teacher education itself is transformed. "What we have today," she observed, "are teacher producing factories that process material from the bottom of the heap and turn out models that perform, but not well enough."[113]

Success in attracting better applicants, she conceded, would depend in part on better pay, better working conditions, and greater professional autonomy for teachers. More exacting college and university entrance requirements likewise were needed, Kramer believed, which in turn would necessitate higher standards of achievement within lower schools. But more urgent still was the need to reconceptualize how teachers were trained. At present, she alleged, repeating a familiar refrain, teacher preparation programs were turning out "experts in methods of teaching with nothing to apply those methods to." Neither possessing nor respecting knowledge themselves, Kramer asked rhetorically, how could teachers imbue their students with any enthusiasm for learning? "Nowhere in America today," she declared, "is intellectual life deader than in our schools—unless it is in our schools of education."[114]

Kramer was persuaded that everything teachers need to know about teaching "could be learned by intelligent people in a single summer of well-planned instruction." She left open the possibility that there could be an upgraded undergraduate education major for elementary teachers. But, like Conant before her, for prospective secondary teachers, Kramer's recommendation was that a meaningful liberal arts degree in an academic subject, followed by a period of supervised practice teaching, ought to be the norm.[115]

DÉJÀ VU

Looking back on a 30-year career in teacher education, Marvin Henry of Indiana State University expressed his personal feeling in 1988 that little had changed in the field—indeed, that matters had practically come full circle. "In the late 50's when I entered the field of teacher education," he reflected, ". . . the likes of Arthur Bestor and Max Rafferty were crossing the country blaming the 'educationists' for their soft curriculum for teachers and advocating rigorous college study. . . . " Decades later, he observed, the same arguments were being heard once again, eliciting much the same responses and coun025charges.[116] The issues had not changed materially, in his view; and neither had less than cordial relations between teacher educators and professors in other disciplines. Many other commentators gave expression to much the same perception. "In spite of a multitude of recommendations published over the past 50 years," one writer observed, "teacher education has been remarkably resistant to substantive change."[117]

B. O. Smith, writing in 1980, felt that over the preceding half century "the basic pedagogical program" for teachers had changed hardly at all.[118] Richard Wisniewski was of the opinion that teacher education in the 1970s was very much like teacher education in the 1960s, which was but slightly modified from teacher education as it was conducted in the 1950s, the 1940s, and so on.[119] One could compare 1980 college of education bulletins with those of the late 1920s or early 1930s, one critic declared, and demonstrate that patterns of preparing teachers had not changed substantially at all in the intervening period.[120]

Seymour B. Sarason, writing in *The Case for Change, Rethinking the Preparation of Educators* (1993), repeated the same sentiment. "As I look back at the reform efforts in the post–World War II era," he remarked, "it is truly remarkable how cosmetic the changes have been . . . amounting to little more than add-ons to conformity-reinforcing programs."[121] Yet another analyst in 1986 summed up a common theme: "The . . . sobering lesson to be learned from the past 50 years of attempted reform of teacher education is that there has been no fundamental reform during that period. The improvements made—and there have been some—have been gradual, slow, and in small and halting steps."[122]

Teacher education critics acknowledged that if the ways in which teachers were prepared for their work had not changed significantly, it had not been for lack of suggestions. The many books, blue ribbon commission reports, and studies published since the 1930s offered a plethora of proposed solutions to problems allegedly resulting from defective training. A certain redundancy was also obvious—there were (and are) only so many elements of a teacher preparation program that can be manipulated: the structure of the program, including its duration; the content of the training, including either its liberal and general education elements and/or its specialized pedagogical components; the students admitted to the program; and so on.[123]

Toward the end of the century, there was growing appreciation for the fact that a clear pattern had repeated itself over and over in the postwar era. First, there would be an intense period of public criticism of schools, as had occurred with the appearance of the report of the National Commission on Excellence in Education entitled *A Nation at*

Risk (1983). There would then ensue a flurry of other reports, commission studies, and books analyzing the nature of the problems identified. Most would labor to the almost inevitable conclusion, as had Rita Kramer, that whatever was wrong with the schools was owed to incompetent or unqualified teachers.

Teacher deficiencies in turn, it would be argued, were caused by shortcomings and failings in teacher preparation. (The 1985 report entitled *A Call for Change in Teacher Education* afforded one illustrative case in point.) The argument would climax with prescriptions for reforming teacher education, whereupon, it was usually implied, teachers would become more effective and schoolchildren would learn more as a result. (The Carnegie Commission's 1986 Report of the Task Force on Education and the Economy, *Teaching as a Profession,* supplied an eloquent example.) The most common measures called for to remedy teacher education since the late 1940s had now grown predictable: more stringent admission standards, better screening of teacher applicants, an increase in the number of academic courses required, more—or, alternatively, fewer—prescribed professional education courses, a beefing up of the number and quality of clinical experiences, and, possibly, standardized testing of teaching and subject matter competence prior to certification.[124]

Accounting for *why* so few reforms of teacher education had been carried out, and identifying the factors responsible for their having failed to take hold when they were enacted, posed a major challenge for teacher educators. To this question, in part, discussion turned in the last decade of the twentieth century. Meanwhile, if anything had changed, perhaps it was the sheer scope and ambition of reform proposals in teacher education emanating from teacher educators themselves. Among the more comprehensive and controversial of several initiatives undertaken from the mid-1980s onward were two reports: *A Nation Prepared: Teachers for the Twenty-First Century* (1986), a document produced under the sponsorship of the Carnegie Forum on Education and the Economy; and *Tomorrow's Teachers: A Report of the Holmes Group* (1986), the first of a trilogy of manifestos generated by a group of deans of education colleges in select research universities.

With exceptional candor, the authors of the trilogy's third volume, *Tomorrow's Schools of Education* (1995), laid out the age-old problem: "The public and much of the university itself harbor suspicions about education schools and wonder whether they serve a useful purpose. Teaching, according to the average person, involves merely knowing something and explaining it to others. Can't any reasonably intelligent person with a decent general education carry out this job without special training? Perhaps a few courses in classroom management might help, but all those other education courses? In truth, education schools have failed to make their case."[125] Making that case anew, now set in the context of urgings to revamp teacher education from top to bottom, was to occupy the attention of teacher educators throughout the closing years of the twentieth century. All told, it promised to be an era marked by more intense soul searching and scrutiny of conventional patterns of teacher preparation than anything witnessed throughout the half century or more preceding.

PART II

THE
CONTEMPORARY
CONTEXT

3

ISSUES OLD AND NEW

MARKET CONSTRAINTS
ON TEACHER EDUCATION

Practically everyone writing on the topic of teacher preparation nowadays acknowledges some degree of discontent with existing training programs on all sides. It has always been open season on teacher education; and today, as in the past, detractors are free with criticism. David F. Labaree of Michigan State University comments: "Everyone seems to have something bad to say about the way we prepare our teachers. If you believe what you read and what you hear, a lot of what is wrong with American education these days can be traced to the failings of teachers and to shortcomings in the processes by which we train them for their tasks. We are told that students are not learning, that productivity is not growing, that economic competitiveness is declining—all to some extent because teachers don't know how to teach."[1]

Recent indictments of teacher preparatory programs for their alleged deficiencies differ from one another considerably, in emphasis and tone if not always so much in substance. But prescriptions for reform vary even more widely. Clark Kerr's wry observation about the university's tendency to gallop off in opposite directions simultaneously seems to apply equally well to the rhetoric of contemporary teacher education reform. Some recommend disbanding professional teacher-training programs entirely, for example, trusting that any well-educated college graduate can learn to become an effective classroom teacher through a brief apprenticeship and practical on-the-job experience. Others would modify the several components of existing undergraduate baccalaureate-level programs, adjusting this or that element, bolstering their entry or exit criteria, changing field experiences, revamping methods courses, or strengthening general education requirements, and so on, but otherwise leaving the structure of programs basically intact. Still others argue on behalf of so-called alternative certification routes whose evident purpose is to bypass traditional training programs entirely.

One expedient might amount to little more than enrollment in a short preparatory regimen offered within a public school district. Again, the idea of having an abbreviated course of study offered cooperatively by a public school in partnership with a college- or university-based department of education attracts support. The presumption in both cases, of course, is that teacher training needs to become shorter, less theoretical, and more practical. Protagonists of this stripe frankly avow their preference for the devolution of teacher education into something akin to practice-oriented apprenticeship. What seems to be wanted, in effect, is a species of craft training.

Consistent with a modern tendency to escalate credentialing, at the opposite end of the spectrum repose reformers who would greatly expand the scale of present-day teacher preparation so as to make it more nearly resemble legal or medical training. Where there is agreement among critics, it tends to be limited only to the judgment that today's schools of education, like their predecessors of yesteryear, fail to provide an education for teachers that is either academically solid or pedagogically effective.[2]

Labaree's own analysis is instructive. He argues that both the form and content of teacher education have always been shaped by market influences and most particularly by the dominant purposes public schools have been called upon to serve, those of social efficiency and social mobility. (The former expresses the top-down perspective of the educational provider; while the latter reflects the bottom-up perspective of the educational consumer.) In terms of social efficiency, the purpose of schooling is held to be one of training students as future workers within a stratified occupational structure. The school's task, runs the argument, is to produce skilled workers and to do so cost-effectively, such that job slots at various levels within the hierarchy are occupied by capable people. Society therefore functions more efficiently.

Social mobility as an educational goal, on the other hand, reflects parents' desires to utilize schooling as a means for their offspring to "get ahead," to acquire the necessary educational credentials for achieving—

or retaining—a desired level of socioeconomic status within society. Credentials (diplomas, degrees, and so forth), in Labaree's phrase, serve "as currency in the zero-sum competition for social status."[3] Both purposes link education to the job market. The net result of their combined influence, Labaree contends, besides their effect on lower and collegiate schooling alike, has been to undermine efforts to enrich the quality, duration, rigor, and aims of teacher education.

Teacher shortages defined the original problem. The advent of near-universal elementary education in the nineteenth century generated a demand for a large number of elementary instructors. That need was met in part with the opening of urban normal schools sponsored by school systems. At about the same time, state normal institutions were first created. The expansion of elementary schooling was followed in the early twentieth century by a swelling of high-school enrollments. Once again, the demand for high-school teachers outstripped the supply available. A response came in the form of state teachers' colleges. In both cases the imperative was for a type of training capable of mass-producing teachers in short order. As Labaree expresses it, "The consequence of the goal of social efficiency was that it put emphasis on the creation of a form of teacher education that could produce the most teachers, in the shortest time, at the lowest cost, and at the minimum level of ability that the public would allow."[4]

Popular reliance on schooling as a mechanism for social mobility has affected teacher preparation in much the same way. Programs in the 1800s were intended on pragmatic grounds to be as accessible and relatively undemanding as possible. Yet as normal educators soon discovered, much to their dismay, consumer pressure to provide general learning for students who had no intention of teaching proved well-nigh irresistible. What ambitious students and their parents wanted from normal schools in many cases was not specialized training for a single vocation but, rather, a route to middle-class status. The result was that many normal schools rather quickly evolved into multipurpose high schools, just as state teachers' colleges were transformed in the 1920s and 1930s into something resembling liberal arts schools and then, in the 1960s and 1970s, into general-purpose public universities.[5] Pressure to provide social mobility forced teacher education to become "unobtrusive in character and minimal in scope for the convenience of students seeking a general education." Teacher education, in short, was to be modest in the demands that it placed on students in order not to block access to the degrees they sought.

In Labaree's view, the importunate demands for social efficiency and mobility over the years continue to undermine efforts today to strengthen teacher education programs. "In fact," he claims, "everything urges toward superficiality (providing thin coverage of both subject matter and pedagogy), brevity (keeping the program short and unintrusive), accessibility (allowing entry to nearly everyone), low level of difficulty (making the process easy and graduation certain), and parsimony (doing all of this on the cheap)."[6] Indicative of how little popular toleration and support strong teacher-training programs enjoy is the public's readiness to circumvent their strictures and to turn to alternatives when teacher shortages are especially acute. To put it bluntly, aside from a handful of critics who would do away with them entirely, practically everyone professes support for robust teacher education programs—but only so long as it is expedient to do so.

HISTORICAL TRADITIONS OF THOUGHT AND PRACTICE IN TEACHER PREPARATION

Before turning to the literature of teacher education reform and some of the issues that animate contemporary discussion, it is helpful to recall briefly those historical traditions that have shaped thinking about teacher preparation and thereby helped define the intellectual context for practically all debate today. Each tradition has been associated with a different institution or training agency, each conceptualizing the task at hand in a different way, each offering a different type of preparation for its own specific constituency.

The first, predating teacher education as a distinct and explicit enterprise in its own right, derives from the liberal arts tradition. Essentially, the "academic" or "liberal" view (for want of a better label) has always held that general learning of a broad and generous character *of itself* constitutes the best preparation for teaching, most particularly at the secondary level.[7] Throughout most of the first half of the nineteenth century, it will be recalled, liberal arts colleges regularly turned out graduates intending to teach in secondary academies. The faith that a classical education by its very nature was fully adequate to meet the preparatory needs of future teachers, no less than those of students bent on pursuing other careers, went virtually unquestioned.

Under the arrangement then prevailing, a fixed curriculum introduced students to a common body of knowledge embodied in the traditional texts of Greco-Roman antiquity. Successful performance demanded that the student acquire specific habits of mind, skills, and the self-discipline considered essential for success in life. Upon completing his studies, the learner would emerge steeped in the humane values of the Western cultural tradition, conversant with the best that had been thought and written on life's great questions. Thus imbued with the wisdom of the liberal arts, college graduates would go forth equipped to teach, and to do it well.

Long before the end of the nineteenth century, proponents of the notion that only certain subjects, such as rhetoric, dialectic, and moral philosophy, were inherently liberalizing (or that they possessed a unique capacity to help strengthen and discipline the several potencies or "faculties" of the mind) were clearly on the defensive. The rise of the modern university, together with the emergence of new specialized disciplines in the social, biological, and physical sciences, eventually spelled an end to the idea that retaining a uniform, fixed regimen of studies common to all was feasible. Yet even when classical studies gave way to a much broader array of subjects, concern for breadth or scope of learning as a leading educational imperative was not lost sight of entirely. Instead, a compromise of sorts emerged.[8]

First, the principle of free election of courses by students was established, beginning in the post–Civil War era with pioneer experiments at Harvard under the leadership of President Charles W. Eliot. Partly in reaction to the excesses of uncontrolled choice, the common pattern subsequently became one of requiring students to "distribute" their studies across a range of different disciplines or subjects. Finally, as an attempt to balance the liberal arts ideal of a common course of study with growing specialization, it became customary to present undergraduates with a more or less structured and prescribed curriculum for the first two or three years, together with an elective concentration or emphasis in a particular discipline (the academic "major") in the junior and senior years. The former was intended to provide scope and breadth of "coverage." The latter aimed at supplying "depth" in a given discipline or field of study. Some such balancing act still prevails as the norm in American higher education today.

In spite of the conceptual disarray and confusion so painfully apparent in the typical undergraduate curriculum, the faith still persists (not surprisingly, running strongest among liberal arts professors) that values traditionally associated with liberal learning—disciplined intelligence, critical and reflective thinking, breadth of perspective, depth of understanding—are both integral to and perhaps exhaustive of qualifications for the work of teaching. What the liberal tradition speaks to first and foremost is the education of teachers as individuals and citizens, as persons engaged in the process of taking on certain humane attributes and distinctive intellectual characteristics. Claims that knowledge of the subject matter to be taught is of paramount if not exclusive importance and that in some final analysis most well-educated people are competent to teach without needing to be taught how to do so have been characteristic tenets of the "academic" tradition applied to teacher preparation.

The normal school tradition, in contrast, came to the question of how best to prepare teachers for their work from exactly the opposite direction.[9] Normal schools, it will be recalled, appeared on the scene at a time when most prospective primary teachers themselves had barely completed the elementary curriculum. What was called for, quite understandably, was little more than a brief review of the common branches of learning to be taught. To this was appended instruction in those pedagogical techniques considered most useful for imparting that same learning to young children. The issue was not necessarily that of promoting breadth or depth of knowledge in the minds of those preparing to teach. Still less was it one of instilling certain humanistic values associated with liberal learning. The more modest and realizable goal was that of assuring minimal acquaintance with a limited, highly circumscribed curriculum and engendering the practical competence needed to convey its substance to schoolchildren.

Normal schools were much criticized for their limitations and shortcomings, and sometimes deservedly so. But for all of their faults, it must be said, normal institutions at their best did undeniably hold themselves to a clear if sometimes narrow interpretation of their mission. Their job, as they saw it, was to foster a strong sense of professionalism and esprit de corps. It was to exalt teaching as a calling or vocation and thus to inspire candidates to make classroom instruction their life's work. Above all, the goal was to provide a training in pedagogy that was eminently practical. This they sought to accomplish autonomously within a setting devoted exclusively to teacher preparation. Left to their own devices, their goal was to furnish an institutional environment free of the blurred purpose resulting from the pursuit of goals other than those involved with teacher preparation. Finally, their appointed task was to provide teacher candidates with closely supervised practice before releasing them to teach in school classrooms.[10] What normal preparatory programs lacked in depth or scope, it may be observed, they tried to compensate for in terms of clarity of purpose and sharpness of focus.

Associated with the development of university schools and colleges of education in the opening years of the twentieth century was a third formative strain of thought. Lacking any better designation, it is sometimes referred to as the "education-as-applied-science" or "technical-professional" tradition.[11] Under either label, it was to produce the university-based model still dominant in the field today. Part and parcel of the story of how teacher education won a place in academe was the struggle for legitimacy and status waged by school administrators and teacher educators. Having arrived relatively late on the college scene and burdened by their association with lower-level normal schools, educationists found themselves ill-equipped to compete for professional standing within the scholarly community.[12] Roughly paralleling the aspirations of their peers in such fields as law and medicine, teacher educators of the early 1900s hoped that the installation of teacher preparation programs in universities would elevate education as a professional field and confer greater dignity on teaching as a career.

In order to gain academic respectability, teacher education needed to be established on a sound intellectual footing. This imperative in turn required—or so it seemed at the time—that its defenders make good on the claim they were privy to an underlying "science" of education. Earlier attempts to ground practice on the theoretical constructions of the likes of Pestalozzi and Herbart were now mostly abandoned. The pervasive trend instead was to draw upon the experimental and quantitative methods of the newly developing social sciences (psychology and sociology in particular) in hopes of building up a true scientific discipline.

Researchers set about the task of trying to devise better ways of testing for intelligence and achievement. Attempts were begun to confirm and analyze general "laws" of learning. Inventing more powerful and discriminating pupil classification schemes became a major concern, as did the work of trying to develop empirically validated principles of curriculum construction. Still another initiative was the move to measure the specific effects of alternative approaches to instruction. Meanwhile, those responsible for the development of graduate programs in school administration were turning increasingly to survey research, amassing prodigious amounts of data on school functions and activities. Innumerable studies and polls were undertaken, and on a scale never before attempted. The tacit assumption throughout seems to have been that with more data in hand, policymakers could make more "scientific" decisions about educational policies and procedures.[13]

What seems to have escaped notice was the growing tendency of research rituals to move farther and farther away from the practical concerns of prospective classroom teachers, those enrolled in preparatory programs in colleges and universities. Rarely, for example, was the individual school classroom itself made the focus of much attention and study. Despite protestations to the contrary, the chasm between the praxis of education as viewed from the perspective of a classroom teacher and the theoretical concerns of researchers continued to widen with each passing decade. In retrospect, all the research activity may have done something to enhance the respectability and prestige of the education professorate. But the seeming lack of "fit" between the abstract findings of educational science and the needs of classroom teachers did little for the utility of the preparatory programs over which they presided. Still heard today is a common complaint that the translation of teaching and learning theory into forms adapted for application by classroom practitioners has not yet been satisfactorily achieved.

Early on, a more or less "standard" undergraduate teacher preparation program emerged. As a model, it derived more than anything else from an archetypal pattern laid down in the first two decades of the twentieth century by Dean James Earl Russell and his colleagues at Teachers College, Columbia University.[14] As Russell expressed it, a proper teacher education program should encompass four basic elements: "general culture" or knowledge; "special scholarship" (by which he meant integrative and synoptic learning across several disciplines); "professional knowledge," or systematic inquiry into the theory and practice of education; and "technical skill," or, roughly, practical pedagogical expertise. Each component (or something resembling Russell's formulations) has since found its place in the traditional four-year undergraduate preservice program, now the most common blueprint for teacher preparation.

According to the formula followed by most colleges and universities engaged in teacher training, the first two years of the undergraduate curriculum are devoted—primarily if not always exclusively—to general studies. In theory, general learning, expressed in terms of "distribution" requirements, is supposed to ensure exposure to, and acquaintance with, a coherent array of subject matter in the humanities, social sciences, mathematics and the natural sciences, and fine arts. What happens, unfortunately, is that the reality of course requirements and credits imposed all too often amounts to little more than a chaotic smorgasbord of offerings, each unrelated to the other and wholly lacking any sort of integrative architecture. As critics of higher education never tire of complaining, the undergraduate curriculum (for prospective teachers and nonteachers alike) most closely resembles a supermarket where students freely choose from independent offerings across a wide range of categories. And only rarely, or so it is claimed, does the result afford learners broad cultural knowledge or the type of disciplinary integration so frequently called for in the rhetoric of colleges' recruitment literature, catalogs, and commencement addresses.

Questions about the quality and organization of general learning aside, sometimes overlooked by liberal arts critics of teacher education is a salient point. Most undergraduates preparing themselves for teaching careers complete the majority of their course work outside the academic unit responsible for professional education. Whereas lay critics frequently assume that the bulk of a future teacher's undergraduate preparation is given over to pedagogical courses, in actuality the opposite is true. Reasonable opinion may differ on what balance ought to be struck between general learning and more specialized, technical training. Liberal arts proponents, for instance, regularly complain that the ratio of "academic" to "professional" courses is too low. In the case of elementary education majors especially, it is said, the constraints imposed by a program requiring the equivalent of three or four full semesters devoted to pedagogical course work allow insufficient space for liberal learning. The fact still remains, however, that education students take considerably more courses outside of a school, department, or college of education than they do within it.

Typically, the general liberal arts portion of a future teacher's coursework accounts for about 35 to 40 percent of the total elementary or secondary preparation program. Additionally, students intending to become secondary teachers satisfy all, or nearly all, of the requirements for a teaching major in some academic field or fields, most commonly running to slightly less than 40 percent of all courses completed. On average, no more than 21 percent of the degree program for high-school teachers involves education courses.

The professional sequence in education—which rarely if ever is articulated in any deliberate way with requirements in general education—tends to differ by teaching levels. Future high-school or middle-school teachers complete an average of 21 to 26 hours out of a total of 120 to 125 hours required for the baccalaureate degree. Mandated course work usually includes a course in adolescent psychology or educational psychology, a general methods course, a subject-specific methods course, some credit-bearing preliminary field experiences, and possibly one or more courses in the social and cultural foundations of education, followed by student teaching.

Elementary education students usually do not major in a single field but complete courses in subjects presumed to be related to the K-6 course of studies they eventually will teach. (Secondary education students are expected to become specialists, while elementary education students usually are required to be generalists.) Primary-school teacher candidates most commonly complete an average of 50 hours in professional education, including an overview or introductory course in education; sometimes a cultural or historical foundations class; a course in educational or child psychology and learning; upward of half a dozen pedagogical courses devoted to the teaching of reading, art, music, mathematics, science, and social studies; supervised field experiences; and student teaching. On average, professional studies courses constitute about 44 percent of the total baccalaureate program, including about 24 percent devoted to methodological or pedagogical courses. These latter classes, considered as a whole, constitute the elementary student's professional major.[15]

Quite predictably, the "typical" four-year undergraduate preservice program—precisely because it serves as a benchmark—has been the object of much criticism from those seeking to enhance the status and quality of teacher preparation. Sometimes the question is about the *quality* of students allowed to enter and to graduate from teacher education. Other times the focus of concern is the overall *structure* of the preparatory program itself and the interrelations among its component parts. Almost as often the locus of debate centers on its *duration,* with protagonists variously clamoring for the prolongation or abbreviation of courses of study. Closely related are urgings to change the *placement* or *sequencing* of teacher preparation by moving it to the postbachelor's level and making it an exclusively graduate-level enterprise.

Finally, the question of the most appropriate *site* for teacher preparation is hotly debated. Many continue to defend the college or university as the proper and most fitting home for teacher education, convinced that the rich intellectual environment of an institution of higher learning is essential to the work of teacher preparation. To abandon teacher education's hard-won place in academe, it is said, would be a tragic mistake. Those on the other side argue on behalf of reversing the history of the development of formal teacher education. Their claim is that because neither contemporary colleges nor universities are well adapted to the task of preparing teachers, programs should be moved wholly or in part out of academe and into the schools where they allegedly belong.

CRITERIA GOVERNING ENTRY INTO TEACHING

Lax standards purportedly governing admission to teacher preparation programs and thence into classroom teaching have been the subject of severe criticism for decades. If the nation is to have first-rate teachers, it is said, colleges and universities offering preparatory programs must "tighten up" standards and make admission criteria more stringent. Only the brightest and best applicants should be accepted. Those of lesser ability should be firmly excluded. Not until education schools begin upgrading themselves and start attracting a better caliber of students, critics avow, can they have any hope of success in shedding their long-standing notoriety on campus as bastions of academic mediocrity. Academic excellence could be achieved in large part if teacher-training units would simply refuse to afford refuge for the scholastically incompetent. They should declare unequivocally that henceforth only academically talented candidates need apply. Until then, as matters now stand, their evident willingness to accept students who could not qualify for admission elsewhere will only continue to lend credibility to the tired old cliché, "Those who can, do, and those who cannot, teach." For just this reason, runs the criticism, schools and colleges of education have unwittingly allowed themselves to become the laughing-stock of higher education. Their continued presence within the groves of academe, some will claim, remains a scandal and an embarrassment.

Research findings dating back to the mid-1970s do tend to confirm the widespread perception that in years past it has been relatively easy to gain admission to teacher education. There is no lack of evidence to show that, on average, those accepted into preparatory programs have compared unfavorably on measures of academic ability with those of their peers preparing for careers other than teaching. This being said, evidence accumulated over the past decade and a half or so indicates that the situation has been changing significantly over time on both counts. Admission to teacher-training programs at most schools has become far more selective than might have been the case just a few years ago. Similarly, the academic quality of teacher candidates appears to have registered significant improvement in contrast with the situation prevailing in decades previous. Meanwhile, there also is growing appreciation for the point that research findings commonly adduced to support charges of a mediocre teacher talent pool require far more careful interpretation than they have heretofore received.

Surveys of admissions procedures employed by North Central Association colleges and universities accredited by the National Council for Accreditation of Teacher Education (NCATE) indicated in the early 1980s that despite lengthy lists of entry criteria, most institutions actually were denying admission to fewer than 10 percent of those who applied to teacher education programs. Virtually all in that period were stipulating a minimum grade point average as a standard for admission or retention. But the minimum required was set low; and even among the country's leading institutions, "conditional" admissions were commonplace. Almost 50 percent of all institutions of higher learning affiliated with the American Association of Colleges for Teacher Education (AACTE), for example, as surveyed in one study cited in 1983, reportedly demanded nothing higher than a 2.0 or less on a four-point scale for admission; about a third required a grade point average between 2.01 and 2.25; and less than 14 percent used an academic average between 2.26 and 2.50 as the criterion.[16]

Since the mid-1980s, thanks partly to a continuing teacher oversupply in most fields, among programs requiring a given grade point average for admission or retention, the trend has been to raise requirements substantially. Currently, at some institutions, only second-semester sophomores with successful academic records are allowed to transfer into education or to declare their candidacy for eventual certification. A common expectation is that applicants will have achieved a collegiate grade point average ranging upward between 2.60 and 2.75 on a four-point scale, either prior to admission or before being allowed to graduate.

As a rule, if admission standards to teacher education traditionally have been low, among a growing number of colleges and universities today this is clearly no longer the case. Compared with the stringency of standards governing admittance to other professional programs in such fields as engineering, nursing, journalism, business administration, library science, pharmacy, and architecture, criteria employed to control entry into professional education seem to fare quite well.

A great deal of attention has been paid to identifying the academic abilities and qualifications of students seeking teaching as a career. A widely reported study conducted by the National Center for Education Statistics of college-bound high-school seniors, by intended majors, between 1973 and 1981, found that the average Scholastic Aptitude Test (SAT) verbal and mathematics scores of those who reportedly planned to major in education fell well below the average for all college-bound seniors tested (27 points below the national average verbal score and 32 points below the national average math score in 1973, 34 points below average verbal and 43 below average math scores in 1976). Moreover, of 19 fields of study reported by the ACT for *enrolled* college freshmen in 1975-76, education majors were tied for seventeenth place on math scores and fourteenth on English scores.[17]

College Entrance Examination Board data showed that not only were scores of intended education majors lower on average than those for all college-bound seniors in 1973 and again in 1976, but by 1981, the gap had increased even further. The mean math scores for those intending to major in education, for example, had dropped 31 points, while the mean score for all students declined by 15 points. SAT verbal scores of intended education majors dropped 27 points, while average scores for all college-bound seniors slipped 21 points.[18] On the whole, the popular impression that students pursuing careers in teaching were academically weak seemed to be amply supported by research data.

The problem with many studies pointing to the supposedly poor qualifications of future teachers, it has been observed, has been their apparent failure to distinguish carefully between the academic qualifications of students who *profess an intention* to enter a teacher certification program and those who are actually *admitted*; or with those who successfully *complete* a program leading to licensure; or, finally, with graduates who actually embark on a career in teaching. The fact of the matter is that there is apt to be considerable "slippage" and attrition between the time a high-school senior declares an interest in teacher education as a possible college major and the point when the person enters teaching. "Assumptions about the limited academic ability of teachers," notes one observer, "appear to be based largely on a handful of highly publicized studies . . . that report the poor performance of teachers or prospective teachers on written tests and the relatively weak performance on college entrance examinations of high-school graduates who *say* that they *intend* to teach." However, it is emphasized, "studies that focus on college entrants tell us very little about teacher education students, much less about teachers."[19] Over half of those who initially express interest in teaching never become licensed and, of those who are certified, almost a third never teach.

Undergraduates actually enrolled in teacher education, as it turns out, appear nationwide to be about as able academically as any other aggregate of college students. A 1985-86 national sample of teacher education students surveyed showed, for example, that they placed somewhere in the middle of the distribution of admission test scores and grade point average performance of all students and in the top third of their high-school graduating classes. Similarly, when compared with students majoring in the arts and sciences or in business administration, teacher education students in recent years consistently have compared very favorably.[20] Again, average prose literacy scores of full-time–employed bachelor's degree recipients, surveyed by occupations in the early 1990s and reported in 1995, indicated that the teachers among them had literacy skills similar to college graduates in most other professional occupations.[21]

Another reason why research findings need to be interpreted with care stems from the fact that knowing something about the *average* capability of prospective teachers does not reveal much about their *distribution* across the spectrum. The problem with many studies using population test scores is that they report measures of central tendency (mean scores) but neglect to pay sufficient attention to the *range* of scores reported. The truth of the matter seems to be that teaching as a career does attract—and, to a lesser degree perhaps, retains—a significant percentage of people of very high ability, at least as high as that of students drawn to any other profession. Unfortunately, perhaps, it also attracts and retains a disproportionately large percentage of those with low measured academic ability and achievement.

What compounds confusion are the differing methods commonly utilized for reporting the percentage of high-ability students in education.[22] One protocol, for example, identifies the full teacher education population, counts the number from that group scoring at the top end of the distribution for all college students (or graduates), and then reports the proportion that this number represents for the teacher education talent pool as a whole. An alternative approach begins with all college students scoring in the upper quintile of a distribution of measures and then identifies the proportion of those students enrolled in teacher preparation programs. The former approach is likely to yield

an exceedingly bleak picture for teacher education. The latter proce-
dure creates a quite different impression.

For example, it was almost certainly not true, as one researcher
reported for the Carnegie Foundation in 1983, that "never before in the
nation's history has the caliber of those entering the teaching profession
been as low as it is today."[23] Still less would any similarly hyperbolic
judgment have been valid a dozen or so years later, in the mid-1990s.
Yet then and now it remains accurate to say that the lowest-scoring
subset of the total college population has seemed to include an excessive
number of prospective teachers. As Judith Lanier and Judith Little of
Michigan State University noted in 1986, "The fact that . . . a large
number and excessive proportion of the lowest scoring college students
are accepted into teacher education and subsequently recommended for
certification explains the genesis of the stereotype that those in teacher
education are the least academically able. . . . The overabundance of
teacher education students drawn from among the least academically
inclined certainly contributes to the characterization that all prospective
and practicing teachers have low intellectual ability."[24]

Actual estimates vary, but the figures most commonly cited today
suggest that about 10 percent of the ablest 20 percent of all students
enroll in teacher education, a quite respectable showing when compared
with other college majors. At the opposite end of the spectrum of ability,
nevertheless, upward of 40 percent of the lowest-scoring students are
recruited yearly to teacher education programs. Less than a third of that
subset actually completes a regimen leading to teacher certification.
Especially troubling in this connection are recurrent allegations—difficult to document but harder to discount entirely—that ranking academic
administrators at certain schools have been prone to *discourage* schools
and colleges of education from becoming more selective. Their inclination instead has been to exploit them as "holding pens" for students of
low ability—those who might otherwise flunk out and thereby raise the
overall student attrition rate. (The attitude seems to be "We need
someplace to keep marginal students. Send them over to the education
school where it doesn't make a difference.")

Even when it is conceded that teaching attracts a high percentage
of academically untalented candidates, it is still worth asking what
would represent education's "fair share" of the brightest and best from
among those scoring in the top quintile of all college students. What
needs to be taken into consideration always is the obvious but often
overlooked fact that *all professions and occupations compete for the*

same top students. Conversely, the question awaiting further consideration is what would constitute a reasonable and acceptable percentage of the least talented that might be expected to enter teaching.

Perhaps it is true, as Frank B. Murray, formerly dean of the College of Education at the University of Delaware, has argued, that some "arithmetical realism" is called for. "The sheer magnitude of the universal schooling enterprise," he notes, "carries with it the requirement that the schools—at all levels—will be operated by large numbers of relatively less-talented persons."[25] There simply are not enough people who score at the top end of any credible measure of academic and intellectual competence to fill over three million teaching positions and still have some left over to engage in the nation's other high-level work. The alternative, inevitably, is to look to more or less average students as well as to the ablest in order to acquire all of the teachers needed in the nation's classrooms. The challenge, perhaps, is to manipulate selection, retention, and certification policies so that the overall distribution of talent is drawn from the average and above, rather than from the average and below, as has traditionally been the case in teacher recruitment.

Unmentioned so far are other forms of "gatekeeping" currently governing entry into teaching. By 1981, according to at least one study, at least 17 states had instituted some form of testing for prospective teachers, either utilizing state-developed examinations or the National Teacher Exam (NTE), or some combination of both. Another study identified 23 states that required academic competency tests for teacher certification or within teacher preparation programs. By 1989, 45 states had mandated some form of independent testing for prospective teachers, including measures of subject-matter knowledge, tests of general knowledge, and tests of professional knowledge and skills.[26]

Sometimes testing is administered prior to formal entry to teacher education. In certain states, testing is mandated upon completion of a preparatory program, as a precondition for certification or permanent licensure. Since the early 1980s, in most cases pressure to institute standardized testing has originated with state boards and legislatures more than it has come from academically based teacher educators. Yet by the late 1990s, a growing number of colleges and universities were expressing cautious support for the idea of requiring teacher candidates to complete a form of examination tied to national teaching standards.

Interestingly, some research has found that among graduating education majors actively seeking teaching positions, those with the highest grade point averages or having the best standardized test scores are not necessarily the same people favored in hiring decisions. In fact, it would appear that even when high-scoring candidates are available, a disproportionate number of lower-ranking applicants are offered positions—suggesting as one hypothesis (adduced by Murray, among others) that school boards and superintendents tend to rely on *other* factors besides academic aptitude and grade scores as predictors of teaching success.

Again, research on the predictive reliability of standardized tests may be illuminating. At the risk of some oversimplification, it would seem that what most of the tests developed so far predict best is a person's performance on any similar examination. The more closely tests resemble one another, the higher the correlation coefficient between them; that is, test performance in the first instance chiefly predicts performance on a similar subsequent test. Unfortunately, what it does *not* predict with much accuracy is success in the classroom, gauged either by observers' ratings of a teacher's performance or by the learning increments students actually register. As Murray concludes with considerable justification, "It has proved impossible, with our existing measurement techniques, to establish any meaningful connection between standardized test scores—or even school grades—and later performance in any of the professions, including teaching. . . . The skills needed to do well on a standardized test seem only remotely connected to the skills needed to teach well."[27]

Superficially considered, findings that grade point averages and performances on standardized intelligence or aptitude tests do not serve as reliable predictors of effective teaching are disconcerting and in a sense seem profoundly counter-intuitive. One would like to think, for example, that bright, high-achieving individuals make the best teachers. (Some such assumption, in fact, defines the position taken by most liberal arts critics of teacher education.) Again, rare indeed are the parents of a school-aged youngster who, all things being equal and given a choice in the matter, would want to have their child assigned to a teacher of mediocre scholastic attainment. Presumably their choice would be a teacher distinguished by an exemplary record of academic achievement. But a moment's reflection suggests why matters are not nearly that simple. In real-life terms, things are rarely equal.

Practical experience and ordinary common sense, if nothing else, should serve as reminders that "excellence" in teaching is a complex equation compounded of multiple, often vaguely defined factors. If a high-school teacher with impeccable academic credentials were found to be emotionally distant and remote, or chronically disorganized, or lacked the ability to communicate effectively with adolescents, or gave evidence that he or she was incapable of motivating youngsters and arousing their interest in the subject matter at hand—that person would not be likely to be perceived as a "good" teacher. Conversely, if a kindergarten teacher was regarded as warm and nurturing, highly motivated, displayed an obvious love of children, and clearly knew how to elicit the best from them, few would trouble themselves over the fact that his or her paper credentials were somehow less than impressive.

Once again, the age-old "criterion problem" surfaces. Deciding what makes for good teaching on the job and who is a competent teacher hinges on the standards by which a judgment is made. Academic ability or attainment alone, it would seem, figures as only one consideration among many. Suffice it to say, if there existed a consensus on what makes for good teaching, and if a test both valid and reliable had been devised for predicting who was most likely to become a good teacher, it seems reasonable to assume some such instrumentality would already have found widespread adoption.

The practical implication to be drawn is that raising admission standards to teacher education programs offers no panacea for curing the ills afflicting contemporary education. The locus of the problem does not rest entirely with academically unpromising candidates being admitted to the field. Nor, within certain limits, do proposals to raise grade point averages required of teacher candidates as a condition for admission or retention within a preparatory program supply a cure-all either. In the final analysis, efforts to create new hurdles to teaching such as imposing standardized tests probably cannot bear the burden that current reform proposals place upon them. As is often pointed out, bright people may score well on various tests of subject-matter competence or professional proficiency but they may not turn out to be good teachers. Conversely, teachers of modest intellectual endowments may turn out to be relatively effective—even outstanding—instructors in school classrooms. The point is, tests do not allow trustworthy estimations to be made before the fact as to who is which.[28]

GENERAL LEARNING FOR TEACHERS

Reform in teacher preparation is unlikely if future innovations are not accompanied by fundamental, possibly far-reaching changes in the nonprofessional component of students' courses of study. This is to say, simply, that without basic reforms in liberal or general education, modifying those aspects of a program for which schools and colleges of education bear direct responsibility is not apt to make a dramatic difference. Conventional wisdom holds that teachers should be "better educated," that they need a stronger grounding in the liberal arts. Typically, appeals for strengthening the liberal arts portion of a prospective teacher's education labor to make the case that students need to become well-rounded, better-informed, more thoughtful individuals. During—and as an outcome of—their course of studies, it is expected they will acquire the distinguishing characteristics of liberally educated persons. As Willis D. Hawley puts it, "There appears to be substantial agreement that at least half of a teacher's undergraduate education should be in the liberal arts and that this coursework should be broadly distributed in the natural sciences, humanities, and the social sciences. The assumption underlying this belief is that such a background will allow teachers to call on a broad range of knowledge in making judgments in general and in giving context and depth to their teaching."[29]

Few question the value of liberal learning for teachers. If anything, many critics would argue that *additional* general course work in the arts and sciences is highly desirable. But simply demanding more of the same will hardly do without also asking about the character and consequences of what is called for. The problem with general education, it is often said, is its quality and coherence, not its length.[30] As dozens of blue ribbon panels, commissions, and national reports have lamented over the past half century, there is very little agreement on baccalaureate goals and priorities. General education nowadays seems to be in a state of growing disarray. There is almost no shared vision of what core learning is essential. Acquiring important skills seems to be left to chance. Finally, current efforts to identify what learning ought to be held in common by everyone, on balance, appear to have been largely ineffectual. "Today there is little consensus on what constitutes a liberal education," declared the Carnegie Council on Policy Studies in Higher Education in 1977, "and, as if by default, the choices have been left to the student." General education, the commission claimed, "is now a disaster area. It has been on the defensive and losing ground for more than 100 years."[31]

Regrettably, there is little to suggest that much has changed in the two decades since the commission's original dire pronouncement. Attempts to analyze causes for the "disaster" have dominated an ever-growing body of literature over the past 30 years. Between 1965 and 1975, the total number of published books and articles treating the condition of liberal learning in higher education registered a tremendous increase, more than doubling the number for the preceding ten-year period.[32] The same trend has continued unabated in the 1990s. Throughout, there has been remarkable unanimity of opinion on what factors threaten to gut the substance of general and liberal education, leaving little more than an empty rhetorical shell. But there has been far less agreement on what should be done to remedy matters.[33]

Critics such as Robert Paul Wolff in *The Ideal of the University* (1969), Brand Blanshard in *The Uses of a Liberal Education* (1973), and Christopher Jencks and David Reisman in *The Academic Revolution* (1977), not to mention some of their more recent counterparts, have all tended to offer the same diagnosis. Institutions of higher learning, they allege, have grown complacent, less reflective about their own practices.[34] Bereft of any guiding intellectual vision and under strong cultural pressure in today's world to vocationalize learning, most colleges and universities have settled for hodgepodge curricula calculated to offer something for everyone. Having abandoned their integrity to marketplace flux and flow, they seem to have lost their will to insist on intellectual coherence or unity in their myriad curricular offerings.

Universities especially, or so it is claimed, have become "knowledge factories," the principal manufacturers and retailers of knowledge as a purchasable commodity. Their buyers include students seeking credentials to guarantee themselves secure futures, industries in search of the skills and products of research, and governmental agencies demanding an array of specialized services. In any such climate or institutional environment, perhaps, authentic liberal learning is bound to become distorted in the service of other ends or simply allowed to languish from neglect.

As many have observed, in the absence of an undergirding scheme of values commanding broad assent within society, intellectual confusion is perhaps inevitable. Elizabeth Coleman, writing in the June 1, 1981 *Chronicle of Higher Education,* noted that the history of American higher education is "strewn with the debris of attempts to create a more integrated curriculum . . . to revitalize the liberal arts." She, like many others, questioned whether a lost common heritage or shared culture could be recaptured through curricular reform, and she was pessimistic about prospects for restoring the splintered curriculum in any meaningful way.[35] Jill Kerr Conway, president of Smith College, similarly felt daunted by the search for a common learning: "We can no longer say, for instance, that students should study the Bible instead of the Koran. Those days are gone forever."[36]

Jerry Gaff, director of the Center for General Education of the American Association of Colleges, feels that the simple imposition of conventional distribution requirements has been a "quick and dirty" approach to curriculum reform. While it reasserts the importance of the liberal arts, he feels it does not go nearly far enough. "Distribution requirements," he claims, "are usually fashioned for political rather than education reasons; more often than not they constitute a trade-off among departments on how to carve up the curricular pie rather than a genuine commitment that certain kinds of knowledge are more important than others."[37] Theodore Lockwood shares Gaff's skepticism. "The current trend at colleges of reviving distribution requirements does not convince me we are improving the quality of education," he comments. "Giving the curriculum more structure doesn't necessarily give it coherence."[38]

Identifying the traditional goals of liberal education has been easier than finding the specific means for achieving them. Always the objective has been to "liberate" or free the learner not just from immediate considerations of utility but, more broadly, from the bondage of ignorance and received opinion. The aim, in Socratic terms, is the examined life, together with the sort of enlarged understanding critical reflection allows. "Liberal education," as Paul Woodring puts it, "is the education that liberates [people] from the bondage of ignorance, prejudice, and provincialism. It enables us to see the world whole and to see ourselves in perspective. It is the education appropriate for free men who must make wise independent decisions—in the home, on the job, in the voting booth, and on the jury panel."[39] And, he might have added, in the classroom.

Jan Blits echoes the same view. Liberal education, he observes, aims to prepare young people for an intelligent life. Its most important goal is to teach them "to become thoughtful about themselves and the world, about their actions and their thoughts, about what they do, what they say, what they want, and what they think." Further, "it seeks to illuminate life, and particularly to clarify the fundamental human alternatives, by delving into the roots of things. Liberal education is thus essentially a recovery or rediscovery of root issues and origins."[40]

Part of the modern problem, perhaps, is that society's internal divisions seem larger and more pronounced than ever before in living memory. As David Saxon comments, up until recently there was always at least one continuing thread that provided a constant over the years. "Liberal education," he observes, "has always attempted to reflect what a particular society thought was important to know and to understand at a particular time. It represented society's collective wisdom about the skills and knowledge a person needed in order to be at home in the world and to make the best use of and derive the greatest pleasure from whatever talents he or she possessed."[41] The question today is whether any such consensus still exists or can be forged anew. Martin Trow, for example, speaks for many observers in judging that contemporary society is witness to nothing less than "a complete collapse of any generally shared conception of what students ought to learn."[42]

When a culture or a society institutionalizes its learning, Martin Kaplan argues, it projects and reifies a particular myth and vision of itself. When it stipulates (or refrains from declaring) what it is that people ought most to know, when it defines (or avoids defining) basic skills and information, when it establishes (or skirts establishing) the rudiments of competence without which a person is thought unable to function in society, it has thereby revealed much about itself. If nothing else, it gives evidence it is hopelessly divided against itself. "A culture's educational ideals for its citizens, and the de facto ideals that its educational institutions carry," he asserts, "are the products of a vision of the good society, of what ought to be. . . . If we have substituted an open curriculum free of requirements for patterned and limited options, if we promote diversity over control, then in our way we, too, have offered moral and political answers to educational—that is, moral and political—questions."[43]

William D. Schaefer, former vice-chancellor at the University of California at Los Angeles, ranks among many commentators and analysts who in recent years have attempted to move beyond diagnosis to more detailed prescription. In his view, institutions of higher learning have "mindlessly mixed vocation and academic courses without continuity or coherence or anything approaching a consensus as to what really should constitute an education." To him, this is the crux of the problem—one that needs to be addressed with thought and deliberation. "I believe," he avows, "that we should be . . . deeply concerned about this confusion of purpose—a confusion that has led colleges and universities to make fraudulent claims about their goals and missions as they package a hodgepodge of unrelated courses and incoherent requirements."

In process of outlining what he feels should be the least a college or university ought to expect its undergraduates to attain in the way of knowledge and analytic skills, Schaefer issues a plea. "What is needed," he observes, "is a commitment on the part of each institution—without qualification, without reservation, without compromise—that through a carefully organized, coherent program of instruction it will share with its students what today it deems to be the best known and thought, through time and space, in this our world." A viable liberal education for the twenty-first century, he adds, demands a "complete rethinking" of what an educated person can and should know.[44]

Commenting on the many national reports and critiques of general or liberal learning issued in recent years, Frank Murray stresses the link between general education reform and prospects for the future improvement of teacher education. "In *all* undergraduate classrooms," he insists, "we need clarity of purpose, effective teaching, high expectations, and student involvement to bring about the educational result we want. The mastery of a core of fundamental and enduring ideas . . . is important for all students, but it is more important for teachers, especially elementary-school teachers, than it is for any other professional group." Summing up a view widely held among teacher educators, Murray concludes, "It is entirely too easy for critics to say that prospective teachers need to take more courses outside the colleges of education. Of course they should, but they must undertake programs of study very different from those found in the modern university."[45]

THE TEACHING MAJOR

Closely allied and often intertwined with appeals for more liberal learning for teachers is the demand that classroom instructors be well grounded in the subjects they teach. Few oppose the suggestion that teachers should become acquainted with a broad range of disciplinary subject matter as part of their general education. Nor would very many people argue the point that teachers also need further in-depth knowledge of whatever it is they are responsible for teaching. As James Conant observed many years ago, "It is risky to assume that a holder of a bachelor's degree from an American college has necessarily pursued a recognized subject in depth, or in a coherent pattern."[46] Taken then as a general principle, making deliberate provision for discipline-based competence based on some concentrated study of a discipline or field is almost unassailable.

What seems more difficult to sort out are the practical details. There appears to be some agreement, for example, that high-school teachers should devote at least a year of study to the subject they plan to teach (despite the fact that few teacher preparation programs currently incorporate any such requirement in full). An academic major is commonly regarded as essential for the prospective teacher's effectiveness in communicating the content of whatever students will be expected to learn, whether it is science, drama, business technology, language arts, mathematics, modern history, or a foreign language.

On the other side, the fact remains that many, perhaps most, high-school and junior-high or middle-school teachers teach *more* than one subject as part of their regular assignment. There appears to be less support among reformers for the idea that high-school teacher candidates must complete a major in each of the subjects in which they receive so-called secondary endorsements. Perhaps in tacit recognition of what is possible within the bounds of a four-year baccalaureate program, few would consider it realistic to require a candidate to complete a full-fledged academic concentration in more than one teaching field. The question always is how much absorption in a subject is necessary as the minimum needed for teaching it responsibly.

The situation involving prospective elementary teachers is even less clear. There is little agreement about whether those planning to teach in the lower grades should be required to major in a single subject, as do future high-school teachers. Some claim it might be more appropriate to have primary-school candidates complete a type of interdisciplinary concentration of studies outside education. At present the nearest equivalent to an academic major for future elementary teachers is comprised of the several methods courses they are obliged to complete as they prepare for teaching the basic elements of the lower-school curriculum. Devising some sort of integrative, synoptic course pattern for elementary teachers might pose an interesting academic challenge. That neither faculty members in liberal arts fields nor teacher educators themselves so far have shown much interest in addressing the task is perhaps more than a little unfortunate.

Greatly complicating matters is the absence of hard evidence to demonstrate that mastery of subject matter is linked directly with teaching effectiveness. Available research, for example, fails to reveal a consistent relationship between the depth or scope of a teacher's subject-matter knowledge and his or her students' understanding of the material when it is taught, with the possible exception of the most advanced high-school courses. Certainly if there is a connection, it is not a simple linear one, such that the extent of a teacher's knowledge of a given field might predict how well he or she can convey it in some meaningful way to younger learners.

It could be argued that, on graduating from college, prospective teachers already know far more about a subject in most cases than they will ever need in order to teach it to children. And once again, knowledge of a subject is not necessarily sufficient of itself to confer the ability to communicate its content to others. As N. L. Gage of Stanford University has rightly observed, "Evidence that knowledge of a subject is not enough to make a teacher is plain to anyone who has ever seen a Ph.D. in mathematics thoroughly confuse a freshman calculus class—or the holder of a bachelor's degree obfuscate the past tense in teaching third-grade reading."[47]

Part of the problem, naturally, stems from the radical difference between how knowledge is organized and conveyed at the collegiate level and how it is imparted at the elementary or secondary levels. In higher education, the thrust of instruction is toward ever-increasing specialization and technical detail. In the lower schools, curricula tend to be more integrative and less well delimited. Hence, reformulating knowledge gained in completing a college major into a teachable form adapted to a high-school or elementary classroom is neither easy nor automatic. As Martin Haberman once commented, "Biology I is not intended as preparation for helping four-year-olds to press leaves," any more than a concentration in literature is easily reshaped to meet the needs of nonliterate adolescents from the urban ghetto. A new teacher observing a group of youngsters who have just built the Alamo and are reenacting its siege might ask, "Is this history, geography, or creative dramatics?" To which a more experienced teacher would respond, "What earthly difference does it make?"[48]

Those who have pondered the matter tend to concur that the best way of learning to teach any particular subject matter is to acquire a thorough understanding of its organizing structure. Effective pedagogy demands that a teacher possess a conceptual "map" of the discipline, a feeling for its most powerful and generative concepts, the modes of inquiry specific to its content, and a sense for how the parts are related to one another to form a whole. (Teacher educators sometimes refer to the need for "pedagogical content knowledge.") The teacher, above all, must come to grasp the logic and rules governing information and be able to sort out what is essential from what is less important. Unhappily, in most cases it appears little attention is given in college teaching to helping students achieve anything remotely approaching this type or level of understanding of what they will teach.

The traditional academic major usually fails to confer the depth or quality of insight needed by a prospective teacher, someone who faces the task of translating what he or she has learned into terms comprehensible to younger, less mature learners. Simply adding on more content courses offers no solution. Unless or until faculty in the various departments and colleges outside of education exhibit greater appreciation for what future teachers truly need from them, urgings that teacher candidates simply complete more training in their teaching fields will need to be treated cautiously. "Research," it has been noted many times, "provides little reason to believe that increasing teachers' knowledge of their subjects beyond that typically required for certification will significantly increase teacher effectiveness."[49]

THE PROFESSIONAL COMPONENT IN TEACHER EDUCATION: METHODS COURSES

Attempting to assess competing claims and counterclaims surrounding the technical or "professional" component of teacher preparation—that portion encompassing required coursework in curriculum theory and development, child or adolescent psychology, teaching methodologies, and techniques for classroom management—is no small challenge. Since the inception of formal teacher preparation, the dominant and most controversial issue always has been the utility or efficacy—or the alleged lack thereof—of "methods" courses. Usually it is framed in terms of the age-old question as to whether good teachers are "made" or "improved" or "born." Depending on what position is taken, it might argued, for instance, that explicit pedagogical training should be considered essential for everyone at the preservice level. Alternatively, the claim could be advanced that the study of instruction and management is helpful, although not necessarily indispensable for most teacher candidates. Finally, some will argue, discrete methodological training in many instances is not needed at all.

While it would be difficult if not impossible to document, the often-heard complaint that methods courses within teacher education programs tend to be poorly taught encapsulates an irony worth savoring. Recurrent surveys indicate that teacher education students also find many of their pedagogy courses more time-consuming than classes they take outside of education. More important, how the former compare with the latter in terms of intellectual challenge and rigor is another question. (Comparisons can easily be overdone, of course, but there is still something discomfiting about the contrast between philosophy majors analyzing a Kantian critique and elementary education majors engaged in the exegesis of children's literature, of architecture students rendering elevations, while teacher education students laminate bulletin board displays, and so on.) Reports of student comparisons further suggest that the level of difficulty between education and noneducation courses tends to be roughly the same, with the exception of coursework in mathematics, the hard sciences, and foreign languages—all of which, in any event, most students strive assiduously to avoid, whether they are in teacher education, the liberal arts, or other professional specializations.

THE TEACHER
EFFECTIVENESS QUESTION

The usefulness of methods courses is only one part of a much broader issue. The core problem for teacher educators since the days of the first normal schools has been, first, to show that, in fact, there are known or discoverable relationships between teacher attributes and characteristics or pedagogical behavior and practices, on the one hand, and the attainment of some valued educational goal or objective, such as increasing learning among schoolchildren, on the other.[50] Essentially, the question involves identifying what specific factors are generally conducive to teacher effectiveness, as judged by prespecified criteria. Second, the problem has been to link the instruction in which a teacher engages to the preparation he or she has received in order to teach effectively. Organizing and applying what is learned about teaching effectiveness, as Gage observes, is the central challenge for teacher education: "Now we are dealing with the teaching that teachers *receive* rather than the teaching that teachers *do*." The root question is whether effective teaching is something that can be taught and learned.[51]

Educators themselves in recent decades appear to remain deeply divided in their views, both about the theoretical and empirical foundation for teaching itself and, more broadly, about the adequacy of the base upon which teacher preparation programs depend. "To speak of a science of education is to speak nonsense," declares Richard D.

Hansgen of Bluffton College. "There is no more a science of education than there is a science of engineering or of medicine." There may be a body of knowledge about techniques thought useful for achieving certain pedagogical ends, he admits. But there is nothing even remotely resembling a full-blown, adequately validated technology for teaching. "Educators," he notes, "cannot even agree on a fixed body of common knowledge that would constitute a discipline of education, let alone a science of education."[52] Even the Holmes Group's *Tomorrow's Schools* expressed a similar perspective in 1990 when its authors observed with considerable understatement, "Educators have not worked out ways and means to articulate principles that represent professional consensus on best practice."[53]

Much of the empirical research, according to Richard L. Turner, is, at best, "of marginal relevance to optimizing teacher success attributable to teacher education." The amount of dependable information available, he judges, compared to what is needed to formulate more effective policies and practices in teacher education, is "minuscule."[54] Symptomatic of the problem, avows Donald Warren of Indiana University, is that an "important and instructive" research literature has been reduced to a supposed "knowledge base" that is "optimistically portrayed as promising more generalized practical applicability than social or behavioral science research can deliver."[55] Acknowledging that the knowledge foundation for teacher education is commonly perceived to be "weak and questionable," Judith Lanier and Judith Little further concede that "research as a whole has not seemed to cumulate into a more coherent understanding of teaching and teacher education."[56]

Teacher training, in common with teaching itself, as two other writers argue, has been "a conspicuous example of practice without theory." Rarely have teacher preparation programs been built according to theoretically relevant criteria, they claim, let alone designed on the basis of empirically valid data. The result is that teacher preparation has been subject to "almost any fad or fanciful idea which pops up from time to time." Certainly there has been no shortage of mindless fads, they allege; and there is little basis for complaining about the emergence of "half-baked ideas and jejune proposals for reform." The "future onslaughts of well-intentioned but misinformed ideologues" can scarcely be avoided until more theoretically sound and empirically confirmed propositions are developed to guide practice.[57]

Teaching-effectiveness research has had a long history, beginning in the early 1920s when the focus was on attempts to derive or extrapolate prescriptions for practice from more general psychological findings and theories. Hoping to generate context-free and scientifically grounded indicators, researchers invested considerable effort in formulating and recommending specific practices derived from controlled studies of learning strategies, behavior modification techniques, programmed instruction, and so on.[58] Subsequently, the locus of attention began to shift toward teacher attributes or characteristics as possible predictors of on-the-job success: beliefs, skills, knowledge, and personality traits. Yet in summarizing a half century and more of inquiry, Walter Doyle of the University of Arizona concluded in 1990 that results were, as he termed them, "discouraging." The search for empirically verified criteria that can serve as predictors of success in teaching—particularly if "success" is defined as a demonstrated ability to foster desired learning outcomes—seems to have yielded few significant findings.[59]

Regarded as more promising by many investigators is the "process-product" or "process-outcome" research paradigm. This approach seeks to relate measures of classroom performance—processes of instruction in which teachers engage rather than personal attributes—to objective measures of outcomes or results—the products of instruction. The goal is to identify those classroom conditions and procedures most conducive to achieving the outcomes sought. According to Jere Brophy and Thomas Good, both of whom rank among the most prolific researchers in the field, "We now know much more about teacher effects on achievement [than formerly]. The fund of available information on producing achievement (especially the literature relating to the general area of classroom management and to the subject areas of elementary reading and mathematics instruction) has progressed from a collection of disappointing and inconsistent findings to a small but well-established knowledge base that includes several successful field experiments."[60]

Flushed by successes registered over the past decade or two, many researchers now seem willing to concur with Gage's verdict that "research has shown that it is possible to change teaching practices enough to make an educationally important difference." While there is yet no systematic theory yet available, educators are now allegedly able to document empirical relationships between variables that collectively possess "some semblance of order, organization, sequence, rationale and meaning; they are not mere random collections of correlation coefficients." Changing teaching practices, Gage concludes, can be shown to *cause* "desirable changes in student achievement, attitude and conduct."[61]

"Life in classrooms . . . has been studied in such a way that fairly convincing and counter-intuitive conclusions about schooling and pupil achievement are now possible," echoes Frank Murray.[62] Again, according to David Berliner, recent research clearly demonstrates, for example, the efficacy under certain conditions of specific techniques for promoting numeracy and literacy among young children. Ostensibly, there is hard evidence to support prescriptions for the management of small-group instruction, promoting time on task, fostering cooperative and collaborative learning, encouraging higher rates of positive social behavior while reducing off-task and deviant behavior among schoolchildren, utilizing "wait time" to facilitate classroom discussion, and compensating for the effects of teachers' expectations on learners' achievement, among other things.

"We have only recently developed a solid body of knowledge and a fresh set of conceptions about teaching on which to base teacher education. For the first time, teacher education has a scientific foundation," Berliner claims. "Research . . . has been very fruitful. Therefore, the last thing we ought to be doing right now is abandoning or reducing the scope of teacher education programs."[63] Today more than ever, he insists, educators are in possession of a solid and reliable body of research data to guide and direct preparatory programs capable of producing effective teachers for the future.

Directly contradicting claims that efforts to develop a knowledge base for teacher education so far have been unsuccessful, allegations abound to the effect that "twenty years of experimental and quasi-experimental research have confirmed that some classroom practices lend themselves well to skills training" and, further, that "teachers can learn a variety of instructional skills and can demonstrate them in simulated or actual classroom situations."[64] Skeptics point to early studies that consisted of direct comparisons of performance by trained versus untrained teachers. Novices, it was found, did as well (or as poorly) as trained instructors, leading researchers to the conclusion that the training involved was poor, unnecessary, or ineffective. But other studies of more recent vintage, or so some argue, tend to support claims that pedagogical training makes for a positive difference among teachers.[65] "It seems clear," writes Carolyn Evertson and her associates, "that teachers who participate in preservice teacher preparation programs are more likely to be (or to be perceived by administrators as) more effective than teachers who have little or no formal training. Further, efforts to teach preservice teachers specific skills and knowledge invariably appear to be effective, at least in the short run."[66]

On balance, perhaps, some authoritative verdict on the efficacy of teacher-training programs has yet to be rendered. Phrasing it another way, it may be premature to pass judgment on whether teacher preparation as now constituted is helpful for most education students or, as some insist, is basically a waste of time. Attempting to isolate and to identify what specific contribution, if any, preservice methods courses offer in helping future teachers prepare for the classroom also is apt to be a perilous enterprise, keeping in mind both the range of talent and ability found among teacher candidates and differences in how the methodological components of individual programs are organized and delivered. Conceivably, it might be shown, for example, that for some prospective teachers, pedagogical studies are indispensable or at least moderately helpful. For others they are likely to be relatively ineffectual. Or perhaps it is true, as one argument has it, that teaching is an art rather than a science and can best be learned, as most college professors say they learned it, on the job.[67]

ALTERNATIVE VIEWS

As-yet unconsidered are alternative views that construe the act of teaching, and the process of learning to teach, in highly personalistic or phenomenological terms. From them stem radically different ways of conceptualizing teaching and, correspondingly, a divergent approach to the "methodological" component of teacher education. Unalterably opposed to the positivist epistemology and reductionism allegedly undergirding the quest for a scientific pedagogy, phenomenologically oriented critics argue from quite dissimilar premises.

What humanistic theorists find especially troublesome about the conventional wisdom of the "technical-professional" tradition is its tacit assumption that teaching as a process entails little or nothing more than the "delivery" of a curriculum. To speak, as many do, about the "transmission" of content, critics argue, is to embrace a simplistic view of teaching that, accepted uncritically, closes off discussion of key questions about the nature of human learning and teaching. What it does, or so it is claimed, is to encourage the "commodification" of vital human relationships. Hence, the human interaction involved in the act of teaching is overlooked, even as instruction is reduced to something resembling a commercial transaction, the delivery of a product to someone. "In this view of the world," Edgar Stones of the University of Birmingham comments sarcastically, "Shakespeare delivers doubt, irony, pity, resentment, pathos, love. We are moved beyond words by the product Mozart delivered now passed on to us, value added, by entrepreneurs such as Stokowski, Kiri Te Kanawa and Menuhin."[68]

No teaching method yet devised is capable of conveying information ready made, Stones insists. The human brain is not an empty receptacle, passively waiting to be filled. "Teaching," he emphasizes, "depends on interaction between human beings, not one-way traffic. Skilled teaching involves structuring learners' environment so that change will occur thus enabling learners to do what they could not do before teaching."[69] Critics of the "professional" approach accordingly look on teaching not as some sort of technical process but rather, as a matter of artistic creation and intuition, an act of personal self-disclosure more than anything else—always unique, idiosyncratic, and inevitably embedded in the particulars of a given life situation.

Distrustful of generalized principles and prescriptions for instruction, humanistic proponents argue that the most useful contribution teacher education can make has little if anything to do with supplying pedagogical rules, procedures, and techniques. Rather, a teacher preparation program should afford opportunities for teacher candidates to involve themselves in the work of sustained reflection and critical analysis, striving always for better understanding of the meaning of the personal encounter that occurs between teachers and learners in classrooms. *Who* one is as a teacher, ultimately, is more important than *what* one does in the act of teaching. From one's identity as a human being derives all of the possibilities for being a teacher.

The future teacher's personal dispositions and values, for example, are taken to be far more powerful and important as subjects of introspective inquiry than is didactic instruction aimed at helping student teachers acquire mastery of a discrete array of classroom skills. As Kathy Carter and Walter Doyle of the University of Arizona express it, personal narrative and life history, not pedagogical technique, need to be placed at the center of teaching practice and the teacher education process. Attention is thus shifted away from the "knowledge base" that teachers are supposed to acquire and "toward the teachers and their understanding of their own teaching." Becoming a teacher, they argue, "involves fundamental issues of achieving an identity as a teacher and working through the difficult tasks of constructing personal images that account for the complex realities of classrooms and schools and provide a foundation for acting as a teacher."[70]

Teaching, according to this sort of personalist view, must be understood at root as a moral and esthetic enterprise more than as a purely technical operation. The teacher, it is argued, is to be seen as a creative artist, not a technician. Still less should the teacher be looked upon merely as someone engaged in the application of formulaic operations designed to achieve predetermined ends.

Gage's contribution to the education-as-art-or-science debate among teacher educators is worth pondering. Teaching, he insists, is an instrumental or practical art, and as such its exercise necessarily transcends or extends beyond the mechanistic application of recipes, rules, unidirectional formulas, and simple algorithms. Good teaching does require improvisation and spontaneity; and the instructional process, just because it is so complex and involves so many interacting variables (including the teacher's own values and personality), is thus irreducible to systematic prescriptions.[71] As Walter Doyle puts it, supporting the same point, it is unrealistic to assume that an effective teaching performance can be reduced to a simple set of indicators or that it is compounded of a finite set of discrete—teachable—competencies, separate and apart from the person who exercises those skills.[72]

Here personalistic views of teaching seem to offer the better argument. But it may be incomplete. While valid, the claim that teaching is an art does not preclude the possibility that instruction can have a scientific base as well. Teaching, in other words, as Gage further insists, is amenable to *both* empirical and artistic scrutiny. The analogy frequently drawn between teaching as a pedagogical art and healing as a medical art makes a telling point. If today's physicians are more effective than their predecessors in centuries past, it is not because they have become more "artistic" in the practice of their craft. It is because they have a more reliable empirical foundation on which to base their work as healers.

All things considered, it seems impossible to assess the value of what currently passes for "state-of-the-art" methodology in instruction. There are reasons both philosophic and technical for doubting whether a true "knowledge base" is possible, at least in the simplistic sense in which overenthusiastic teacher educators make claims for a body of information from which effective teaching and management practices can be derived directly and taught to others. Perhaps, as many are prone to argue, the goal should not be to seek the prediction and control promised by scientific methodology. Possibly instead a more important objective should be to search out the type of insights and wisdom best supplied by moral philosophy, literature, art, and literary criticism. In any event, if the past three-quarters of a century's worth of intensive but ultimately inconclusive research affords any indication, prospects for building up an empirical science directive of what is a profoundly human enterprise are not especially promising. Once again, the hope of ever achieving a pedagogical technology may be fundamentally misconceived.[73]

As for claims that a discipline or science of education already exists, skeptics may be forgiven their doubts. No matter how vehemently some may claim that a pedagogical millennium has arrived, it remains an open question how far experimental research in education has really advanced. On first reading, much of what has been produced seems to amount to little more than a codification of tradition and common sense. What many studies have done, simply, is to provide confirmation for practices long familiar in received pedagogical folklore. Others give the impression of laboring ponderously to explicate what has always been intuitively obvious about teaching, at least among experienced classroom practitioners. And even when findings point to novelty or the unexpected, it is a long stretch from the carefully hedged and highly qualified findings of a few research studies, many of them unreplicated or subject to variant interpretations, to the bold assertion that a full-scale knowledge base for educators is now in place and can be relied on with confidence.

Looked at in the most basic way possible, of course, trying to prepare classroom teachers for their work seems better than not making any attempt at all.[74] To be trained for something seems in principle infinitely preferable to remaining untrained. But regarded another way, given the limited, tentative, and always provisional nature of what is "known" about teaching, dogmatic assertions about the specific ways in which teacher education should be conceptualized, organized, and managed need to be scrutinized with utmost care.

STUDENT TEACHING
AND SCHOOL CULTURE

A prodigious amount of literature has grown up around the so-called clinical phase of teacher education—the now-fashionable rubric for observations in schools, supervised practica, internships, and student teaching.[75] Practically all surveys of teacher education programs find that graduates ascribe the greatest importance to their early student-teaching experiences. Whereas students' attitudes toward the formal study of pedagogy in a college classroom may differ, ranging from positive judgments that methods courses were helpful to estimations they proved useless, there seems to be near unanimity by all parties concerned that practical classroom experience represents an essential aspect of a teacher's initial preparation. When queried about what was the most important aspect of their preservice training, for instance, new teachers are far more likely to single out practice teaching and other field experiences than anything having to do with formal work in learning theory, curriculum development, or teaching methodology.

Partly because practice teaching performance seems to be the single best predictor of future teaching success, would-be reformers invariably hasten to recommend that teacher candidates spend more time in real-life classrooms acquiring and applying practical skills. In leading programs across the country, much is made of the fact that students are increasingly obliged to participate in early field experiences, such that student teaching as the culminating phase of preparation is no longer the first and only interval spent out in "real-world" school settings. The feeling seems to be, the more time spent out in the field, the better. Some give the impression that a field-based apprenticeship is far and away the *only* element of a preparatory program worth preserving. Academic learning, on this view, is represented at best as an obligatory prelude, at worst an unfortunate intrusion into fieldwork, only the latter of which is of import to the novice teacher.[76]

The conventional rationale offered for fieldwork—and for more of it—is familiar enough. "Increased classroom practica can provide opportunities for novices to work alongside expert, veteran teachers for extended periods," declares Peter McDermott and his associates. "The experience of teaching with skilled professionals can accelerate novices' learning of pedagogical skills and strategies not easily acquired in isolated campus-based methods courses. . . . The overall purpose of improved and extended practica is to prepare better teachers by integrating pedagogical study with the practical realities of everyday classroom life."[77]

Ironically, however, demands that apprenticeship training be enshrined as the core of teacher education find only limited research support. There are, in fact, many reasons to question claims for all of the benefits presumed to flow from the traditional clinical field experience. As Evertson and her colleagues sum it up, "The existing research

... provides little reason to believe that supervised practical experience, in itself and as it is encountered in most student teaching situations, is a very effective way to educate teachers."[78] Willis Hawley makes the same point: "Available research," he notes, "suggests that practicums and practice teaching are often not very effective and may be counterproductive in many instances. . . . There also is little evidence to support the investment of greater time in practice teaching."[79]

The "problem" with field experience, if there is one, begins when the novice is first placed in charge of a class of children. As experienced practitioners can readily attest, observing students at work and play is one thing; assuming total or even partial responsibility for their instruction, quite another. The intent, of course, is to allow novices opportunities to "apply" and practice what they have previously learned. Oftentimes, what happens instead is that the student teacher, feeling overwhelmed and stressed by the situation, reacts by jettisoning earlier-learned precepts and teaching methods. The student reverts back to a more primitive survival mode, struggling to establish authority, to keep the children attentive and on task, and to maintain classroom control. The teacher's entire focus is narrowed, fastening on strategies for handling pupils' behavior much more than it is on facilitating their learning.

Oftentimes too the tendency is to regress back to the ways in which the fledgling teacher himself or herself was taught. A common habit among new teachers, for example, is to rely on "telling" or even to resort to the classroom lecturing mode with which they are most recently familiar from their own undergraduate experiences. (The predictable result is likely to be more chaos, not the sought-after control.) As the induction period proceeds, what has been learned in preservice courses may be undone or at least come to seem increasingly irrelevant. Invariably, the norms of the school's culture prove the more powerful, working to separate and disengage the student from what he or she learned in academic courses, all the while shaping behavior consistent with established conventions and procedures.

Cooperating teachers sometimes help reinforce the teaching initiate's growing perception that prevailing practice defines the limits of what is possible—what some have termed the "excessive realism" or "reflexive conservatism" of new instructors. "Forget everything they taught you back in college about teaching," run a familiar refrain. "Now you'll see what it's *really* like." Thus, lessons learned in college classrooms are not necessarily reinforced through practical experience. Indeed, they may be deliberately undermined or contradicted by the experienced classroom teacher to whom the student is assigned, whether he or she affords a model worthy of emulation or not. Inevitably, "success" comes to be defined by how closely the student teacher is able to adjust his or her behavior to conform to the norms of the local school culture. It is not to be wondered at, in such situations, that the student teacher eventually concludes that his or her prior training was "too idealistic" and "impractical."

Even when there is consistency between norms prevailing in a field setting and those taught in preparatory classes, many practice teaching experiences still fall short of yielding the positive outcomes claimed for them. The separation in time that occurs between enrollment in methods courses and opportunities to practice what has been learned is the source of a major problem—an issue addressed by those who recommend that student teaching and pedagogical instruction be offered in closer conjunction with one another. This is not to say that under present circumstances teachers who have graduated and taken jobs invariably or permanently forget everything they learned in previous training. Rather, it is to suggest that it is anyone's guess just how much they actually remember and apply on a long-term basis.

Another chronic problem involves cooperating teachers. Public schools have long acknowledged their responsibility to assist with teacher preparation by supplying field sites for practice teaching. Unfortunately, they are not always able to provide adequately for the supervision of the novice teachers entrusted to their care. Few cooperating teachers are well trained to provide the careful mentoring required; still fewer are afforded adequate opportunities for doing so. All too often, student teaching supervision is an extra responsibility for regular teachers, added on to an already heavy work assignment, and with no reduction in teaching load granted. Lacking released time and without sufficient extra compensation to justify their efforts, cooperating teachers have few incentives, material or otherwise, to supply the tutelage needed. What is surprising perhaps is not that student teachers are sometimes ill-advised but, rather, how often they do receive the assistance and counsel they require.

University teaching supervision is sometimes part of the problem as well. Within small colleges, the institutional environment may well value and reinforce the work faculty do "out in the field" supervising student teachers. In larger, research-focused universities, the same rarely holds true. Faculty members are extremely reluctant to invest much time or effort visiting schools and meeting with teaching interns. Typically, they will oppose efforts to compel them to serve in any such capacity. Education professors know full well that the prevailing academic reward system does not value clinical supervision, no matter how strenuously academic administrators insist otherwise.

Hence it is understandable perhaps that exhortations for regular faculty (teachers of methods courses in particular) to assume responsibility for field supervision fall on deaf ears. Acutely aware that research productivity and grantsmanship offer the most promising route to tenure and promotion, professors are not easily deflected from the single-minded pursuit of their own individual career goals. Sometimes, in fact (another irony worth savoring), outright coercion is needed to induce education faculty to leave the sheltered precincts of the campus and to venture out into the schools—the very work sites for which their students are purportedly being prepared to work.

Given faculty intransigence and reluctance to take on the task, student-teaching supervision tends to be farmed out or delegated to an academic subclass of instructors, adjuncts or nonregular faculty, persons of low rank and lower prestige whose task it is to supply whatever direct supervision student teachers are liable to receive. Poorly paid as a rule, usually overworked, and often saddled with a caseload that allows little time or attention to each individual student teacher, so-called clinical supervisors live out at the periphery of academe, not quite hired hands perhaps but effectively marginalized all the same. Remarkably, it would appear many do an excellent job nonetheless.

Researchers report that by the end of student teaching, significant shifts in the attitudes and beliefs of novice teachers are often apparent. The decrement observed in positive attitudes toward teaching may be unavoidable, particularly since many come to their internships with wildly unrealistic expectations that are bound to go unfulfilled. Still, it is disturbing to contemplate how often buoyant optimism and healthy idealism give way to cynicism and alienation. Even when employment opportunities are plentiful, it may be significant that a fairly large percentage of graduates from teacher education programs elect not to seek permanent positions. Among those who do apply and secure teaching posts, the attrition rate over time is high enough to give anyone pause. (Some undocumented estimates cite a replacement figure close to 90 percent over a ten-year cycle.) Overall, for whatever reasons, it does not appear that many elementary or secondary teachers freely choose to make teaching a long-term career.

CHANGING THE TEACHER WORKPLACE

As neophytes graduate from their preparatory programs and enter the "real" world of school teaching, researchers have found, they rather quickly acculturate to prevailing workplace norms. Prior training is lost sight of or forgotten to some (indeterminate) extent. New teachers thus take on more or less traditional ways of instructing the young. How students are taught accordingly changes only very slowly and gradually—a typical school classroom of the late 1990s could hardly be said to differ in anything but superficial ways from the classroom of a half or even three-quarters of a century ago. Nor have the duties and functions of the teacher changed dramatically (with the partial exception of expanded responsibility for accommodating to learner diversity). Fundamental alterations in how teachers teach and the conditions under which they work, historically, have proceeded at a near-glacial pace.

Salaries have improved. Otherwise, high-school teachers today are still assigned to teach between five and seven classes (often involving different subjects), amounting to perhaps 150 students, just as were their counterparts 50 years ago. The length of the school day, class sizes, and the numbers of students that an elementary teacher confronts—usually in isolation from his or her colleagues—have not been modified much over the years either. Lower-school teachers continue to be burdened with excessively heavy loads; and they retain direct responsibility for supervising their students throughout the entire school day.[80]

Without attending to needed changes in the school as a workplace, critics point out, reforms in teacher education are not going to have much of an impact. Yet in spite of much brave talk about "teacher empowerment" and the near-ubiquitous rhetoric of "site-based management," there is little on the horizon to indicate that systemic change is destined to arrive any time soon. Everything conspires to keep teachers locked in at or near the bottom of a pyramidal, hierarchical governance structure, one where authority is concentrated at the apex and power flows downward. Individual classroom teachers are hemmed in on all sides: by legislative and administrative mandates from state departments of public instruction, by rules and regulations promulgated by local school boards, by directives handed down from superintendents and principals, by the very parents of the children they teach. District contracts stipulate in detail the terms of each teacher's employment, curriculum guides lay out what is to be taught and when, committees decide on the texts from which teachers must teach. In combination, these and other limiting factors closely circumscribe the sphere of discretionary choice and independent decision making within which individual teachers can function.

It may be well and good to claim, as some critics have done, that teachers should not be counted on to countenance a top-down approach to reform, as has often been the case in the recent past, and still be expected to be ready, willing, and eager to perform as instructed.[81] Teachers, it is said, are not hired hands, and they ought not to be treated as such. True or not, the hard fact remains that if teachers are not merely salaried employees, strictly speaking, neither are they regarded by society as true professionals either, entitled as such to all of the prerogatives and privileges enjoyed by members of a bona fide profession. And however urgent or desirable it may be to improve the workplace and conditions of schooling, the likelihood of teaching coming to be regarded as a professional endeavor in the fullest sense of the term seems highly problematic.

TEACHING AS A PROFESSION

Teacher education reform historically has almost always been linked with efforts to win recognition for educators as professionals.[82] Current calls to extend teacher preparation programs, as a case in point, are commonly defended on the grounds that teaching as a "profession" demands nothing less than a protracted initiation process, similar to that which physicians or attorneys must undergo. Again, because a profession grounds its practices on a body of specialized technical expertise, much is made of the "knowledge base" ostensibly conveyed to future teachers in their preparatory programs. Attracting good students to teacher education and retaining them as teachers in schools once they have finished their training, it is said, hinges on whether teaching can win acceptance as an authentic profession; and so on.

Yet claiming the title of a "profession" for education does not necessarily make it so. Most observers will concede, judging from the usual criteria on graduating from college employed, that at most teaching might best be classified as a "semi-profession" or an "aspirant profession."[83] Considered in the abstract, a fairly uniform list of standards is usually thought to apply.[84] First, a profession is conventionally defined as an occupation whose members are reputed to perform a unique, definite, and important social service, one those outside the profession are unable to supply or generate on their own. As corollary, laypersons are thought incapable of making informed judgments on the specifics of how the service or function is to be performed. These matters necessarily must be left to professional experts.

Second, practitioners supplying the service are thought to possess arcane knowledge inaccessible to the untrained. Professionals are presumed to command or have a mastery of information demonstrably essential to the exercise of what is recognized and universally acknowledged to be a type of expertise. Third, accordingly, a protracted period of training is deemed indispensable for successful performance. Fourth, professionals characteristically enjoy broad autonomy, discretion, and independence of action in determining the substance of their own work. Fifth, practitioners assume personal responsibility for judgments made and acts performed in the exercise of their duties. Sixth, the emphasis is on service rendered rather than on whatever economic gain may be realized. Seventh, there exists a comprehensive and authoritative self governing organization to which practitioners give their allegiance and support (such as the American Bar Association or the American Medical Association), some agency empowered to define and pass judgments on what constitutes acceptable or "best" practice.

Finally, a hallmark of a profession is that it has a regulative code of ethics governing entry into the occupation, together with standards and procedures for penalizing those found in violation of its tenets and precepts. Professionals police their own. They retain primary if not near-exclusive authority for deciding the basis on which new practitioners will be admitted to the guild. Further, they bear responsibility for deciding under what circumstances a member's expulsion may be warranted.

Many occupational groups vie for social recognition as professions. However, not all of them succeed. The real difference comes when an occupation's claims to professionalism win public acceptance and are supported as a matter of policy—as seems to be the case with the practice of law, medicine, dentistry, and a few others. The key to professional status, in other words, is not simply the existence or even the validity of such claims but, rather, public acceptance of the legitimacy of what the occupation asserts about itself.[85] Myron Lieberman was thus undoubtedly correct but incomplete when he observed years ago, "A thoroughgoing profession of education would require a transformation of the teacher's job, but it would require much more than this.

It would require basic changes in the legal and administrative structure of public education."[86]

In fact, the issue of teaching as a profession goes deeper still. While it is true to say that structural changes would be required, there would also have to be a profound and fundamental reorientation of popular attitudes and beliefs about teaching and teachers. So long as uncertainty or warranted doubt persists as to whether there is—or can be—a true scientific knowledge base for educational practice, to cite just one example, it is doubtful whether teachers will be perceived by the public as possessing some esoteric competence or expertise closed off to anyone and everyone else, parents especially. Teachers may command public respect but they are not generally regarded as "experts" in the same sense as are most other professionals. Public school teachers in consequence enjoy nowhere near the autonomy or independence of action accorded true professionals. Nor are they likely to acquire it in the future.

There are many other factors at work inimical to the cause of teacher professionalism; and it is a sort of chicken-or-egg question sorting out causes from effects. Partly because the very notion of pedagogical expertise is suspect, lower-school teachers have never achieved hegemonic control over the determination of their own work and, once again, for a variety of other reasons as well, it is improbable to suppose they will ever do so. The well-established tradition of local, grass-roots control over public schooling by laypersons figures in as one factor, naturally, as does the entrenched pyramidal system of bureaucratic control within which teachers work. The fact that teaching and learning go on in many other settings besides schools, and without benefit of certified teachers to direct such processes, certainly must be counted as another.

So far as teacher education itself is concerned, a fundamental and abiding confusion over cause and effect resides at the heart of debate over proposals to prolong preparatory training. Arguing, for example, that *because* teachers are professionals and that teaching is a profession, preparatory programs should therefore be longer or somehow different poses one sort of claim. This argument also happens to be manifestly false—for all of the reasons suggested, teaching has not attained public acceptance as a true profession. Hence the appeal to extant professionalism as a rationale for strengthening training programs is obviated.

The obverse argument fares little better: that longer or different or better training programs will serve to *define* teaching as a profession and materially help win professional status for teachers—neither of which, allegedly for want of the necessary reforms called for, has yet occurred. In order for the argument to have credibility, it needs to be shown that teachers *would* qualify as professionals if their training were more fully adequate than is now the case. Phrasing the same point a bit differently, it would have to be demonstrated that the advent of better training is the central or critical consideration, that it would be *sufficient* (or nearly so) to win public acceptance of teaching as a profession. The supposition that correcting the alleged deficiencies in the training teachers now receive actually would result in their coming to be considered full professionals appears, in the final analysis, to be open to challenge. Phrased this way, the argument seems to depend on the dubious assumption that the length or nature of teacher training, more than the resident expertise teachers acquire, is the critical consideration so far as professionalism is concerned. Needless to add, perhaps, the argument also ignores or minimizes all of the other conditions that would need to be satisfied in order to achieve the outcome anticipated.

More compelling by far is the suggestion that teacher education reforms need to be assessed on their own merits, *without regard to issues involving the social standing of teachers—or of teacher educators.* Considerations of prestige and status afford an exceedingly weak basis on which to endorse or to reject specific reform measures, especially considering the heavy potential costs involved. What seems called for, rather, is a general willingness to look first and foremost to the substantive and strategic advantages or disadvantages of the various alternatives put forth. Specific proposals, in other words, should be assessed not on the basis of what will serve to enhance public approbation for teaching but on what seems most likely to help teachers become more effective; more on what is socially desirable and possible and less on what is conducive to the advancement of a vested interest. Surveying the diverse array of options and reform agendas scattered across the teacher-education landscape today, there is much from which to choose for possible consideration.

4

STRUCTURAL ALTERNATIVES

CALLS FOR EXTENDED PRESERVICE TEACHER EDUCATION

Recent proposals to locate preservice teacher education exclusively or at least partly at the postbachelor's level are not necessarily new. Their precedents date back at least as far as the opening years of the twentieth century. The reform thrust of the early 1900s, it will be recalled, was to establish teachers' colleges and to create training units fully coordinate with other academic departments in existing colleges. More important still was the movement to elevate normal departments within universities and place them on the same footing as other constituent departments, schools, and colleges. Among leading reformers were many who sought to emphasize university-based postgraduate instruction for an elite class of educational leaders. Also, the idea that preservice teacher preparatory programs likewise should be located at the graduate level was sometimes advanced. Only after completing a bachelor's degree, some claimed, should candidates be admitted to a course of specialized training leading to initial licensure.

Still uncommon but heard from time to time throughout the first half of the century and beyond was a similar though somewhat different claim: it was impossible to offer satisfactory teacher preparation within the limits imposed by a four-year program. Preservice training, it was periodically alleged, should be lengthened by at least a year, possibly two. As always, the entry point would be located somewhere in the undergraduate years—most commonly either at the beginning of the freshman year or at the end of the sophomore year. However, extra time beyond the normal baccalaureate schedule would be required to finish the entire certification program. Proponents of a full five-year or six-year regimen generally were agreed that those who completed the entire program would be entitled to some type of graduate degree.

The advent of Master of Arts in Teaching (M.A.T.) programs under Ford Foundation sponsorship in the late 1950s and early 1960s served to renew and heighten interest in a full range of possible "extended" (five-year and fifth-year) alternatives. Briefly, M.A.T. programs were designed to offer liberal arts graduates—students of proven talent and promise who had not majored in education as undergraduates—an alternate route of entry into teaching. The usual pattern, as at Northwestern University and elsewhere, was to require one full academic year and two summers for the master's degree, a period combining intensive didactic instruction in education at the graduate level with additional subject-matter courses in a teaching field, plus supervised practice teaching during the first summer of enrollment. Continuing to take courses during the following academic year, a student intern would be employed part time as a salaried teacher in a public secondary school. The second summer typically was taken up with full-time study leading to graduation and licensure. By most accounts, M.A.T. programs were successful experiments thought to offer substantial promise for the future. Because they tended to be costly to operate and were never permanently institutionalized, however, most disappeared once external funding was withdrawn.

Meanwhile, and in spite of the fact that the number of institutions actually offering lengthier preservice training in the 1950s and 1960s remained small, some observers were already predicting that five-year programs for secondary teachers (if not for elementary teachers) were destined to become commonplace. A few went so far as to claim they would eventually come to define standard practice.[1] By the 1970s, interest in longer programs of several different types had begun to intensify. One writer's unequivocal declaration in 1971 was a harbinger of things to come: "The four-year undergraduate bachelor's degree curriculum," announced Lowell Horton, "is no longer adequate or relevant for the preparation of teachers."[2]

Thereafter and throughout the decade of the 1980s, hard on the heels of a succession of national reports strongly critical of teacher education, more and more reformers were drawn to the idea of making programs better by increasing their duration. Four-year programs continued to predominate nationwide up through the decade following, as they had previously and, indeed, since their inception at the century's beginning.[3] Notwithstanding, the theme of extended teacher preparation seemed to have become almost an *idée fixe* among a growing number of prominent educational reformers of the 1980s and 1990s.

ARGUMENTS PRO AND CON

Hendrik Gideonse, education dean at the University of Cincinnati, was one of many in the early 1980s pressing the case for graduate teacher preparation programs. Speaking before the annual meeting of the American Association of Colleges for Teacher Education (AACTE) in 1982, Gideonse argued that the task of providing teacher candidates with a liberal education of significant breadth and substance, thorough acquaintance with a growing body of professional knowledge about teaching, and a period of intensive, full-time practice teaching—all the while attempting to accomplish everything within a four-year baccalaureate program—was, simply, a practical impossibility.[4] "In no way can the levels of proficiency we must come to demand be achieved in four years," he insisted. "We must do more than merely expose teacher candidates to the wide knowledge they need; we must require that they become masters of how to use that knowledge."[5]

Gideonse was convinced that entry-level training of teachers should require a minimum of six years beyond high school. Achieving the goals of a liberal education, including mastery of content areas to be taught, he believed, was more than sufficient to occupy a four-year undergraduate education. As an integral part of the general curriculum, he suggested that during the junior and senior years a few foundational courses should be offered devoted to the study of educational policies and societal issues directly related to schooling. He further recommended there be a progressive series of field observations and on-site practica conducted throughout the undergraduate years. Such guided experiences would serve to afford students broad, firsthand acquaintance with life in public schools. Otherwise, more specialized training would be deferred until after graduation.

The basic professional education sequence following the baccalaureate, in his scheme, would require a minimum of two full academic years to complete. It would include both didactic and clinical instruction and, ideally, conclude with an intensive internship in a special school designed and operated cooperatively by the teacher-training institution and a local school district (what shortly thereafter came to be called a "professional development school"). To his outline Gideonse appended a suggestion for the creation of hierarchically structured teams of teachers in schools. Leadership would be provided by experienced "lead" teachers—that is, practitioners with several years of successful practice and at least two years of formal training at a level appropriate for a professional doctorate degree (perhaps a "Doctor of Pedagogy").

Gideonse was well aware of the litany of objections that might be brought against his ideas: that good students would not be attracted to postbaccalaureate programs until the financial rewards for teaching were raised substantially; that the knowledge base of teacher education was negligible or nonexistent; that teachers are born, not made; that competent, overtrained practitioners would be reluctant to work in schools as presently constituted; that smaller training programs would be put out of business; that political factors would combine to stall and kill innovation; and that, ultimately, narrow self-interest always would prevail. Undeterred, he reaffirmed his faith that teacher education, like medical education before it, was capable of being transformed and improved in quite fundamental ways.[6]

Indiana University's David L. Clark weighed in with proposals similar to those proffered by Gideonse. The fact that more than 70 percent of all four-year colleges and universities in the nation were operating state-approved teacher-training programs, in his opinion served only to illustrate the willingness of institutions to supply low-level vocational training for their undergraduates. In no way did the ubiquity of teacher training across academe represent a genuine commitment to professional or academic excellence. Many programs, he judged, were "substandard" in one respect or another; a few he termed "dreadful" on all counts. Against the claim that small programs offered richness and diversity in training opportunities, Clark professed to discern only "a bland and mediocre sameness" blanketing the country.[7]

So long as teacher training was conducted at the undergraduate level, he estimated, all baccalaureate institutions would continue to insist on their right to prepare teachers. If, on the other hand, *no* teacher-education programs whatsoever were offered at the undergraduate level, the competitive advantage in student recruitment would not control an institution's interest in preparing teachers.[8] It was infinitely preferable, he believed, to have fewer programs—each of them of high quality and delivered at the graduate level—than a plethora of bachelor's-level programs, the overwhelming majority of them mediocre. Clark strongly concurred with Donna Kerr's judgment that undergraduate education affords an inhospitable, sometimes hostile, environment for teacher education and that training for teachers can be only as good as its placement on the undergraduate level allows—which is "not very good."[9]

The main reason why the undergraduate connection is so debilitating, Clark avowed, is that it severely circumscribes the time available for any truly adequate form of training. The almost inevitable outcome over the years has been professional programs devoid of virtually all their essential elements: a concentrated period of study in an area of specialized expertise, socialization to the profession through intensive work and discussion with other trainees, a clinical apprenticeship offering close and extended mentoring, and an opportunity for practice applying professional skills in a variety of settings.[10]

Clark felt teacher education eminently deserved its low reputation within the university community. If its condition were ever to be improved, the practice of admitting students of indifferent to low academic ability would have to cease forthwith. Courses would need to become more challenging and demanding. Above all, he was persuaded that it was imperative that programs be removed from the undergraduate context altogether. "Teacher educators," Clark declared, "must focus on making teacher education a fifth-year (not a five-year) program." Efforts aimed at anything less would fail, he predicted, leading "ineluctably to an apprentice style training program for teachers, separated from the university and from the knowledge base about teaching."[11]

Others weighed in with similar conclusions. "The prevailing [four-year] model for teacher education in this country," observed Dale Scannell, "has remained relatively constant for over fifty years . . . for more years than has any other in the evolution of teacher education and longer than the models found in virtually all other fields of professional preparation."[12] He took note of the increasing difficulty faced by planners in trying to accommodate within the standard program of study new materials on mainstreaming and exceptionality, on multiculturalism, on instructional and computer technology, and on a host of other items. Trying to incorporate what was needed or even externally mandated, and doing it all within the confines of a traditional four-year program, Scannell emphasized, had become nearly impossible. Even with all duplication of content eliminated, it was a struggle for teacher preparatory institutions to keep their curricula contained within acceptable boundaries.

Scannell announced the time had come to move to a more commodious paradigm. "On a rational basis," he concluded, "it seems unlikely that reform of four-year programs will be sufficient to achieve the full potential of teacher education." The need now was for more adequate and comprehensive courses of study: "Four-year teacher education programs have not produced teachers who can guide students to a level of achievement expected and needed by our society."[13] In short, the four-year program with its superficial and overburdened curriculum was no longer adequate for meeting the preparatory needs of tomorrow's teachers.

Skeptics freely acknowledged the imperative to upgrade standards, to revise curricula, to recruit more academically able students to teaching, and to work toward improving the school workplace. Still, they questioned the advisability of trying to extend teacher training beyond its traditional bounds. Calls for longer programs might be "rational," one commentator observed, but "unrealistic," given tight budgets at all levels, the low status of teacher education within institutions of higher education, the relatively poor salaries paid public school teachers, and expanding job opportunities in more lucrative fields for women and minorities.[14]

But Scannell, among others, felt that opponents of extended teacher preparation were missing the point. He conceded the difficulties of attracting the brightest and best as teachers and of enhancing salaries and working conditions for teaching. At the same time he felt that the need to strengthen teacher education was equally urgent. "Why a choice between the two must be made," he complained, "has never been satisfactorily explained."[15]

As the drumbeat for extended programs continued, Arnold M. Gallegos spoke for those who harbored serious reservations about moving beyond the format of the four-year baccalaureate teacher education model.[16] Most discussions surrounding extended programs, he noted, had been linked to proposals for collaborative training arrangements with practitioners in school settings. He questioned whether there was a sufficient "critical mass" of public school people willing and able to commit time and resources to support such programs. As for university faculty, Gallegos doubted whether very many of them, accustomed to working exclusively on campus, would be willing to assume responsibility for making collaborative ventures work.[17] Besides, any extended postbaccalaureate program of initial certification, he believed, would be far more costly. Finally, he questioned whether it might not become more difficult to attract low-income and minority students to extended programs. "Many of the gains we have made in attracting qualified minority students into the profession would quickly be lost under costly extended programs," he alleged. "Admittedly, we cannot prove that this would occur," Gallegos added, "but the logic is such that a different conclusion is not readily available."[18]

Frederick R. Cyphert and Kevin A. Ryan of Ohio State University felt in 1984 that there was insufficient evidence in hand to warrant a shift over to longer teacher education programs. Reporting on the results of an Ohio survey, they found that if given a choice, fully 90 percent of those queried would elect a four-year program over one lasting five years. About 40 percent of their respondents indicated they would not have chosen to become teachers if required to complete an initial preparatory program extending beyond the bachelor's degree. Many of those polled expressed concern over the extra expenditure of time and money required. Cyphert and Ryan concluded, "This is probably not the time for a mass or mandated movement to extend teacher education programs."[19]

Willis Hawley, writing two years later, felt it was time to subject proposals to lengthen teacher preparation to closer scrutiny than they had so far received. Most of the arguments advanced to date, he alleged, consisted of "unsubstantiated claims and assumptions."[20] He reiterated the now familiar objection that without significant improvements in teachers' working conditions and salaries, both the quality and quantity of candidates in the applicant pool would decline if five-year programs were imposed as a common pattern. The expense of implementing extended programs, he believed, would deny resources to support other, more productive reforms. Meanwhile, increasing the cost of becoming a teacher would reduce the attractiveness of teaching as a career unless it was offset by benefits not now available. But the latter necessarily would have to precede the former. Otherwise, Hawley predicted, "those who will drop out of the pool will be those who are brightest, have the best interpersonal skills, are the most imaginative, and thus have broader career options."[21]

Hawley took issue with the assumption that increasing the amount of entry-level training required, of itself, results in higher status for any given profession (the rationale often invoked to justify longer programs at the graduate level). Engineers, journalists, and businesspeople, he pointed out, already enjoy higher prestige than do teachers. Yet they are not required to possess more than a college degree for induction into their respective occupations. The critical consideration is not length of preparatory training but, rather, the nature of the job itself. What low-status academic units in universities such as schools of library and information sciences, nursing, social work, or public health share in common with colleges or schools of education is that they prepare persons for relatively low-paying careers, most of them in the public sector.[22]

As for the argument that fifth-year programs (as distinct from five-year programs) would allow teachers a better grounding in pedagogical theory, his feeling was that they actually would be afforded less. That is, a one-year postbachelor's certification program would limit students to fewer education courses than they might take in most undergraduate programs, especially if teachers' initial training in extended programs resulted in the conferral of a master's degree. The total amount of formal professional education completed, in other words, probably would be halved, compared with that taken to satisfy the requirements of a four-year course of study. Moreover, Hawley doubted whether it could be shown that graduate courses in extended programs would necessarily be more intellectually demanding than their current undergraduate equivalents. On balance, there was no guarantee that students would necessarily learn more about how to teach.[23]

Along with many other critics, Hawley questioned whether a one-year graduate program would open up much space for teacher candidates to complete additional courses in their teaching fields either—and he was dubious whether the increment, if it occurred, would make for any practical difference anyway. Nor was he impressed by the argument (even if it were true) that there was now more knowledge about effective instruction that teacher candidates needed to acquire before entering the classroom. "This argument," he commented, "assumes that what teacher candidates learn before they become teachers is often put to good use in the classroom." Quite the contrary, he asserted, "Recent research clearly demonstrates that much of what teachers learn in the preservice stage of their career is undone or substantially mitigated during the first year or so of teaching and, perhaps, by the practice teaching experience." Hawley concluded, "Increasing the amount of information and skills teachers learn in college is an inefficient and, perhaps, futile strategy." The likelihood that extended programs would improve teacher performance, he judged, was "not great."[24]

Prominently featured in many proposals for longer programs was the idea that teacher candidates would be organized into student "cohorts," that is, classes whose members would begin working and learning together on a full-time basis, beginning a program at the same time and progressing within groups more or less in lock-step fashion through to its completion, much like medical students in training. The advantage, proponents claimed, was that assigning trainees to cohorts would encourage closer mentoring, better professional socialization, and a smoother induction into teaching. At the same time, assuming everyone moved at the same rate, it would make course scheduling more efficient and render possible much tighter program planning.

The rejoinder from skeptics—the merits of forming cohorts aside—was that an arrangement that might have been workable a generation or so ago was no longer feasible today. Many of today's collegians, it was pointed out, depend on outside employment to support part-time attendance in school and are forced to drop out temporarily at various intervals for economic reasons. Hence, critics argued, it seemed unlikely that the stability of cohort groups could be preserved over the entire course of their training. And if cohorts could not be held together, the original purpose of having students grouped together in the first place would be defeated.

Cautious about the supposed benefits of longer programs, more than a few teacher educators moved to defend existing baccalaureate approaches to teacher education. The trend toward extended or graduate programs, skeptics alleged, probably had much more to do with a quest for status and prestige on the part of teacher educators than with the substantive merits of longer training. The tendency of practically every social system ever devised, it was suggested, always is to seek outward expansion and upward growth, sometimes mindlessly and irrationally. Perhaps teacher education in this respect was proving itself no exception. Expanding the system undoubtedly would work to the advantage of its professorial incumbents, although possibly at the expense of their student "consumers." The truth of the matter, it was said, was that the current dimensions of the professional component within four-year preservice programs were about right, especially taking into consideration the contested status of education's knowledge base. With careful planning, four years allegedly offered ample time to allow for an integration of general and professional education as well as a clinical internship or supervised induction into the field.

For all of these reasons, defenders of traditional programs claimed the four-year option remained by far the more cost-effective alternative. Note too was taken of the attitude of public policymakers across the country. Many outside the education establishment, those whose support would be needed to bring about reform, reportedly were opposed to extended teacher preparation. Legislators in more than a few states, for example, had been discussing, if anything, ways of limiting or *shortening* publicly assisted teacher education programs—not making them longer and more expensive.[25]

THE CARNEGIE AND
HOLMES GROUP INITIATIVES

With the debate over extended programs well under way, the mid-1980s brought a whole new succession of national studies and reports calling for systemic changes in teacher education. A task force of the Carnegie Forum on Education and the Economy led off with a strong endorsement for making a bachelor's degree prerequisite for entry into a teacher education program. Entitled *A Nation Prepared: Teachers for the 21st Century,* the Carnegie report issued a clarion call for the restructuring of lower schools and colleges of education alike. Among the more provocative recommendations put forth by the Forum's Task Force on Teaching as a Profession was the proposal to introduce a system of differentiated staffing in schools, headed by a new class of "lead" teachers—much as Gideonse had urged. Others included the development of expanded curricula in graduate schools of education; abolition of the traditional four-year undergraduate version of teacher preparation; and the creation of a rigorous Master in Teaching degree as an entry-level credential for beginning teachers.[26]

Similar in at least some of its major recommendations was a report prepared by the National Commission for Excellence in Teacher Education, also released in 1985. Entitled *A Call for Change in Teacher Education,* its authors urged broad innovations in teacher preparation, increased funding for preparatory programs, more rigorous academic and performance standards for teacher candidates, and the development of special recruitment programs to attract members of minority groups to teaching careers.[27]

A reported entitled *Improving Teacher Education: An Agenda for Higher Education and the Schools,* sponsored by the Southern Regional Education Board, took the position that any movement away from undergraduate teacher education was premature and that efforts aimed at improving existing programs should be explored further before abandoning the four-year model.[28]

One year after the release of the Carnegie study, the first of three major reports issued by the Holmes Group (originally an informal network of education deans that had subsequently evolved into a formal consortium of teacher education units within research-oriented universities) appeared.[29] *Tomorrow's Teachers,* issued in 1986, was the first of the Holmes Group's publications. It was basically a revision of an earlier document entitled *Goals for Educating Teachers as Professionals: An Interim Report,* circulated the year before. *Tomorrow's Teachers* was followed four years later by a second and much-discussed manifesto, *Tomorrow's Schools: Principles for the Design of Professional Development Schools.* In 1995 came a third, long-delayed monograph entitled *Tomorrow's Schools of Education.*[30]

The first of the three, *Tomorrow's Teachers,* set forth the Holmes Group's agenda for the simultaneous reform of teacher education and the teaching profession at large. Five basic goals were enunciated: (1) to make the preparation of teachers more intellectually solid; (2) to acknowledge and to institutionalize differences in teachers' skills, knowledge and career commitments; (3) to create entry standards for teaching that would be "professionally relevant and intellectually defensible"; (4) to link institutions of higher education more closely with schools; and (5) to make schools better places for teachers to work and to learn.[31]

The second, *Tomorrow's Schools,* outlined in greater detail the concept of professional development schools.[32] The third, *Tomorrow's Schools of Education,* reiterated support for extended programs of teacher preparation offered in collaboration with special training sites of the type called for previously.[33]

Integral to both the Holmes Group's and the Carnegie Forum's agenda was a strong commitment to raising the occupation of teaching to the level of a true profession. Any such transformation, it was affirmed in both cases, would necessitate improving the quality of teachers recruited to teaching and substantially increasing their preparation—in the case of the Holmes Group, by instituting a two-year, postgraduate master's degree program following a four-year baccalaureate, or, alternatively, following the Carnegie Forum's proposal, by inaugurating the Master in Teaching degree program. Both *A Nation Prepared* and *Tomorrow's Teachers,* needless to say, urged an end to the traditional undergraduate major in education.

Common to both also was a recommendation for the creation of a career ladder for teachers—a differentiated system offering teachers opportunities for career advancement and graduated salary increments. The Carnegie Forum, for its part, proposed the creation of a National Board of Professional Teaching Standards. It would issue two different certificates: an entry-level certification for beginners and an "advanced" certificate for "lead teachers" of proven experience and leadership potential.

The Holmes Group's proposed nomenclature differed only in its details. It was to encompass an initial "instructor" certification for bachelor's graduates who still lacked full professional preparation; a more advanced "career professional" designation for those who had completed a full six-year certification program; and, finally, "career professional teacher" status for teachers who had finished doctoral-level study (the last of which more or less corresponded with the "lead teacher" Carnegie designation). The Forum urged that school practitioners assume major responsibility in helping to develop national professional standards for teaching. The Holmes report, however, clearly favored top-down leadership and direction from university-based teacher educators, those it termed "emissaries from higher education."[34]

REACTIONS AND RESPONSES

Reactions to the two sets of proposals in the months following their release varied tremendously, ranging from enthusiastic endorsements, to qualified or tepid support, to outright rejection and condemnation. Some considered the Holmes initiatives quite radical. Almost as many expressed keen disappointment, claiming the ideas really were quite conservative and unexceptional.[35] The Teacher Education Council of State Colleges and Universities, in particular, praised the Holmes Group's efforts to improve teacher education on university campuses. But it qualified its accolades with a demurral that there was no one "right" way of educating teachers that was irrefutably superior to all others. The Council took special exception to the idea that in all cases teacher development should be delayed until after completion of a bachelor's degree, terming it "unwise."[36] Baccalaureate colleges with their own teacher education programs to protect, understandably, were not at all enthusiastic about being urged to relinquish their involvement in teacher preparation. Few seemed prepared to accede to programs being placed under the exclusive control of large research universities.

With many important vested interests at stake, it was not surprising that both the Carnegie and Holmes reports should have stimulated so much acrimonious discussion. Yet five years later, in spite of extensive debate, scant headway appeared to have been made in upgrading teacher preparatory programs along the specific lines suggested in the reports. "There is little indication," observed Barbara Schneider and Stafford Hood in 1994, "that the Holmes group has been successful in its efforts to increase the status of teacher education programs in research-oriented schools and colleges of education." Furthermore, they noted, "there is little evidence that institutions have responded to the Holmes group by establishing a reward system that would encourage faculty to take up teacher training rather than research. Finally, many faculty in schools and colleges of education directly or indirectly involved with teacher education continue to have little knowledge of the Holmes group's reform agenda. These matters remain formidable obstacles."[37]

Some counseled patience, alleging that more lead time was needed for institutions to revamp their programs. Any verdict on the eventual success of the reforms so recently urged, it was said, was still premature. Others felt that the storm of protest surrounding some of the more controversial Holmes proposals was portentous in and of itself, serving perhaps to indicate how few were destined to win eventual acceptance.

What was clear was that the work of creating professional development schools had not progressed at the rate some had anticipated or at least hoped for. "While the professional development school model has gained acceptance within the Holmes Group," Schneider and Hood commented, "there is little evidence that the grassroots support from the public schools for the establishment of professional schools has materialized." They noted too that few Holmes institutions had developed close ties with inner-city schools. "The complexities of these schools and the diversity of the educational needs of their students is new territory for most Holmes Group member institutions. If the Holmes Group's reform agenda is to be judged in the future, its success in working with urban schools and preparing teachers for these schools will be perhaps its most difficult test."[38]

A still more fundamental question posed by some critics, once again, had to do with the expanded knowledge base that allegedly warranted and made imperative the creation of lengthier teacher-preparation programs in the first place. The earliest Holmes report, for example, had asserted that the reform of teacher education depended on "engaging the complex work of identifying the knowledge base for competent teaching and developing the content and strategies whereby it is imparted." Asserted as factual but not documented was the claim that "studies of life in classrooms now make possible some convincing and counter-intuitive conclusions about schooling and pupil achievement."[39] *Tomorrow's Teachers* confidently assured its readers that "dramatic strides" had been made in developing a scientific body of research on teaching as the foundation for the professional knowledge needed by teachers; that "scholarship and empirical research in education" had matured; that "within the last twenty years . . . the science of education promised by Dewey, Thorndike and others . . . " had become "more tangible"; and, finally, that "the promise of a science of education" was "about to be fulfilled."[40]

William Johnston of the University of Maryland, among several others, was quick to point out in 1987 that the Holmes report of the year before had offered virtually no hard evidence to buttress its contention that a true science of education was eminent. The authors of *Tomorrow's Teachers* had observed simply that novices lacking professional training would make "predictable pedagogical mistakes" and that effective strategies of instruction required "disciplined practice that typically exceeds even that offered by extraordinary teacher education programs."[41] What those strategies might be was left unexplained, apart from illustrative references to the importance of making use of "wait time" to facilitate student discussion, and the need for a teacher to increase the number of higher-order questions posed, to decrease the preponderance of teacher talk, and to provide advance organizers, plans, and clear directions for classroom activities.[42] The question as to why such relatively mundane strategies, and much else besides, could not be imparted within even the most ordinary training program likewise went unanswered.[43]

FURTHER CRITICISM

Unimpressed by exhortations to embrace the extended teacher preparation concept, proponents of more traditional programs continued to defend reforms that would leave existing patterns substantially intact. "A reasonable case can be made," Alan Tom asserted, "that the rethinking of general education and subject matter preparation is a far more

significant reform than the expansion of either of these areas of study."
He continued, "The present size of the professional curriculum is
sufficient for the inclusion of pedagogical knowledge which has been
developed in recent years, providing redundant and unnecessary professional content is removed from the current professional curriculum."[44]
Other critics agreed that observing a four-year limit had a salutory
disciplinary value. Once freed of traditional time constraints, they
feared, there would be little incentive for sponsoring institutions to
tighten up their teacher education curricula and dispense with extraneous and nonessential material. Hence, the danger latent within five-year
programs—those combining undergraduate and graduate training
within a single preservice certification program—was that they might
end up simply offering "more of the same." In this sense, some critics
noted, proposals to lengthen programs offered the *least* fundamental
challenge to the dominant mores, values, and structures of today's
education colleges—and for just that reason might still win support in
spite of stiff opposition and criticism from some.

Many took the position that there were no compelling reasons
for radical changes of any sort whatsoever. "We are very pleased with
our program," one education dean reported. "We get positive feedback
year after year from those who employ our students. Students who
want to teach in this state seek us out. . . . I can't imagine why we
would want to expand our present efforts."[45] Others were willing to
consider five-year baccalaureate-level programs, particularly if they
included lengthier and better induction periods for new teachers. But
they saw little reason to move programs in their entirety to the
postgraduate level as Carnegie Forum and Holmes reformers had
insisted was imperative.

Some critics questioned whether prospective teacher candidates
would be attracted to longer programs while shorter alternatives were
still available. Many also wondered whether graduates of extended
programs would not be placed at a disadvantage when it came time to
seek employment. Hiring a beginning teacher with a master's degree
would be costlier to a school district than employing someone without
the advanced degree; and school officials would be unlikely to offer the
former a position without evidence he or she was demonstrably more
competent and better prepared. Whether five-year and fifth-year programs actually could provide persuasive evidence that extended program graduates were in fact more skillful and effective, it was said,
seemed more than slightly problematic.

Yet another potential problem for institutions contemplating the move to postbaccalaureate training was the practical difficulty of differentiating graduate courses for beginners without prior classroom experience from those offered for veteran teachers returning to campus to seek graduate degrees. Unless universities were prepared to offer two entirely separate and parallel graduate "tracks" for some years to come, it was predicted, chaos would likely ensue. More specifically, what would happen to the traditional Master of Education degree (M.Ed.) or the Master of Arts in Education (M.A.) in an environment dominated by Master of Teaching graduates remained more than a little unclear.

Especially disquieting to many teacher educators in the 1990s was the paucity of hard evidence to support or refute any given structural configuration for teacher education. One study done in 1990 reported that graduates of a five-year program at the University of New Hampshire were more likely to pursue teaching careers than graduates of the four-year program. Further, contradicting earlier studies, a higher percentage of five-year program graduates reportedly had remained in teaching.[46] Other studies from the late 1980s onward tended to indicate that extended programs were attracting high-quality students and that their graduates professed a strong degree of satisfaction with the training they had received. Some performance comparisons between five-year and four-year programs also had been attempted on a limited basis, although the results were either inconclusive or open to divergent interpretations.[47]

Summarizing a common stance among many observers, Kenneth Howey and Nancy Zimpher of Ohio State University, writing in 1986, expressed their conviction that teachers probably could be prepared to teach effectively in initial assignments at *either* the baccalaureate or postbaccalaureate level, and that for some time to come there would be teachers prepared at *both* levels. What was needed now, they urged, were better, more rigorous cost-benefit evaluations of each type of program.[48]

Howey, for one, issued a cautionary warning about the hazards of concluding that all four-year undergraduate programs were fatally flawed. The impression fomented by reform hyperbole, he alleged, was that traditional programs were all alike and uniformly mediocre. He insisted this was not necessarily the case. Citing several studies of recent vintage, Howey pointed out that fully 81 percent of all faculty members surveyed in baccalaureate institutions were reporting that four years afforded enough time to mount a viable teacher-education program and that 75 percent of those in master's and doctoral institutions felt the same. Among 1,140 students polled, Howey found that 73.5 percent rated their elementary-education programs as "above average" or "excellent," while 80 percent of all students claimed their preparatory programs were "better than average" or "excellent." Almost 90 percent of 250 faculty members surveyed in undergraduate schools reportedly rated their elementary teacher education programs as being above average; and three-quarters or more in graduate institutions concurred. "Many good things are happening," Howey declared, and positive assessments of existing programs needed to be more widely acknowledged and shared.[49]

To the extent that it could be said that most faculty preferred to leave programs as they were, it followed that broad support among educators for extended programs was still lacking. Schools and colleges of education with both undergraduate and graduate education programs, it was reported in 1993, had responded only slowly if at all to urgings for the extension of teacher education programs beyond the four-year baccalaureate. It was apparent, for example, that most students seeking teacher certification were still enrolled in four-year programs.[50] In fact, according to the American Association of Colleges for Teacher Education, between 1986 and 1991 there had been practically *no* change at all in the actual proportion of students enrolled in four-year versus extended programs.[51]

"The education reform movement of the 1980s and 1990s has produced disappointing results," judged David L. Clark and Terry A. Astuto of New York University in 1994. "Most teacher preparation programs," they observed, "continue to be undergraduate degree programs with little space or time for intense professional preparation. And these preservice training programs are spread across 1,300 colleges and universities, many of which commit few resources and little energy to teacher education."[52]

Seeking reasons to account for the seeming lack of results achieved to date, Clark and Astuto identified a root cause of the failure of reform as one of "limited imagination" on the part of some reformers, coupled with popular acceptance of unchallenged but erroneous assumptions about the process of institutional change itself.

The resilience of traditional teacher education and its apparent imperviousness to reform, they claimed, owed more than anything else to a lack of consensus within society at large about teaching and teachers: "Everyone does not agree on whether the work of teachers involves only the mastery of relatively specific technical skills or the development of a professional repertoire of instructional options, in-depth understanding of the content of instruction, sensitivity to the wide range of student needs, and a comprehensive understanding of the principles of child and adolescent growth and development." "These competing beliefs," they asserted, "are played out in the choice of reforms for preservice teacher education . . . and for the improvement of school and classroom practices."[53]

Landon E. Beyer of Knox College offered an alternative explanation for why fundamental change of any sort was so slow in coming. Having been involved in an attempt to reconfigure one particular institution's teacher education program, he reported, "We sought to create [a program] that would lead neither to a bifurcation of academic and professional studies nor to a model based on technical rationality and vocationalism." The effort failed. It had succumbed, as Beyer characterized it, more than anything else to the "aloof scholasticism" of defenders of the status quo and to the "technical/vocational narrowness" of others equally opposed to the structural innovations proposed. Beyer drew the lesson that in planning reform, an institution's local "micro-context" of competing and vested interests needed always to be taken into account in estimating prospects for success.[54]

Meanwhile, stung by charges of "elitism" and perhaps chastened by complaints that university behemoths were trying to crowd smaller colleges out of the business of preparing teachers without regard for the merits of individual programs, the Holmes Group appeared in the mid-1990s to have lost at least some of its former militancy. More conciliatory in attitude and seemingly less assured of the self-evident validity of the reforms they had championed, some of the Holmes leaders in the latter half of the 1990s were talking openly about regrouping and about the need for greater institutional "inclusivity" in future reform initiatives. In the aftermath of a decade or more of turmoil, polarized opinion, and sporadic attempts by some universities to refurbish programs, the future of academic teacher education thus seemed as uncertain and volatile as ever.

PROFESSIONAL
DEVELOPMENT PARTNERSHIPS

If neither the Carnegie Forum report nor those of the Holmes Group precipitated any headlong rush to initiate extended teacher preparation programs, all the same they did serve to expand discussion throughout the 1990s on a long-standing and important issue, namely, the relationship between public schools and teacher-education units in colleges and universities. In advocating teacher empowerment, urging changes in the teaching workplace, and supporting the idea of professional development schools, both reports helped encourage reexamination of how institutions of higher learning might work more effectively in concert with public schools. Academic teacher educators and classroom practitioners alike were drawn to considering anew the possibilities of improved linkages, of closer cooperative ties between their respective work settings. Ironically enough, the net outcome of some of the debate, as it began to build, was that it seemed to open up possibilities for quite novel program configurations, patterns sometimes almost diametrically opposed to those originally recommended by both the Holmes Group and the Carnegie Forum's Task Force on Teaching as a Profession.

The theme of academic culture as a force antithetical to the practical work of educating teachers in colleges and universities, for example, was a familiar one, and had been remarked on extensively in the teacher education literature for years. Martin Haberman, an education professor at the University of Wisconsin–Milwaukee, writing in 1971, reiterated the claim that the "clutching bear hug" in which universities held teacher education had dulled everyone's senses and perpetuated the "delusion" that colleges and universities were well adapted to educating classroom teachers. Teacher educators, he argued, needed to reconsider more carefully what had been given up in return for membership in the university club.

The faculty reward system in higher education, Haberman claimed, lay at the heart of a major dilemma faced by teacher educators: "The real criteria of academe are too well known to need lengthy rehearsal. . . . In order they are: research, writing, consulting, teaching graduate seminars, teaching classes, administration, and working with students in field experiences." Unfortunately, he felt, because the bottom priority was what teacher education was mainly all about, it was least likely to receive the attention it deserved from faculty encouraged to engage in more rewarding pursuits. "The less one is available to students, the less time spent on campus or in the field, the more one is rewarded."[55]

James R. Delisle, a part-time fourth-grade teacher and a special education professor at Kent State University, writing over 20 years later, registered almost exactly the same point. Reflecting on his experience as a university faculty member, he recalled, "I began to notice a disproportionate amount of time being focused on scholarship at the expense of students. It's not that the two cannot coexist; it's just that the university rewards *only* those who do *both*. Gone is the time when an excellent professor and student-teacher supervisor received the benefits of tenure and promotion." Published research or scholarship, not teaching or clinical supervision of student teachers, was what counted. "In the dog-eat-dog 'culture' of higher education," Delisle observed, "a two-page article in some obscure journal ranks higher than a semester full of excellent teaching evaluations. Go figure."[56]

Haberman was skeptical about the pretensions of college faculty members to link pedagogical theory with practice and their ability to offer much in the way of useful advice to teacher candidates. All too often, he claimed, education professors perform in a "neverland" falling somewhere between abstract theory and empirical practice. "Most education faculty have a few generalizations that we pass off as theoretic principles, and a few illustrations that we pass off as practical expertise." Nor was he any more sanguine about the claim that institutions of higher learning were performing a useful role in providing the necessary research, demonstration, and dissemination programs needed for reforming lower schools. "After much time and money," he asserted, "there isn't a single example of school change which university faculty have researched and advocated that is now accepted practice." Haberman believed the same was true of the university's supposed capacity for self-improvement. "Our record for self-change is even more dismal," he alleged. "After decades of massive aid for innovation, which university has been significantly changed?"[57]

Haberman was just as skeptical of claims that the key to teacher education reform lay with creating closer working relationships between schools and colleges; and he likened prospects for rapprochement to the predicament of "slow-witted lumbering elephants" circling each other warily, "only to discover they are both males and incapable even of friendship."[58] The organizational gap would not be bridged easily. Lower schools, he pointed out, benefit from the instructional help supplied by student teachers. Colleges and universities for their part operate programs that depend heavily on schools as practice training sites. Yet the two seemingly congruent interests do not necessarily always coincide. Nor are there many incentives and resources available to facilitate cooperation between the two types of institutions. On the contrary, Haberman judged, the more either institution becomes involved in the work of the other, the more it costs and detracts from its own major purposes.

As if working in dissimilar organizations with different reward systems were not enough, personality and value differences are always common. Public school personnel, he alleged, are inclined to regard academics as too theoretical and more concerned with the analysis of problems than with finding practical solutions to those same problems. Faculty, in turn, look upon schoolteachers as anti-intellectual, excessively pragmatic, and overly conservative. Both groups are experts in maintaining the status quo in their respective organizations, all the while espousing drastic reforms in the other.[59]

From the vantage point of a quarter century later, Douglas Simpson of Texas Christian University spoke of the "incredible complexities" of a collaboration resulting from the bringing together of any two such "radically different" institutions. "For a [professional development school] to succeed," he asserted, "all participants must understand and bridge enormous orientation and relational gaps. . . . Many professors must become more like teachers, and many teachers must become more like professors. We professors must learn to think like teachers, to see things through their lenses, and to understand their problems and interests." Likewise, he observed, "teachers must learn to think like us and understand why theory, research, experience, and practice are vital elements in developing future educators and educating students." Simpson concluded, "Building these experiential and conceptual bridges is a time-intensive . . . process."[60]

Lee Teitel of the University of Massachusetts at Boston concurred, noting that genuine partnerships between schools and colleges would be difficult to build.[61] He wrote at some length of the "contradictory pulls" latent within professional development schools. The goal of working collaboratively toward the simultaneous renewal of both teacher education programs and schools was a vital one, he believed, but he emphasized how difficult it might be to reorient the parties involved. Teachers would need to adjust to new demands entailed by their expanded role in working with preservice students. Faculty members, meanwhile, would need to accustom themselves to functioning in an environment quite unlike that of a university campus.

The free movement of the two between campus and school—teachers, for example, serving as resource personnel within preservice programs and faculty members immersing themselves within school routines—would not be achieved easily. School contracts would need to be revised in order to allow lower-school teachers to teach part-time in universities. Powerful disincentives for faculty to become more extensively and intensively involved in student-teaching supervision—especially those involving criteria governing tenure and promotion—would have to be addressed.

Left unmentioned by Teitel and others (perhaps because it would have been impolitic to do so) was still another relevant consideration. Traditionally, many education professors have been former lower-school teachers who subsequently moved "up" through the ranks. Some, of course, would be quite comfortable going back to work part-time in a consultative or supervisory role within elementary and secondary schools. But presumably many others would not. That is, having departed from the schools to secure advanced degrees and to pursue an academic career in higher education, few could be expected now as college faculty members to welcome the prospect of returning to the same classroom settings they had left behind.

To more than a few contemporary observers, the notion of attempting to change the culture of academe such that off-campus involvement with public schools can become a respected and valued activity, one for which faculty can expect to be appropriately rewarded, poses a near impossibility. No less formidable in the minds of many is the prospect of attempting to transform the governance structure of public schools. Yet unless the entire system of authority, power, and control is challenged and perhaps at least partially dismantled, there can be little scope or opportunity for the meaningful—as distinct from "cosmetic"—empowerment of individual classroom teachers. Charging them to serve as leaders in redesigning schools could prove an exercise in futility and ultimately serve no real purpose—if, as seems to be the case, the real locus of power to effect change lies elsewhere, mainly with school administrators and other state or local bureaucratic functionaries.

The fact that the typical teacher education unit, considered as the anchor point at one end of the connection between an institution of higher education and a public school, has rarely functioned as a unitary or cohesive entity at all represents another complicating factor, as many writers on professional development schools have hastened to point out. Arts and sciences professors ensconced in their respective academic departments, for example, while they may have many education majors attending their classes and—knowingly or not—depend on future teachers for their course enrollments, have tended always to identify with their subject-matter disciplines more than anything else.

Most are poorly informed about and largely indifferent to any broader academic enterprise beyond their own specialties. The work of teacher education affords a conspicuous case in point. As many more hold such training—not to mention those who conduct it—in ill-concealed if not open contempt. "Teacher educators," Edward Ducharme once remarked with considerable justification, "are among the least welcome guests at the educational lawn party of the establishment of higher education."[62]

Given the low status attached to teacher preparation, it is not surprising that even members of the education professoriate itself have been reluctant to identify themselves in a generic but explicit way as teacher educators. Many of them, as Walter Doyle of the University of Arizona pointed out several years ago, prefer to affiliate themselves with supposedly more prestigious specializations, such as educational psychology, education policy studies, technology and instructional design, curriculum development, or psychometric assessment and evaluation. By inclination and temperament, it is often charged, faculty members are more disposed to study *about* teachers and schools than to engage in the actual hands-on work of helping to train the one to work in the other. Nor, given the reward structure of academe, do they find it prudent to invest any more time in teacher education (field supervision especially) than absolutely necessary.[63] In consequence, what is supposed to be the shared intellectual and organizational responsibility of the entire academic community for teacher preparation, as it turns out, sometimes becomes the responsibility of no one in particular.

Paradoxically enough, schools, and colleges of education themselves, in recent years have seemingly tried to diffuse and blur their own identity as preservice teacher-training agencies. It is a tendency vividly illustrated by the propensity of some of the larger training units to concentrate almost exclusively on research and inservice graduate training. It is shown too by the willingness, even eagerness, of some education colleges to incorporate functions and academic units wholly unrelated to initial teacher preparation—rehabilitative and agency counseling, recreational studies, allied health technologies, nursing, public hygiene, and a host of others (however valuable and important such enterprises might happen to be in their own right). The goal, in current parlance, appears to be one of becoming a "comprehensive" school or college. The fact that education deans are thus prone to emphasize to outsiders "We are not just about teacher training" says something perhaps about the lack of centrality assigned to teacher preparation.

Mirroring the same phenomenon has been the trend among education units toward eschewing straightforward designations for themselves as colleges devoted to the preparation of school personnel. Favored instead are more inclusive appellations or titles such as "Education and Human Services," "Education and Human Resource Management," or "Education and the Helping Professions."

There was a time, it might be said, when teachers' colleges sought to divest themselves of their normal school origins with a name change and thereafter identified themselves as multipurpose regional colleges or, preferably, universities. Now, conceivably, the same process of disengagement from a nonprestigious enterprise is to be found at work within university schools and colleges of education. Having finally "arrived" in academe, if only on the intellectual periphery, they now seek to distance themselves from the enterprise they originally brought with them and that gave them their original reason for existing.

What has long been true of many universities—that preservice teacher education tends to be deemphasized and hence marginalized—is equally true of public schools, where teaching children, not helping train teachers, of necessity has always been looked upon as the overriding consideration. At best, school personnel traditionally have been apt to view teacher education as an extra responsibility added on to their regular duties. "In sum," as Doyle remarked several years ago, "there are powerful centrifugal forces that pull the enterprise of teacher education apart. Indeed, the epicenter of teacher education lies somewhere between the university and the school systems," with little glue to hold the components together.

Doyle noted that structural problems are not unique to teacher preparation. "All university-based professional education is torn between the academy and the practitioner community," he observed. "Nevertheless, the structural features of teacher preparation make planning and program operation cumbersome and often confer marginal status on those in universities or school systems who function as teacher educators."[64]

Formidable obstacles notwithstanding, and despite all of the logistical and psychological difficulties entailed (most of them commented on extensively well before the appearance of the Holmes reports and still more frequently thereafter), some teacher-training institutions in the early 1990s appeared determined to explore better ways of bringing clinical and academic experiences closer together. Madeleine R. Grumet of Brooklyn College, for one (albeit in a somewhat different context), issued an impassioned plea for reconceptualizing what teacher education could become and what roles teachers in schools had to play in contemporary society.[65] Elizabeth Hunter, on the other hand, felt the key to optimal teacher preparation lay in better student mentoring and a pattern of alternating campus-based classroom instruction with on-site teaching and part-time classroom apprenticeships. She was persuaded it could be done within a four-year period. "We have been hearing a good deal lately about the importance of permitting only graduate level preservice preparation in order to upgrade teacher education," she observed, "but I doubt that this step will make much difference in teacher quality."[66]

The real solution, she was convinced, lay with qualitatively better training, not lengthier preparation. "I believe most people who are capable of graduating from a respectable college are capable of becoming effective teachers," she declared. "There are some persons who are too rigid and unbending, and some who are too loose and disorganized, but contrary to current wisdom about the nincompoops who become teachers, I think that with proper training most college graduates *can* be good teachers."[67]

A stripped-down but more cohesive professional curriculum, she felt, was essential. "Currently," Hunter alleged, "we seem to be caught in an escalating pattern of required courses on everything from the disadvantaged, the bright, the handicapped, the bilingual, the ethnically and racially different, and so on and so on." This sort of mindless and uncontrolled proliferation of education courses needed to be curtailed, she insisted. "Teachers do not need 'a course for every kid.' They need to know how to build a curriculum which permits them to find out about every youngster, and provide for every youngster, with some appropriate consultant help when the need arises."[68]

Profiling three different school and university partnerships that had undertaken comprehensive reform initiatives, Judy Swanson, a research associate in Andover, Massachusetts, judged in 1994 that some preservice teacher preparation programs involving school and university linkages offered useful exemplars of change.[69] Singled out for attention was the Learning Consortium at the University of Toronto, the Southern Maine Partnership and the University of Southern Maine Extended Teacher Education Program, and the Benedum Project at West Virginia University. In all three cases, she reported, programs were emphasizing extensive field practice, selective admission standards, expanded requirements for initial certification, and school partnerships designed to enhance and reinforce the connection between theory and practice. Swanson stressed the point that university teacher educators and school-based educators in all three cases were engaged in a genuinely collaborative effort, one encompassing team teaching, jointly developed curricula, shared student teacher supervision, and program assessment. At all three sites, she noted, valuable lessons were being learned that deserved to be shared with others engaged in school reform.[70]

ALTERNATIVE AND
SITE-BASED PROGRAMS

Teacher-education reformers in the Carnegie-Holmes mold of the 1980s and 1990s have long been calling for greater collaboration between two groups that, historically, have not always been successful in aligning themselves with one another or in working closely together. But even as appeals are issued for school and college partnerships and for more protracted programs of academic preparation, there are others who had come to the conclusion that meaningful reform lies in exactly the opposite direction: in *reducing* the involvement of institutions of higher learning in preservice teacher preparation. "We are witnessing a growing movement to prepare teachers outside traditional college/university programs," observes Robert Roth of California State University, Long Beach. It has been a movement, as he represents it, founded on a growing suspicion that the university is inherently incapable of training teachers effectively.[71]

As of 1990-91, Roth reports, between 34 and 48 states had generated a total of over 40 alternative certification avenues, administered by various combinations of state agencies, school districts, and colleges or universities. A few were sponsored solely by public school districts. Some were being offered jointly by school districts and state education agencies. Others were shared ventures of schools and colleges. Still others involved public schools, colleges, and state licensure boards. Between 1985 and 1990, the number of candidates certified through alternatives to approved collegiate teacher education programs had more than doubled and was still on the rise.[72] Indicative of growing interest in alternative teacher education throughout the 1980s and beyond has been the founding of a National Center for Alternative Preparation of Teachers, headquartered in Georgia; the establishment of the Texas Alternative Certification Association; and the creation of several similar organizations elsewhere.

Among the best-known private groups to become involved in teacher preparation in recent years has been "Teach for America" (TFA), a self-described national teacher corps initiated originally as a senior thesis project by Wendy Kopp at Princeton in 1989. With funding from business and industry, TFA set about recruiting graduating seniors, all of them without education degrees, from over 160 different colleges and universities across the country. New recruits then and now are enrolled in a six-week preservice institute, using local schools for practice teaching, followed by a two-week supervised induction at a selected school site. Thereafter, graduates are placed in teaching positions as full-fledged teachers with a minimum two-year guarantee of employment.

Within three years of its founding, Kopp's organization had attracted support from over 300 corporations, foundations, and private donors; and its budget had reportedly grown to an astounding total of almost $8 million annually. Having secured state approval as a teacher preparation program in Maryland and in the process of applying for it in other states by the middle of the decade, TFA had become one of the largest producers of teachers in the entire nation.

Local school districts have shown a willingness to go it alone (or nearly so) as well, without substantial university involvement. California's District Intern Program, first authorized in 1983 and sponsored through 20 different school districts, offers direct, albeit temporary certification from the state upon completion of a 120-hour "professional development plan" that includes pedagogical instruction and practice teaching. More extensive still is the Texas Alternative Certification Program implemented by the Houston Independent School District. Throughout the state, over a dozen alternative certification programs have been initiated, many of them requiring only minimal course work from an institution of higher learning. Elsewhere, as in Maryland and New Jersey, school-based teacher preparation and provisional certification programs have become increasingly widespread and continue to attract growing numbers of resident interns.

Whereas most alternate programs originated as temporary expedients to increase the supply of teachers in areas of critical need during periods of teacher shortages, some have since evolved into more or less permanent, standing alternatives to regular programs. Many are intended to attract candidates who otherwise would be unwilling or unable to complete a traditional regimen. Featuring drastically abbreviated preparatory training, flexible scheduling of instruction, and close mentoring and supervision in a classroom setting, alternative teacher certification routes now offer direct competition to the more demanding if traditional avenues of entry into teaching sponsored through colleges and universities.[73]

Verdicts on the merits of abbreviated programs so far have been mixed.[74] Some findings indicate teachers certified from a regular program are likely to be rated higher in terms of self-confidence, classroom management skills, ability to meet students' needs, and fostering academic achievement. Teachers from short-term programs, in contrast, have been thought to be less comfortable in a teaching role, less reflective about their own practices, and less well able to adapt and adjust instructional strategies to meet students' differing needs. Other research has indicated that condensed pedagogical preparation and a supervised internship *do* pose a reasonable and workable alternative to traditional teacher preparation, at least for persons already possessing degrees in the subjects they will teach.[75]

Roth's major contention is that the "decreasing credibility" of traditional, university-based programs has been a major factor responsible for helping to create a niche for alternative certification programs. What the alternatives do in a minimal sort of way, he judges, is to allow novices to survive in classrooms and to fit themselves into local school settings—although usually not much beyond that. On the other hand, for all their apparent defects and limitations, it needs to be said, short-term preparatory programs on balance have proven themselves less expensive; they do help supply teachers for at-risk students in rural or urban settings; they have been far more successful than university programs in attracting bilingual and minority candidates to teaching; and in other ways they have helped fill in lacunae not dealt with effectively by traditional programs.

Roth foresees a scenario for the future in which alternative, school-based programs will continue to expand at the expense of university courses of study. If accurate, the shift in locus of preparation would move teaching even further in the direction of trade training. "On-the-job training is not characteristic of a profession," he cautions. "Dismissing the requirement of professional preparation and a credential prior to practice is also uncharacteristic of a profession." But unless colleges and universities increase the number of students prepared to work in hard-to-staff schools, strive to attract more minority candidates, and jointly develop and operate professional development schools instead of simply placing teachers in existing schools and using them for observation sites, he believes, some such future almost certainly will come to pass.

Always, Roth insists, academically based teacher educators must pose themselves a critical question: "What can the university do different from and/or better than the schools in preparing teachers?" Without cogent and persuasive answers to that query, Roth concludes, and "as long as the public or governing agencies believe the university cannot train teachers, its credibility will continue to wane." As for the potential long-term impact of alternative programs, his summary judgment is abundantly clear: "It . . . must be recognized that one of the most significant transformations in the history of teacher education has already begun."[76]

THE GOODLAD PROJECT

Among the more widely discussed studies of schooling and of American teacher education undertaken in the waning years of the twentieth century was that spearheaded in 1985 by John I. Goodlad, director of the Center for Educational Renewal at the University of Washington, Seattle. The basic intent of the center's "Study of the Education of Educators" was threefold: to undertake "a comprehensive study of the conditions and circumstances of educating educators for the nation's schools"; to review preparatory programs in other professions as "possible exemplars" for teacher education; and to examine "the development of school-university partnerships for purposes of simultaneously improving schools and the education of those who work in them."[77] Out of that effort in 1990 were to come three major published works: *Teachers for Our Nation's Schools, The Moral Dimensions of Teaching,* and *Places Where Teachers Are Taught.*[78]

Goodlad and his associates undertook to examine 29 different programs in eight different states. Surveying the landscape of teacher education as they found it in the several institutions they studied, he and his colleagues uncovered ample reason for consternation and dismay. Few programs, they determined, seemed to be infused with any coherent sense of mission or some larger guiding vision of the basic purposes of schooling. Teachers, Goodlad wrote, first and foremost need to have a clear understanding of the requirements of citizenship in a democracy and the role of the school in helping its citizenry meet democratic expectations. Second, they must attain a mastery of the intellectual tools needed for effective participation in the "human conversation" and the ability to introduce young people to that conversation. Third, they should possess the pedagogical knowledge and skills essential for arranging optimal conditions for educating the young. Finally, of course, they must understand the commonplaces of schooling: goals, organization, curriculum, instruction, evaluation, and so on.[79]

Goodlad's verdict was that most programs had been attempting to accomplish the fourth objective and in some cases at least were making an effort to address the third. But regarding the first and second, he believed, most programs had fallen far short; their failure to address issues of purpose and values may owe more than anything else to a wrongheaded notion of teaching as a purely neutral, value-free, technical endeavor. By the same token, he pointed out, "To expect teacher education to have a clear mission and identity in settings that attach little importance to it is to expect a great deal."[80]

Only rarely, for example, did a university president interviewed during the course of their survey spontaneously identify the preparation of teachers as central to his or her institution's mission. Nor as a general rule did Goodlad and his fellow researchers find teacher education lodged in any single unifying location within the regional university institutions comprising the bulk of their study sample. Typically, what they observed instead were multiple, independent units engaged in teacher training within a single given university, especially in such fields as home economics, music, health and physical education, the fine arts, and vocational education—each of them operating parallel programs without any overall coordination of effort by a department, school, or college of education. Even where there was an oversight committee or coordinating body, the typical pattern was one of business conducted in desultory fashion, without much sense of urgency about the need to draw the disparate elements together to form a cohesive whole.

Enumerated throughout the pages of *Teachers for Our Nation's Schools* were all the factors conspiring to keep teacher education weak and ineffectual. The prevalence of a faculty reward system designed to emphasize research and published scholarship over teaching and clinical field supervision came in for special criticism. Ironically, Goodlad felt, expanded attention to pedigreed research appeared neither to have brought greater prestige to professors of education nor materially improved the image of teacher education on campus. Preparing teachers, as always, continued to rank low on the scale of academic respectability. Faculty preoccupation with activities most likely to lead to promotion and tenure, moreover, was resented for perfectly understandable reasons by students who often felt their own educational needs were being neglected. Goodlad observed, "It takes enormous strength of imagination and extraordinary faith to believe that . . . we can have the best schools in the world, while we continue to neglect the education of those who will teach in them."[81] And teacher education, he emphasized, was most decidedly a "neglected enterprise" in academe.

Goodlad lamented the tendency of many of the programs he and his associates examined to allow casual entry of students into, and unimpeded passage through, courses of study. A distressingly high percentage of the education schools surveyed appeared to lack identifiable classes of students or formal admissions criteria. With few notable exceptions, institutional efforts to strengthen the professional socialization process among students also was weak, sporadic, or nonexistent, he believed. Instead, the burden of effecting the transition from student to practitioner fell almost exclusively on the formal curriculum. As for preparatory studies themselves, Goodlad and his peers judged that education course requirements in a majority of cases too closely mirrored the "technocratic simplicity" of state mandates and licensure requirements—regulations likely to change with every turn of the political breeze.[82]

In order for academic teacher education to be truly successful, Goodlad argued, new "centers of pedagogy" would need to be created—and these would not necessarily be identical or coterminal with existing schools and colleges of education. Each would be designed as a clearly identifiable unit bearing responsibility for organizing and maintaining the teacher preparatory program as a whole. A pedagogical center, properly conceived, would enjoy parity with other campus programs and be recognized for its involvement in an academically legitimate undertaking, an enterprise for which faculty participating would be properly rewarded.

A center should be autonomous and secure in its borders, with a clear organizational identity, a stable budget, and full decision-making authority, Goodlad insisted. It would need to be staffed by faculty for whom teacher education was the primary if not exclusive professional priority. The faculty would be responsible—and accountable—for selecting students, monitoring their progress, developing curricula, evaluating and improving programs, and facilitating the transition of student graduates into teaching careers. Teacher preparation, rightly conducted, would make available to students a broad array of laboratory settings for observation, hands-on experiences, and internships and clinical residencies, much like a medical teaching hospital. Finally, a center would not admit more teacher candidates to its programs than could be assured academic experiences of uniformly high quality.[83]

Goodlad repeatedly stressed the point that there was little room for complacency about what he termed the current "disjuncture" between university campuses and schools. An essential first step in implementing the reforms he felt were necessary would be for education faculty from colleges and universities and classroom teachers to begin working together in the planning, delivery, and assessment of preparatory programs for future teachers.[84] Just as it would be a mistake to have academics attempt to dictate to classroom teachers (a common pattern in the past), an equally egregious error would be to allow students' acculturation to teaching to be dominated exclusively and uncritically by practitioners. As Goodlad put it, "The connecting of schooling and the education of new teachers has virtually guaranteed that the status quo would be protected: tomorrow's teachers are mentored by today's. The irony is that this hoary practice is so frequently couched in the language of school reform."[85]

Goodlad conceded there was ample ammunition in his findings to lend support and credibility to the "shortsighted" who would remove teacher education from the knowledge-producing context of the university. Chester Finn, director of the Washington-based Education Excellence Network, in fact, drew just that conclusion in reviewing Goodlad's project. "Perhaps someone living on a remote island has not already deduced that teacher education is one of the great debacles of American education," he remarked sarcastically. Goodlad's error, he claimed, lay in confining his horizon to the "ivied campus walls" in the first place. The teacher education field, Finn alleged, had long been "awash in nonsensical ideas and assumptions about education itself" that would probably endure longer than any specific rearrangement of campus responsibilities. He argued that the most promising changes in teacher preparation and licensure were *not* those to be found in colleges and universities but those occurring elsewhere: in school-based programs, alternative certification routes, and apprenticeship arrangements that would match a novice teacher with a skilled classroom veteran for the purpose of mentoring and development.

"Goodlad is stuck in the model that says one must prepare as an undergraduate for a lifetime commitment to the teaching profession, that the university is the only legitimate route into that profession, that one learns most of what one needs to know about education from professors, and that the academy is itself the source of change and improvement in education and teaching particularly," Finn declared. Those sharing such assumptions, he predicted, would welcome Goodlad's recommendations for reform. But those who no longer subscribed to any of them, he opined, would be more apt to regard the center's analysis as little more than "a learned blast from the past."[86]

Goodlad struck back hard at his critics. His findings, he alleged, offered scant support for the assumptions undergirding panaceas currently most popular: that an emphasis on general education and subject matter, unaccompanied by courses in pedagogy, is sufficient; that undergraduate teacher preparation should be done away with; or that simple apprenticeship provides sufficient preparation for teaching. Referring to so-called alternative programs in particular, his judgment was that "putting in a quickie to substitute for what we've got" offers no viable solution either.[87] Yet abbreviated certification regimens, he argued, for the most part were based on just the sort of unwarranted assumptions cited.

At present, Goodlad thought, conditions necessary for building up "vigorous, coherent, and self-renewing" programs of teacher preparation were simply not yet in place. Responding to critics who had faulted him for not having laid out detailed prescriptions for curricular reform, for example, he remarked, "The malaise in teacher education runs deeper and is far more complex than problems with the curriculum. It will not be cured by agreement on a remedial curriculum package, even though renewal of curricula must be a central component of any reform." As for the broader question about prospects for genuine systemic change, Goodlad retained his optimism for the future. He emphasized, among other things, how important it would be to identify leaders who were comfortable in both the lower schools and in higher education, those who could provide the "vision and the know-how for preparing a new breed of teachers." If efforts to enlist the help of dedicated leaders capable of moving all of the essential actors "from dialogue to action" were successful, he predicted, the simultaneous renewal of schooling and the education of educators still remained a live possibility for the years ahead.[88]

ASSESSING OPTIONS

Reflecting on the differing recommendations for improving American teacher education advanced in recent years, a contemporary observer cannot help being struck by just how divergent are the points of view argued for by various protagonists. In trying to evaluate the respective advantages and weaknesses of competing proposals, it is helpful perhaps to think of a broad continuum of opinion, ranging at one end from those who deny the need for any teacher preparatory programs whatsoever to those at the other who, given the opportunity, would institute far more elaborate and complex systems than any now in existence. In some respects at least, the gamut of opinion offers an intriguing parallel to debate in the late nineteenth century between critics who urged an end to normal academies of any sort and those who aspired to create more comprehensive, multi-tiered normal schools to address teacher training at every level.

Today, no less than 100 years ago, at one extreme stand those who regard the whole business as an absurd charade and advocate the abolition of formal teacher preparation in virtually any shape or form. Next come those who argue for simple apprenticeships, abbreviated courses of instruction, and other "alternative" routes to teacher certification, with or without benefit of collegiate auspices or academic sponsorship—something vaguely reminiscent perhaps of the old-time teachers' institute of the mid-nineteenth century. Whereas those of this persuasion grudgingly acknowledge a need for some prior training, they urge that academic involvement be kept to an absolute minimum. A few would eliminate the role of higher education in teacher education entirely and house preparatory programs entirely within schools—possibly after the fashion of what some of the larger urban school districts attempted to do in the last century when they took on the responsibility for training their own teachers.

Of a similar mind are those who, skeptical of efforts to reform existing schools and colleges of education, urge the creation of entirely new types of university-based preservice preparatory units, something modeled after the training conducted in teaching hospitals. (Again, modern prescriptions like Goodlad's for pedagogical centers bear more than a superficial resemblance to what normal schools once aspired to become. The *form* of the argument, on the other hand, is eerily reminiscent of late-nineteenth century calls for the replacement of normal schools with university-based teacher education.) Advocates tend to favor closer collaboration between pedagogical training centers and professional development schools. Their basic inclination, however, is to recommend that a teaching center be coupled only loosely with an academic institution. Depending on how the argument is framed, colleges of education either would be expected to serve as research and development centers or would occupy themselves with graduate in-service training. More typically, their role (if any) is left unspecified.

Adjacent, so to speak, are advocates for the idea that responsibility for teacher preparation should be academically based but shared throughout the entire university community—again, an idea first intro-duced for consideration in the 1800s. In its modern incarnation, the argument is that a separate school or college of education either should be done away with entirely or, at most, should be incorporated as a modest-sized coordinating entity or department within the college of arts and sciences.

Somewhere in the middle of the spectrum stand those who defend existing preservice programs and argue for retaining them more or less in their present state. Many profess to be committed to working toward the improvement of traditional programs, although they do not neces-sarily endorse changes that would affect their existing structure. (As many more, one suspects, have hunkered down to wait out the storm, hoping it will pass by and leave them untouched, just as previous flurries of reform have done in the past.)

Next on the spectrum are proponents of expanded preservice teacher education. Here the call is for a five-year program encompassing instruction at both undergraduate and postbaccalaureate levels, to in-clude a protracted induction period for teacher candidates. Somewhere within this same range on the continuum are those who would move the center of teacher education out of its now-traditional campus setting and relocate it midway between colleges or universities and professional development schools.

Overlapping but distinguishable from the position taken by sup-porters of five-year programs is that advanced by proponents for fifth- and sixth-year extended teacher education programs, conducted exclu-sively at the graduate level. Once again, the recommendation is to link campus preparatory units more closely with school-based clinical train-ing sites, the whole encompassed by an elaborate credentialing and differentiated staffing system. Some advocates would go so far as to require pedagogical doctorates for the most advanced class of school practitioners.

Of all the teacher education reforms currently touted, abandoning formal preparatory programs altogether is perhaps least worthy of serious consideration. It may be true that there are "natural-born" teachers, persons solidly grounded in their subject matter who have an immediate instinctive grasp of what is needed without benefit of methodological training. Undeniably too, there are those rare few individuals who seem bound to succeed on the basis of sheer charisma and personality alone, regardless of putative deficiencies in background or experience. They are, as it were, able to surmount or compensate for whatever disadvantages presumably accrue from not having been prepared in some formal fashion for the work at hand.

What percentage of the teacher candidate talent pool is accounted for by these exceptional individuals is anyone's guess. It is reasonable to assume, nevertheless, that the figure is rather small. As for all the others who enter teaching, the vast and overwhelming majority appears to benefit materially from some type of systematic instruction and planning. Denying that formal preparation is necessary or at least helpful overlooks the possibility that even talented teacher candidates could do better with benefit of training. It further discounts the point that the transition from student to teacher can be greatly facilitated when candidates are taught before the fact what they need to know in order to function most effectively on the job (assuming, of course, that information apart from whatever is acquired through on-the-job learning actually contributes to performance).

As a matter of public policy, placing large numbers of inexperienced, untrained novices in schools appears neither wise nor prudent. It would be grossly unfair, or so it would seem, to consign young students to the ministrations of wholly unprepared classroom practitioners. Nor would it be realistic in most cases to expect the uninitiated to achieve proficiency at the outset. Even if it were true that instruction involves nothing more than the simple exercise of a craft or trade—an impression unwittingly fomented by many teacher educators themselves—delivering up hundreds of thousands of ill-prepared teachers annually and leaving them to their own devices, with virtually nothing by way of a fund of information to draw upon for guidance and support, hardly seems defensible.

In reality, of course, practically no one contends that hiring people literally off the street to staff the nation's classrooms offers a viable possibility. And if nothing else, historical experience dating back to the early nineteenth century suggests the practice—in the unlikely event it were to regain popular acceptance—would likely fail to protect the public interest or ensure even rudimentary quality control. Yet some critics come close in claiming that an apprenticeship might suffice, that a brief period of supervised student teaching could serve to foster the requisite competency, provided only that candidates were already proficient in the subjects they intended to teach.

Here experience with so-called alternative certification programs may prove relevant in the long run.[89] For the moment, however, it appears that not nearly enough is known about comparative outcomes to allow any confident verdict one way or the other. Some informed opinion about the most typical level of teacher competency fostered through abbreviated training, however, is certainly not reassuring.[90] It is important to bear in mind that even alternative programs include a prior period of didactic instruction and that in most cases interns already hold baccalaureate degrees. The issue, then, devolves into questions about how much formal pedagogical training at the entry level is necessary as an absolute minimum and what would be optimally desirable as an ideal.

Proposals for creating quasi-independent teaching centers share with arguments supporting abbreviated alternative programs a common conviction, as Warren Corbin expressed it, that "universities are structurally and philosophically incapable of providing the kind of training that practicing teachers and school administrators need."[91] Who would staff and offer instruction in pedagogical centers—education faculty members drawn from colleges and universities, or experienced classroom teachers recruited from public schools, or some combination thereof—is not always made clear. "Clinical" professors almost certainly would enjoy less standing and academic prestige than their research-oriented counterparts working in a traditional college of education. But if only exemplary public-school teachers were utilized, it is difficult to see how a teaching center could benefit professionally and intellectually from its association with a university. (Self-contained, inward-looking pedagogical centers easily could become the twenty-first-century equivalent of the much-derided nineteenth-century normal seminary.) Furthermore, it is doubtful whether much support could be garnered for sustaining the expense of operating a college of education and a separate pedagogical training center. Even if their respective functions and roles were clearly delineated, the impression of institutional redundancy would likely loom large.

The notion that responsibility for teacher preparation should be spread across all academic departments within an institution and that there should be no independent college or school of education presents its own array of difficulties. Superficially considered, the proposal has a certain appeal to it. It affirms that teacher education should be the business of the whole university and that all faculty, no matter what their disciplinary specialties, ought to model exemplary instruction. In theory, the process of induction into a discipline would become inseparable from learning how to teach the subject matter of that discipline. Students, according to this model, at one and the same time would learn content and pedagogical methodology. Hence, it is argued, there would be no real need to have a separate teacher preparation unit.

But critics object that even outstanding collegiate instruction in no way affords a useful model for teaching young children whose needs and capabilities are vastly different from those of mature collegians. The caveat seems cogent enough applied to instructing young children and has perhaps only slightly less validity in the context of high-school teaching. But there are more fundamental obstacles to consider.

The hard truth is, not all—perhaps not very many—faculty have an interest in good teaching. (Or, more precisely, faculty typically exhibit a high tolerance for mediocre or indifferent teaching among themselves.) Within larger institutions at least, teaching excellence is a low priority and it will remain so, exhortations and protestations to the contrary notwithstanding, so long as the present-day faculty reward system endures. Changing that system would be no small challenge. Teaching (and the study of pedagogy), after all, is a low-priority concern compared with other activities in which faculty are expected to engage, most notably the productive work of scholarship and research. Hence it would be extremely difficult, if not impossible, to persuade faculty to invest much effort in an enterprise in which they have little interest and less expertise and for which there are few extrinsic rewards to be had. Critics also register a persuasive case in pointing out how improbable it is that college faculty members in the various disciplines would have much awareness of, or appreciation for, the complexities of teaching in the lower schools.

There are many other questions left unanswered, not the least of which has to do with where responsibility would repose for coordinating and supervising teacher candidates' field assignments if there were no school or college of education to assume the task. Moreover, to the extent that traditional academic departments afford an inhospitable environment for pedagogical specialists, it is difficult to imagine who, if anyone, would engage in the work of educational research and policy analysis, helping to build up a fund of knowledge about curricula, instruction, and related matters. Presumably, all such concerns could be addressed without having to resurrect education colleges. But how *desirable* it might be to allow teacher preparation to "float" through and across academic departments, reduced as it were to the status of a stepchild of other academic endeavors, remains questionable.

Occupying a sort of "centrist" position are those who would defend teacher preparatory programs more or less as they now exist. If nothing else, the last few decades of debate over teacher education reform illustrate how vulnerable to criticism is the traditional four-year undergraduate preparatory program. Its practical advantages are often overlooked; its shortcomings are obvious for all to see. Seldom appreciated is the fact that the traditional route to teacher certification represents the complex product and outgrowth of a whole series of historic compromises and strategic trade-offs. Whether in combination they support a defensible organizational pattern still worth preserving, of course, has been a topic hotly disputed for years.

One presumption common to most baccalaureate programs, not just the standard teacher preparation regimen, is that within a four-year period, students receive a solid grounding in the various arts and sciences; that they are furnished with a good general education compounded of exposure to a range of subject-matter disciplines. The possibility that in many instances the liberal learning they do acquire is shallow and disorganized, that little intellectual integration takes place, and that the whole often fails to cohere in any intelligible way is less frequently acknowledged. Sensitive to the problem, the National Commission for Excellence in Teacher Education declared in 1985, "Liberal education [for all undergraduates, not just education majors] should be a cohesive planned program—not merely an accumulation of courses scattered across a number of departments."[92] To the extent that allegations of disorder within the sphere of liberal arts education are valid and real, therefore, there may be much to find fault with in programs where many classes are poorly taught, where courses tend to be unconnected with one another, and where courses of study exhibit no underlying architecture or logical form whatever.

A second assumption is that four years are sufficient to allow students to achieve not only breadth of content in their general studies but also depth in a specialty area—for prospective teachers, usually the field or fields in which they intend to teach. Again, the AACTE's National Commission for Excellence in Teacher Education reaffirmed the importance of the academic major: "We contend that one cannot be liberally educated without in-depth study in at least one academic subject. All prospective teachers, as part of their liberal education, should be educated in at least one academic major. This is as true for the person who will teach first grade as it is for the person who will teach high-school physics."[93]

It is often observed that while there is little agreement on the basic purpose of baccalaureate education, there is a general consensus that it can be satisfied within four years. It may be thought feasible, for example, for a liberal arts major to acquire a general education within four years and simultaneously pursue the study of a particular academic discipline. But so far as teacher education is concerned, adding on professional training greatly complicates matters, since it represents yet another demand on the time and space constraints of an undergraduate degree program. Given finite limits on a program's length, in the "zero-sum" game of curriculum, professional training can be had only at the expense of general academic learning (not to mention studies devoted to an academic major), or vice versa. Depending on the balance struck between the two, a teacher education program is liable to be faulted for overemphasizing pedagogical studies and not allowing sufficient room for liberal learning. Or it can be assailed for slighting the former in favor of the latter. Either way invites criticism. The only other solution—as proponents of extended programs argue— is to expand the limits within which both general and professional learning are accommodated.

Four-year teachers' programs as currently constituted almost inevitably come in for other types of criticisms as well. Most arrange for no more than 8 to 16 weeks of student teaching, an induction period critics fault as being far too brief, even when it is managed competently—which often seems not to be the case. The fact that it is logistically difficult to articulate methods courses with clinical experiences and that the two are therefore often widely separated and isolated from one another also is held to be a major defect. That programs fail to supply enough early field exposure prior to practice teaching represents yet another common complaint.

Not directly dependent on structural considerations are other alleged defects, not the least of which is the widespread impression that pedagogical methods courses tend to be shallow and are poorly taught (in this respect confirming anecdotal evidence abounds), are too formulaic or, alternatively, are too theoretical and detached. Education courses as a whole, critics allege, generally fail to reflect the realities of contemporary schooling and thus poorly prepare practitioners for the challenges they will confront in the real world of public schooling. (Small wonder, it is observed, considering how many teacher educators themselves have not stepped foot in an elementary or secondary classroom in years.)

Sometimes too, it is said, preparatory classes seem to mirror a narrow technocratic mentality, an attitude or cast of mind that has infiltrated and insinuated itself to the point where it has become virtually hegemonic within today's teacher education establishment. A major result, allegedly, is that little or no attention is paid to furnishing teacher candidates with anything resembling a critical, normative, and interpretive context within which they can come to understand the meaning and purposes of their future work. Instead, students are supplied, on the one hand, with theory largely detached from its applications and, on the other, with cookbook formulas and recipes drawn from the grab bag of teachers' tricks of the trade. Lacking is any larger or intelligible sense of purpose and direction to inform the work of teaching.

Again, in part because public schooling itself is the repository of so many disparate and conflicting social aspirations, sooner or later everyone with an ax to grind and an agenda to pursue fastens on teacher education as a possible vehicle for advancing a particular interest. The external ideological freight, so to speak, that existing programs are asked to carry is apt to be considerable. Social reformers are prone to arguing, for example, that among many other things teachers must be enlisted to help combat racism, sexism, and prejudice within contemporary society at large, and that courses devoted to those ends should be included in their preservice preparation. So too, teachers-in-training must be taught how to advance multiculturalism, globalism, internationalism, and heightened ecological consciousness or awareness as contemporary societal imperatives, each entailing the addition of another course or courses to an already overcrowded curriculum. Again, above and beyond the basic skills and subjects of the standard curriculum, so it is claimed, teachers must be taught how to encourage greater interpersonal sensitivity and nonviolence among those entrusted to their care.

Always, by precept and example, classroom teachers and other educational specialists should promote popular responsiveness to the needs of "exceptional" children and the handicapped. Additionally, they must inculcate civic virtue within young learners, foster public and personal morality, and teach responsible ethical values. Regardless of their teaching specialties, the nation's pedagogues should work to help reduce teen pregnancies, to compensate in myriad ways for the erosion of the traditional family unit, to warn their impressionable young charges of the dangers of sexually transmitted diseases and assist in waging the war against drug and alcohol abuse—each end requiring mastery of a separate fund of information and a specialized set of instructional strategies. The list of specific and worthy concerns put forth at any given time is endless. Therefore, it is not to be wondered that teacher educators, no less than curriculum planners in the lower schools, have a difficult time organizing courses of study that conform to reasonable limits. Presumably the problem would be much the same regardless of the length of any particular preservice program.

On a more positive note, the very real and substantial advantages of the traditional undergraduate teacher preparation pattern as it now exists ought not to be discounted either. A four-year program can be offered at relatively low cost and within the same time frame common to many other forms of professional training. And although advocates for longer programs make much of the need for more curricular space, according to some reckonings there is real benefit in compelling faculty to confine their offerings within sustainable boundaries, recognizing that there can be only so many classes required of a candidate seeking certification. (When it comes to matters of curriculum and instruction, it has been observed, more is not necessarily better.) Under current circumstances, it is feasible for smaller institutions with limited resources, no less than for larger research universities, to involve themselves in the work of preparing teachers at the undergraduate level and thus make viable programs accessible to their students. The usual program also imposes few demands on schools as practice teaching sites (although, naturally, there is nothing inherent in a four-year course of studies forestalling closer ties and collaboration if those responsible deem it advisable).

Finally, some argue, that portion of an undergraduate's total program represented by professional education is roughly proportional to what is necessary and appropriate, taking into consideration what preservice candidates actually require at an entry level and what the market will bear relative to the status and extrinsic rewards attached to a teaching career in elementary and secondary schools. For all of the foregoing reasons, the conventional teacher education program has many defenders. They remain convinced that improving preparatory courses of study, not making them longer or more complex, is what really matters.

On the other hand, the very arguments commonly adduced to support retaining undergraduate teacher education—its relatively modest cost, accessibility, and manageable curriculum responsive to market needs—are now increasingly recast as reasons for instituting longer programs instead. The contours of the case for and against extended teacher preparation are by now more than a little familiar.[94] Chiefly, they reduce to disagreements over whether there is more knowledge prospective teachers must possess than can be imparted responsibly within a four-year program, and whether it is possible to supply adequate clinical training within a traditional program. Often appended is the disputed claim that extended graduate training will help enhance the status and prestige attached to teaching or, running the argument backward, that teaching as a profession demands nothing less.

As the twentieth century draws to its close, the gamut of teacher education reform proposals under active consideration as policy options has never been as broad and diverse as it is today. Whether any one single pattern can continue to dominate the scene, as the four-year undergraduate program has done for over three-quarters of a century, remains to be seen. Many will likely endure for years to come. But provided public support is forthcoming for more extended programs, it may turn out that five-year or fifth-year courses of study eventually will supplant the standard prebaccalaureate pattern. Or the two alternatives may continue to compete for acceptance—with one another and, conceivably, with entirely new types of training agencies such as the so-called pedagogical training center or some latter-day equivalent to the old-fashioned teachers' institute. At the same time, short-term alternative certification programs appear to have gained a place for themselves as well, and so long as they continue to satisfy needs unmet elsewhere, prospects for their future look good.

That responsibility for teacher preparation will come to be accepted as a general responsibility of all members of an academic community seems highly unlikely in any immediately foreseeable future. The prospect that teacher education critics who would dispense with all training will prevail is more improbable still. Some existing teacher preparation programs probably will continue to function as always; some are already in the process of evolving into extended or graduate-level programs; and further experimentation with entirely new configurations and structural patterns beyond the conventional bounds of academic teacher education may be expected.

Often overlooked or not sufficiently well emphasized in debates over teacher education reform is the fact that programs are rarely if ever self-contained constructions of faculty members and administrators in particular colleges and universities. Nor do preparatory programs operate in a sort of policy vacuum, somehow immune from external pressures exercised by other stakeholders besides academic teacher educators. The reality is that national norms and accreditation standards, those of the National Council for Accreditation of Teacher Education (NCATE) in particular, exercise a powerful determinative force on upward of half the nation's preparatory programs for teachers and perhaps a suasive influence on as many more. Accreditation standards specific to teaching specialties or specialized areas within professional education, propounded by a dozen or more national professional associations and societies, likewise establish program guidelines that must be taken into account. More influential still are the detailed prescriptions and recommendations set forth in each state's own teacher licensure or certification requirements, rules and regulations with which programs in individual colleges or universities invariably must comply. Hence no discussion of the future of teacher education is complete without considering the many external mandates and constraints to which programs must remain responsive.

5

ACCREDITATION AND CERTIFICATION STANDARDS

STATE INFLUENCE AND CONTROL OVER TEACHER PREPARATION

Authority for teacher licensure and certification by specialty areas rests ultimately with the 50 separate states. State education agencies, variously constituted and designated by legislative action, bear statutory responsibility for defining minimal requirements for entry into teaching. Directly or indirectly, virtually all state regulations go further in establishing basic criteria or standards to which teachers' preparatory programs must conform.[1] Requirements are apt to vary considerably from state to state, differing from one another both in terms of how they are organized and according to their specific provisions.[2]

Oversimplifying somewhat, two overlapping approaches may be said to predominate. The first stipulates particular features or constituent elements a preparatory program must incorporate and exhibit in order to garner state approval and hence authority to recommend its graduates for state licensure. The other focuses on the specific qualifications individual applicants must possess to attain licensure eligibility. In the latter case, "credit counting" is most common—that is, the candidate must give evidence that he or she has taken the number and types of preparatory classes demanded. An alternate formula enumerates particular "performances" or "competencies" a teaching candidate must be able to demonstrate. Whatever the approach followed, there are conflicting answers as to whether the differences among state certification standards and procedures are truly significant, as state officials represent them to be, or whether collectively they reflect a high degree of uniformity in accreditation, certification and training patterns nationwide, as some observers are prone to allege.

Most states (as in Indiana, Kansas, New Jersey, Maryland, Missouri, and Virginia) require an applicant for licensure to be a graduate from a state-recognized "accredited" institution. The regulations in over two dozen, or roughly half of the states include an additional proviso that the applicant must have completed an "approved" baccalaureate teacher education program. Standards in eight other states (Alaska, Arizona, Arkansas, Florida, Delaware, North Dakota, Oklahoma, and Washington) make dual reference to accredited institutions and approved preparatory programs. A few states, such as Minnesota, identify approved in-state institutions by name.

Most of the states impose requirements tied to a hierarchy of types and levels of teaching certificates, as in South Carolina, where credentials are classified according to three different categories and titles, including "Class III-Professional," "Class II-Professional," "Class I-Professional," "Class I-Specialist Professional," and "Class I-Advanced Professional." Pennsylvania offers an "Intern Certificate," followed by a provisional "Instructional Certificate I" and an "Instructional Certificate II." New Hampshire offers a "Beginning Educator Certificate" and an "Experienced Educator Certificate." Nebraska's system includes an "initial" certificate, followed by a "standard" teaching certificate, and, finally, a "professional" certificate. Utah has a "basic" and a "standard" certificate. New Mexico's regulations provide for a Level 1 type of nonrenewable "initial" licensure, followed by renewable Level 2 "continuing" licensure and a Level 3-A "instructional leadership" license. Maryland's certificates include "standard professional" status and "advanced professional" standing, and so on.

In practically all cases, graduated levels in teaching licenses or certificates are linked with an ascending order of required qualifications and longer periods of renewability. Permanent lifetime teacher licensure is far less common than it once was. Marking a departure from usage prevailing up until a decade or so ago, most states today require that even "advanced" teaching certificates be renewed periodically, contingent on successful classroom performance ratings and continued in-service training.

Much of the complexity surrounding state requirements for teachers stems from the varying levels at which certification is conferred. Most states set out specific qualifications, depending on whether a candidate intends to work in a preschool setting, in the elementary grades, in a middle or junior high school, or at the high-school level. Requirements for teaching various subjects at the secondary level differ as well, depending on the particular subject matter "endorsement" sought. Additionally, in all states certification as a school librarian or "media services specialist," for example, carries with it its own particular requirements, as does licensure as a special education teacher, a school counselor, a reading specialist, a curriculum coordinator, and so forth.

The last 15 years or so have brought extensive revisions in state teacher certification and licensure standards.[3] Galvanized in the early 1980s by reports of falling test scores and inferior academic performance among American schoolchildren; by recurrent charges that the nation's schoolteachers were incompetent and poorly prepared; and by often-repeated, highly publicized claims in the late 1980s and early 1990s that teacher preparation programs themselves lacked coherence or rigor, state legislatures bestirred themselves to "do" something. Public policymakers for the most part apparently assumed that changes in state licensing policies would afford a "quick fix" for the ills allegedly besetting the education establishment.[4] Whether that expectation was warranted, the result today is state requirements considerably more detailed and prescriptive than ever before. The broader question as to whether revisions to state directives and guidelines actually have made them better adapted to their ostensible purpose—providing minimum quality assurance and protection of the public interest against pedagogical incompetence—remains in dispute.

STATE STANDARDS FOR
TEACHER LICENSURE
AND CERTIFICATION

At least 18 states incorporate detailed prescriptions governing the pattern of courses in general education a teaching candidate must complete as a precondition for licensure. Where regulations differ is in their specificity of detail. Alabama, Arizona, Delaware, Illinois, Louisiana, Texas, Maryland, New Mexico, South Dakota, and Virginia all mandate minimum hour totals, ranging from 46 to 71 semester hours, distributed by credit-hour subtotals for each discipline identified. Florida, Kansas, Ohio, Oklahoma, and Indiana, on the other hand, prescribe distribution requirements or hourly totals, but without assigning minimum credit-hour requirements to each discipline within the general education distribution.

New York requires a bachelor's degree with a "concentration" in one of the liberal arts and sciences, including college-level work in English, mathematics, science, social studies, and a foreign language. (California and Connecticut rank among the states that specifically disallow a major in education at the baccalaureate level, except for applications from out-of state candidates.) Missouri's general education requirements mandate completion of courses in English composition and oral communication, American history and government, mathematics, and the physical and biological sciences. Elective choices are allowed among music, art, foreign languages, Western and non-Western cultures, philosophy, literature, classical studies, theater and drama; and among geography, economics, sociology, anthropology, and psychology.

Indiana and Oklahoma require, respectively, 40 and 50 semester hours of general education, but without delineating any particular spread of courses to satisfy their requirements. Kansas stipulates that applicants must have completed a general education designed "to develop the student's skills of analysis, synthesis, and evaluation, competence in written and oral communication skills, understanding of and the ability to use basic mathematical properties, processes and symbols, and the study and application of modes of inquiry and the characteristics of the disciplines in the arts, humanities, natural sciences, and the social sciences."

As the number of required semester hours of general studies differs among states, so also do minimum hour requirements for course work related to secondary-level teaching fields. A teacher in some states may be authorized to teach a given subject with as few as 20 hours completed in the discipline. In other cases, as in Louisiana, to cite but one instance, as many as 62 hours are mandated for teachers of vocal or instrumental music. Twenty-four of the 50 states outline specific numbers of semester hours a prospective teacher must complete before seeking a teaching endorsement in a particular field or subject.

Minimums required vary not only state by state but by subject matter within a single state. In Virginia, a physical education teacher is required to complete 33 hours of course work in his or her endorsement area, compared with 53 hours for teaching physics or chemistry. New Mexico's requirements also vary by subject field, ranging from a low of 23 to a high of 36 semester credit hours. In Arizona, Delaware, Florida, Idaho, Iowa, Michigan, Utah, Missouri, Montana, Ohio, and Rhode Island, the most common minimum is 30 hours for any given teaching field. Elsewhere, as in Illinois, Indiana, Maine, Nevada, Massachusetts, New York and Virginia, the total runs slightly higher, ranging upward from 33 to 36 hours as the required minimum. In many states, including Montana, Nevada, Idaho, Illinois, Michigan, and Utah, the number of hours mandated for a "minor" endorsement in a second field is considerably lower than that for the "major" teaching area, and typically ranges between 16 and 24 credit hours.

About two-thirds of the states follow some version of an "approved-program" approach to teacher certification. Thus, any successful graduate of a state-recognized teacher preparation program who has satisfied all of the program's own internal requirements may be recommended for licensure. But states differ in the extent to which their respective regulations set forth standards to which state-sanctioned programs must conform. Some states, such as Alaska, declare basically that an approved program is one accredited by the National Council for Accreditation of Teacher Education (NCATE), or one in compliance with standards set forth by the National Association of State Directors of Teacher Education and Certification (NASDTEC).

NCATE, for example, currently has "partnership agreements" with more than 35 states that provide for some degree of linkage between its own programmatic standards and state program review standards or processes. Among those not included are Alaska, Arizona, Colorado, Connecticut, Delaware, Louisiana, Missouri, New Hampshire, New Jersey, New York, Rhode Island, South Carolina, Texas, Utah, and Vermont.

Some states traditionally have considered regional accreditation of the institution offering the program in question sufficient for state approval. In most cases, rules governing teacher education as laid out by one or another of the regional accrediting bodies are quite broad and nonspecific. Those of the Commission on Schools of the North Central Association of Colleges and Schools, for example, require only a bachelor's degree and a relatively low number of professional education courses, depending on the level at which an applicant intends to teach. A prospective secondary teacher, according to North Central's rules, need have no more than 20 to 24 semester hours to qualify for a teaching endorsement in a particular field.

Standards of the Commission on Schools of the Northwest Association of Schools and Colleges are more permissive still, requiring only that a prospective teacher complete a minimum of 14 hours of professional training, to include educational psychology, methods courses, and practice teaching. The Commission on Elementary Schools and the Commission on Secondary Schools of the Southern Association of Colleges and Schools each require no more than 12 hours of professional preparation, plus another 24 hours in a teaching field.

At the opposite extreme, individual states have developed their own standards boards and charged them with devising specific criteria against which to assess preparatory programs. An increasing number of states—among them Kentucky, Massachusetts, Ohio, Pennsylvania, Vermont, and Wyoming—have devised performance-based program assessment schemes or systems detailing the specific "competencies" a program graduate must possess. Wyoming, as a case in point, sets forth no fewer than 23 standards (each with multiple subsections) with which a professional education program must comply. Massachusetts, for its part, details eight teacher certification competencies pertaining to subject-matter knowledge, communication, instructional practice, evaluation, problem solving, equity issues, professionalism, and pedagogical content knowledge. After additional competencies for specialized certificates are added in, the listing of regulations alone runs in excess of 100 pages. Ohio's most recent revision of its licensure rules requires about 117 pages of text. Kentucky's recently approved "New Teacher" standards, eight in all, with a combined total of no fewer than 56 explicit performance criteria, are equally detailed and lengthy.

The common tactic employed by most states is to specify the minimum course or credit-hour requirements of the "professional education component" of a teacher preparation program. Depending on how regulations are framed, the state's specification of elements supplies the criteria to which a preparatory program must conform in order for it to receive state approval. Alternatively, it outlines the education course requirements an individual candidate must satisfy before making application for a teaching license. At present, almost two dozen states set forth minimum credit hours for course work in professional education. Credit-hour requirements typically are highest for persons intending to be certified in early childhood or elementary education, ranging from 18 to 45 semester hours, including a prescribed internship or supervised student teaching (which itself may vary by credit hours or actual clock hours spent in a classroom setting). Among the 22 states where it is possible to calculate required hourly minimums, the average total amount of education course work demanded is around 29 credit hours.

For those seeking to work at the secondary or middle-school level, required credits in professional education are slightly lower, ranging between 16 and 30 hours, or on average, 22 hours, once again including student teaching. (The difference between the two levels is accounted for by the greater number of subject-specific methods courses required of elementary-education majors.) As a percentage of the total hours required for completing a baccalaureate degree, elementary-education majors are obliged to devote approximately one-fourth of all course work to education classes in order to comply with minimum state norms. For secondary-education teacher candidates, about 18 percent of all courses taken are completed to satisfy state-mandated professional education requirements.

These tallies, it should be emphasized, reflect only *minimum* state stipulations. Preparatory programs themselves can and often do require *additional* credit hours in education courses. On average, in the late 1990s, elementary-education majors enrolled in baccalaureate degree programs actually were required to take more than one-third of all their course work in education (not counting electives), or between 42 and 45 semester credit hours, inclusive of student teaching and other clinical experiences. With electives added in, the total amount of education course work was somewhat higher. About one-fifth of a typical prospective secondary teacher's program was comprised of education courses, or between 24 and 27 semester hours, including practice teaching but exclusive of additional elective credits in education or courses needed for multiple teaching endorsements.

Among the two dozen or so states where professional education requirements are enumerated by credit hours or numbers of courses, there is little variation in terms of constituent elements specified. Most required elementary-education sequences include an introductory education course; one or more courses in the social, cultural, historical, philosophical, or sociological foundations of education; at least one course in educational psychology; an organization and administration course; a special education course dealing with learner exceptionality; a general curriculum or methods course; specialized pedagogical courses devoted to methods of teaching reading, art, mathematics, the sciences, social studies, music, health and physical education, and the language arts; assessment and evaluation; and classroom management. Sometimes course work in human relations, legal and ethical aspects of teaching, multicultural education, or computers and instructional technology also is required.

To these are added various clinical practice and supervised classroom observations or aiding, as well as student teaching. Practice teaching requirements typically are the most detailed. They may be variously expressed in terms of mandated duration (one-half semester or an entire semester), course credit hours, or actual clock hours. Most state-approved programs are obliged to include at least five credit hours of student teaching; some states require 9 to 12 credit hours.

Secondary-education requirements laid out in state regulations also tend to follow a common pattern. Virtually all programmatic sequences include a course in the social and cultural foundations of education and a course in educational psychology or basic learning theory and human development. Other courses sometimes required include organization and administration of secondary schools; special education; a generic curriculum theory or methods course; at least one specialized methods course for each teaching area where certification is sought; a course devoted to methods of teaching reading; assessment and evaluation; classroom management; and multicultural education. Less often an instructional technology course is mandated as well. Practice teaching is stipulated; minimum requirements range between 5 and 12 hours.

To these more general requirements, some states append specialized elements or courses all teacher candidates must complete, including one in nutrition (Louisiana), environmental education and "education for employment" (Wisconsin), and a "whole language" approach to the teaching of reading in the primary grades (Maine). Alaska has its own unique "Alaska studies" requirement; most states have embedded requirements pertaining to each state's history and constitution. Further complicating matters are the so-called preprofessional courses in arts and sciences some teacher preparation programs—as distinct from state regulations—require of their students. Usually preprofessional courses do double duty in satisfying general studies requirements. Less often they are required as prerequisites for enrollment in education classes but are not counted as part of the general-education portion of an undergraduate course of study.

All but a handful of states now offer some type of probationary or alternative certification route. Most, like West Virginia's Alternative Program for the Education of Teachers (APET), are intended to serve only as short-term expedients, especially in teaching areas where there are severe teacher shortages. Some programs, as in Mississippi and Virginia, grant credit for previous teaching experience in lieu of satisfying formal course requirements or otherwise temporarily relax regular standards. In the great majority of cases, alternative certification routes are designed primarily to allow a prospective teacher additional time to meet criteria governing regular provisional licensure.

TESTING TEACHER CANDIDATES

At least 30 states now require applicants to teacher preparation programs to complete examinations designed to provide measures of basic academic achievement and academic skill proficiency. Some are common to all undergraduates enrolled in publicly assisted institutions of higher learning. Most tests are administered either roughly halfway through a student's academic program of study or toward the completion of the baccalaureate program. Arkansas' so-called rising junior examinations, mandated by the state's legislature, affords one model widely emulated elsewhere. Equally often, states require those completing teacher preparation programs to submit themselves for testing within their professional area of specialization.

Eight states—Arizona, California, Colorado, Connecticut, New York, Oregon, Texas, and West Virginia—employ special examinations developed in-state. In Arizona, prior to receiving a temporary or basic standard certificate, licensure candidates must complete the Arizona Teacher Proficiency Examination, or ATPE, a proficiency test in the areas of reading, grammar, and mathematics. California mandates use of the California Basic Educational Skills Test (CBEST); and Oregon has authorized its use as an alternative to portions of the National Teacher Examination, or NTE, for its own teacher candidates.

Colorado applicants must pass one or more of the state's PLACE assessments (Program for Licensing Assessments for Colorado Educators). Connecticut has its own Connecticut Elementary Education Certification Test (CONNECT), which it utilizes in conjunction with subject assessment tests (Praxis II) developed by the Educational Testing Service (ETS) of Princeton, New Jersey. New York uses its own New York State Teacher Certification Examination's liberal arts and sciences test (LAST) and a written assessment of teaching skills, the ATS-W. Texas relies on its own Examination for the Certification of Educators in Texas (ExCET); while West Virginia utilizes a content test of proficiency before granting any secondary-level endorsement area to an out-of-state applicant.

A growing number of states employ one or more of the core battery tests of the National Teacher Examination, including measures of general knowledge, communication skills, professional knowledge, and specialty area exams. Their numbers include Arkansas, Florida, Hawaii, Idaho, Indiana, Kansas, Louisiana, Maine, Maryland, Mississippi, Missouri, Montana, New Mexico, North Carolina, Oregon, Pennsylvania, Rhode Island, South Carolina, and Tennessee. Six states make exclusive use of the core battery only; nine further mandate one or more specialty tests from the accompanying ETS Praxis II test series. Delaware, Kansas, Minnesota, Nebraska, and several other states also require the Pre-Professional Skills Test (PPST) of reading, mathematics, and writing, each a one-hour multiple-choice exam developed by the Educational Testing Service.

CRITICISM OF STATE REGULATIONS

On the whole, state regulations are more stringent today than they were just a few years ago. Typical revisions reflect a movement toward more rigorous screening of applicants prior to acceptance into a preparatory program, mandatory standardized testing for proficiency in basic academic skills, competency testing over general and professional knowledge prior to initial licensure, heavier general education requirements, lengthier preservice clinical training, and a virtual end to permanent or lifetime teacher licensure.[5] (Significantly, few reform initiatives originating *outside* of academe have called for augmenting the number of pedagogy courses required of teacher candidates. Quite the contrary; although the situation is sometimes otherwise represented, most pressures to expand the education curriculum come not from external constituencies but from faculty *within* schools or colleges of education or from the multiple professional associations of their fellow educationists.)

Despite the many changes effected in recent years, critics of state teacher licensure remain unmollified. For all of the effort expended over the past decade or so, complains Arthur Wise of the National Council for Accreditation of Teacher Education, "there has not been much change in teaching and learning" to correspond with upgraded certification statutes. Some innovations have shown promise, he believes. But on the whole the gains registered to date have been negligible. Licensing tests that have been introduced, he points out, "are still tests of basic skills and general knowledge geared to minimums," and examinations intended to determine the adequacy of a prospective teacher's knowledge "have been normed to low achievement." Even where competency- or performance-based measures have been brought into play, more often than not the performance component has been "a single data source of one to three observations plus an interview—an isolated snapshot."[6]

Particularly objectionable in Wise's view has been the trend in most states to develop alternative avenues to licensure, routes designed to circumvent the very standards and admission requirements the states have created. As he phrases it, "Existing state regulations regarding teacher licensure are so poor that the majority of states have now created emergency routes to gaining a license to teach in order to place teachers in areas experiencing shortages. . . . Since existing regulations have been deemed, by the very legislators that sanctioned them, a hindrance to recruiting and keeping a high quality work force, they have created an 'end run' around the system by creating 'alternate' routes."[7]

David L. Clark and Robert F. McNergney of the University of Virginia judge that the entire elaborate apparatus of teacher certification and licensure relies heavily on formal displays of confidence in order to effect its legitimacy.[8] That is, initiatives to upgrade entrance requirements, bolster programmatic requirements, institute competency testing, and so forth may all be defensible and well intended. But given their lack of predictive validity, the real purpose they serve appears to have more to do with providing a public appearance of quality assurance than with supplying its reality. The increasing use made of standardized multiple-choice tests in teacher licensing programs affords a case in point. The empirical fact of the matter, long acknowledged but not widely publicized, is that only a very low correlation has been found between scores on any formal test yet devised and measures of teaching effectiveness. "The available evidence," it is reported, "indicates that teacher tests have little, if any, power to predict how well people perform as teachers, whether that performance is judged by ratings of college supervisory personnel, ratings by teachers, student ratings, or achievement gains made by students."[9] Nevertheless, reliance on testing as an obligatory feature of teacher preparation has, if anything, actually increased in most states and is now officially enshrined within their rules and regulations.

Traditional licensing requirements, claims Harvard's Richard Murname, coauthor of *Who Will Teach? Policies That Matter* (1991), "are not effective because, while the state can mandate that teachers graduate from preservice training programs and can specify the material that must be covered in those programs, no set of requirements can guarantee that the material will be taught well enough to benefit participants or to attract academically able students."[10] Although "raising standards is important," Murname concedes, ". . . increasing the number of preservice courses that aspiring teachers must take to obtain a teaching license does not accomplish this objective. Neither does raising the minimum scores that applicants must achieve on. . . . tests such as the current version of the NTE."[11] The attraction of policy changes of this nature, he concludes, is that they are easy to implement, cost very little, and do not require expensive research and development for their support. They are good public relations mechanisms. Unfortunately, they carry little potential for improving teacher quality.

Underscoring just how precarious and uncertain are the empirical foundations upon which state certification and licensure requirements depend, Robert Roth of California State University, Long Beach, and Chris Pipho of the Education Commission of the States, writing for the 1990 edition of the *Handbook of Research on Teacher Education,* reviewed several key assumptions on which recent reforms in teacher education standards appear to rely.[12] Some standards rather clearly have been designed to promote greater in-depth knowledge of subjects to be taught. Demanding subject-matter proficiency of prospective teachers—requiring that they achieve a thorough and in-depth knowledge of what they will teach—certainly poses a worthwhile, eminently reasonable aim practically everyone would support. Yet relevant research suggests a point of early diminishing returns, beyond which increased knowledge of subject matter (as measured by number of courses taken and by grade point average) contributes nothing measurably significant to pupil performance on standardized tests. The point is not that subject-matter competency is *un*important but, rather, that beyond a certain minimum level, it does not demonstrably affect teacher effectiveness in ways that can be documented empirically.

Bolstering general education requirements has been a prominent theme in reforming standards. Again, however, evidence to identify and confirm the nature of the contribution additional study in the liberal arts makes to teaching effectiveness is still largely lacking. Nor have efforts been very successful in showing how teacher success is related to the completion of more professional education courses, or more preservice practice, or overall length of preservice training. Tested intelligence likewise seems to be an unreliable predictor, as are scores from tests of basic skills and general knowledge. Once again, intuitively, it seems essential and reasonable to stress the critical importance of general knowledge, professional knowledge, and thorough conversance with the subject matter to be taught. But by the same token, it has proven difficult to validate any particular set of standards based on some type of formal test performance by teacher candidates.

Often noted too is the problematic status of claims that longer preparatory programs will help ensure better quality among those pursuing teaching careers or enhance teachers' status as professionals. Actually, or so some analysts claim, the esteem (or the lack thereof) in which teaching is held by the public at large appears to have little if anything to do with how much graduate-level training teachers receive or how many advanced degrees they hold. As for the quality issue, the now-familiar counterargument is that today's teacher labor market probably already exhibits a rough equilibrium between the rewards for teaching as an occupation currently made available and the size and quality of the candidate talent pool. Increasing the costs and demands of entry into the profession, it is argued, may have exactly the opposite effect than the one intended—that is, as costs increase without a commensurate increase in benefits, the quality of those attracted to teaching may actually decline.[13]

Gary Fenstermacher of the University of Arizona offers an interesting rejoinder of sorts to complaints about the presumptive lack of stringency and rigor characteristic of state licensing standards.[14] "If completion of teacher training leads to licensure by the state," he observes, "then the state is presumed to have the authority to regulate the activity leading to issuance of the license." In a democracy, however, "the state is often highly constrained in the exercise of regulatory authority. It must balance assuring the welfare and safety of the public it serves against the possibility of unwarranted interference with individual (and corporate) liberties and rights."

In order to achieve the critical balance needed, the state is obliged to exercise its power in ways that allow as many service providers to enter the market as seek to do so, on condition they can meet certain minimum standards and performance levels. "These minimum standards are those believed essential to preparing a license holder who will not do harm as a result of ignorance, lack of skill or flawed character, and who is prepared to learn and improve as a result of further experience."[15] But the democratic political imperative always is to cant state rules and regulations toward inclusivity rather than exclusivity. The result is that standards must be kept relatively low. Consequently the state's practical ability to impose standards of sufficient stringency to exclude marginal preparatory programs, even if it wished to do so, is severely limited.

Practitioners in a given occupation, such as teacher education, may elect to adopt a second tier of standards more rigorous and demanding than those mandated by state agencies, as indeed has occurred with the advent of new accreditation standards developed by the National Council for Accreditation of Teacher Education. The tendency then is to urge each state to raise its own standards or to replace them with those advanced by some voluntary accrediting agency, such as NASDTEC or NCATE. If the state elects the first option—raising its own standards—it runs the risk of becoming more restrictive than public opinion (or rival institutions preparing practitioners for the field) will tolerate. Or the effect becomes one of rendering the more stringent standards of the oversight agency superfluous. If the second alternative is chosen, the state may choose to withdraw from the standard-setting business altogether, accepting instead the review processes and judgments of the accrediting agency or simply duplicating them in its own review procedures.

At present, teacher licensure more nearly reflects a balanced two-tiered system within which the state sets minimum standards that are considered politically viable, while national agencies, such as NCATE, are free to impose what they represent to be their own more rigorous demands. In the closing years of the twentieth century, the impetus toward a significant strengthening of the system's second tier has advanced steadily. Already some states stipulate that NCATE accreditation is to be a prerequisite to program approval, or—what amounts to practically the same thing—they accept NCATE standards as the basis for their own respective reviews. Meanwhile, even as NCATE moves to subordinate individual state *accreditation* standards to a single set of national requirements, a parallel attempt is well under way to institute a uniform set of advanced teacher licensure or national *certification* standards as well.

NATIONAL ACCREDITATION STANDARDS

Attempts to standardize teacher education admission requirements, preparatory curricula, and programmatic requirements on a national scale have a long if sometimes uneven history.[16] Among the first were pioneering efforts undertaken by the American Normal School Association (ANSA), founded in 1858. In 1885, the ANSA appointed its first committee charged with preparing a formal report on teaching standards for normal institutions.[17] In 1899, a successor body issued a series of recommendations governing minimal requirements for teacher preparatory courses of study.[18] In 1923, the American Association of Teacher Colleges, predecessor to the American Association of Colleges for Teacher Education (AACTE), first adopted a list of nine minimal standards for normal schools and teachers' colleges.[19]

In 1946, the National Education Association took matters one step further, acting to create a National Commission on Teacher Education and Professional Standards (NCTEPS) as an official agency empowered to establish and enforce a national set of teacher education standards for all colleges and universities engaged in teacher preparation.[20] It soon became apparent, for a variety of reasons, that NCTEPS was not destined to play the governance role in teacher education originally envisioned for it. The outcome was the convocation of yet another national conference, this time involving representatives of NCTEPS, AACTE, NASDTEC, and the Council of Chief State School Officers (CCSSO). From that meeting of alphabet-soup agencies came the establishment three years later (in 1954) of an entirely new organization, the National Council for Accreditation of Teacher Education, or NCATE.

In the half century or so since its inception, NCATE has evolved into a national regulatory body superintending an elaborate system of voluntary teacher education accreditation. NCATE's avowed mission nowadays is "to provide professional judgment of the quality" of schools, colleges, and departments within member postsecondary institutions that bear primary responsibility for "the initial and continuing preparation of teachers and other professional school personnel." Colleges and universities seeking to comply with NCATE accreditation standards, procedures, and policies are required "to provide quality professional education that fosters competent practice of graduates" and are encouraged to meet "rigorous standards of excellence developed by the profession."

NCATE's declared role today is to implement a process of voluntary peer review, one that "ensures that requirements for accreditation are related to established knowledge and sound professional practice"; that "establishes and upholds national standards of excellence; and strengthens the quality and integrity of professional education units."[21]

NCATE's membership includes professional and academic associations representing four different constituent groups: teacher educators, classroom teachers, state and local policymakers, and professional specialty areas. Represented on NCATE's governing boards are the nation's two major teacher educator organizations, the Association of Teacher Educators and the American Association of Colleges for Teacher Education. Teachers' organizations include both the National Education Association and the American Federation of Teachers. Public policy-making agencies, such as the Council of Chief State School Officers, the National School Boards Association, and the National Association of State Boards of Education, are NCATE members. So also are several school administrators' organizations, including the American Association of School Administrators, the Association for Supervision and Curriculum Development, the Association of School Business Officials International, the National Association of Elementary School Principals, and the National Association of Secondary School Principals.

The complete roster of specialized-interest groups comprising NCATE's constituent members is lengthy. It includes the American Alliance for Health, Physical Education, Recreation, and Dance; the International Reading Association; the National Council for the Social Studies; the National Council of Teachers of English; the National Council of Teachers of Mathematics; and the National Science Teachers Association. Still others include the Association for Childhood Education International, the Council for Exceptional Children, the National Association for the Education of Young Children, the National Middle School Association, the Association for Educational Communications and Technology, the International Society for Technology in Education, the International Technology Education Association's Council on Technology Teacher Education, the Association of School Librarians of the American Library Association, and the National Association of School Psychologists.

Besides other assorted public and student representatives, still other member organizations include the National Board for Professional Teaching Standards and the Council of Learned Societies in Education. The latter, in turn, functions as an "umbrella" organization and advocate in professional matters for such academic groups as the History of Education Society, the Philosophy of Education Society, the Comparative and International Education Society, the American Educational Studies Association, and many regional specialty organizations.

Despite a hefty dues structure, virtually no agency or professional association with a vested interest in teacher education, it appears, feels it can afford politically to be excluded from some type of representation within NCATE. Among other things, as its leaders are quick to point out, NCATE is the sole authority for teacher education recognized by the Commission on Recognition of Postsecondary Accreditation (CORPA) and by the U.S. Department of Education. So far as the mainstream American educational establishment is concerned, therefore, in matters of national standing involving accreditation and teacher education standards, NCATE (together with NASDTEC) represents just about "the only game in town."

Nevertheless, while virtually all of the major professional associations feel constrained as stakeholders in teacher preparation to affiliate themselves with NCATE and to be represented on its multiple governing boards, the same is not necessarily true of individual institutions. As of late 1994, only 516, or 40 percent, of the nation's 1,290 state-approved colleges and universities engaged in teacher preparation belonged to NCATE; and several prestigious universities in recent years (for differing reasons) have seen fit to drop their NCATE affiliation. Whereas all of Arkansas' 17 institutions were in the NCATE system, for example, only 6 percent of schools in New York, or 6 out of 103 held NCATE accreditation; 1 out of 12 in Vermont (8 percent); and 10 out of 68 (15 percent) in Texas. NCATE-approved schools and colleges of education are in the minority in over half the states, including California, (13 out of 70 institutions), Iowa (7 of 31), Maine (3 of 13), Maryland (4 out of 20), New Hampshire (3 of 13), South Carolina (7 of 28), Vermont (1 out of 12), Virginia (14 of 37), and Wisconsin (14 out of 32).[22]

Factors behind nonaffiliation vary according to individual cases. A given institution's unwillingness to bear the expense involved in undergoing accreditation or its presumed inability to meet NCATE standards undoubtedly figures as a major consideration in many instances, especially among smaller programs. But the great majority of teachers are produced by larger state institutions, virtually all of which hold NCATE accreditation. In any event, unlike state approval systems for teacher education programs, where few schools fail to win endorsement, it has been reported in recent years that one in every five schools or colleges of education seeking NCATE approval has initially failed to win full accreditation. (Equally significant, perhaps, is the fact that no fewer than 500 colleges and universities do hold accreditation, suggesting perhaps that compliance with NCATE standards is not nearly as difficult as it sometimes is reputed to be by its representatives.)

The latest version of NCATE's standards were designed in the late 1980s, first implemented in 1987, and revised as of 1995. In their current iteration there are now no fewer than 20 standards and 69 "indicators" organized according to four categories (program design, faculty, students, and the unit for professional education). Substantively, NCATE requires that candidates complete "general studies courses and experiences in the liberal arts and have developed theoretical and practical knowledge." The content of this requirement goes unspecified, except for a reference to "the arts, communications, history, literature, mathematics, philosophy, sciences, and the social sciences"—which, it is added, must "incorporate multicultural and global perspectives." Preparatory units also are called upon to ensure that "teacher candidates attain academic competence in the content that they plan to teach"—including its "structure, skills, core concepts, ideas, values, facts, [and] methods of inquiry."

Besides general studies, teacher candidates are required to complete "a well-planned sequence of courses and/or experiences" in "professional" and "pedagogical" studies. So far as the first are concerned, teacher candidates are to "acquire and learn to apply knowledge" about "the social, historical, and philosophical foundations of education, including an understanding of the moral, social, and political dimensions of classrooms, teaching, and schools; the impact of technological and societal changes on schools; theories of human development and learning; inquiry and research; school law and educational policy; professional ethics; and the responsibilities, structure, and activities of the profession."[23]

With respect to "pedagogical studies," teacher candidates are to "develop understanding and use" of "research- and experience-based principles of effective practice for encouraging the intellectual, social, and personal development of students." They are supposed to acquire the ability to employ "different student approaches to learning for creating instructional opportunities adapted to learners from diverse cultural backgrounds and with exceptionalities" and a "variety of instructional strategies for developing critical thinking, problem solving, and performance skills." Prospective teachers likewise are expected to utilize "individual and group motivation for encouraging positive social interaction, active engagement in learning, and self-motivation."

"Effective verbal, nonverbal, and media communications for fostering active inquiry, collaboration, and supportive interactions in the classroom" are mandated (although it is not entirely plain how one goes about mandating "communications"). Similarly required are "planning and management of instruction based on knowledge of the content area, the community, and curriculum goals." Both "formal and informal assessment strategies for evaluating and ensuring the continuous intellectual, social, and physical development of the learner" are deemed essential.

Teaching graduates must be prepared to understand and use "collaboration with school colleagues, parents, and agencies in the larger community for supporting students' learning and well-being." They should be able to conduct "effective interactions with parents for supporting students' learning and well-being." Programs also should afford teacher candidates opportunities "to reflect on their teaching and its effects on student growth and learning." Finally, prospective teachers must know about "educational technology, including the use of computer and other technologies in instruction, assessment, and professional productivity."[24]

NCATE emphasizes that its current standards are oriented to outcomes rather than to discrete courses. Prospective teachers, it is said, "are expected. . . . to demonstrate specific skills as a result of their preparation." Assessment criteria for programs "emphasize the unit's role in monitoring candidates' progress throughout their program of study, and in requiring specific outcomes—assessed through a variety of performance measures—for program completion." They must demonstrate, once again, that in fact they can apply "instructional strategies for developing critical thinking, problem solving, and performance skills" and can adapt instruction for "learners from diverse cultural backgrounds and with exceptionalities." Additionally, they must exhibit the ability to promote "active inquiry, collaboration, and supportive interactions in the classroom."[25]

For specific recommendations involving actual curricular content, NCATE relies on 18 of the professional specialty associations among its constituent members—the National Council of Teachers of Mathematics, the National Science Teachers Association, the National Council for the Social Studies, and the others—to set standards for each program area.[26] Until very recently, however, guidelines supplied by associations whose respective interests are specific to particular teaching areas or subjects (English and language arts, art, music, physical education, and so forth) have in no way been even roughly isomorphic to one another. Nor until recently in most cases have they been well adapted to the new performance-based NCATE format.

Some organizations have offered only standards for instructional programs within public schools, not criteria against which to judge preservice teacher programs at the collegiate level. The American

Association of School Librarians and the Association for Educational Communications and Technology, for example, supplies only guidelines for assessing school library media programs. The National Academy of Early Childhood Programs conducts its own independent accreditation for collegiate programs preparing early childhood teachers, utilizing benchmarks framed rather differently from those developed by the National Council of Teachers of Mathematics or, again, those of the National Science Teachers Association. Again, the formatting of standards for English and language arts as developed by the International Reading Association and the National Council of Teachers of English, to cite another example, little resembles the ways in which criteria intended to govern teacher preparation programs in certain other content fields are formulated.

The response from NCATE has been to encourage its constituent members—those specialty associations that participate in its accrediting system—to revise their teacher preparation guidelines so as to emphasize instructional outcomes. It is anticipated that within the very near future performance standards for elementary and secondary students in each teaching field or area will be complemented by teacher preparation standards framed in terms of competencies and performances—what a teacher legitimately may be expected to do in a classroom setting. Those expectations are then to be incorporated as the instructional goals of teacher preparatory programs subject to NCATE scrutiny.

NATIONAL TEACHER LICENSURE AND CERTIFICATION STANDARDS

In 1987, a National Board for Professional Teaching Standards was created with substantial foundation funding for the purpose of developing nationwide standards for advanced teacher certification. The announced goal was to help improve the status of teaching as a profession by establishing a voluntary national system of board certification, a review process designed to identify and reward exceptional elementary and secondary teachers.[27] Recognizing accomplished teachers, the Board declared, would work to enhance the professional practice of teachers and thereby provide assurance of high quality. It would further serve, or so it was claimed, to invigorate and vitalize the entire country's educational system.[28]

To accomplish these ends, the Board proposed to generate standards reflecting "what teachers should know and be able to do." Five "core propositions" were articulated as the basis on which national teacher standards would be formulated: (1) "Teachers are committed to students and their learning"; (2) "Teachers know the subjects they teach and how to teach those subjects to students"; (3) "Teachers are responsible for managing and monitoring student learning"; (4) "Teachers think systematically about their practice and learn from experience"; and (5) "Teachers are members of learning communities."[29]

Accompanying the development of standards, the Board explained, would be assessment procedures for determining compliance. Protocols would include interviews, portfolios, simulated performances, and on-site observations. Successful applicants would be granted official national certification in any of 20 or so different teaching areas, from generalist certificates in early and middle childhood, to subject specialist certificates for middle childhood and adolescence as well as certification at multiple levels, as in music, art, special education, and the teaching of English-deficient learners. Each certification would reflect four areas of teacher proficiency: general professional knowledge, knowledge specific to the developmental level of students taught, breadth or scope of subject-matter knowledge, and depth of teaching-content knowledge.

Weighing in with support for the National Board's ambitious agenda was the American Federation of Teachers (AFT), among others. Inaugurating national standards for advanced certification, the AFT avowed, held promise for "upgrading the status of teachers, for expanding and codifying the knowledge base for teaching" and for providing a means for recognizing excellent teachers. Board certification, it was promised, would serve to encourage such needed school reforms as "increased collaboration among teachers, reduced bureaucratic control over the forms of their work, and more productive use of their talents."[30]

NCATE president Arthur Wise was effusive in his predictions. "National Board advanced certification," he declared, "will be an important form of recognition for many teachers. . . . Advanced certification will provide formal recognition of and rewards for excellence in teaching. It will create an opportunity for excellent teachers to remain in the classroom and to expand their roles, and thus, create a new tier of teaching professionalism." Already, he claimed, the teaching profession had been helped by the National Board "by bringing attention to the inadequacies of licensing and teacher preparation programs, and stimulating parallel change in those quality assurance systems."[31]

In the same year the National Board was founded, the Council of Chief State School Officers undertook to create an Interstate New Teacher Assessment and Support Consortium, or INTASC. It was charged with the task of seeking ways to enhance collaboration among states engaged in effecting changes in their own initial licensing standards for teachers. The National Board for Professional Teaching Standards and INTASC were united, it was announced, in their view that "the complex art of teaching requires performance-based standards and assessment standards and assessment strategies that are capable of capturing teachers' reasoned judgments and that evaluate what they can actually do in authentic teaching situations."[32]

INTASC moved quickly to establish a task force to consider what kinds of changes in state licensing regulations would be required in order to create "Board-compatible" standards for entry into teaching—criteria that would embody the "knowledge, skills and dispositions" needed by beginning teachers. Seventeen states supplied representatives for INTASC's standards-drafting committee: California, Connecticut, Delaware, Florida, Georgia, Kentucky, Louisiana, Massachusetts, Minnesota, New York, North Carolina, Pennsylvania, South Carolina, Texas, Vermont, Washington, and Wisconsin.

These states were joined by representatives from most of the major national organizations involved in establishing teacher preparation standards, including the National Board for Professional Teaching Standards, AACTE, NCATE, NASDTEC, the National Association of State Boards of Education, the AFT, and the National Education Association. A State Networking Committee, composed of 22 additional states, also was established to work closely with INTASC in facilitating a public review of its draft standards.

In the initial presentation of its model standards for beginning teacher licensure, the INTASC task force stressed what it saw as the distinction between state licensing and board certification. The function of the former, the drafting committee explained, was to ensure compliance with standards of minimal competence established by each state to protect the public from harm. Professional certification by the National Board for Professional Teaching Standards, in contrast, was to be more exacting in character, relying on criteria analogous to those developed by the National Board of Medical Examiners for physicians or the National Architectural Registration Board. Board certification for teachers would require "additional education or supervised intern-ship as well as greater knowledge and more skilled performances in specific areas."[33]

INTASC foresaw a system in which states would continue to license beginning teachers, as always, whereas the National Board would award advanced certificates only to those who met the prereq-uisite experience level of at least three years of practice and who successfully passed its voluntary examinations. INTASC's task mean-while was to work toward a closer performance-based alignment between minimal initial licensing requirements developed by the states and the more demanding advanced standards under development by the National Board.[34] Ten basic principles were drawn up, each ac-companied by varying numbers of "knowledge" descriptors, congru-ent teacher "dispositions," and several discrete "performance" indicators. The ten INTASC precepts were subsequently incorporated with very few changes in NCATE's 1995 revision of its own program accreditation standards.[35]

It has thus become abundantly apparent in recent years that major teacher preparation organizations at the national level have begun joining forces to bring about a uniform, consistent, and all-encompass-ing national system of accreditation, licensure, and advanced certifica-tion. Nowhere is the movement toward convergence and mutual reinforcement of one another's efforts more vividly illustrated than in NCATE's New Professional Teacher Project (NPT), a $2 million effort financed by the Carnegie Corporation and other leading foundations. Its purpose, clearly, has been to draw all the disparate threads together: National Board certification, INTASC licensing principles, the stan-dards of specialized professional associations, and its own program accreditation function.

As NCATE represents it, the overarching goal is to create a "new professional teacher," someone "guided by professional and clinical knowledge and supervised experiences . . . a beginner with a solid foundation of knowledge and skills who becomes a reflective and effective practitioner . . . and a professional teacher who is well prepared to help all students learn [ellipses in original]."[36] This new breed of teacher, according to NPT promotional literature, will be someone "who will measure up to demanding standards and a performance-based quality assurance process."[37] Interestingly enough, it might be noted, the "continuum" of teacher preparation urged by NCATE as a way of achieving quality assurance assumes a four-year undergraduate preservice preparatory program followed by a year-long internship as its norm (a five-year program in total). It does not embrace, for example, the extended fifth-year or six-year program model urged by the Holmes Group and other reform groups of the late 1980s.

Reminiscent of a script for a public-service film or a corporate-industrial public relations effort, NCATE offers a narrative "portrait" of a prototypical new professional teacher as she progresses through an idealized accrediting system. "Karen" is beginning her first year of teaching in an urban elementary school. She is purportedly "well prepared" to assume her new duties because she commands a "foundation of knowledge upon which she bases classroom decisions." Attentive always to "research and best practice," she can readily explain the grounds on which her many choices rest. The "research-based program of studies" from which she graduated, the narrative continues, has "provided her with a research-based foundation in the liberal arts, content knowledge, the latest in pedagogical knowledge and professional practice, and many clinical experiences."[38]

As a sophomore in college, Karen first "began to develop her clinical skills by observing and analyzing effective teachers." As a junior, "she tutored one-on-one and small groups of students, under the supervision of expert school personnel." As a senior, she spent ten weeks in a classroom, "assuming greater and greater responsibility for instruction."

But her clinical preparation had just begun. Karen then completed "a year-long internship in an urban setting and developed an array of teaching skills" by working with and observing a number of expert teachers. She knew from the time of her acceptance into the school of education that she would be required "to demonstrate specific performance outcomes for graduation." She had to be successful "as assessed in a variety of ways, including portfolios, interviews, performance, grades, and standardized tests."

She has since passed state licensing examinations—"both written tests and performance examinations—at an assessment center and in the classroom—with flying colors." She has "demonstrated that she has the classroom management, interpersonal, content and pedagogical skills necessary to be a new professional teacher." Karen regards herself as a professional and is already "looking forward to participating in various professional development activities and assessment by the National Board for Professional Teaching Standards."[39]

The preservice phase of NCATE's projected teacher preparation continuum thus incorporates several distinct elements, beginning with an NCATE-accredited four-year preparatory program encompassing field observations, supervised tutoring in a school classroom, and a ten-week regimen of "clinical studies." Immediately prior to graduation, according to the NCATE schematic (assuming it were adopted), students would be obliged to undergo a formal state-mandated assessment of their subject-matter knowledge and knowledge about teaching. Thereafter, teacher candidate graduates would complete a year-long internship in a professional development school setting. In the next phase, the state would intervene once again with a licensure examination designed to reveal how well applicants could apply their knowledge and skills. Those who were successful would receive their regular teaching licenses. In the third phase, having completed three or more years of practical classroom experience, qualified teachers could present themselves for assessment by the National Board for Professional Teaching Standards. If successful, they would be awarded advanced board certification. Teachers who elected not to seek the Board's imprimatur would still be obliged to involve themselves in ongoing "professional development" activities leading to license renewal.[40]

DISSENTING VIEWS

Both the National Board's effort to establish uniform teacher certification standards and the National Council for Accreditation of Teacher Education's attempt to create a common, national system of accreditation have come in for strong criticism. Much of the debate centers on the supposed knowledge base for teacher preparation on which both presumably depend for their authority and legitimacy. Both NCATE and the National Board not only assume the existence of such a base, but go further in representing it as a corpus of accredited and valid scientific findings already known and available for application to instructional practice.

While it acknowledges that teaching is an artistic activity in certain respects, the Board, for example, lays greater stress on the theme of the accomplished teacher as pedagogical technician, as someone who has mastery of a codified professional knowledge base and is technically proficient in "applying" that knowledge directly in the classroom.[41] NCATE invokes the term "conceptual framework" to reflect the same architectural metaphor: a knowledge base on which teacher preparatory programs are erected. The "knowledge-based" conceptual framework insisted upon by the National Council is represented as an edifice built on "established and contemporary research," buttressed by "the wisdom of practice, and emerging education policies and practices." Rather confusingly, a normative component is mandated as well, since the framework must include a "commitment to acquire and use professional knowledge on behalf of students"; and, further (presumably as a way of acknowledging current canons of political correctness), it is stipulated that the framework must "reflect multicultural and global perspectives which permeate all programs."[42]

As always, what some critics question is whether the field in fact possesses a sufficiently substantial "knowledge base" to warrant the imposition of standards, criteria, performances, and procedures based on that foundation. Gary Fenstermacher, for example, argues that critical errors have been made in how a knowledge base for teacher education needs to be understood.[43] Basically, the argument he and other critics of monolithic standards put forth recapitulates caveats first issued by Josiah Royce, William James, John Dewey, and others almost a century ago. The point is reiterated once again that pedagogical practices are never directly deducible or derivable from scientific findings in and of themselves. Systematic observations of lawlike regularities in human growth and development or learning (assuming they exist and have predictive reliability) do not generate specific applications of their own accord in some linear, straightforward fashion. Intervening between general theoretical axioms in the abstract or particular empirical "facts," on the one hand, and particular classroom usages on the other—practices that inevitably must be adapted to fit concrete contexts and settings—are complex processes of mediation, translation, and interpretation. In some cases, important normative judgments are required as well.[44] Fenstermacher sums it up: "We have been too quick to accept research rooted in a highly conventional epistemology, one embedded in the ideology of determinism and positivism."[45]

Leaving aside the norm-laden prescriptions and judgments embedded in the language of NCATE and National Board standards (with all of the attendant conceptual confusion they may engender), the fact remains—as critics have emphasized—that teaching cannot be understood as an entirely neutral, value-free undertaking in the way often implied by official invocations of a professional knowledge base undergirding teacher education.[46] Teaching of any sort is a normative, which is to say in this instance a moral, enterprise. Once again, as Fenstermacher phrases the point, "The issue is not that a knowledge base is unimportant; rather that a knowledge base without a moral base simply fails to provide a conception of teaching that accords with any well-developed theory of education."[47]

David Labaree of Michigan State University, as well as several others, makes the related point that a purely technical view of teaching as process deflects attention from the content of instruction, the purposes thereby served, and the larger political context in which teaching occurs. To cite one obvious example, an exclusive techno-methodological construction of teaching can easily obscure the meaning of instances where what is taught highlights the knowledge, history, and culture of certain people while ignoring or consigning to the margins of attention the accomplishments of others. In fact, practically any instructional undertaking is infused with, or carries with it, political significance at some level or another. "One potential danger of professionalization," Labaree observes, ". . . is the way in which it pushes technical questions into the foreground and political questions in the background as either unscientific or unproblematic."[48]

Many critics regard the impetus toward technical professionalism, all-encompassing licensure standards, uniform assessment, and National Board certification as nothing short of "alarming" and a major "threat" to democratic ideals.[49] Teacher professionalism cast primarily if not exclusively in terms of specialized technical expertise, Labaree argues, is antidemocratic insofar as it is intended to "distance" schoolteachers and insulate them from students, their parents, or the community at large. If teachers alone are considered the only certified experts in educational matters, he fears, efforts to set the direction or to shape the content of education by the laity will not be regarded as defensible and appropriate acts of democratic participation in decision making. Rather, attempts at oversight will be seen as tantamount to unwarranted interference by laypersons who are considered incapable of passing informed judgment.

Precisely because proponents of professionalism are fond of drawing parallels between teachers and physicians, for instance, Labaree anticipates that the implication invited will be that laypersons should have no more say than about how a teacher conducts a class than about how a surgeon conducts an operation. (The field of medicine, of course, unlike public education, has neither been rooted in nor associated with a tradition of local support and grassroots control.) In any case, erecting barriers to public influence over classroom teaching via a particular conception of professional autonomy challenges a very basic tenet of democratic authority over a public-service function—or so critics claim.[50]

M. Bruce King of the University of Wisconsin–Madison expects that National Board certification will come to represent a new commodity, a marker of social distinction much sought after by ambitious teachers imbued with a technocratic ethic of professionalism. "What the new teaching certificate represents, it seems, is the spread of the mechanisms for social distinction to a field that, until recently, has had little differentiation in status or rank," he observes. "What national board certification is about, at least in part, is extending to teachers the symbolic struggle for cultural capital within their occupational field." Thus, with the certificate, "the Board joins merit pay plans, career ladders, and other proposals that will inaugurate more rigorous classifications and distinctions among educators."[51] Whether more status differentiation among teachers will conduce to better teaching, however, remains to be seen.

In King's view, the effect, if not the intention, of a program of national certification will be "to institute a particular conception of teaching as *the* official and legitimate point of view." It is, he alleges, "an attempt to universalize a dogma, to conceal the indeterminacy of the exercise of power of one over another, to ultimately deny the impact of specific local conditions." It is probable, moreover, he alleges, "that the construction of professional standards, with the force of national certification behind them, will be another instance of educational policy being mandated 'from the top.' This will, more than likely, inhibit opportunities to critically examine schools and teaching, and to grapple with policy issues in their distinct and diverse settings."[52] King concludes that the work of creating national teaching standards must therefore be challenged and perhaps actively opposed.

Other critics, for all their misgivings, are not prepared to go quite that far. Many simply caution against the supposed dangers of replacing broadly based democratic control over education with a narrower form of professional hegemony. Simultaneously, they insist that rigorous teacher standards must remain purely voluntary. Sensible public policy, it is argued, must avoid placing the power and authority of the state behind a particular construction of good teaching: "It is not the business of the democratic state, whether it be a local, state or federal government," Fenstermacher remarks, "to enforce upon its citizens some conception of best theory or best practice."[53] At a time when the knowledge base for teaching is itself in dispute and the moral and political underpinnings of education are just beginning to come under sustained scholarly investigation, no one epistemological and moral ideology should be state-sanctioned. It follows accordingly, or so he claims, that efforts such as those of NCATE to displace a state-level minimal review and substitute for it the accredited profession's conception of high standards is "an unjustified and potentially harmful policy direction."[54]

MISCONCEIVED STANDARDS

Critics of uniform accreditation and certification register what may be a valid point when they warn against the dangers of imposing a monolithic system of technocratic controls on all teacher candidates or programs. Unfortunately, these same critics seem to offer little in the way of viable alternatives. Looked at one way, the logic of the argument advanced by detractors leads back to state criteria as the only remaining option—rules and regulations whose supposed advantage, paradoxically, is that they are neither selective enough to exclude marginal preparatory programs from producing teachers for the field nor sufficiently rigorous to guarantee competent teaching graduates from programs that *are* state approved. But to just the extent that they are somehow more "acceptable"—or at least less objectionable—because of their weaknesses, they must inevitably fail in their intended purpose of providing a meaningful level of quality assurance.

From another perspective, the fears of those who oppose national standards may be almost completely unfounded. It seems extremely doubtful, for example, whether competency-based or performance-based requirements of the sort touted by NCATE or the National Board for Professional Teaching Standards will in fact prove capable—as INTASC puts it—of "capturing teachers' reasoned judgments" and evaluating what teachers "can actually do in authentic teaching situations."[55] For all practical purposes, they may turn out be even more innocuous—and ineffectual—than some of the governing regulations already in place.

Superficially considered, outcomes-based evaluation appears to offer an attractive alternative to traditional forms of assessment, if only because it circumvents the seeming futility of trying to gauge teacher quality as a direct function of credit hours or specific courses completed. Instead, the process focuses directly on results, attempting to determine what it is prospective teachers actually can do. Yet for all its surface plausibility, on both theoretical and practical grounds, there would seem to be ample reason for doubting whether National Board certification criteria and NCATE accreditation standards *in their present performance-based forms* can succeed in fulfilling their intended purposes.

Critics of PBTE, or performance-based teacher education in the 1960s and 1970s, it is worth recalling, took strong exception to the assumption that the act of teaching ever can be exhausted by, or fully translated into, a discrete set of competencies or performances; and they assailed the entire notion that it was possible to do so as woefully atomistic and reductively behaviorist in nature. Much was made as well of the confusion and ambiguity generated by combining or intermingling "knowledge" propositions (knowing *that* something is the case), "dispositions" (hypothetical or potential tendencies or inclinations to engage in some particular activity), and "performative" statements (assertions requiring some actual manifestation or demonstration of the fact that one knows *how* to do something) in evaluative judgments governing teachers. Little has changed since; and today's attempted resurrection of the PBTE concept by official accrediting and certification agencies likely will fare no better at critics' hands this time around. In the meantime, on a more pragmatic level, the current adaptation of PBTE for both licensure and program approval purposes offers a quite limited and tractable set of issues for reconsideration.

Only in a narrow ex post facto sense, for example, does it seem feasible to make any judgment about the actual quality of a teacher preparation program based on whether its students have an "understanding" of "collaboration with school colleagues, parents, and agencies in the larger community for supporting students' learning and well-being." Again, the NCATE prescription for teachers to engage in "effective interactions with parents for supporting students' learning and well-being" seems unexceptional—desirable even. But as formulated, it hardly can be made to serve in any meaningful fashion as an actual standard or criterion against which to judge the adequacy of a teacher's preparatory program.[56] Similar difficulties attend most of the other core standards expressed as outcomes: They appear to say something concrete and specific but, on closer inspection, their vagueness and generality precludes any possibility of grounding real and meaningful judgments upon them.

Few teachers' programs, for example, would have difficulty making the case that they afford their students opportunities "to reflect on their teaching and its effects on student growth and learning."[57] Likewise, the NCATE requirement that program faculty "use a variety of instructional strategies that reflect an understanding of different models and approaches to learning" is sufficiently inclusive as to mark out almost nothing in particular by way of instruction.[58] Similarly, few faculty in colleges or schools of education, if obliged to do so, would have much trouble pressing the claim (whether justified or not) that their instruction encouraged "the candidate's development of reflection, critical thinking, problem solving, and professional dispositions."[59]

For all of these reasons, it is difficult to resist the conclusion that many—although not necessarily all—of the standards so much feared by critics are in fact "empty." Expressed as "performances" or "competencies," they are broad enough not to exclude much of anything; or they are ambiguous and allow an almost infinite range of interpretations and applications; or, finally and most commonly, they do not link back to identifiable features or aspects of the programs they are supposed to govern.

Ironically, in a few instances much-maligned state regulations actually reflect a more coherent and intelligible use of teacher performance indicators and criteria than do standards developed so far at the national level. Kentucky's guidelines, to cite a case in point, elucidate standards, specify performance criteria for applying the standards, and also supply a contrasting descriptor to help clarify each criterion more precisely. It is stipulated, for example, that a teacher's instructional plan should integrate "skills, thinking processes, and content across disciplines"—which is then narratively contrasted with a plan that "focuses on discrete skills and knowledge in separate disciplines." Again, the teacher is called on to provide "learning experiences that encourage students to be adaptable, flexible, resourceful, and creative," as opposed to one that only requires students "to follow prescribed or teacher-directed processes and strategies."[60]

Needless to add, while these sorts of indicators undoubtedly could be helpful for evaluating teachers (either experienced practitioners or student interns completing their practice teaching), their linkage back to the substance or content of a preparatory program would be exceedingly difficult to document. That is, it would be hard to show that the performances enumerated had ensued in any specific way as the direct consequent of some particular form of preparation completed prior to student teaching.

Leaving aside the question of whether PBTE offers desirable features outweighing its disadvantages, there may be nothing inherently unworkable, at least in principle, about employing performance-based standards for teacher *licensure*—provided always that certain critical conditions are satisfied and it is understood that no finite enumeration of performance indicators of themselves would be sufficient for ascertaining overall teaching competence. Briefly, and at the risk of reiterating what ought to be self-evident, locutions combining "knowledge" or "understanding" of information would have to be carefully sorted out and held distinct from purely descriptive statements about discrete "performances," that is, demonstrations of a capacity to engage in certain actions. (A teacher could have knowledge or an understanding of something, after all, while still lacking the ability to convey that knowledge to others.) Confusion arises when different orders of knowing and behaving are conjoined.

Second, specifications of what it is teacher candidates ought to be able to do would need to be as specific, unambiguous, and exact as possible. Some rudimentary degree of conceptual precision would be needed in terms of agreed-upon operational definitions for each term employed. (A hypothetical counterexample might read, "The teacher encourages a positive learning environment reflective of best practice in teaching.") Unless it is known what qualifies as markers for "a positive learning environment," for example, it would be impossible to ascertain whether the environment the teacher provides is in fact "reflective of," or congruent with, "best practice"—further assuming, of course, some general agreement attends the meaning of "best practice."

Third, and more important still, performative declarations would have to be susceptible to an observer's decision that the requisite behavior either had or had not occurred. (A contrary example of a declaration unlikely to permit any such determination might be "The teacher strives to facilitate and foster the holistic intellectual, emotional, and moral development of students.") The verdict, in other words, ought to be dichotomous: Either the standard has been met or it has not; and it should be possible to determine which is the case. Alternatively, if the objection is made that standards should allow judgments about *graduated degrees of compliance*—that the performance in question partly fulfilled the standard but did not fully meet its intent—then it would be necessary to have at hand some means to guide judgments about the degree of conformity exhibited.

Fourth, as much as possible, normative considerations would need to be isolated, or more clearly distinguishable, from purely factual or empirical considerations than is now the case. The more common pattern today is to find the former embedded within the latter, well illustrated by such statements as "The teacher seeks to provide the least restrictive learning environment possible for exceptional learners," or "The teacher strives to facilitate student awareness of cultural diversity and the importance of social harmony within today's multicultural society." There is nothing indefensible about incorporating normatively evaluative elements within the text of a standard, of course, so long as they are clearly stated and recognizable for what they are. But overall, in this respect and others, judged by each of the foregoing "standards for standards," national licensure criteria would still seem to stand in need of much further refinement.

Finally, and minimally, adequate provision must be made in a performance-based teacher evaluation system for multiple observations of a candidate's behavior. There needs to be a system for repeated sampling and judging of the prospective teacher's performance over some extended period of time, presumably as it occurs in a "real-world" classroom setting. If the argument is made that a candidate's recorded responses to test items on some paper-and-pencil examination ought to qualify as "performances" as well, as should the student's assembly of a portfolio, or responses made to questions posed during the course of a personal interview, the only possible rejoinder is to claim that the concept of "performance" has been so expanded and trivialized as to render its meaning unintelligible for all practical purposes.

For reasons already alluded to, an outcomes-based or performance-based approach to teacher-education program *accreditation* seems fraught with even more formidable obstacles. The biggest problem lies with trying to exhibit the linkage or causal connection, if any, between how a prospective graduate performs in some clinical setting, according to some set of standards, and previous training received. It might be thought self-evident that prior training was responsible for whatever success a teacher candidate enjoyed in being performatively evaluated. But assuming a connection between the two and demonstrating it as fact might be two different matters. It is at least conceivable, for instance, that factors responsible for an intern's successful performance assessment might have little, if anything, to do with courses he or she completed during the preparatory program; that preclinical training was superfluous or irrelevant; that student outcomes owed more to intervening learning that had taken place during the clinical internship; or that entirely fortuitous variables of one sort or another were at work, perhaps such that the candidate was able to compensate for deficiencies or shortcomings in training. In sum, even the most exacting of performance standards would be ill-adapted for assessing the overall quality of a teacher's preparatory program of studies. As for outcomes-based program accreditation standards now in existence, the most charitable estimation must be that most fall far short of accomplishing their goal of ensuring authentic teacher competence.

Most regulatory standards governing teacher preparation make ritual obeisance to general education, for example, although few attempt to specify its recommended substance or content. In this respect rules and regulations appear to miss an important point, one often emphasized by outside critics of education—namely, that most of today's teachers are poorly grounded in the liberal arts and more deficient still in their knowledge of the subjects they presume to teach. Admittedly, as undergraduates, prospective teachers are required to take far more liberal-arts courses than education classes; and both schools or colleges of education and state regulatory agencies often do go to great lengths in specifying minimum hour requirements or in controlling how general-studies patterns are to be distributed across the various disciplines. The National Council for Accreditation of Teacher Education, however, makes only cursory reference to the general-education component recommended for teacher candidates.

Baird W. Whitlock of Midwestern State University in Texas claims "we all really know what is needed in the training of good teachers." What is required, he argues, "is a good, strong general education with courses that require hard work and real knowledge on the part of future teachers."[61] Yet the preponderance of evidence shows that students intending to pursue a teaching career today typically are not broadly or liberally educated persons upon graduation, even though many were trained in "accredited" teacher education programs. Hence, the relative lack of attention paid to general education requirements reflected by licensure and certification requirements—or, more precisely, their tendency to emphasize minimum hour totals or courses rather than their actual content—is all the more unfortunate. If findings from a 1985 study of the transcripts of 3,283 education graduates and 2,760 arts and science graduates at 17 major state universities throughout the South, conducted by the Southern Regional Education Board (SREB), are still applicable or typical nationwide, for example, there seems to be cause for concern.[62]

Revealed by the SREB study was the fact that three-quarters of all teachers from the 17 universities included in the survey had graduated without taking any courses in foreign languages, economics, philosophy, chemistry, or physics. Almost half had taken no political science whatsoever. Fewer still had completed a course in geography. Elementary-education majors, it was discovered, had taken an average of only 6 percent of their college course work in mathematics and 9 percent in English, the two subjects that elementary teachers spend most of their time teaching; whereas pedagogical and physical education courses combined occupied nearly half their college studies. It was further reported that prospective secondary teachers had taken significantly fewer courses in their major teaching field than had arts and science graduates who had specialized in the same disciplines, partly because many institutions held education students to a less demanding standard than that required of liberal arts students.

Detailed transcript analysis showed that the academic courses future high-school teachers completed, either to satisfy their general-studies requirements or those within their majors, were mostly lower-level and introductory courses. In practically every field except foreign languages, in fact, prospective secondary teachers had completed fewer advanced or upper-level courses in their academic major than had arts and science students majoring in the same disciplines. While regular science majors, for example, had completed half or more of their credits in upper-level courses, students intending to become science teachers in the lower schools had earned no more than one-third of their major credits in advanced courses. Students specializing in some other field besides mathematics completed no more than one-fifth of the total mathematics credits they earned in advanced-level courses, compared with over half for arts and sciences students not majoring in mathematics. Many education majors satisfied their requirements only by completing remedial classes intended specifically for teacher trainees.

Suggestive of the same general pattern, fully 83 percent of all future teachers not majoring in English had never taken an upper-level English course. Once again, many fulfilled their English requirement only by taking watered-down remedial courses.[63] Consistent with the SREB findings were those from a 1984 study of academic transcripts for graduates of Arizona State University's education college, where fully 95 percent of the science, mathematics, and English credits earned by teachers in training were completed by enrollments in introductory courses at the freshman level.[64] Equally disturbing were findings from both the SREB study and the Arizona State survey indicating that education students often met liberal-arts course requirements late in their programs by transferring credits earned in less stringent courses taken at community colleges, many doing so only after having failed equivalent university courses at their home institutions.

Additional evidence for the weak academic preparation of teachers was furnished in a 1985 study of 101 graduates of the elementary-education program at Central Washington University. It was found that out of a combined total of 3,479 courses taken by education students during their preparatory training as undergraduates, only 49 were in history, and 44 of those were in regional Northwest history. Only one student from the sample of 101 undergraduates had taken a course in Western civilization.[65]

Changes in state certification requirements have since begun to address these deficiencies, although to what extent and how successfully are not always evident. If genuine reform is to occur, it should be argued, what will be needed is a clearer, more comprehensive specification (although not necessarily some lengthy enumeration) of the actual substance or content—the basic knowledge, terms, conceptual apparatus, modes of inquiry, and so forth—specific to each discipline or field future teachers are obliged to study. In the final analysis, nothing less will suffice when it comes to setting usable standards for general education.

If both state and national program accreditation or licensure standards tend to describe the content of required general-studies courses in fairly vague and abbreviated terms, the same is equally true, if not even more so, when it comes to education courses—as in Oklahoma, where a mandated sequence anticipates that students "shall demonstrate a knowledge of" the "appropriate use of a variety of communication patterns within the classroom"; "cultural pluralism as it relates to the public schools"; "appropriate organization of instructional resources and materials for effective teaching"; "the development of education as a profession"; and so on.[66] Rules in Kansas are somewhat more detailed and specific in outlining 17 different "competencies" a student must demonstrate relative to "knowledge of the importance of self esteem, and techniques to foster the development of positive self esteem in students"; "knowledge of communication theory and techniques to foster the development of verbal and nonverbal communication"; "knowledge of techniques for teaching goal-setting and decision-making"; and "knowledge of major categories of exceptionality, and the application of this knowledge to teaching."[67]

What conventional standards such as these cannot do, even though they may be dressed up in the appurtenances of outcomes, competencies, and performances, is to ensure that education courses no longer deserve the calumny heaped on them by a long succession of critics. In the 1940s and 1950s, Alfred Bestor's broadside (*Educational Wastelands*) dismissed pedagogy courses as a stupendous waste of time; James Koerner's diatribe in the early 1960s (*The Miseducation of American Teachers*) derided pedagogical courses as "repetitious, dull, and ambiguous." In the same vein was the critique offered by Charles Silberman in 1970 (*Crisis in the Classroom*), which faulted teacher education as a whole for its endemic "mindlessness." In the 1980s, grammarian Richard Mitchell (*The Graves of Academe*) offered another noteworthy illustration, when, with devastating effect, like Koerner, he poked fun at jargon-ridden educationist rhetoric and judged that the entire teacher education enterprise was presided over by intellectual "pygmies." More recently, it will be recalled, it was investigative journalist Rita Kramer in the 1990s (*Ed School Follies*) who concluded that most education courses she had personally observed were "deadly dull." Joining in the indictment have been countless others, as in the SREB study, where, as education correspondent Thomas Toch complained in 1991, it was painfully obvious that so far as most education courses required of students were concerned, there was not much substance to be found and still less rigor. The typical professional education sequence, as he judged it, could be said to amount to little more than "a profoundly anti-intellectual enterprise."[68]

Sweeping condemnations of all education courses as unreservedly vacuous and puerile are manifestly unfair, of course, particularly since, as many students themselves often will attest, at least some of them can be as intellectually challenging, exciting, and relevant as any others to be found in collegiate curricula. Licensure and program accreditation standards of themselves, of course, cannot be relied on to ensure that preparatory courses for future teachers are well managed and competently taught. But the real point of having criteria in the first place, it would appear, is to ensure that the preparatory curriculum accomplishes what it is supposed to achieve, as reflecting good practice and the best thinking in the field. And if performance-based measures for courses cannot be made as detailed and specific as is required without becoming hopelessly cumbersome, then the best alternative is to devise ways of spelling out in summary form the *substantive* outlines of whatever knowledge and skills are supposed to be conveyed within programs (whether the unit of assessment is a specific course, a workshop, independent study, a learning "module," or whatever).

It may matter little whether colleges and universities assume primary responsibility for accomplishing the task, provided the work is subject to some type of external surveillance, or whether state departments of education undertake to draw up the requisite specifications. The critical consideration is that the work be accomplished in such a way that standards for checking on whether learning has occurred are truly functional and meaningful. If performance outcomes, courses, or minimum credit hours are not sufficient to identify what it is prospective teachers must come to know, to value, to appreciate, and to be able to do, then the best remaining alternative is some concrete specification of what it is they are expected to learn during the course of their programs of study.

Sometimes the rejoinder is heard that standards do not stand alone and that quality assurance is reinforced through teacher examinations— one of the most widely adopted reforms in recent years within teacher preparation. Unfortunately, as critics such as Thomas Toch and many others hasten to point out, as currently constituted, "the tests are keeping only the most grossly incompetent teachers out of the nation's classrooms; they aren't tough enough to do more than that." Compared with the rigorous entrance and licensing examinations common in medicine, law, and other professions, the majority of the teacher tests currently in use do little more than measure rudimentary academic and literacy skills. "Rather than promoting the cause of teacher professionalism by setting high standards that signal to talented candidates that teaching is both a serious and prestigious profession," Toch judges, "the majority of the state teacher tests aspire only to ensure that teachers are literate."[69]

In more than a few instances, for example, teachers are still tested at a level *below* that demanded of their own students—knowledge of simple percentages, fractions, geometric shapes, basic grammar, reading ability—information and skills any well-educated elementary or junior high student ought to be able to manage with ease. Even the National Teaching Examinations, the tests most widely relied on in state licensing procedures, tend to be relatively undemanding, despite their pretensions to selectivity and rigor. Much the same could be said of most of the state-mandated tests of teachers' academic subject-matter knowledge. Tests that purportedly measure so-called professional knowledge about teaching tend to be even easier still.

Not only are most state teacher examinations absurdly simplistic, but reportedly the scores needed to pass them have been set astonishingly low. In some states it is customary to allow teacher candidates to take the examinations as many times as necessary in order to pass.[70] Even so, failure rates reported offer few grounds for much confidence in the basic literacy proficiency of the teacher talent pool nationwide.

The problem of "misconceived" standards thus amounts to an ineluctable failure on the part of many state education officials and most of the rest of the so-called educational establishment to specify whatever is deemed important or essential in the training of teachers; an inability or unwillingness on the part of many to contemplate meaningful and specific criteria for determining whether in fact programs are accomplishing what they claim to be doing; and a manifest reluctance to hold prospective teachers to whatever standards are agreed on to govern initial licensure.

Creating minimum standards for teacher preparation is both feasible and potentially useful. It can and should occur within individual programs, within institutions, at the state level—perhaps even at a national level. But bringing about substantive reform equal to its rhetoric will not prove possible until stakeholders at all levels in the enterprise of teacher preparation begin to appreciate the full dimensions of the challenge they confront. Growing evidence at state and national levels suggests instead that teacher educators are more preoccupied with extending and elaborating the machinery of accreditation and licensure—generating formal displays of public accountability—than they are in engaging the authentic substance of what meaningful reform demands.

PART III

FUTURE POSSIBILITIES

6

WHAT EXPERIENCED TEACHERS RECOMMEND: A SURVEY AND ANALYSIS

INTRODUCTION: TEACHERS AS PROGRAM EVALUATORS

A traditional method of evaluating a teacher education program relies on follow-up data supplied by recent graduates. Those polled are asked to complete a survey, providing judgments as to the worth of the program and its various courses in helping former students in their new teaching positions.[1] Program assessments of this type have become quite common. Dorothy H. Mayne, for example, reported the results of an extensive survey undertaken by the University of Alaska to improve its teacher-training program and services to teachers using an instrument completed by 52 principals and teachers in 46 rural Alaskan high schools.[2] Similar in purpose was a study of the Master of Education degree program in Special Education at the University of North Carolina at Chapel Hill.[3] Data collected both from students and from teachers who were program graduates were utilized to revise the content of certain courses, to change the overall pattern of courses required, and to modify preservice student teaching assignments.

A study by the University of North Florida was conducted to ascertain how beginning teachers who were former students and who had subsequently been hired by Florida school systems evaluated the quality and relevance of their preparation.[4] Respondents were asked to rate themselves on 27 generic teaching competencies and to write comments on their self-estimated strengths and weaknesses during their first year of teaching. Graduates were further requested to supply specific suggestions for improving North Florida's preservice program. Beginning teachers reportedly wanted a more "reality based" preparation, with more field experiences and opportunities for "hands-on" interaction with schoolchildren. Also recommended were support groups for new teachers, telephone hot lines, and seminars on problems most likely to be encountered by first-year teachers.

Somewhat more ambitious in scope was a postgraduate assessment effort initiated by the Planning and Evaluation Unit of the Colorado State Department of Education.[5] Survey forms were received from 1,991 first- and third-year teachers who had been asked to rate each of the components of their respective preservice programs on a five-point scale according to its estimated importance for effective teaching and on the basis of the adequacy of preparation that particular program component had supplied. Once again teachers reported a need for more practical experience in real classroom settings during their preservice training. Specific applications of instruction were more highly valued than theory or research in the early stages of their careers. Among other aspects of programs allegedly needing improvement were courses in classroom management and instruction to help neophyte teachers deal with parents as well as with special populations of students—multicultural, the gifted, slow learners, and at-risk learners. Frequently cited also was the need to provide trainees more thorough preparation for grading and assessing student performance.

Don Holste and Don Matthews reported on a program evaluation survey initiated by the Council on Teacher Education of the College of Education at the University of Illinois.[6] The 1991 survey was the first of several reports using data collected from graduates one and three years following graduation, from current students prior to and upon completion of student teaching, from employers of former students (superintendents and principals), and from cooperating teachers. Graduates were asked to assess their own knowledge and skills, to evaluate the quality of their preservice training, and to indicate how the University of Illinois preservice program might be improved. Once again items identified as in need of strengthening included instruction relating to classroom management techniques, multicultural issues and perspectives, theory and principles of how students learn, and information on child and adolescent growth and development.

A three-stage study conducted by Indiana University at South Bend relied on telephone surveys of 201 out of 400 recent teacher-education graduates. Responses to a 46-item questionnaire were elicited, on the basis of which several important program improvements were made.[7] Results from annual follow-up studies at North Dakota State University of graduates of a secondary education preservice program likewise reportedly led to significant changes in the areas of teaching about classroom management, multicultural education, and evaluating student learning.[8] Consistent with similar findings from other studies were those forthcoming from a follow-up assessment of the University of Kentucky's graduates who were first-year teachers participating in the Kentucky Beginning Teacher Internship Program.[9] Respondents were asked to assess the degree of difficulty they were experiencing in each of 20 competency areas. Responses indicated a need for more field experience during preservice training, a better linkage of theory with practice, and a closer articulation or coordination of training courses. The importance of fostering a network of colleagues and university faculty to provide continuing guidance and support to new teachers was stressed by third-year teachers who had graduated from an experimental five-year program sponsored by the Comprehensive Teacher Institute in California.[10]

Many similar follow-up studies utilizing former students' feedback for purposes of program improvement have been undertaken in recent years.[11] Most common are studies that query first-year teachers about the specific strengths and shortcomings of the preservice programs from which they graduated.[12] Some studies have focused on specific aspects of teachers' preservice preparation, such as student teaching or some special type of internship experience, polling students immediately following the experience or subsequent to their graduation.[13] Institutions engaged in the process of changing over from one particular teacher education program to another often have used survey instruments to compare graduates' opinions about the changeover, or to contrast features of the former program with its successor.[14]

Anecdotal data derived from personal interviews with beginning teachers reportedly have been found useful for assessing the quality of training they received as well as for tracking how teachers' viewpoints have changed from their previous expectations as students.[15] A study conducted by Frances O'Connell Rust, for example, examined two beginning teachers' first-year experiences and the contrasting beliefs they expressed over time as indicators of how new teachers manage the transition from being students to autonomous classroom practitioners.[16] In a similar context, Robert P. Craig utilized a narrative account to describe the attitudinal changes, shifts in values, and skills development of a new teacher, changes purportedly useful for redesigning teacher preparatory programs.[17]

Sometimes found useful are independent assessments of the abilities of graduates made by third-person observers rather than direct retrospective assessments supplied by program graduates themselves. A study by Judy Reinhartz and Don M. Beach, for example, sought to determine the effectiveness of a teacher education program by garnering evaluations of its recent graduates from the principals who had hired them after graduation.[18] It also has been suggested that a standing board of former graduates might provide a still more useful source of information for monitoring any given teacher-education program on an ongoing basis.[19]

New teachers (typically those in their first year of service) have been most commonly called upon to assess their own pre-entry training. Less often have experienced teachers been utilized as program evaluators, except perhaps those who were graduates of the particular program under scrutiny, and rarely after their third year or so of classroom experience. In a few isolated instances, however, retired educators with many years of teaching behind them have been invited to offer advice and counsel regarding program changes and improvements. Edwin G. Ralph, to cite a case in point, reported on the results of a survey conducted by the University of Saskatchewan that enlisted the cooperation of retired teachers from western Canada, asking them to offer recommendations for enhancing the institution's undergraduate teacher preparatory program.[20]

Among other suggestions, respondents urged more rigorous screening of program applicants, including the use of such selection measures as personality inventories, personal interviews, and aptitude tests in order to ensure a higher-quality pool of teacher candidates for training. They also endorsed more attention to teaching about differences in instructional and learning styles, more school-based experiences, a restructuring of courses in a more cohesive pattern, and the transfer of responsibility to schools for specific task training.

Researchers at the Educational Testing Service (ETS) in Princeton, New Jersey, have made extensive use of teacher's opinions in identifying knowledge and skills needed by beginning teachers. M. Rosenfeld and R. J. Tannenbaum, for example, asked 2,269 classroom teachers to rate the importance to an entry-level teacher's job of generic "enabling" skills (that is, skills needed to prepare and organize instruction) as applied to the teaching of reading, writing, mathematics, listening, speaking, and interactive communication. Items judged "extremely important" or of "moderate" importance included the ability to determine the main ideas expressed in textual material, skill in performing computations, recognizing basic grammatical errors, and organizing important ideas contained within a text.[21]

An ETS study by Anne Reynolds, Tannenbaum, and Rosenfeld utilized 167 teachers to rate the importance of a series of descriptors organized by "domains" within the elementary curriculum, including (1) elementary school students, (2) professional issues, (3) reading, language arts and literature, (4) mathematics, (5) social studies, (6) science, (7) physical education, (8) health, and (9) visual and performing arts.[22] Highest-ranked items included the need to recognize the signs and symptoms of child abuse, understanding conventions of language and text structure, knowledge about the effects of teaching style on learning, and the affective development of learners. Those polled also were asked to rate the relative importance of statements pertaining to content-specific pedagogy under the same organizers. Highest-ranked statements included those involving motivational strategies in reading, language arts, and literature; ways of presenting mathematics; teaching strategies in reading, language arts, and literature; motivational and instructional strategies in mathematics; and ways of presenting and teaching science.

Closely related in purpose and structure was a survey in which 335 teachers were asked to rate the importance of general principles of teaching and learning that newly licensed teachers allegedly need, regardless of subject matter or grade level taught.[23] Organizing categories included (1) human development and the learning process, (2) curriculum planning and design, (3) management of the learning process, (4) assessment and the learning process, and (5) professional issues related to teaching and learning. Highest-rated areas included motivational techniques, disciplinary strategies and styles, teaching strategies, relationships of instructional activities to learner characteristics, stages or patterns of affective development among learners, learning climate, structuring evaluation plans, and organizing lessons according to instructional objectives. Lowest-rated knowledge statements included those pertaining to the social, political, and historical events that influence curricula planning; roles and functions of professional organizations; political issues affecting public education; and definitions of education held by curricula planners. In general, knowledge related more distantly to the teacher's immediate interaction with students (professional issues, measurement principles, philosophical and sociological influences on curricula) was deemed to be of "moderate" importance only.

Assistance from 3,434 teachers was called for in yet another ETS study of "tasks" demanded of beginning instructors.[24] Respondents were asked to rate the importance of a list of explanatory descriptors organized according to six "domains": (1) planning and preparing instruction, (2) managing the classroom, (3) implementing instruction, (4) evaluating student learning and instructional effectiveness, (5) administrative responsibilities, and (6) professional responsibilities. Likewise solicited were estimations of the contribution of each to teaching effectiveness and judgments as to how well each teacher's own preparatory training had provided an opportunity to achieve proficiency in performing each task listed. Cited as most important were the tasks of enhancing students' confidence and self-esteem, monitoring in-class student behavior, establishing rules and procedures, managing classroom time effectively, facilitating student learning, and encouraging pupils' efforts.

Judged highly important to teacher effectiveness was the ability to encourage a variety of critical thinking skills, facilitating student learning and effort, and enhancing student confidence and self-esteem. Respondents identified as strengths of their preservice training opportunities for learning how to prepare lesson plans, to develop a variety of teaching approaches, to write instructional objectives, to use motivational techniques and activities, and to enhance student confidence and self-esteem.

Reynolds has argued that the apparent discrepancy between what school and state administrators and teacher educators feel they are entitled to expect of beginning teachers and what first-year novices actually know and can do should be a matter of some concern.[25] Newly licensed elementary teachers, it is argued, should be able to perform in a "competent, if not proficient," manner most of the teaching skills that more experienced teachers perform. Beginning teachers should have a command of the pedagogical principles that will enable them to perform essential teaching tasks, especially those required to implement lessons and manage the learning environment. Finally, first-year teachers should have a thorough knowledge of the traditional academic disciplines

incorporated within school curricula (reading, language arts and literature, mathematics, social studies, science—and to a lesser degree—
health, physical education, and the visual and performing arts).

Evidence adduced from ETS studies suggests that beginning
teachers need more time for planning than do their more experienced
colleagues. Neophytes typically lack multiple contingency plans for
organizing lessons they can implement as the need arises. They experience difficulties in adapting to the needs of individual students. They
lack facility with basic managerial routines such as classroom organization and discipline. Last, beginners appear to lack content-specific
pedagogical understanding—that is, they do not know subjects in ways
that allow them to explain them to their students. According to Reynolds, each generalization, to the extent that it is valid and accurate,
carries with it implications for the preservice preparation of teachers.[26]

Whereas experienced teachers—as distinct from novices—have
been recruited to make judgments on the relative importance or relevance of teacher tasks and competencies in the abstract, and beginners
often are asked to assess the adequacy of their own preservice preparation, few attempts have been made to involve teachers with years of
practical experience in discussions of teacher education programs.
Experienced practitioners have been utilized as respondents in formal
studies of teaching as an activity or process. Yet, ironically, scant
attention has been paid to the potential contribution seasoned classroom veterans might make to discussions regarding the specifics of
teacher education programs in general. Accordingly, the study here
reported was undertaken as an attempt to explore teachers' opinions
about the appropriate content and proportions of entry-level preservice
teacher preparation.

THE SAMPLE AND SURVEY INSTRUMENT

Prior to the development of a survey questionnaire, lengthy individual
interviews were conducted with a total of 23 public school teachers in
three mid-sized school districts, located in the northwest portion of the
state of Arkansas, in the northeastern corner of Oklahoma, and adjacent
to the southern border of Missouri. Six males and 17 females in all were
interviewed. Thirteen were elementary teachers; ten were certified to
teach at the secondary level. Their teaching experience ranged from ten
to 17 years, averaging 14.5 years. Respondents were asked to list and to

describe briefly in open-ended narrative form the content of various "knowledge areas" or "professional studies components" each considered essential to the formal preservice preparation of beginning teachers. Interviewees were asked to confine their respective enumerations to descriptions of essential *knowledge content* rather than specific skills, abilities, or competencies teaching neophytes ought to possess.

The pilot sample group collectively generated 83 descriptors of information or knowledge judged to be important for beginning teachers. Once duplicated content was eliminated, the list of knowledge was reducible to a total of 11 information clusters. These remaining descriptors were then combined and recast in order to parallel closely the ten major "professional studies components" stipulated as essential ingredients of basic preparatory programs in the then-current 1990 version of teacher education accreditation standards of the National Council for Accreditation of Teacher Education.[27] Categories included: (1) curriculum development and design; (2) instructional planning and management; (3) evaluation, assessment, and measurement methodology; (4) classroom supervision and behavior management; (5) instructional technology; (6) student development and learning; (7) learner exceptionality; (8) school law and legal aspects of education; (9) multiculturalism and globalism; and (10) social, historical, and philosophic foundations of education.

A survey instrument subsequently was developed to elicit three data sets: first, basic demographic characteristics and background information for each respondent; second, his or her estimation of the relative degree of importance of each of the knowledge areas specified; and, third, the number of hours of instruction considered sufficient for imparting essential information within each category. The response rate from the 2,110 surveys distributed exceeded 69 percent. Altogether, responses were collected from a convenience sample of 1,471 elementary, middle-school, and high-school teachers currently employed in the state of Arkansas (drawn from 50 different school districts ranging from large urban to small rural), Oklahoma (two mid-sized districts), Texas (three districts), Missouri (three districts), and New York (one district). Whereas no formal effort was made to derive a statistically rigorous microcosm of the total relevant population, the demographic characteristics of those polled did not appear to differ markedly from those of teachers nationwide.

Of the respondents, 117 (8 percent) reported two or fewer years of full-time classroom teaching experience; 171 (12 percent) indicated three to five years of experience; and 988, or 67 percent, had completed more than five years of teaching experience. (The full range of years of experience cited extended from 1 to 40 years; the sample average was 17.) These figures compare with an estimated 9.7 percent of all teachers nationwide with less than three years of experience; 26 percent having 3 to 9 years of teaching; 39 percent with 10 to 20 years of previous experience; and about 25 percent reporting more than two decades of experience, as supplied in a 1990-91 national survey conducted by the National Center for Educational Statistics.[28]

Those polled in the present study included 259 males, or 18 percent of the total, and 1,183 females, representing 82 percent of those responding. Males were slightly underrepresented, as compared with National Center statistics indicating that as of 1990-91 roughly 28 percent of all teachers nationwide were males. In the present study, females were correspondingly overrepresented, based on a reported national percentage figure of 72 percent for all female teachers for the same school year.

Nationally, slightly over 51 percent of all teachers employed in public schools in 1990-91 (an estimated 1.3 million in all) were teaching at the elementary level and 47 percent (1.2 million) were reported to be teaching at the secondary level.[29] Of the estimated 2.5 million teachers employed in the fall of 1992, according to National Center tallies, 54 percent, or 1.3 million were elementary instructors, and 36 percent, or nearly 918,000, were postelementary teachers.[30] A total of 846 teachers, or almost 58 percent of those included in the 1995-96 sample studied, were certified to teach at the elementary level. Taking into account multiple certifications, 101 teachers participating in the current study were licensed to teach at the preschool or early childhood level; 555 were employed as middle or junior high teachers; and 751 reported holding certification to teach at the secondary level (grade seven and above).

Nationwide, it has been estimated, nearly 52 percent of all public classroom teachers are holders of the bachelor's degree, 42 percent have a master's degree, and 5.4 percent possess a specialist or doctoral degree.[31] Within this study sample, 894 teachers, or 63 percent, listed the bachelor's degree as the highest credential attained; 442, or 31 percent, held the master's degree; 81, or 6 percent, reported possessing a specialist degree or certificate; and 9 respondents reportedly had been awarded a doctoral degree. The average number of academic credits earned beyond the bachelor's degree was 16 hours.

MAJOR FINDINGS

Preservice instruction designed to help teacher candidates become proficient in *curriculum planning and development,* organizing instructional units, lesson planning, and utilizing appropriate learning resources was judged to be "essential" by 913, or 62 percent, of the sample surveyed. A total of 421 teachers judged such instruction to be "important" (29 percent). Only 82 respondents, or less than 6 percent of the sample, judged the relevant instruction to be "fairly useful" or as "relatively unimportant." Thirty-nine percent of those polled (569 respondents) reportedly felt that the curriculum planning and design component of a preservice teacher education program could be covered adequately in a single three-credit-hour course. One in every four believed the material could be addressed within the confines of a two-credit-hour or one-credit-hour course, or in a brief workshop or short course. About one-third of the sample indicated more time, ranging from 90 to 135 hours of formal instruction, might be required to provide adequate training.

Close to 38 percent of those queried (557) considered *instructional planning and management* as a second "essential" knowledge category. Almost half (45.3 percent, or 667 respondents) judged preparation in this respect to be "important." Close to three-quarters (1,107), however, felt that the necessary information and skills entailed could be imparted either by means of a brief workshop (6 percent), a one-credit-hour course consisting of 15 hours of instruction (17 percent of the sample), a course involving 30 hours of instruction (14 percent), or by means of a three-credit-hour course consisting of 45 hours of instruction (41 percent). Slightly over one-fifth of those responding (302) indicated still more time might be necessary.

An instructional component devoted to *evaluation and assessment methodology* was deemed "essential" by 467 teachers (nearly one-third of the total sample), as "important" by 667 respondents (45 percent), as "fairly useful" by 17 percent (252), and as "relatively unimportant" by 29 individuals (2 percent). Fully 83 percent of those responding (1,216) indicated they felt the necessary material could be conveyed with 45 or fewer hours of instruction.

Ninety-four percent of the sample (1,378 respondents) reportedly considered information about *classroom supervision and behavior management* to be "essential" or "important." About 21 percent (312) believed the necessary content could be dealt with in a two-hour or a one-hour course or a workshop; and 36 percent (526) indicated they felt a three-credit-hour course consisting of 45 hours of instruction would be necessary for the purpose. Twenty-six percent (387) recommended two three-hour courses; and 10 percent (154) were willing to devote three courses to the topic.

Almost one in every three persons surveyed (459) characterized instruction in the use of *teaching technology* as an "essential" component in preservice teacher preparation. Almost half the sample, 46 percent (684), judged it "important." The remainder, or slightly over one-fifth of those polled, assigned the topic a lower degree of importance. About 9 percent felt the information could be handled in a short workshop; 20 percent felt the information might require a one-credit-hour course (15 hours of instruction); 247 teachers (18 percent) suggested a two-credit-hour course; and nearly 35 percent (490) indicated that a single three-hour course would suffice. The remaining one-fifth or so of the sample (283) recommended more than 45 hours of instruction.

Almost 72 percent of those surveyed (1,051) judged information about *student development and learning* to be "important" or "essential." Over 78 percent (1,157) indicated coverage could be achieved within the confines of a single three-hour course (42 percent), in a course bearing one-credit-hour (15 percent), a two-credit-hour course (17 percent), or a workshop consisting of less than 15 hours of instruction (7 percent). The other one-fifth or so of the sample indicated additional time might be needed.

Teaching about *learner differences and exceptionality* and strategies for teaching special-needs children was characterized as an "essential" preservice preparatory program component by 42 percent of those queried (611) and as "important" by another 616 individuals (42 percent). Approximately 22 percent (319) indicated the information could be addressed in a workshop, a one-credit-hour course, or a two-credit-hour course. Thirty-six percent (528) suggested a three-hour course. Another 416, or 28 percent, felt that material on exceptionality would require more than 45 hours of instruction.

Teaching about *school law* and *legal aspects of education* was considered "essential" by 21 percent of those polled (312) and as "important" by 673 teachers, or nearly 46 percent of all respondents. Thirty percent (443) considered law-related information "fairly useful" or "relatively unimportant." About 19 percent (276) felt a short course or workshop would be sufficient for considering all essential information under this category.

Another 23 percent (336) thought it might require a one-credit-hour course consisting of 15 hours of instruction. Eighteen percent (267) urged a two-credit-hour course; and 29 percent (431) felt 45 hours of instruction in a three-hour course were warranted. The remaining 7 percent (107 respondents) urged more time devoted to legal matters.

Consideration of issues involving *multiculturalism and globalism in education* was considered "fairly useful" by 44 percent (654) of those responding. Only 30 percent (437), however, viewed this potential program component as "important" (345) or "essential" (92); and nearly a fifth of those responding (291 teachers) dismissed it as "relatively unimportant." Approximately 96 percent were *un*willing to devote more than a single three-credit-hour course to multicultural or international perspectives on education; and 75 percent (1,105) recommended considerably *less* time and attention assigned to them.

Much the same pattern prevailed with respect to the *social, historical, and philosophical foundations of education* as a proposed program element. Almost a quarter (336) of those questioned downplayed the importance of the category, regarding it as "relatively unimportant." Slightly under half (49 percent) deemed it "fairly useful," and another 23 percent (330) of the sample identified educational foundations as "important." Less than 4 percent (56 individuals) selected "essential" as a descriptor. Seventy-four percent (1,083) indicated a workshop, a one-credit-hour course, or a two-credit-hour course would suffice for treating issues of social policy and issues in education. No more than 17 percent (257) indicated a willingness to reserve a single three-credit-hour course for treating the foundations of education; and less than 3 percent (42) felt more emphasis was needed.

Teachers in the sample polled were afforded opportunities to supply open-ended responses within an "other" category (that is, to identify preservice program components besides those included within the first ten knowledge areas specified). Altogether, 581 narrative comments were recorded. A total of 88, or 15 percent, spoke to the need for beginning teachers to receive formal training in communication and public speaking, managing school-community relations, and parent-teacher conferencing. More specifically, the need for teachers to be trained in ways of encouraging parental involvement in, and support for, the work of the school was frequently cited.

In descending order of frequency, other areas of identified need included strategies for effecting cooperative planning and collaboration among teachers in the work setting; strategies and techniques for addressing the needs of at-risk students and, more generally, for dealing with issues of child abuse, drugs, dysfunctional families, gangs, divorce, and so forth; assistance with managing record keeping (budgets, inventories, reporting requirements); techniques for effective time management; dealing with job-related stress; teacher professionalism (duties and obligations); methods of teaching nonnative children; fostering cooperative and individualized learning; professional organizations; and questions involving the sponsorship of students' extracurricular organizations.

Besides being asked to identify the major component elements or areas of knowledge that ought to be incorporated within an ideal teacher preparation program, respondents were asked to indicate the optimal length of the student teaching experience. A majority (828 of the sample, representing 56 percent of the total) endorsed the traditional 16-week period, corresponding to the duration of a typical academic semester. Another 24 percent or so (359 respondents) urged a full year's experience. Twelve percent (172) indicated that eight weeks would suffice. Other responses ranged from a recommended length of as little as two weeks up to two full years. Eleven respondents (less than 1 percent) cited a half year to a full year as the ideal duration of student teaching; 16 (slightly over 1 percent) cited an experience lasting between 18 and 27 weeks. Nineteen teachers (less than two percent) endorsed a 12-week regimen; while another 12 (less than 1 percent) cited figures ranging from 6 to 10 weeks. One respondent spoke for many, however, in commenting that the "length [of student teaching] doesn't matter; it's the environment that counts."

Narrative comments often addressed particular specific features of student teaching. Most often cited was the need for early observation and supervised "hands-on" experience in an actual classroom setting; the desirability of close supervision and tutelage from experienced teachers; the importance of effecting a smooth transition from initial observation, through one-on-one tutoring, to full classroom independence and autonomy; and the need for novices to gain experience teaching with different teachers, at different levels, and in different schools where possible. In many instances, those supplying commentary did not distinguish carefully between initial student teaching and some type of more prolonged internship, perhaps encompassing a neophyte's first year or two of full-time teaching. Frequently mentioned also was the need for close mentoring and the importance of providing beginning teachers with a peer support system.

Teachers in the sample also were asked to indicate agreement or disagreement with the following statement: "I believe undergraduate college students who intend to become teachers after they graduate should concentrate on acquiring a broad, general education, and to learn as much as possible about the discipline or subjects they want to teach, *even if it means postponing or limiting the number of courses they take in professional education at the undergraduate level"* (original italics). Nearly two-thirds (65 percent, or 958 respondents) checked "tend to agree" while the remaining third (465) chose "tend to disagree."

Two-thirds of those polled (915 teachers) indicated agreement with the statement "I believe it is useful, and should be possible, to major in professional education at the undergraduate level." The remaining one-third of the sample, or 467 respondents, registered disagreement. However, when the responses were broken down by certification levels, the ratio between those indicating agreement and those expressing disagreement shifted significantly. Whereas fully 72 percent of all teachers certified at *other than* the secondary level reported agreement with the practice of allowing students to major in professional education, only 60 percent of all secondary teachers in the sample concurred.

Thirty-two percent of those in the sample (478) reportedly agreed with the statement "I believe it is useful, and should be possible, to require students who are intending to become teachers to complete a *fifth* year of concentrated training in professional education prior to receiving their bachelor's degrees and licenses to teach." About 65 percent of all respondents (955) disagreed. Response patterns to the statement, however, differed markedly according to highest degree attained among respondents. Seventy-two percent of all teachers whose highest earned credential was the bachelor's degree disagreed with the idea of a mandated fifth year of preparatory training, while 28 percent supported the idea. Among the 442 teachers who were holders of a master's degree, 40 percent supported the proposal to require a fifth year of training; the remaining majority did not. Among the 81 teachers with specialist credentials, over 47 percent supported a fifth year of preparation. Five of the nine teachers with doctoral degrees, or 56 percent of the subsample, indicated support for a fifth-year program. The decreasing size of each subsample makes generalizations hazardous, but as a trend, the tendency to endorse the idea of a fifth year of training did appear to be associated with type of credential possessed.

By an overwhelming margin—90.8 percent to 9.2 percent—those surveyed disagreed with the statement, "I believe future teachers should complete a *master's* degree in education before they are allowed to become certified teachers." Avowed support for master's-level training, once again, appeared to be associated with respondents' academic credentials. Fewer than 7 percent of all teachers holding baccalaureate degrees only (a subset representing 62.5 percent of the total sample) supported the hypothetical proposal to require a beginning teacher to have completed a master's degree. About 13 percent of all teachers with master's degrees reported agreement with the statement; about one-fifth of those holding specialist degrees likewise were supportive. Two teachers with doctorates indicated agreement with master's-level teacher preparation. Overall, narrative comments appended reiterated the theme that current teachers' salaries do not warrant the imposition of lengthy graduate-level training prior to the point of initial entry into teaching.

Finally, when asked to rate the quality (academic rigor, professional relevance, helpfulness, practicality) of the professional preparation for teaching they themselves had previously received, 195 respondents (13 percent) rated it as "very high." Thirty-five percent (512) rated it as "fairly high." Thirty-eight percent (561 responses) characterized prior training as "adequate." Ten percent rated it as "fairly low" (151) or "very low" (29 teachers). In more than two dozen instances, teachers volunteered comments highly critical of professional education courses, ranging from their blanket dismissal as "useless" to charges that they tend to be "unrealistic." In no cases were comments praising education courses forthcoming.

Education professors similarly came in for severe criticism in numerous instances. A common theme was that those who bear primary academic responsibility for training teachers tend to be "out of touch" and isolated from the realities of teaching in a present-day public school classroom. One suggestion repeatedly volunteered was that professors involved in teacher training should be required to return to teaching in lower-level classrooms periodically and for stipulated periods of time in order to remain connected with the future work environment of elementary and secondary teacher candidates.

DISCUSSION

Respondents exhibited a striking degree of unanimity of opinion on the major component elements to be included within a preservice, entry-level teacher preparation program. However, views differed considerably on the *relative importance* assigned to the various knowledge categories stipulated. The knowledge area or domain deemed essential by the highest majority of respondents (83 percent) was that pertaining to classroom supervision and behavior management (maintaining discipline, pacing of activities, time management, techniques for keeping students on task, dealing with disruptive or inattentive students, and so forth). But a clear majority (60 percent) felt all essential information could be conveyed within 45 or fewer hours of didactic instruction, or a single three-credit-hour course.

Almost two out of every three queried felt it was "essential" to include information on curriculum planning and design, including how to organize instructional units, prepare lesson plans, and select learning resources. About the same-sized majority (65 percent) felt the necessary information could be imparted within the time normally taken up by a single three-credit-hour course (40 percent) or, alternatively, within a more abbreviated time frame (25 percent). Thus, even with respect to the two highest-rated categories, in both instances a majority of all teachers surveyed indicated that the information involved could be dealt with adequately *within the limits of a single semester-long three-credit-hour course or its equivalent.* In both cases, between a fifth and a fourth of all respondents indicated the time needed might be considerably less.

Ranking third highest in terms of number of teachers judging the area to be essential was that pertaining to learner differences and exceptionalities (41 percent), followed, in descending order, by instructional planning and management (38 percent), assessment and evaluation (32 percent), instructional technology (31 percent), student development and learning (25 percent), school law (12 percent), multiculturalism and globalism (6 percent), and social foundations of education (3 percent).

Not surprisingly, the smaller the percentage of respondents designating a given component as essential, the higher the percentage of those unwilling to devote more than a single three-credit-hour course to instruction within the given category. For example, 68 percent estimated 45 hours of instruction *or less* should be devoted to treating issues about learner exceptionality. Over 75 percent thought instructional planning and management could be handled in a three-credit-hour course *or less.* For measurement and assessment, the comparable percentage was 83 percent; for instructional technology, 77 percent; for student development and learning, 79 percent; for legal aspects of education, 89 percent; for multiculturalism and for the social foundations of education, 91 percent.

Overall, among those surveyed, there was very little support shown for any form of lengthy teacher preparation. Seventy-four percent, for example, felt the social foundations of education could be dealt with in 30 or fewer hours of instruction. Ninety-one percent said the same of multicultural issues. Sixty percent indicated a workshop or a one- or two-hour course would provide adequate coverage of legal issues. Nearly half (44 percent) claimed essential information beginning teachers might need to know about instructional media and computer-related instruction could be handled in less than 30 teaching hours. The same was judged of evaluation and assessment (43 percent).

Additional confirming evidence that teachers in this study typically were not supportive of extensive or lengthy teacher preparation is suggested by the fact that fully two-thirds of all those polled did *not* accept the necessity or desirability of a fifth-year undergraduate program. More dramatic still, more than nine of every ten respondents indicated that they disagreed with the idea of preservice teacher training conducted at the master's level. Finally, consistent with the same antipathy toward extended teacher preparation, over two-thirds of all teachers queried indicated that they felt it was important to emphasize general learning and proficiency in a teaching field at the undergraduate level, even if it might mean limiting the number of courses mandated in professional education at the prebaccalaureate level. An even larger proportion of secondary teachers endorsed the importance of having a thorough mastery of teaching content, even if secured at the expense of professional instruction in education. But narrative commentary from teachers at all levels, elementary and secondary alike, repeatedly made mention of the need first and foremost to ensure that all prospective teachers be well grounded and proficient in the substance of their teaching field or fields.

Relatively few respondents availed themselves of the opportunity to append additional concluding comments or remarks regarding the organizational specifics or structure of a teacher preparation program. The most common refrain (60 instances) was insistence on the importance of having students involved at an early point in their training in on-site visits to schools and directed observation, followed by field practice, and then by mentoring at the hands of master teachers. Several commented on the need for more stringent admissions criteria for entry into preparatory programs and higher assessment standards thereafter.

Some teachers expressed a feeling that the student-teaching experience should be utilized as a gatekeeping mechanism, serving to exclude those whose potential for long-term success was judged minimal. Also mentioned by several respondents was the need for a closer articulation or integration of theory with practice in teaching.

Because the survey instrument was not designed to elicit forced choices among mutually exclusive or alternative program formats, it was impossible to identify any single pattern preferred by a majority of respondents. But some inferences seem plain enough. Given the fact that fully 90.8 percent of those polled opposed requiring teacher candidates to complete a master's degree prior to certification, it seems probable to suppose that most teachers comprising the sample studied, if asked to do so, would have registered a preference for conducting teacher preparation primarily if not exclusively at the undergraduate or prebaccalaureate level. Confirmation for the inference is supplied by the fact that two-thirds indicated agreement with the proposition that it ought to be possible to major in professional education at the undergraduate level.

On the other hand, it is important to recall that over 67 percent of all respondents agreed that the number of undergraduate education courses required of students ought to be limited in the interest of having them obtain a broad, general education and adequate concentration in a teaching field or discipline. Clearly, therefore, the sort of regimen of education courses preferred by most respondents would not be extensive or lengthy. As previously noted, even with respect to the category of classroom supervision and behavior management (discipline, pacing of activities, time management, dealing with disruptive or inattentive students, maintenance of classroom control), rated as an "essential" component of teacher education by over 79 percent of all respondents, no more than 39 percent felt that something more extensive than a single course might be required to impart the necessary information involved. Curriculum planning and design (developing curricula, organizing instruction, and lesson planning) was identified as an "essential" component by 62 percent of all respondents. But once again, no more than a third indicated a need for more than a single three-credit-hour course devoted to the relevant material.

The same pattern prevailed so far as each of the remaining knowledge categories were concerned. Dealing with learner exceptionality was cited by 41 percent of all those responding as an essential area for inclusion in a teacher-training program. Yet only 28 percent indicated that a single three-hour course might be insufficient for the purpose of teaching future teachers how to adjust instruction to meet the needs of exceptional learners. Similarly, 38 percent indicated that instructional planning and management should be considered an essential program element, but only 21 percent of all teachers in the sample recommended more than a single three-hour course in special education or a related specialty.

Assessment and evaluation issues were considered essential by 32 percent of all respondents. Only a small minority—14 percent—indicated any need for more than one course given over to testing, measurement, and assessment. Thirty-one percent designated the area of instructional technology as an essential knowledge category to be included, yet less than a fifth (19 percent) urged devoting more than one course to technology-related issues. A quarter of the sample surveyed reportedly believed that information about student growth and development in relation to learning ought to be treated as essential. However, no more than 18 percent felt the task would demand more than a single course. Twelve percent claimed school law and legal issues in education represented an essential component as well, but only 7 percent indicated the need for more than one pertinent three-hour course. For multiculturalism and globalism, cited as essential by 6 percent of the sample, only 2 percent expressed support for the idea of requiring more than a single course in the area. Those urging more than one course in the social foundations of education likewise represented only 2 percent of the total.

It appears reasonable to assume, therefore, that the great majority of teachers surveyed might have been willing to endorse *no more than* the equivalent of one full academic year (two semesters' worth of formal course work, representing one three-hour course in each of the ten knowledge areas) to undergraduate professional education, exclusive of student teaching and other clinical practica. Further, it seems reasonable to infer that an indeterminate but presumably substantial percentage of respondents might have endorsed considerably less—in some instances amounting to little more than a series of short courses or workshops, each incorporating fewer hours of instruction than that associated with a regular one-credit-hour course.

Respondents' opinions differed dramatically on the question of an appropriate length for the initial student-teaching experience, ranging from less than six weeks upward to a full year or more. The traditional pattern of a full semester (16 weeks) won endorsement from most teachers, followed by a 12-week plan. Judging from narrative commentary, many teachers were less concerned with the precise duration of the experience and more concerned with its quality. Themes frequently mentioned included the need for early observation in schools, the importance of making provision for a gradual or phased entry into teaching, the necessity of close supervision throughout, and the desirability of having student interns work at differing grade levels, with more than one cooperating teacher, and in a variety of practice sites. Also cited was the advisability of having beginning teachers complete a first-year internship under the direction of a mentor, with ample opportunities for the neophyte to receive advice and counsel from more experienced practitioners. Some teachers in the poll took pains to underscore the point that a beginning teacher should receive renewable or permanent licensure only upon successful completion of the first year or so of paid, full-time teaching.

Considered as a whole, the results of this study tended to be consistent with findings from previous teacher surveys. As other studies have shown repeatedly, practicing classroom teachers believe more field experiences are essential for teacher candidates. They tend to emphasize the importance of better preparation with respect to classroom management and student discipline, learner differences and learning styles, and dealing with parents. Judging from narrative comments supplied, teachers tend to be relatively uninterested in theoretical considerations apart from their immediate practical applications. They are narrowly focused on "how-to-do-it" skills and strategies rather than broader contextual and interpretive understanding; and they value hands-on experience over didactic instruction. Even among experienced teachers, the felt need is for better counsel on how to work more closely and collaboratively with peers, on how to manage time more effectively, and how to deal with job-related stress. Although skeptical about the value of some education courses, teachers still tend to think in terms of formal credit-bearing instruction as the most appropriate vehicle for imparting needed information and skills. The sole exception was student teaching, where coaching and modeling were deemed most effective in engendering the pedagogical proficiency teachers must attain.

As yet, or so it would appear, there exists no professional consensus among teachers in support of extended teacher preparation leading to initial certification. Few who work in lower-school settings seem prepared to endorse initiatives from academic teacher educators to conduct teacher training at the graduate level. Likewise, requiring certification candidates to complete a master's degree attracts little enthusiasm from experienced classroom practitioners. Most tend to express a preference for undergraduate instruction combining a limited number of preparatory courses with extensive clinical field experiences. At the same time, many teachers appear to appreciate the value of a supervised first-year internship or probationary period before full licensure is granted.

POSSIBLE IMPLICATIONS

Insofar as the rhetoric of teacher professionalism needs to be taken seriously, it seems to follow that classroom teachers in elementary and secondary schools ought to have more of a voice in helping to shape teacher preparation policies and practices than they commonly receive. That is, the expressed preferences and opinions of teachers themselves should receive more of a hearing and be attended to by public policy makers more than has been typical in years past. Whereas teachers alone may have no monopoly on wisdom in matters of how best to prepare tomorrow's classroom practitioners, collectively they do offer a unique and invaluable perspective on what is required in the way of preparation for effective on-the-job performance. All too often, or so it would seem, national debates over teacher education are conducted primarily (if not exclusively) among collegiate-based teacher educators, state education officials, public school administrators, legislators, college trustees, and assorted special interest groups and professional associations. Even when teachers' representatives at the national level—the NEA and AFT, for example—are included, what ensues in the way of recommendations from high-level blue-ribbon panels and commissions may not necessarily reflect closely the opinions and beliefs of those engaged directly in the instruction of the nation's schoolchildren.

Hence the potential fruitfulness of further research on teachers' beliefs about teacher education ought not to be underestimated. Further inquiry may reveal that teachers have much to offer in the way of well-considered opinion about how teacher preparatory programs ought to be mounted in future. Preliminary indications from research and opinion polls conducted in recent years suggests possible directions quite at odds with innovations now fashionable within teacher education circles.

Unwittingly or not, for example, many teachers tend to favor views that would preserve or refashion teacher education as a species of craft training rather than as a full-fledged professional development process analogous to that engaged in by trainees within the better-recognized professions such as law and medicine. Whether warranted or desirable or not, antipathy among teachers toward extended teacher preparation affords a possible case in point. There is also evidence to suggest that teachers are consistently identifying deficiencies and weaknesses in the training present-day teacher candidates receive that tend not to be addressed adequately in many "top-down" reform movements. Helping teachers learn how to function effectively and in an integrative way so far as curriculum development and planning are concerned may be just one area deserving closer scrutiny, particularly given the rhetoric of teacher "empowerment" now common among reformers. Specifics aside, the point, of course, is not that teachers somehow should exercise a decisive say in how initial teacher training is conducted. Rather, the point is that teachers by right ought to be allowed to contribute whatever they are capable of offering in the way of advice and counsel. Much-touted "partnerships" between public schools and colleges or universities engaged in teacher training, as one illustration, must become exactly that: genuinely collaborative ventures between equals, where the opinions of all the players involved receive due consideration.

At the very least, public debate over the directions of teacher education in the years ahead needs to be informed more adequately by what teachers believe and prefer. In response to external critics who urge the abandonment of all formal training whatsoever, experienced classroom teachers—many of them by no means uncritical advocates for education courses as these are currently conducted—might offer powerful testimony in support of discrete formal training. At the opposite extreme, in response to those who aspire to lengthen preparatory programs to five or even six years, classroom teachers might be found to offer cautionary caveats or recommendations to the contrary well worth considering. Again, it is not unreasonable to assume that if teachers' opinions were heeded, they would collectively pose a significant challenge to defenders of the status quo, those who would retain today's programs substantially unchanged. It is virtually certain, for example, that if given the opportunity to do so, schoolteachers would urge specific changes in how early field experiences and student teaching programs are conducted.

Against the backdrop of continuing controversy and disagreement, it remains to sketch out the essential outlines of one possible reform pattern for teacher education in America. It is informed but not necessarily determined by the literature on teachers' own convictions and beliefs about teacher training. What follows in Chapter 7 is a necessarily abbreviated discussion of a model as-yet infrequently considered, one that attempts to offer the advantages of brevity and economy while simultaneously avoiding the seeming superficiality of so-called "alternative" certification programs. Whether the proposals to be put forward are capable of attracting support or are destined to be summarily dismissed as ill-advised and inadequate is uncertain. They are advanced, however, in the interest of contributing something of merit to the national debate over how students can be prepared for their entry into teaching.

7

SOME PROPOSALS

DISAGREEMENTS IN REVIEW

The claim that people aspiring to become elementary or secondary classroom instructors need formal preparation for their work, it is abundantly apparent, has yet to win universal acceptance at the close of the twentieth century. Every so often, an editorialist or a self-styled critic brandishing a book with an inflammatory title such as *The Collapse of American Education, How Our Schools Are Failing and Why the Crisis Is Worsening* will attract wide attention by rehearsing the claim that teacher education is bankrupt. Instructional acts are natural occurrences in the repertoire of human behaviors, runs the argument; and there were teachers long before someone seized upon the curious notion they needed to be trained in order to exercise abilities they—and practically everyone else—already possess.[1]

As for the argument that instructional skills can be further developed and expanded on through training, the rejoinder is that practice alone is almost always sufficient for improvement. Formal means are superfluous. All that is really needed, first and last, is that a person be well versed in the subject matter he or she wishes to impart. Critics are fond of noting, for example, that whereas anyone teaching high-school seniors aged 17 or 18 in a public school must hold a state-issued license, no comparable demand is made of faculty instructing 18-year-old freshmen in college. Skeptics doubt whether the two settings are so radically dissimilar as to warrant the imposition of lengthy training in the former situation, while requiring nothing but knowledge of content in the latter.

In an address to the Southern Legislative Conference several years ago, former Secretary of Education William Bennett urged legislators to consider dropping requirements that teachers complete professional programs to earn credentials, arguing "We need to attract the best people to teaching, whether they are professional educators or not. Get rid of the mindless paper credentials."[2] Bennett went on to suggest that prospective teachers should be obliged to demonstrate evidence only of their subject-matter knowledge, their good character, and, possibly, an ability to communicate with youngsters in order to qualify.

Recounted with ironic relish by critics of the present system are professedly infuriating incidents where well-educated persons bent on entering teaching, otherwise competent but who lack the necessary education credits, find themselves up against the state's elaborate licensing and certification system. Or (in some cases amounting to the same thing) they run afoul of the lengthy preparatory requirements of a state-approved school or college of education. They quickly discover that in order to satisfy initial licensure standards, they must complete a formidable array of education courses bearing such titles as "Instructional Materials and Media in the Classroom," "Teaching of Reading," "Psychological Dynamics of Child Development and Learning," "Introduction to the Social and Cultural Foundations of Education," and perhaps a host of others. Facing the prospect of a long regimen stretching out before them, they give up in disgust, abandoning all hope of pursuing a career in the schools. Hence many good people allegedly are lost to the field.

On the other side of the issue, it may be true that complex licensure requirements undoubtedly serve to discourage some promising would-be teachers from applying. But, it must be said, most careers generally do require some formal preparatory training for entry into the trade or profession. Why teaching in the lower grades should be an exception (assuming defensible entrance requirements) remains a mystery. Only if one has already decided that no requirements are necessary beyond competence in a subject field or that they are inherently unreasonable does it make sense to criticize them for precluding anyone who wants to teach from doing so.

The fact of the matter is, even the most acerbic detractors of teacher education who have given the matter some thought will concede, finally, that some sort of training and/or practice is both prudent and necessary. If all that were needed were a thorough understanding of one's subject, any well-educated person could become an effective classroom instructor. But common experience rather clearly suggests otherwise. Not even bright people who command something approaching an exhaustive knowledge of a subject or field are able always to survive—much less flourish—in a public school classroom (or, for that matter, in a college classroom either). More than native intelligence and good academic training are demanded, particularly when it is a matter of keeping immature, usually involuntary learners on task and making their instruction as interesting, understandable, and enjoyable as possible. "Good teaching," it has been rightly observed, " is far more than a smart person taking the knowledge of the university and teaching it to younger students at a lower level or a slower pace."[3]

The conclusion usually invited is that future teachers need an extensive and detailed program to supply all of the requisite knowledge, skills, and practical experiences they will be expected to have on the job. Besides content classes, customary usage holds that teaching candidates must complete a long sequence of courses in pedagogy and related subjects, plus field experiences and clinical practica. But of course it is by no means obvious or self-evident that because effective teaching demands *some* type of preparatory training, the *only* means or even the *best* way of supplying it is through an elaborate and protracted system of formal instruction. Still less is it clear why training must occupy a third or more of a baccalaureate degree program, as is often the case under current circumstances. Much depends naturally on just what sort of preparation is thought necessary to accomplish the task at hand. And the answer to that question, in turn, depends on how the nature of the work to be done is understood.

Meanwhile, there is certainly nothing remotely resembling a national consensus on the question of how best to train teachers for the classroom, even among teacher educators themselves. Even the ways in which people think about the process are apt to vary tremendously. Some view preparing teachers as a purely technical enterprise concerned with the adaptation of means efficient to given ends. Others look on it as a species of low-level craft training, something requiring little more than imitative learning of a select few skills. Then there are those who construe the process more phenomenologically, portraying it as a sort of personal journey of holistic self-discovery and personal development. Still others would recast teacher training as a kind of political project—an undertaking intended to raise the critical consciousness of teacher candidates and to arm them for ideological struggle within an allegedly unjust social order.

So far as structure or format is concerned, it has been noted how at one extreme are those who urge that teacher preparation be confined to some rudimentary form of school-based apprenticeship training, directed and superintended exclusively by classroom practitioners themselves. Others at the opposite end of the spectrum now increasingly argue the case that a lengthy and elaborate regimen of academic instruction and clinical experience must be mandated for optimal effect, one spread out over some protracted period and usually involving a year or two of expensive, full-time graduate study. Somewhere in the middle repose those who would defend the traditional, four-year undergraduate pattern. Commented on previously is the point that the four-year model, with all of its inevitable compromises and trade-offs, invariably furnishes a target for criticism by academics, editorialists, and the lay public—not to mention, in moments of candor, by more than a few teachers themselves.

The literature on teacher preparation is almost stupefying in its proportions. It amounts to literally hundreds of books, published conference proceedings, governmental reports and studies, thousands of articles in professional journals, and specialized newsletters of one kind or another. Yet even a cursory perusal of that vast corpus quickly reveals deep divisions of opinion and few areas of agreement among the professionals. In no sense has scholarship coalesced around any one particular theory of teaching or of teacher education. Defining "good" teaching in some generic, context-free sense, as it turns out, is extraordinarily difficult. Devising an authoritative specification of the "effective" teacher's attributes likewise seems almost impossible. And accomplishing either goal with the precision or exactitude needed for the ideal to serve as a criterion for judging "best" practice has proven a still more elusive goal.

Part of the reason, of course, is that embedded within the constructed idea of instructional excellence and of the outstanding teacher are quite complex considerations of normative judgment and preference, both of them inextricably bound up with matters of empirical fact. Because there is so little consensus on what *constitutes* the exemplary teacher, there is scant agreement on what conduces to *produce* that paragon. In short, there is no all-encompassing, systematic, or authoritative body of scholarly knowledge to which one may appeal. Pretending otherwise is simply a sham or a delusion.

For all the bold talk among technocrats about a solid knowledge base for teacher education and vehement assertions that the advent of a true scientific pedagogy is imminent or has already occurred, for instance, the hard truth is that solid, empirical evidence to support one way of preparing teachers in preference to another is largely lacking.[4] This is not to deny the existence of an enormous number of well-informed opinions available for consideration. In fact, they abound. Many thoughtful recommendations have been proffered for discussion in recent years. Nor is it to allege that nothing whatsoever is known about what it is teachers must learn in order to teach. But compared with the accredited knowledge typical of many other fields, the extent of reliable, validated data about teacher preparation and about teaching itself is, finally, minuscule. Thinking of it as a social and cultural artifact, the work of preparing teachers, like most other complex human enterprises, is indeterminate and fraught with ambiguity.

For quite understandable reasons, therefore, it is probable that experimentation with multiple ways of managing teacher education will continue in years to come. If as yet there exists no one way of training teachers that is clearly superior to all others, the work of institutions in trying out various policy choices and arrangements must go on. So-called alternative preparatory programs of brief duration that make few demands on teacher candidates will not easily be legislated out of existence, no matter how much some would like to see them shut down entirely. Institutional inertia alone, if nothing else, should allow many traditional four-year programs to endure pretty much as always, some of them perhaps adopting no more than whatever cosmetic changes the public comes to demand at any particular point in time. For much the same reasons, the politics of teacher education are such that it is equally likely that a niche will continue to exist for lengthier extended programs within certain of the nation's larger schools and colleges of education.

Overall, the most probable pattern for the immediate future is that no one form of teacher education will come to predominate nationwide, certainly not to the exclusion of all others. In the meantime, particularly in the absence of any single controlling paradigm or some uniform model commanding universal assent, anyone is free to recommend ideas for possible consideration.

GENERAL LIBERAL STUDIES

*Prerequsite to meaningful teacher education reform is the
reinvigoration and resuscitation of the idea of liberal
learning. Teachers need a broad, general education at the
undergraduate level, one marked by both breadth and
depth of content. Liberal learning is an essential
foundation of professional teacher training.*

Contemplating the directions teacher education reform might pursue in future, first and foremost must come acknowledgment that most of today's collegians (not just prospective teachers among them) typically do not receive an adequate liberal education marked by either scope or depth of substance. The attempt by four-year colleges and universities to mix academic learning and vocational training within the confines of a baccalaureate program is bound to fail. It simply is not credible to suppose, given the limits of an undergraduate degree program, that students can be supplied with a broad-based liberal education of meaningful proportions and at the same time be trained effectively for any particular career, including teaching. In attempting to do both, academic institutions in fact succeed in doing neither particularly well.[5] "Educating students liberally in the arts and sciences and preparing them to be public school teachers are distinct functions with dissimilar means and ends," it has been rightly observed. "The attempt to combine liberal education and professional training in a single undergraduate program has been unsuccessful for so long at so many institutions it is reasonable to conclude that something is wrong with the model."[6]

*Colleges and universities must affirm liberal learning
for personal and social development, not discrete job
training, as the primary purpose of
undergraduate education.*

In an ideal world, institutions of higher learning would stop trying to shoehorn academic learning and vocational training directly applicable to occupations within the boundaries of a four-year time span. They would further disavow any intent to prepare their students directly for employment at the baccalaureate level. Prospective applicants and their parents thus would be firmly disabused of the notion that the primary purpose of attending college is "to get a better job." Undergraduate

liberal studies, of course, have much to do with preparing for employment and, more broadly, for future participation in society's economic
order. But the contribution of liberal learning should be recognized for
what it is: a broad, albeit indirect building up of an undergirding
structure or foundation of basic knowledge, values, and skills. Proficiency specific to a given profession or occupation can and should come
later. It certainly ought not to be had at the expense of essential
foundational learning. (Students bent exclusively on securing employment, of course, would be better advised to repair to a two-year vocational school immediately upon graduating from high school.)

*The goal of liberal education reform ought to be the
creation of an integrative and cohesive course of
undergraduate studies.*

*Redesigning an intelligible program of interdisciplinary
liberal learning would challenge virtually all of the
systemic conventions that now fragment and
divide the academy against itself.*

The first step on the road to genuine reform would be to concede openly
that general or liberal learning at the undergraduate level in most
American colleges and universities has long been in disarray. Now more
than ever, it stands in need of drastic revamping. Without becoming
overly prescriptive, a necessary measure—undoubtedly accompanied
by indignant cries of protest from faculties—would be for colleges and
universities to divest themselves of their existing departmental structures as mechanisms for organizing undergraduate study. Academic
departments in their current form serve mainly to reinforce and accentuate a broader movement toward disciplinary fragmentation and intellectual anarchy. They tend almost always to operate in ways that impede
interdisciplinary collaboration and integration, or at least make them far
less likely to occur than might otherwise be the case if faculty members
were not so preoccupied with defending their own turf. The case for
doing away with autonomous departments, of dispensing with them
entirely as a basis for organizing instruction at the baccalaureate level,
deserves thoughtful consideration.

More than anything else, the organizational fragmentation of arts
and sciences colleges encourages faculty scholars to retreat even further
into their respective academic specializations. It often has been observed

how rarely scholar-specialists from different disciplines in academe even talk with one another about the substance of what they do, much less work together, in ways apt to influence curricula and student instruction. Unsurprisingly, the usual undergraduate arts and sciences course of study that results tends to exhibit little coherence or integration of its own. What ensues in the vacuum left by lack of collaboration and genuine intellectual cooperation is more nearly an inchoate artifact, a product of the intense horsetrading and bartering for credit hours that occurs among competing departmental rivals whenever the general curriculum is revised. Preferable by far would be some regrouping of faculty by overlapping "clusters" or programmatic teaching "areas"— that is, more informal and loosely organized units not always aligned precisely along the boundaries of the established academic disciplines.

Experimentation with different institutional structures and configurations, together with less reliance on lecturing and more emphasis on imaginative pedagogy, would be helpful to the cause of fostering a meaningful, integrative type of undergraduate experience. Reconfiguring the faculty for instructional and curricular purposes could take several possible forms. One pattern might involve no more than three broad aggregations, organized respectively around the sciences and technologies, the social sciences, and the arts and humanities. Another possibility might entail five different "divisions" or schools.

The first, Physical and Quantitative Sciences and Technologies, would bring together mathematics and statistics, computer science, inorganic chemistry, physics, astronomy, and possibly geology for purposes of shared curriculum planning and integrative teaching. Biological Sciences and Technologies would encompass biology, microbiology, botany, zoology, genetics, organic chemistry perhaps, paleontology, and probably some few others. Social and Human Studies (including psychology, sociology, anthropology, political science, economics, political geography, archaeology, and possibly comparative religion) would constitute a third grouping. Fourth, art, theater, dance, aesthetics, music, some elements of architecture, and art history would fall under Fine and Performing Arts. Finally, Arts and Letters would afford the pedagogical home for English, comparative and world literature, linguistics and semiotics, mythology, philosophy, classical studies, speech, languages, and communications.

Other configurations could be devised, given sufficient thought and planning, whether clustered around similar or shared modes of investigation and inquiry or broadly defined knowledge domains (possibly as few as three or as many as six or seven cross-disciplinary groupings), or some other heuristic approach deemed worth exploring. Details as to the optimal number of groupings and which disciplines belonged where could be left to trial and error as well as local preference. (Cybernetics, certain branches of higher mathematics, and some aspects of geography, for instance, do not seem to fit neatly within any particular category, any more than do many interdisciplinary hybrids, such as biochemistry, now commonly taught in universities.) The point in all cases, however, would be to assign to each faculty aggregation responsibility for designing and developing a two-and-a-half-year sequence of courses (or their equivalents), each of whose major elements or "modules" would be required of all students throughout their first five semesters as undergraduates.

In terms of deciding on and expressing instructional goals, it should be possible to negotiate a middle course between the Charybdis of too much generality and the Scylla of excessive specificity. Conventional statements of curricular and instructional objectives limited to broad and lofty generalities could hardly be helpful since, inevitably, they would fail to mark out the particular learning needed. Conversely, any near-encyclopedic enumeration of content would soon become unwieldy and cumbersome. The aim in all cases, rather, would be to give expression to goals in such a way that they would be capable of furnishing general standards or criteria against which to measure the congruence and efficacy of whatever courses of study actually were developed.

The fundamental aims of liberal learning can and
should be expressed as specific desired outcomes
or as the intended consequences of instruction
and other educative experiences.

Institutions of higher learning, it should be emphasized once again, may tinker endlessly with their breadth requirements, fiddle with the specifics of a curricular core, or modify existing courses and devise new ones, as colleges and universities are prone to do from time to time. But lacking some shared vision of the larger purposes served—goals defining the meaning and significance of the baccalaureate degree as a whole—all such exercises are likely to remain futile and ultimately self-defeating. What must be achieved is some explicit consensus about the knowledge, abilities, skills, and values expected of students after two or more years of undergraduate education—attributes and characteristics that would make them educated in ways *different* from (and implicitly better than) those who elected not to attend college or who attended a different type of institution.[7] Only after outcomes have been decided on—and only then—can the work of curriculum design and development proceed in devising courses of study adapted to helping attain the goals set forth.

Despite the undoubted difficulties involved, the logic behind the redesign of undergraduate liberal education along the lines proposed seems both attractive and compelling. If it is conceded that the incoherence of today's curricular "smorgasbord" is undesirable, and if the usual pick-and-choose, hit-or-miss approach needs to be avoided, ultimately some working agreement on basic purposes and aims appears essential. The overriding need, in some final analysis, would be for a *substantive* specification of hoped-for outcomes, one that would go beyond minimum credit hours spread across disparate disciplines or the usual simplistic listing of subject fields: so many hours to be taken in history, so many in political science or biology, a choice between anthropology or sociology, and so on.

Elements entailed would include skills and competencies essential to academic success (computer literacy, basic numeracy, facility in written and oral communication); "conversancies" (knowledge about and familiarity with generative concepts, motive ideas, major findings, dominant figures, central themes, and the basic terminology of a given disciplinary domain); and the values and habits of mind considered integral to the enterprise of liberal learning at large (intellectual curiosity and love of learning; tolerance and respect for honest differences of opinion; some grasp of the importance of critical analysis and logic; respect for the role of evidence in argumentation; academic and intellectual honesty; awareness of the differences among opinions, beliefs, judgments, and facts; a developing sense of style; esthetic sensibility, and so on).

Designing course sequences of an appropriate character would amount to a major intellectual challenge for faculty scholars. Much time and energy would be required to think things through afresh; to identify the basic organizing conceptual structures characteristic of each disciplinary combination; to uncover ways of linking ideas together to form intelligible wholes; to exhibit the modes of inquiry and of knowing distinctive of different subjects; to draw out integrative themes and continuities; and to sequence information in ways most helpful to novice learners. Specialists in the various disciplines might find it difficult—

although certainly not impossible—to "step back" and plot out the routes along which the uninitiated would need to be guided. (It should be noted in this connection that several experimental colleges—and a very few major universities—already have embarked on such reform courses, sometimes with intriguing and promising results.)

Certain elements within each sequence—not necessarily free-standing courses—might be adjusted to take into account differences in students' aptitudes, abilities, and interests. Inaugurating interdisciplinary course sequences of a general nature, in other words, would *not* necessarily need to signal a return to the now-discredited fixed and uniform curriculum of yesteryear. A limited number of choices and alternatives within each sequence might prove unobjectionable but only so long as the scope of elective choice did not serve to revive the excesses of conventional "distribution" requirements. (Flexibility would be essential throughout, particularly for students in the performing arts, where concentration and continuity of training are usually essential.) The full gamut of possibilities, ranging, for example, from "remedial" to "intensive," from "standard" to "enriched" to "accelerated" to "honors," would be limited only by the imagination and ingenuity of the curriculum planners themselves.

Care would need to be exercised to prevent courses of study from degenerating into mere surveys of a superficial nature ("dibs and dabs" of this and that), or simplistic "introductions" to the disciplines, or watered-down versions of more advanced courses. Nor, of course, would beginning courses be offered to learners as hurdles to be surmounted en route to more specialized studies. Still less could they be exploited as tools for recruiting prospective majors to some given field, as now seems often the case under the present system. The objective, always, would be to find ways of drawing learners "inside" various fields of study; to explore with them, as it were, the multiple worlds of humanity's physical, biological, social, and cultural environments; of contemporary civilization, its achievements and historical antecedents; and of the "inner space" of the human mind, its workings and creative products. Introducing students to the "syntactical" structure of various academic disciplines and fields of knowledge is yet another metaphor helpful for thinking about what might be required.

Sometimes conventional courses would be found to afford the best means of achieving the outcomes agreed upon. However, faculty would not need to rely solely on the traditional three-hour course format as the vehicle for accomplishing everything. Constituent building blocks for each interdisciplinary sequence could be built up from many different combinations of learning experiences and activities, involving differing instructional formats and "segments" of varying duration: free-standing courses in some cases, certainly, but also so-called minicourses, short courses, workshops, seminars, colloquia, tutorials, independent study, internships and practica—the list of possibilities worth exploring might be quite extensive.

As for academic skill-building, provision certainly could be made to allow students already proficient in specified areas to "test out" of certain elements in each sequence through some type of competency assessment. (Facility in a foreign language, for example, is best determined through a student's interrogation in that language, not by how many language course credits he or she may have piled up. The only meaningful assessment of computer literacy is the user's demonstrated ability to do word processing, build a data base, run a spreadsheet, locate and download information from the Internet, perform calculations and data entry, manipulate a graphics program, and so on.)

Assuming semester hours as the units of measurement involved, 15 or 16 hours (or their quarter-hour or trimester-hour equivalents) of work completed each academic term should represent full-time study at the undergraduate level. Hence, the average student would have completed between 75 and 80 credit hours at the end of the fifth semester, midway through the junior year. Assuming it has been carefully designed and properly managed, the total course of study extending up into the third undergraduate year ought to be more than sufficient to provide students with a broad, liberal foundation for their remaining academic work.

Parenthetically, although future teachers and nonteachers alike would be required to satisfy the same general studies requirements regardless of their respective career aspirations, in principle there is no reason during the undergraduate years to exclude the liberal study of education and schooling as sociocultural phenomena. Courses in the history, philosophy, psychology, politics, or sociology of education, for example, represent perfectly viable specializations or subdivisions within their respective cognate disciplines, and they seem eminently deserving of a place in the undergraduate liberal-arts curriculum.

Much ink has been shed over the years about who should be considered competent to teach such courses, how instructors should be trained, and where the faculty involved should hold their academic appointments—in education or in the undergirding liberal disciplines, or jointly in both. But so far as undergraduates are concerned, all such controversies should be matters of some indifference. The larger point, perhaps, is that there is no a priori reason to proscribe the study of education as an aspect of students' undergraduate liberal education, regardless of whether the learners anticipate becoming teachers. Especially useful for those students already contemplating teaching careers would be organized study in the areas of basic learning theory and child or adolescent psychology and development.

Comprehensive third-year baccalaureate candidacy examinations should be administered prior to allowing undergraduates to select a major field of concentration or interdisciplinary academic specialization.

At a point halfway through the third year, provision should be made for administering comprehensive upper-level candidacy examinations, both written and oral, prior to permitting students to select their major fields of concentration. Testing would serve not only to check for academic achievement but also to focus effort and attention away from individual courses and isolated learning, as they are now, and to place them where they belong, on more global learning outcomes.

To the usual objection that professors would be tempted to "teach to the test," the most sensible rejoinder would be to ask "Why not?" Each institution involved could devise comprehensive examinations in such a way that criterion-referenced student performances would serve as valid indicators of what had been learned (or at least a reasonable sampling thereof). Under such circumstances, the testing process itself would be unobjectionable and, in fact, could be extremely helpful for diagnostic and remedial purposes. Minimally, examinations adapted to perform a gatekeeping function might help reduce the frequency with which functional illiterates nowadays are allowed to pass through untouched and unscathed, emerging from colleges and universities bearing unearned degrees.

Contingent upon passing candidacy exams, a student would be allowed to elect a more specialized concentration or academic major in arts and sciences (although not quite one in the traditional single-discipline mold). Three semesters' worth of full-time course work or its equivalent, culminating in some appropriate sort of integrative "capstone" experience, would yield 45 to 48 semester hours of study, or close to 40 percent of all academic work completed for the baccalaureate degree (totaling 120 to 128 semester hours). This seems a reasonable portion to reserve for greater in-depth absorption in a particular discipline or, better yet, a linked array of related disciplines, especially if considered in conjunction with the underlying foundation laid down during the freshman and sophomore years. A concentration also would serve to establish the content fields for someone intending to pursue a teaching career.

The undergraduate "major" or academic concentration should ground a prospective teacher in his or her intended teaching field.

Once again, the armature for an academic concentration could be supplied by something along the lines of a tripartite or fivefold clustering of fields. A student would "major" in certain of the quantitative disciplines or sciences (physics and chemistry, biology and zoology, mathematics and computer sciences), or the social sciences (psychology and sociology), or the arts and humanities (communications, language and literature), choosing electives from among advanced-level specialized courses. Once all requirements were satisfied, the successful graduate would receive his or her bachelor's degree in General Studies, perhaps with a subdesignation reflecting whatever specialized concentration was completed.

Teacher education should be removed from its traditional undergraduate setting and repositioned as the first phase of postbaccalaureate training.

Needless to say, training in more applied fields such as engineering, journalism, horticulture, business administration, accountancy, library science, and so on would be postponed to the postbachelor level. In no way would professional study be allowed to encroach on the time and space available for undergraduate liberal education, as now seems to be the advancing tendency. Basically, few if any professional degrees, as in elementary or secondary education, would be offered at the bachelor's level except perhaps in single-purpose postsecondary institutions.

Few other promising alternatives suggest themselves, except perhaps a pattern trading off time spent in completing a major concentration for a final semester devoted to preprofessional studies. Yet another option revived from time to time for consideration but that rarely attracts much popular enthusiasm would be to redefine the baccalaureate degree as a three-year program. In this case, the first year and a half might be devoted to general studies (45 to 48 hours) and the latter half of the second and first half of the third to an academic major or concentration within arts and sciences (30 to 32 hours). This would leave 15 to 16 hours in the last portion of the third and final year for additional electives or specialized preprofessional studies and the "extra" postgraduation year thereafter for applied study. With the four-year pattern so firmly established by hallowed precedent and tradition, however, it seems quite unlikely that a three-year bachelor's degree program would ever win broad acceptance.

PRESERVICE PRACTICA

On balance, the value of having all students complete a broad, general, and nonspecialized liberal education at the bachelor's level far outweighs the supposed advantages of an earlier career decision about entering teaching or of positioning a course of studies in education at the undergraduate level. Among other things, requiring systematic exposure to the various arts and science disciplines over a four-year span would better serve to place all prospective teacher candidates at the same entry point for further, more specialized professional study following graduation. Anyone intending to teach would be expected to hold a general degree in the arts and sciences—one reflecting considerable breadth and depth of liberal learning—together with a concentration serving as a teaching field or fields—a minimally adequate level of knowledge of what is to be taught—and to have acquired both *prior* to embarking upon teacher training. The common problem of trying to balance out professional and liberal studies within a conventional program (usually to the detriment of both studies) would be avoided by excluding education courses at the undergraduate level.

Prospective teacher candidates should complete a practicum or a series of clinical field experiences prior to embarking upon direct professional training.

The sole variation that would distinguish future teachers' preprofessional preparation prior to graduation would be a series of extracurricular practica in school settings—or, the next best thing, the establishment of a record of paid or volunteer service working with children of appropriate age in various settings (public service literacy programs, summer camps, and so on). Field observations, serving as a teacher's aide, and tutoring experiences with schoolchildren could be completed within any maximum time limit stipulated during the four undergraduate years. For those late in coming to a decision about a teaching career, the practicum still could be completed toward the end of baccalaureate studies.

A total of somewhere between 80 and 100 clock hours does not seem unwarranted as a minimum requirement for the preservice practicum (or practica), especially if time spent observing and working with children in schools under the tutelage of one or more experienced teachers were spread out over time and could be completed within any one of the four years of undergraduate study. Segments might be scheduled between academic terms when public schools were still in session. An optimal arrangement, however, would be one allowing for some continuity of involvement over time. Student participants thus would be in a position to observe pupils' progress throughout the entire school year (involving an average of three hours weekly) or over the course of a 16-week semester (six hours weekly).

Practica would not necessarily need to fall within the formal purview of institutions of higher learning. Nor would they offer college credit. In fact, probably it would be better to delegate primary responsibility for coordinating and administering teacher candidates' initial clinical experiences to a school district functionary, perhaps in cooperation with someone associated as a director of field experiences with a student's own college or university. Once practica sponsorship was firmly established as a regular, ongoing responsibility of every self-respecting school, local districts could make admissions somewhat selective or competitive, thus allowing them greater control over whom they admitted for tutelage. Within very broad limits, provided only that practicum students were given a chance to interact with youngsters instead of being consigned always to the role of passive observers, school districts could experiment with varying degrees of structure, direction, and control. Practica might be conducted in many different yet still fruitful ways.

Specifics aside, completing an approved series of supervised practica ought not to pose an undue hardship on someone planning on teaching—indeed, students who already are required to complete early field experiences generally report them helpful rather than burdensome. The practical advantage is that they afford prospective teachers opportunities to familiarize themselves with real-world work settings in schools. Given the scheme under consideration, candidates could better decide in consultation with on-site mentors whether to pursue their career ambitions. And they would be in a position to make a decision well *before* having embarked upon and invested themselves in formal training.

In any event, there is something profoundly disquieting about the prevailing system where many students elect to major in education as a professional degree, only to discover too late they have no desire to pursue a career in teaching. The point is not that they cannot "do" something else with their degree. Rather, it is that they have devoted a significant portion of their undergraduate studies to specialized training for which they have little direct use. To that same extent, they have lost an opportunity to profit from more generalizable liberal studies.

INITIAL TEACHER CERTIFICATION

Excluding professional education courses from the undergraduate curriculum would solve multiple problems without necessarily creating commensurate difficulties. First, the absence of professional training at the prebaccalaureate level would leave space and time needed for general studies and for concentrated study in whatever major was selected as a subject-matter teaching field. The point should be underscored: Those two preliminary tasks are fundamental and can best be accomplished during the undergraduate years.

Second, with teacher training postponed until after graduation, the need to articulate college-based coursework with related field-based experiences would be obviated. The latter would be strictly ancillary rather than an integral element of the future teacher's academic program of study. Further, and more important, pedagogical methods courses would not have to be offered at a time when teacher candidates had yet to complete their study of the disciplines involved, much less spent much time observing how science or the language arts, for example, actually are taught at lower levels.

Finally, to future elementary-school teachers no less than to their prospective secondary-level colleagues would accrue the benefits of in-depth exposure to a discipline or combination of fields as an academic concentration. As matters now stand, elementary majors typically substitute additional methods courses for an academic major. Devoting a large amount of time to pedagogical activities, frequently offered before the students enrolled are adequately prepared to appreciate their relevance or applicability, is an indefensible waste of effort and energy.

In proscribing undergraduate courses in education, the overall pattern proposed, of course, marks a significant departure from the traditional four-year baccalaureate model. It would diverge almost as much from the format of so-called integrated, extended five-year programs leading to a bachelor's degree or to both a baccalaureate and a master's degree. Some programs, such as those begun in the early 1980s at the University of Kansas, divide up the hours needed for a baccalaureate degree among general studies, course work in one or more teaching fields, practical fieldwork, and professional studies in education. These are followed in a fifth year by a combination of extended clinical experiences, advanced course work in education, and a semester-long, unpaid student teaching internship.

Other preparatory programs, such as that initiated by the University of Virginia in 1986-87, similarly require five years to finish, except that two degrees are awarded simultaneously on completion: a bachelor's degree in arts and sciences and a master of teaching degree in education.[8] The very real problem with these "integrated" five-year programs is that they still have the drawback of trying to combine several different pedagogical elements—liberal learning, a teaching concentration, professional training, and clinical experience—at the undergraduate level. They compensate for this disadvantage in no small measure, of course, by deferring most of the last two components into an extra year or so at the graduate level.

The other major alternative pursued by some teacher-preparation institutions is a fifth-year ("4+1") program leading to conferral of a master's degree. The University of Maryland offers an illustrative case, where undergraduates must complete an arts and sciences regimen before embarking upon postbaccalaureate, graduate-level teacher training in the fifth year. First implemented in 1985, the Maryland Master's Certification Program (MMCP) requires postbachelor's candidates to commence their studies early in the summer and continue through two six-week summer sessions and an academic year. Besides a professional core of courses, students register for a three-hour practicum working in schools during the fall semester. During the spring term, they are enrolled for a 12-week internship as well as two week-long workshops. The MMCP program concludes with submission of a student research project and comprehensive examinations. Graduates are awarded a master's degree.[9] A similar program was begun at the University of

Arkansas in the early 1990s. However, 18 hours of preprofessional course work at the undergraduate level were added on as prerequisites for pursuing the fifth-year master's degree, making for 50 or more hours of course credits needed for initial state licensure.

More ambitious still but nowhere yet adopted in full is the six-year ("4+2") program model leading to a master's degree first proposed by B. O. Smith in *A Design for a School of Pedagogy* (1980). Building on a foundation comprised by a four-year arts and science program, Smith recommended an additional two-year period of pedagogical preparation, including formal course work and clinical observations throughout the first two semesters. These were to be followed in the second and final year by clinical seminars and work in a laboratory or field setting.[10]

Extended programs, whether five-year or fifth-year, share the virtue of opening up more room for additional subject-matter courses, pedagogical studies, or longer field experiences—although oftentimes education courses offered at the graduate level tend to differ little from their undergraduate counterparts, and allegedly are just as repetitive. Moreover, no incontrovertible evidence exists to show that the results of extended programs are discernibly different from, or necessarily superior to, those achieved in more traditional four-year programs. Whatever the eventual verdict on their presumed benefits, integrated programs still have the disadvantage of trying to combine several different pedagogical elements at the undergraduate level—liberal learning, a teaching field concentration, professional training, and clinical experiences.

Teacher training for initial licensure should neither involve graduate education nor should it demand that a candidate satisfy the requirements of a master's degree.

Extended programs (integrated or not) that culminate with the awarding of a master's degree raise yet another issue: *the questionable advisability of tying graduate-level training to initial teacher licensure and certification.* Although it would be difficult to document empirically, it seems plausible to argue there are many candidates capable of becoming satisfactory teachers who lack the academic ability needed to pursue credible master's degree study, at least not at the level at which graduate studies ought to be conducted—or, in fact, at a level comparable with that long maintained in many other fields. The fact that most school district policies link teachers' salary increments and licensure renewal to the attainment of one or more postbaccalaureate degrees only accentuates the problem, because it adds to the demand for graduate training. In some cases—it is perhaps anyone's guess how many—the pressure issues from teachers ill-equipped to handle the work but who under today's system need the credential in order to remain in good standing for certification purposes.

Making a master's degree prerequisite to entry into teaching can only exacerbate matters, and for much the same reasons. "Credential inflation" seems a foregone outcome as the master's degree becomes the minimal qualification for literally thousands of teachers each year. Almost certainly its scarcity value will plummet with the passage of time. In the face of strong (albeit artificially stimulated) consumer demand, moreover, it is a safe bet that academic stringency and rigor will continue to decline. So also will the prestige attached to a graduate degree in education—which already is exceedingly low among those outside the education establishment.

Not often mentioned is another consideration: the plight of experienced teachers who are graduates from four-year programs and who now must seek the equivalent credential already possessed by novices who have graduated from five-year or fifth-year programs. Whether graduate institutions can manage to meet the postbaccalaureate training of both constituencies without entangling their curricula remains to be seen. Meanwhile, although proponents of the fifth-year Master of Teaching degree earnestly claim it is a bona fide graduate credential fully comparable with the traditional Master of Education degree (M.Ed.), a side-by-side look at the academic course- and credit-hour requirements for each usually indicates otherwise.

More to the point, it seems very dubious that the level of training offered in the concluding phases of a five-year or fifth-year teacher program lends itself well to graduate crediting. By their very nature, introductory courses in pedagogy and related studies are just that: relatively low-level introductions to the theory and practice of teaching, designed to meet the needs of teaching novices. Regarding programs that lay heavy emphasis on practical field-based experiences, it is difficult to know what to make of the practice of awarding graduate credit for work completed. No matter how invaluable and indispensable clinical training may be, the nature of what beginners do in school classrooms makes assessment and evaluation of their work according to *academic* criteria exceedingly difficult, if not impossible.

*Entry-level teacher training ought to combine a field
experience correlated with intensive didactic instruction
and should be organized as a postgraduate sequence of
limited proportions and relatively short duration.*

If a three-year baccalaureate degree program is unlikely ever to win
acceptance, the same could be said of a five-year or fifth-year undergraduate program of the sort some "integrated" teacher education institutions seek to provide. Postponing the awarding of a bachelor's degree
until a fifth year of education study is completed, in other words, hardly
seems warranted. A logical and far more defensible alternative would
be simply to *institute a separate, semester-long postgraduation sequence of studies devoted exclusively to teacher training* (including a
clinical component). This addendum to an arts and sciences degree
program, in effect, would mark the main route to entry-level teacher
certification. Preparatory studies and experiences would carry neither
undergraduate nor graduate academic credit as such; nor would they be
tied to any formal degree program whatever. In its entirety, the 16-week
internship would constitute a free-standing licensure program leading
directly to initial state certification.

Several important considerations favor some such arrangement
(assuming, of course, that any type of teacher training should be conducted wholly or in part under academic auspices, a presumption remaining to be considered). Awarding undergraduate credits subsequent
to graduation, of course, would be rather pointless. But neither would it
be necessary or justifiable to award credit toward a graduate degree.
Absent either choice, the training could be designed solely and exclusively to accomplish its own circumscribed purpose, without its having
to be adapted to fit the special requirements of, or to conform to the
criteria appropriate to, a full-fledged graduate program.

A nondegree certification sequence would serve to keep the role
that graduate master's programs perform (fulfilling licensure renewal or
advanced certification requirements) separate from that of a training
sequence leading to initial licensure. Candidates seeking initial or entry-
level certification, after all, are presumably engaged in an enterprise with
its own unique set of demands. These are—or should be—quite different
from those appropriate for experienced teachers pursuing academic
graduate study at a more advanced level.

Finally, in principle, if initial certification did not entail graduate-level work, the door would be left open for high-quality undergrad-

uate institutions lacking graduate-level programs of their own to retain their involvement in teacher preparation. Otherwise, in an environment dominated and controlled by graduate research universities, only institutions capable of sustaining postbaccalaureate education could hope to offer credible teacher education programs for their students. The prospect that teacher education within some of the nation's outstanding undergraduate liberal arts colleges might be legislated out of existence ought to be deeply troubling. Contrary to what some advocates for extended graduate programs allege, not all small teacher education programs, even as currently constituted, are irredeemably flawed or necessarily inferior in quality to those offered in larger institutions. Some may be decidedly better.

FIELD-BASED TEACHER PREPARATION

Teacher training ought to be a genuinely collaborative and cooperative venture shared by academic teacher educators and experienced classroom practitioners. The former should assume primary responsibility for didactic instruction. The latter should be charged with taking the lead in helping novices develop practical instructional and managerial skills.

Before exploring the possible organization and specific content of postbaccalaureate teacher training along the lines here suggested, the question as to whether institutions of higher learning have any viable and defensible part to play in the initial training of teachers beyond supplying a foundation in the liberal arts is one that ought to be confronted squarely.[11] By now the case for field-based teacher education is fairly widely known. It does have a certain plausibility about it.[12] What colleges and universities do best is to generate and impart basic knowledge. Learning to become a teacher necessitates practical training, however, and of a sort academic institutions characteristically are ill-adapted to convey. Many education students report their university-based courses are taught in a vacuum, so to speak, and that they are not particularly effective in helping them develop their teaching abilities. Graduates of conventional programs often find upon first entering a classroom that they are woefully underprepared for the challenges they confront. Part of the problem, paradoxically, is that traditional teacher education programs usually supply *too much* training, far more perhaps than novices lacking the practical experience that otherwise might give it meaning can absorb effectively. Training is offered prematurely, at the wrong time, and in a setting divorced from the context in which the learning will be applied.

Teacher candidates, it is said, cannot be expected to learn how to become teachers by listening to professors of education talk about instruction. Teaching is a practical art unlikely to be mastered through academic study. What is needed instead is supervised practice, trial and error, and repeated effort. As James Conant observed decades ago and many have reiterated forcefully ever since, it is as improbable that a novice can become a good teacher by enrolling in education courses as it is that an aspiring artist will attain proficiency as a painter or musician by attending lectures on art or music theory.

Preferable by far, some argue, would be state-operated, field-based teacher preparation programs designed and organized by state departments of education, conducted in public schools, and staffed by school personnel.[13] Already the states bear responsibility for setting licensure standards. There is nothing to prevent them from assuming direct control of teacher education itself if they chose to do so. In fact, many believe encouraging states to do just that might prove a very good idea.

One obvious benefit would be that in a school-based preparatory program, coaching would be done by classroom veterans, practitioners whose skills were honed by years of practical experience. It would be more helpful, runs the argument, to have prospective teachers taught by those who supervise schoolchildren daily and who work closely with the realities of elementary or secondary classrooms than by campus-based academics who may not have been in a public school classroom for years, if ever. Professors have their own professional agendas to pursue, few of them pertinent to supervising student interns in public school settings.

Institutions of higher learning are notorious for their apparent unwillingness or inability to adjust or link student admissions to specific programs with prevailing marketplace demands. All too frequently, colleges and universities continue to churn out graduates for fields where there is low demand (as is currently true in elementary education) while at the same time fail to promote enrollments to prepare teachers for such high-demand teaching fields as high-school science and mathematics. Bilingual teachers, meanwhile, already much in demand in certain parts of the country and in growing demand in others, are simply not to be had. Presumably, state-operated programs based in schools would be more adept when it came to matching teacher demand with an appropriate-size supply of qualified candidates. And throughout, it could be safely assumed that whatever training was offered would be more continuous with actual school practice than anything taught in classrooms on a college campus.

ACADEMIC SPONSORSHIP OF
INITIAL TEACHER LICENSURE

All of the foregoing notwithstanding, the weakness of the argument for school-based teacher preparation perhaps is that it tends both to oversimplify and to overstate its case. In principle at least, there is nothing to preclude the possibility of having some university-sponsored education courses taught on-site in professional development schools, assuming locating them off-campus was considered necessary or desirable. The claim that pedagogical methods courses should be offered simultaneously, or in closer conjunction with, field experiences and practice teaching is well taken. But neither argument necessarily affords a basis for deciding *who* would be best equipped to direct the instruction, collegiate teacher educators or classroom teachers, or some combination of both. It may be true, in other words, that the best place to acquire a complex set of skills is the setting in which those skills are practiced. But from that it does not follow that *only* practitioners of that expertise have something meaningful and vital to offer teacher candidates during their training.

A great deal depends on how the relationship between theory and practice in teaching is conceived. If indeed it were the case that the act of instruction amounted to nothing more than the exercise of a discrete set of skills, bereft of any theoretical setting or foundation, it would follow that learning skills drawn from the teacher's grab bag of tricks and practicing their application through simple apprenticeship would be all that teacher preparation required. That any such view is simplistic and misconceived ought to be obvious. Teaching is a fairly complex phenomenon and not something mechanically rule-bound, involving as it does a whole array of judgments and evaluative considerations, most of which are grounded in what the teacher knows, understands, and values as well as what he or she is able to *do* performatively.

Skepticism about the existence of any extensive scientifically validated knowledge base for teaching is not equivalent to an outright denial that teaching is information-based or that little or nothing is known to help guide the process. In fact, there is a significant amount of relevant information to be had about child psychology and adolescent development; about learning processes; about classroom management, learner differences, assessment and evaluation of instruction; about cultural differences and their impact on learning; about education in its larger societal setting; about the political, social, cultural, and economic dimensions of teaching and learning, within school settings and without. Contextual knowledge of this sort is critical not only to anyone's understanding of the "technology" of teaching and learning but also to comprehension and full appreciation of its larger meaning and purposes.

But even only insofar as teaching itself is concerned, a full and generous conception of the modern teacher's role extends far beyond the image of someone serving simply as a purveyor of facts or transmitter of a received body of fixed knowledge. "The challenges teachers face today are prodigious and likely to mount," it has been observed. "Teachers are . . . expected to promote very high levels of cognitive skill and to open up for students diverse and wide-ranging bodies of knowledge. . . . This is significantly different from earlier aspirations, which . . . had less to do with developing complex student competencies than with transmitting knowledge and information."[14] Again, exemplary teachers "help students do more than memorize and recite. Good teachers show students how to reason; to sort through competing ideas and arrive at sound conclusions; to speak and write effectively; and to decide what knowledge is most worthwhile."[15] The means by which teachers learn how to strive toward the accomplishment of these important goals go beyond practice-bound prescriptions and formulas. They are in a very real (if as-yet imperfectly understood) sense the complex products of different kinds and levels of knowing possessed by a teacher.

A cherished but now largely discredited tenet held by advocates of the "science of education" movement earlier in the twentieth century was that teaching was a generic, rule-governed activity bounded by a finite number of pedagogical laws and principles, regulative ideas whose applications were direct and straightforward. More recent thinking has helped advance awareness that matters are not nearly so simple. Teaching expertise is now viewed increasingly as something that is context-specific and that is thought by some to depend to a certain extent (among many other things) on the teacher's "pedagogical content knowledge"— that is, on an understanding of and appreciation for "the most useful forms of representation" of the content of any specific subject that is taught, including "the most powerful analogies, illustrations, examples, explanations, and demonstrations" of that subject matter, the ways of "formulating the subject that make it comprehensible to others," and "an understanding of what makes the learning of specific concepts easy or difficult: the conceptions and preconceptions that students of different ages and backgrounds bring with them to the learning."[16]

Experience and practice are helpful. But pedagogical content knowledge is also something susceptible to being taught didactically and, indeed, can constitute the bulk of the content of pedagogical methods courses, together with a knowledge of support resources and techniques. (The basic concept of pedagogical content knowledge has been greatly refined and expanded upon in recent years, although, it might be noted, in its original incarnation simply as "teaching knowledge," the idea traces all the way back to the formative years of the normal school movement in the mid-nineteenth century.)

Teaching challenges aside, there is a certain amount of information that is useful—some would say, essential—that even rank novices must possess in order to function effectively. After all, teachers do more than engage in serial acts of teaching. They diagnose, assess, evaluate, plan, judge, remediate, intervene, facilitate, counsel, and manage, among many other things. Throughout, they need to be aware, for example, of the ethical obligations and responsibilities attached to their actions, not to mention their legal rights and liability as teachers. Presumably they should have at least some basic information about the governance and administration of the public education system of which they are a part. Knowledge of the rudiments of curriculum development and instructional planning is probably important, as are the fundamentals of student testing; the effective use of teaching technologies, and probably much else besides—*almost none of it reducible to direct or linear application based on simple rules and procedures.* Nor, once again, does it seem plausible to claim that all of the knowledge of this sort that teachers need can best or most effectively be learned on the job, through slow trial and error, or by informal processes of socialization and acculturation to school norms and customs.

Pivotal to any discussion of teacher preparation must be due regard for the type of teachers contemporary schooling demands. The point can easily be exaggerated, but it would still seem that there is a choice to be made between instructional technicians employed to keep children preoccupied with worksheets and texts and informed decisionmakers with some pretension to being considered "professionals." Those who would "de-skill" teaching appear to harbor a penchant for automaton-like hired hands who "fit in," who do as others instruct and direct them, and who adhere closely to the detailed curricular prescriptions and bureaucratic formulas imposed on them from above. The alternative suggests teachers who in some sense are autonomous instructional leaders; true pedagogues capable of assisting in the work of designing, implementing, and evaluating curricula and instruction; instructors who can exercise a degree of independent judgment in determining what actually transpires in classrooms.

Sometimes overlooked by enthusiasts for field-based apprenticeship training, too, is the point that in the final analysis, public schools cannot be expected to be their own critics. It simply is not at all realistic to anticipate that schools, left to their own devices, will train teachers who are critical minded and who might challenge conventional wisdom and prevailing usage. The aim of teacher education (especially in its more advanced stages) therefore ought not to become one of simple social reproduction—especially since public schools themselves often fail to provide exemplary models for educational practice. Some, of course, are outstanding in quality. But many are mediocre or fairly undistinguished. And, quite bluntly, it must be conceded that a distressingly high number of them are execrable. Hence, it seems highly inadvisable to place prospective teachers in virtual thralldom to the norms of any given school workplace.[17]

What the foregoing suggests, instead, is an approximate sharing or division of labor in which experienced teachers are charged with helping to "coach" novices, while college- or university-based teacher educators assume primary responsibility for designing and supervising didactic instruction of a broader and more theoretical character. Ideally, a synergy would emerge out of the collaboration and partnership between the two. Working closely in concert with one another, academic specialists would supply the directive "contextual" and "interpretive" knowledge or background information thought to be essential. Their school-based clinical colleagues would assist candidates more directly with the "hands-on" specifics of classroom management, instructional planning, and actual teaching.

CLINICAL PREPARATION

Much recurrent controversy surrounding teacher education boils down to the question of how much training genuinely is needed at the preservice level. How the question is phrased is important, because what an *entry-level* novice needs for *initial* certification is a rather different query from how much professional training teachers ought to acquire generally. The answer to the former—or, rather, one possible response—is that minimum preparation for beginners should be substantially more than what abbreviated "quick-and-dirty" alternative programs supply. It could be about the same as that typically required of undergraduate secondary-education majors in a conventional baccalaureate program and slightly less than that required of undergraduate elementary majors in the same type of program. Substantially less than what is imposed in a five-year, combined or integrated undergraduate-and-graduate regimen would be more than adequate. Preservice training roughly the same as that given in a fifth-year, graduate-degree program, although offered at a lower level and on a more intensive basis, likewise should be sufficient.

Whatever the amount or length of training, it figures as a foregone conclusion that a type of Gresham's law will ensure that instructional content expands to fill up whatever space and time are afforded. For present purposes, the assumption is that all (or nearly all) of the essential elements of preparatory training for postbaccalaureate liberal arts graduates could be incorporated within a relatively brief regimen of carefully selected education course work combined with intensive clinical practice. In its entirety, it would be possible to complete the whole sequence satisfactorily *in about half an academic year*—or, roughly, within the equivalent of a 16-week semester. Teacher education's harshest critics might consider this stipulation far too generous while most teacher educators would dismiss it as patently insufficient—suggesting perhaps the proportions are about right.

On pedagogical grounds, if on no other, there are many ways in which the initial preparatory curriculum could and should be pared down to fit a program of short duration. (Again, for the same reasons, what is taught should be conveyed in a more intensive way than what the usual leisurely pace of academe affords.) So-called generic or general courses in teaching methodology, for example, would give way to subject-specific pedagogical courses. General curriculum theory probably could be safely dispensed with or incorporated within sequences devoted to human development and learning. Courses in the social foundations of education possibly would be omitted as well or offered in abbreviated form.

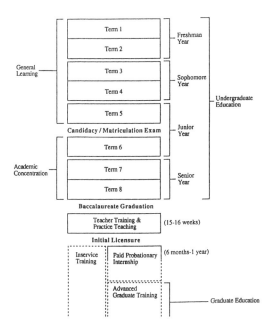

Opportunities for teachers to acquire a broad historical or philosophic perspective on their work are undoubtedly important. So also is looking at education in a global context, or exploring the political, ideological, and economic dimensions of contemporary schooling. The problem with most foundational courses in the undergraduate teacher education course of study is that they come too soon (at least when framed in the context of specific professional preparation rather than liberal studies). What they do, essentially, is attempt to induce students to grapple with problems and questions they have not yet confronted for themselves, or for which in most instances they are not intellectually and emotionally ready. Moreover, students usually lack the fund of real-life professional experience that would make social, historical, and philosophic issues compelling or in some respects even intelligible.

Hence the better alternative by far would be to defer "foundational" offerings to the graduate phase of inservice training where they could make a more meaningful contribution. If it were thought useful to retain a critical foundational element in preservice teacher education, an intensive but short-term seminar treating selected philosophic and sociological themes might be in order. It could involve, for example, closely focused discussion on educational goals and objectives, issues of equity and access, and an abbreviated analysis of some of the sociocultural determinants of learner achievement in schools.

The advisability of postponing certain theoretical elements applies with equal force to the bulk of what is ordinarily supplied in traditional courses in educational psychology, human development, and learning theory. Most offer a surfeit of riches: child and adolescent psychosocial, emotional and moral development (Piaget, Vygotsky, Erikson, Kohlberg); language acquisition and maturation; intelligence measurement; ability differences; cognitive and learning styles; memory; motivational theory (Bandura, Maslow); attribution theory; learning theory (behaviorist, cognitive, constructivist); creativity; multiculturalism and human diversity (cognitive, gender, linguistic, social class, ethnic, and racial); and so on *ad infinitum*.[18]

Once again, however, it needs to be appreciated that teacher candidates nearing entry into their profession (for perfectly understandable reasons) are preoccupied mostly with questions of basic "survival." Their primary interest lies in acquiring the practical competence needed to enter and manage an actual classroom. Given this mind-set, it seems doubtful that many are prepared to assimilate or use very much of the abundant theoretical and empirical material commonly presented. As in the case of social foundations, while a few key elements ought to be retained within preservice training at the postbachelor's level, much of what is taught in psychology of education courses—*or, for that matter, in most preservice courses*—ought to be reserved for greater in-depth treatment at a still later time, when teachers are involved in graduate study.

An optimal 16-week or half-year program for entry-level, preservice teacher preparation would combine intensive theoretical and didactic instruction with supervised student teaching. A major consideration ought to be the articulation and close correlation of clinical practice with instruction in teaching methodology.

Details about the instructional content and organization of a preservice internship might best be left for experimentation. One possible pattern could feature a four-week period of intensive, full-time instruction (five or six 50-minute classroom contact hours daily), followed by 12 weeks of half-time supervised student teaching (three or four hours daily for a

weekly on-site total of 15 to 20 clock hours), accompanied simultaneously by half-time didactic instruction (two or three hours daily, or
ten to 15 hours weekly). An alternative would be an eight-week period
of clinical field experience positioned in between two four-week academic sessions. Or an intensive two-week period of instruction might
be arranged prior to student teaching, followed by a series of workshops
or seminars coming at its conclusion, and so on. Still other possibilities
worth trying might include a "2+12+2" or a "4+12" sequence, or perhaps
a "3+10+3" or "2+10+4" arrangement.

*The ideal format for the initial certification program
would "bracket" classroom teaching with theoretical and
didactic instruction, before and after, while leaving room
for pedagogical instruction throughout the practice
teaching experience.*

No matter what the configuration, it ought to be possible for interns to
earn the nondegree equivalent of 19 to 20 academic credit hours, based
on the total number of classroom contact hours completed over 16
weeks, *excluding* student teaching. For any pattern chosen, the overriding consideration would be to ensure that methods courses were scheduled *concurrent* with student teaching. The optimal placement of
pedagogical course work, as most former students who are now teachers
will heartily attest, is immediately prior to or, better yet, during the
opening phases of the clinical field experience itself. Considering the
low regard in which students tend to hold conventional methods courses,
special pains would need to be taken to ensure that pedagogical instruction was pertinent, helpful, and applicable to specific situations and tasks
students would be likely to face during student teaching.

Another important piece of testimony from former preservice
students worth heeding is the often-reiterated complaint that teacher
preparation fails to give sufficient attention to issues of classroom
management. Specifically, teacher candidates are most apprehensive
about how to handle student discipline problems. Yet this is an area in
which they feel they receive the least guidance.[19] Experience indicates
that separate courses devoted to management considerations may not
necessarily be effective. A better approach, it has been suggested, would
be to integrate classroom management issues, concepts, and recommended strategies within methods courses, field experiences, and
student teaching.[20]

Didactic instruction could be arranged within many different formats, ranging from short courses to seminars to workshops. Some topics or content areas would lend themselves to drastically abbreviated treatment, occupying no more than a few teaching hours. Discussions of the structure and governance of public education, or of its legal aspects, for example, might last no more than a few days. The equivalent of a brief introductory course in educational psychology, an overview of special education, and teaching about testing and assessment might each require more time and involve several weeks of concentrated attention.

Fostering students' competency in the utilization or production of instructional media would be more time-intensive still. Probably an instructional media and materials course would require extended instruction across the entire span of the internship (although, of course, the assumption ideally is that all baccalaureate graduates would already be fully computer-literate, which would help facilitate learning some facets of the material). Subject-specific methods seminars for secondary teachers, on the other hand, would need to be coordinated closely with the timing of student teaching. So also would comparable methodological courses and workshops for elementary teachers in language arts, reading, mathematics, science, and social studies. The optimal mix of theory and practice within pedagogical instruction for either level would require fine-tuning and adjustment.

> *Beginning teachers need to know something about the*
> *structural organization of schooling, legal and*
> *ethical aspects of teaching, testing assessment,*
> *curricula and learning, learner development,*
> *and instructional media.*

Offered for illustrative purposes are some of the major instructional elements that immediately suggest themselves for possible inclusion in a preservice teacher internship. The following enumeration of concepts, terms, and skills cited is by no means intended to be exhaustive or all-inclusive. No given program would be limited to them, nor would it necessarily encompass all of the topics cited.

Structure, Governance, and Organization:

Composition, functions, and statutory authority of the state department of public instruction; state teacher licensure and certification rules and regulations; powers, functions, and roles of federal, state, and local governments in the governance and financing of public education; composition, functions, and statutory authority of local school boards; role and responsibilities of the district superintendent; line and staff positions within local school districts; organization, management, and administration of local instructional, personnel, and support services; role and responsibilities of building principals and staff; site-based management, and administrative leadership; local district hiring and promotion policies and practices; national and local teachers' organizations; school policies governing curriculum development and instructional resources; teacher compensation and career ladders; parent, teacher, and student organizations and community relations; home schooling; policy issues and trends affecting public and private schooling.

Legal and Ethical Aspects of Teaching and Public Schooling:

Terms of eligibility and conditions of teacher employment; work contracts; conditions of evaluation and assessment of district employees; personnel records and teacher evaluation; collective bargaining and teachers' professional associations; teacher unions; termination of employment (due process, procedural requirements, nondisciplinary dismissals, dismissal for cause); tort liability; First Amendment rights of teachers and students; teachers' reporting obligations (physical, emotional, and sexual abuse of students); sexual harassment; academic record-keeping requirements; teacher and student privacy rights and confidentiality; discrimination and equity issues; student discipline (expulsion, suspension, corporal punishment, academic sanctions, behavior codes, search and seizure); applicable laws, rules, regulations, and procedural safeguards involved in the management of student behavior; special considerations and liabilities governing off-site instruction and supervision; major judicial decisions affecting schooling (e.g., school prayer and religious observances); censorship; legal responsibilities relative to student disabilities and exceptionality; academic freedom; learners' freedoms; professional ethics and teachers' ethical responsibilities.

Education in Its Social Bearings:

Types of knowledge and modes of knowing; education as initiation and enculturation; changing functions and aims of formal schooling; teaching and learning as social reproduction; historical and contemporary criticism of American schools; modern issues and trends; societal and cultural determinants of curricula and instruction.

Human Development, Curricula, and Learning:

Child and/or adolescent development (cognitive, social, moral); psychology of learning and learning styles; student self-concept and self-esteem; dynamics of language acquisition; classroom motivation; individual differences (socioeconomic, cultural, and gender); instructional planning and organization (organizing instructional units, developing lesson plans, pacing and sequencing instruction, resource utilization, time management); at-risk students; classroom organization, management, and supervision; effective teaching and learning skills; grading and assessment; social, cultural, economic, and environmental factors affecting learner performance and achievement.[21]

Learner Exceptionality:

Learner differences and the nature and effects of exceptionalities (visual impairment, hearing impairment, speech impairment, mental retardation, behavior disorders, orthopedic disabilities, learning disorders, giftedness); diversity issues relative to culture, language, gender, religion, race, ethnicity, and sexuality; basic terminology for defining and identifying students with exceptional learning needs; due-process rights, ethical concerns, and legal provisions related to the assessment, eligibility, and placement of exceptional students; similarities and differences among the cognitive, physical, cultural, social, emotional, and developmental needs of typical and exceptional learners; characteristics of normal, delayed, and disordered communication patterns among exceptional learners; cultural, social, and biological etiology of exceptionality; typical procedures utilized for screenings, referrals and classification of students; identification and use of curricula, instructional methods, materials, equipment, supplies, and other resources appropriate for meeting the needs of students with exceptionalities; development and use of assessment instruments and procedures for special-needs learners; terms and conditions governing the administration of medication to students; effects of medication and other intervention techniques on the cognitive, physical, social, and emotional behavior of individuals with exceptionalities; basic classroom management methods and techniques recommended for use with students with exceptional learning needs; strategies and programs for gifted and talented students; typical concerns of parents of students with exceptional learning needs and appropriate strategies for helping with parental concerns; standards, policies, and recommended practices of professional organizations such as the Council for Exceptional Children and similar national, regional, and state associations.[22]

Testing, Measurement, and Evaluation:

Formative and summative evaluation and performance assessment; processes and procedures for student grading (point systems, percentage grading, contract systems, incremental difference); differing types of learner assessment; nontraditional and "authentic" assessment (portfolios, exhibitions, demonstrations); fundamentals of test design; aligning testing with instructional objectives; basic principles of objective and subjective test construction; summarizing and interpreting measurements; typical assessment errors; item analysis (discrimination and difficulty indices); practice effects; reliability and validity of measurements; rating scales and indices; nominal, ordinal, interval, and ratio scales; selecting, utilizing, and evaluating standardized tests; culture-fair and culture-free tests; criterion- versus norm-referenced testing and evaluation; interpretation and use of standardized test results; test norms; rudiments of applied descriptive and inferential statistics: frequency distribution, sampling, range, measures of central tendency (mean, median, mode) and variance, standard error of measurement, standard scores, correlational measures, correlation, and causation.

Instructional Media:

Role of media in instruction; systematic planning of media utilization; elements of visual design; nonprojected visuals (still images, graphics, models, displays); projected visuals (slides, overheads, filmstrips, opaque projection, film); audio media; motion media (video and film); computers (operating systems and applications, LCD panel projection; animation, CD-ROM, task-based software classifications and evaluations, word-processing, spreadsheets and spreadsheet gradebooks, graphics, electronic mail, sending and receiving messages, accessing data bases and downloading information, desktop publishing, image scanning); multimedia systems (sound-slide sets, interactive video, computer multimedia systems, hypermedia); telecommunication systems (interactive, noninteractive, and pseudointeractive, one- and two-way audio and video, compressed video, radio, and television); distance education and teleconferencing; fundamentals of the Internet (networks, servers, Websites, home-pages); basic photography and image digitalization; simulations and games; utilizing media setups (overhead projectors, filmstrip projectors, video recorder/players and playback systems); basics of dry mounting, laminating, graphics production, thermal transparencies and overlays, video editing.[23]

Making a concentrated, intensive teacher preparation program work effectively would require careful articulation of each curricular element with all others, not to mention a degree of instructional coordination and correlation rarely found today in college and university settings. Several other equally important conditions would need to be satisfied in order to make any postbaccalaureate, semester-long internship of the sort contemplated truly viable. First, there would have to be a cadre of dedicated teacher educators charged with overall authority and responsibility for designing the internship experience. Each would be a specialist in his or her respective area, and each would work closely with other team members in program planning, development, and instruction.

Second, the internship would have to be a genuinely collaborative effort or partnership between schools or colleges of education and public school districts. It would be staffed not only by professors of education but also by experienced classroom teachers who had been specially trained to act as clinical supervisors for student teaching. Pedagogical clinicians would serve in all respects as equals with their academic colleagues, dividing their time between working with teacher candidates and regular classroom instruction at the elementary or secondary level.

Third, colleges and universities would need to devise whatever special arrangements were necessary for enrolling prospective teachers and collecting tuition for noncredit instruction (presumably offered twice yearly, during both semesters in any given academic year). Most large institutions of higher learning already have mechanisms in place for awarding credit for participation in special workshops and conferences unconnected with formal degree programs.

Fourth, some thought would have to go into deciding how best to handle the logistics of instruction and whether classes ought to be convened in a campus setting or sometimes within the precincts of a cooperating school. Current reform wisdom to the contrary, it seems a relatively inconsequential choice where classes actually would be conducted, so long as adequate arrangements were made for linking theory and practice, and demonstration with application, throughout the course of the internship. In fact, logistical considerations (including geographical proximity to school sites in sufficient numbers to accommodate internship student enrollment) might become paramount, determining in the final analysis which academic institutions—regardless of size— were able to mount viable training programs.

Obviously, only applicants already holding bachelor's degrees would be eligible to apply for teacher training. Whether additional entrance requirements should be imposed—minimum undergraduate grade point average or class ranking, a recommendation from a practicum supervisor, test scores—would remain to be decided. How best to offer subsequent training for specialized types of certification also would need to be considered: for reading specialists, special educators, and so forth. Training for those intending to teach subject specialties included in lower schools but not at the undergraduate level in colleges and universities, such as health and physical education, business education, vocational and technical education, and so on, would pose a separate challenge.

Also awaiting resolution would be the question as to whether students completing their training should be required to submit themselves for further assessment prior to being recommended for state licensure, as, for example, by means of the NTE or some other state- or nationally normed evaluation instrument. State licensing standards and requirements might have to be adjusted in some cases to accommodate graduates of a half-year program, at least until the program's credibility was well established to everyone's satisfaction. In all likelihood, many other issues and complications would need to be confronted and dealt with before the half-year pattern won widespread acceptance as an accepted route to initial certification.

POSSIBLE CRITICISMS AND RESPONSES

Instituting a half-year teacher-training program in lieu of some more extensive and prolonged course of study undoubtedly would prove controversial. Some critics would view it as little more than a thinly disguised effort to reduce teacher preparation to apprenticeship training, especially in light of the proposed net reduction of pedagogical instruction, compared with lengthier programs. Some would dismiss the entire idea as just another minor variation on the theme of "alternative" certification. Still others might question whether it offers any real advantages over a five-year baccalaureate degree program of the type already pioneered by some schools and colleges of education.

Its relative brevity would do nothing to recommend it to partisans of extended fifth-year programs now offered partly at the graduate level, nor to those who are otherwise persuaded that length and complexity of training eventually will help elevate teaching to the status of a true profession. Again, proponents of school-based teacher-training programs might object to the retention of academics as teachers or to the fact that the internship would still fall ultimately under the authority of a college or university, even though linked in partnership with selected school training sites. The very fact that postbaccalaureate training would be required at all might well be challenged. Many other questions could be raised about how training might be articulated with licensure renewal, or with advanced certification, or with master's-level graduate study in education. In sum, the proposed pattern probably offers something to offend or trouble almost everyone—which at least should commend it for attention.

The very real strengths and advantages of short-training ought not to be discounted or minimized, however. The argument here presented on its behalf accepts as its first premise that a major key to improving the education of teachers lies not with adjustments to professional training per se but with reforms in general education. The value and relevance of liberal arts learning are accepted as a given; and it is assumed for present purposes that the case for liberal learning requires no further adumbration. At the same time, the defense for a new and different form of teacher preparation resting on a liberal arts foundation does not automatically assume that "more" of the same is necessarily "better"—that is, that teacher candidates simply should be required to take more courses of the traditional sort in the various arts and sciences.

What is called for, rather, is a more coherent and cohesive undergraduate course of studies, something far more integrative in character than what colleges and universities today customarily supply. With a proper reconstitution of liberal learning would come an end to the need for colleges of education and state departments of instruction to stipulate specific general studies courses a teacher candidate had to complete. It could be safely assumed, rather, that students were already well acquainted with a broad range of disciplines, as attested to by the very fact they had attained a degree. (A return to the notion that a baccalaureate degree might mark out something substantive by way of academic achievement is a pleasant prospect to contemplate.)

Second, the argument takes a clear and unequivocal stance in judging as futile any attempt to accommodate both liberal learning and professional training within a four-year undergraduate program. Virtually all of the baccalaureate degree course of studies should be given over to liberal arts education, without compromise. Specialized teacher education therefore would have to be deferred or postponed to the postbachelor's level.

Due allowance is made for the fact that teachers must be reasonably well versed in the subjects they essay to teach and that they must have acquired mastery—or at least a significant command—of the key elements of whatever discipline or subject matter is selected as a teaching field. The presumption is that 45 to 48 academic credits of course work, representing approximately 40 percent of all credits earned toward the degree, would be adequate for the purpose. Three semesters of study can hardly be expected to make someone an expert in his or her field (or a combination of related fields), naturally, but it would substantially exceed what many existing programs and state regulations now require of teachers.

Comprehensive matriculation examinations administered to all undergraduates halfway through the third year would go far to satisfy the need now addressed by the separate testing of prospective teachers for basic literacy skills as a prerequisite for licensure. Criterion-referenced scoring tied to knowledge of academic subject matter halfway through the junior year of college certainly would better serve the purpose of trying to determine whether prospective teachers among the total student body had achieved some minimal level of competency. Presumably it would be feasible to maintain higher standards than those now controlling current assessments. Overall, the entire evaluation process could be made more rigorous and meaningful than current practice allows.

Under conditions now prevailing, there are several points of entry into teacher education scattered across the undergraduate years. Some students are accepted directly into programs as freshmen. Others do not declare a major until the end of the sophomore year or the beginning of the following year. Making completion of an entire baccalaureate arts and sciences degree prerequisite to admission to teacher education might go far in helping to ensure a better pool of teacher candidates because the pool would now consist of students whose academic ability already had been demonstrated as successful undergraduates. By the same token, if internship admission standards are reasonably selective, it should be possible to recruit academically talented applicants without insisting that they qualify for admission to graduate-level studies or commit themselves to extended graduate training.

Holding a degree "hostage" until candidates complete their licensure preparation, as now occurs in five-year programs, hardly seems necessary either, even assuming a full extra year of training were deemed indispensable. In any event, under the terms outlined in support of a four- or five-month apprenticeship, students who elected not to pursue a teaching career would still have satisfied all of the requirements for a baccalaureate degree and could turn elsewhere for postbaccalaureate training.

Although critics might find the "minimalist" approach to teacher education objectionable, there is much to be said for imposing stringent restrictions on the time and space set aside for pedagogical training. That preservice tutelage must encompass nearly everything teachers need to know is a precarious assumption; and it especially fails to make much sense given the popularity of the idea of career ladders for teachers, licensure renewal requirements, and advancing or staged levels of certification—all of them tied to further training. Pedagogically, it seems indefensible to overwhelm novices with more theory and detail than they can profitably assimilate as they first prepare themselves to enter classrooms. And from an economic standpoint, it seems logical to do everything possible to keep costs down and not to prolong expensive training any longer than absolutely needed.

Above all, considering how often students in education schools and colleges across the country complain about the repetitiveness or duplication of content typical of the methods courses they are obliged to take, the time and space limits of a single 16-week semester might have a salutory effect. If nothing else, it would encourage teacher educators to decide at the outset what is really critical or essential and compel them to adjust their instruction accordingly. Nothing so wonderfully concentrates academic attention or encourages a sharper focus on matters at hand than stringent constraints placed on the time allowed for instruction.

A noncredit preparatory sequence as the vehicle for attaining initial licensure would help to preserve the intellectual rigor and academic integrity of graduate study in education. With matters of prestige, status, and professionalism excluded as extraneous considerations, there is little about initial teacher preparation to warrant its being offered at the graduate level. Formal programs of instruction leading to a master's degree and beyond ought to be reserved for advanced study, not for lower-level preparatory programs for classroom teaching. Alternatively, if the tendency to push teacher education upward into graduate-level training continues unimpeded, it is difficult to know where the process will stop—probably with something resembling Doctor of Pedagogy degrees required of everyone (not just for so-called master teachers, as has already been suggested in some quarters).

Yet another presumed advantage of the proposed training program would be its close linkage of pedagogical instruction with practical field experience. In order for the instruction to fulfill its intended purpose, genuine partnerships between collegiate education units and public schools would become not simply desirable but absolutely essential. Academicians would be set the task of accomplishing what they do best: bringing together an array of theoretical perspectives and detailed information on the work of teaching and then presenting it in usable, applied forms. Experienced teachers, for their part, would co-teach methods courses or otherwise help introduce novices to resources and strategies thought useful for success in student teaching.

Graduates would be eminently employable. They would have devoted four full years or its equivalent to grounding themselves in a broad array of liberal arts disciplines plus a preservice practicum. Their academic competence and general literacy would be attested to by the fact they had successfully completed a baccalaureate degree, one exhibiting some coherence of structure and specifiable substance. Additionally, they would have satisfied the requirements for a teaching field or fields as an integral part of their studies. Then they would have spent four or five months in intensive, concentrated training of a more specialized character, combined and integrated with an extensive period of practice teaching. Now recommended for licensure, carrying with it the expectation of further inservice training prerequisite to renewal (workshops, conferences, attendance at professional meetings, and possibly master's-level graduate study), successful candidates would be well prepared to assume their duties as classroom educators. If anything further seemed necessary, "probationary" internship status could be conferred on graduates throughout their first year of contractual employment as teachers.

*An initial certification program for teachers might
culminate in a year-long probationary internship under
the supervision of an experienced mentor and would lead
to renewable licensure. Continuing inservice development
thereafter could be facilitated through workshops, short
courses, conferences, and—for academically able
candidates—formal graduate study.*

It is difficult to judge whether a semester-long program for teacher education could attract widespread support. Certainly in spirit, although not in substance or structure, the concentrated preparation it reflects is consistent with the popular trend toward "alternative" certification programs. The theme also is congruent with growing national interest in outcomes assessment and performance-based standards for teacher certification. The economic advantages of shortening the typical state-assisted regimen should prove popular with state legislators, if not with some members of the education professoriate, and might prove tolerable to critics inclined to deny that any training beyond practice teaching is needed.

Academic faculty in arts and sciences almost certainly would embrace the emphasis placed on more and better liberal-arts learning. But whether they would be as enthusiastic about effecting reforms of the sort needed and called for seems less certain. Smaller colleges with an investment in teacher education could not help but support the short-term training idea if the only alternative offered were longer graduate programs they are unsuited to support and maintain. Students contemplating careers as teachers might welcome the advent of a shorter training period as well, as would their families, assuming the only options involved postbaccalaureate graduate study. Public school teachers and administrators who now *sotto voce* criticize existing programs as too impractical likewise might endorse programs in which they were made full-fledged partners and in which they shared more direct responsibility for their success. To the extent that professors of education felt their own interests were not directly threatened, some might be willing to give the idea a fair hearing—at one time or another, after all, practically everything else has been tried out somewhere.

Stiffest opposition to the half-year program would most likely issue from the teacher education establishment, chiefly from national accrediting bodies and education faculties within larger, graduate-focused universities. Having secured support—or at least acquiescence—from the powers that be for the installation of longer, graduate-level teacher education programs, it seems highly unlikely many would now consider the idea of a shorter, more concentrated program either compelling or especially desirable. Between a program format allowing expansive curricular space and one forcing hard choices from an array of instructional possibilities, the decision would not be difficult for faculty to make. Powerful disincentives, in other words, militate against the current practice of "front-loading" entry-level teacher education.

On the other hand, it is worth recalling the fate of normal training institutes in the waning years of the nineteenth century. Even as their supporters advanced ever more grandiose plans for all-encompassing teacher education programs, offered at multiple levels, their institutions were poised on the brink of extinction. And within a matter of a scant few decades, normal academies and seminaries, together with the lofty ambitions of their leaders, had been swept away and their functions assumed by entirely new preparatory institutions. Whether a similar fate awaits today's schools and colleges of education with their equally ambitious proposals and aspirations and whether they might be superseded by something altogether different in the twenty-first century remains to be seen. All things considered, however, it does not seem likely that the body politic will tolerate and support indefinitely the ever-increasing length and excessive complexity of today's efflorescent teacher education systems.

NOTES

PREFACE

1. Carnegie Foundation for the Advancement of Teaching, *Report Card on School Reform: The Teachers Speak* (Washington, D.C.: Carnegie Foundation, 1988).
2. Ibid., p. 11.
3. Benjamin R. Barber, *An Aristocracy of Everyone, The Politics of Education and the Future of America* (New York: Ballantine Books, 1992), p. 11.
4. National Center of Education Statistics, *The Condition of Education 1994* (Washington, D.C.: Office of Educational Research and Improvement, U.S. Department of Education, 1995), p. 154.
5. Ibid., p. 158.
6. National Center for Education Statistics, *America's Teachers: Profile of a Profession* (Washington, D.C.: Office of Educational Research and Improvement, U.S. Department of Education, 1993), p. 5. See also Carnegie Forum on Education and the Economy, *A Nation Prepared: Teachers for the 21st Century* (Washington, D.C.: Carnegie Forum on Education and the Economy, 1986), p. 79.
7. Arthur E. Wise, "Teaching the Teachers," *American School Board Journal* 181 (June, 1994): 22.
8. Thomas Toch, *In the Name of Excellence, The Struggle to Reform the Nation's Schools, Why It's Failing and What Should Be Done* (New York: Oxford University Press, 1991), pp. 158-161.
9. David F. Labaree, "An Unlovely Legacy, The Disabling Impact of the Market on American Teacher Education," *Phi Delta Kappan* 75 (April, 1994): 595.
10. Wise, pp. 22-23.
11. Jurgen Herbst, *And Sadly Teach: Teacher Education and Professionalization in American Culture* (Madison, Wisc.: University of Wisconsin Press, 1989), p. 3.

CHAPTER 1

1. Lawrence A. Cremin, "The Heritage of American Teacher Education," *Journal of Teacher Education* 4 (June 1953): 163-164. See also, for example, Jon Teaford, "The Transformation of Massachusetts Education, 1670-1780," *History of Education Quarterly* 10 (Fall 1970): 287-307; and Robert T. Sidwell,

"'Writers, Thinkers and Fox Hunters'—Educational Theory in the Almanacs of Eighteenth-Century Colonial America," *History of Education Quarterly* 8 (Fall 1968): 275-288.

2. Lawrence A. Cremin, *American Education: The Colonial Experience, 1607-1783* (New York: Harper & Row, 1970), p. 187.

3. See Wilson Smith, "The Teacher in Puritan Culture," *Harvard Educational Review* 36 (Fall 1966): 394-411; and David F. Allmendinger, Jr., *Paupers and Scholars: The Transformation of Student Life in Nineteenth-Century New England* (New York: St. Martin's Press, 1975), pp. 91-93.

4. R. Freeman Butts and Lawrence A. Cremin, *A History of Education in American Culture* (New York: Holt, Rinehart and Winston, 1953), p. 133.

5. Guy F. Wells, *Parish Education in Colonial Virginia* (New York: Bureau of Publications, Teachers College, Columbia University, 1923), p. 20.

6. Cited in Willard S. Elsbree, *The American Teacher, Evolution of a Profession in a Democracy* (New York: American Book Company, 1939), p. 32.

7. Walter H. Small, *Early New England Schools* (Boston: Ginn and Company, 1914), p. 93.

8. William H. Kilpatrick, *The Dutch Schools of New Netherland and Colonial New York* (Washington, D.C.: U.S. Government Printing Office, Bureau of Education Bulletin No. 12, 1912), pp. 170, 174.

9. Small, pp. 109-110.

10. John H. Crippen, *Character of the School Master in the Colonial Period.* Unpublished Master's Thesis, Columbia University, 1907, p. 104; cited in Elsbree, p. 30.

11. Quoted in David B. Tyack, *Turning Points in American Educational History* (Waltham, Mass.: Blaisdell Publishing, 1967), p. 413.

12. Consult James P. Wickersham, *A History of Education in Pennsylvania* (Lancaster, Penn.: Inquirer Publishing, 1886), p. 60; and quoted in Francis N. Thorpe, *Benjamin Franklin and the University of Pennsylvania* (Washington, D.C.: U.S. Government Printing Office, Bureau of Education Circular of Information No. 2, 1889), pp. 245-246.

13. Cited in Cremin, *American Education,* pp. 187-188. See Norwood M. Cole, "The Licensing of Schoolmasters in Colonial Massachusetts," *History of Education Journal* 8 (Winter, 1957): 68-74.

14. Caleb Bingham, *The Columbian Orator* . . . (Hartford, Conn.: Lincoln and Gleason, 1807), pp. 158-165; reprinted in Tyack, pp. 421-425. The perfunctory character of teacher interviews by local selectmen often inspired commentary. From the Civil War period comes an account of the school superintendent of Oxford, Ohio, crossing a muddy street with a prospective teacher candidate in hand while conducting an interview. The superintendent asks, "What is the gender of boy?" The candidate answers, "Masculine." "Of girl?" "Feminine." "Box?" "Neuter." "Children?" "Common." The superintendent concludes, "Well, I guess you know enough to teach, so I'll write you out a certificate." Cited in C. Neale Bogner, "Teaching—Progress?" *Journal of Teacher Education* 29 (May-June 1978): 59.

15. Donald Warren, "Learning from Experience: History and Teacher Education," *Educational Researcher* 14 (December, 1985): 6.

16. Samuel Hall, *Lectures on Schoolkeeping* (Boston: Richardson, Lord & Holbrook, 1829), p. 16.

17. Tyack, p. 414.

18. Quoted in Elsbree, p. 179.

19. Cited in Charles A. Harper, *A Century of Public Teacher Education* (Washington, D.C.: American Association of Teachers Colleges, National Education Association, 1939), p. 13.

20. James Bowen, *A History of Western Education,* Vol. 3 (London: Methuen & Company, 1981), p. 359.

21. Ibid., p. 361.

22. Cremin, "The Heritage of American Teacher Education," p. 164. Note the discussion in S. Alexander Rippa, *Education in a Free Society, An American History,* 2nd ed. (New York: David McKay, 1971), pp. 102-118, and in Jonathan C. Messerli, "Controversy and Consensus in Common School Reform," *Teachers College Record* 66 (May 1965): 749-759.

23. Catherine Beecher, *Suggestions Respecting Improvements in Education, Presented to the Trustees of the Hartford Female Seminary* (Hartford, Conn.: Packard and Butler, 1829), p. 7.

24. Catherine Beecher, *A Treatise on Domestic Economy, for the Use of Young Ladies at Home, and at School* (Boston: Marsh, Capen, Lyon and Webb, 1841), p. 9.

25. Quoted in G. Lerner, ed., *The Female Experience* (Indianapolis: Bobbs-Merrill, 1977), pp. 235-236; and also cited in Warren, p. 9.

26. E. W. Knight and C. L. Hall, eds., *Readings in American Educational History* (New York: Greenwood Press, 1951), p. 415.

27. The point is registered in Warren, p. 9.

28. Edward H. Reisner, *The Evolution of the Common School* (New York: Macmillan, 1930), pp. 384-388.

29. Walter S. Monroe, *Teaching-Learning Theory and Teacher Education, 1890-1950* (Urbana, Ill.: University of Illinois Press, 1952), p. 42.

30. Lawrence A. Cremin, *American Education: The National Experience, 1783-1876* (New York: Harper & Row, 1980), p. 398.

31. Cited in Cremin, "The Heritage of American Teacher Education," p. 164.

32. Wickersham, p. 60.

33. Jurgen Herbst, *And Sadly Teach: Teacher Education and Professionalization in American Culture* (Madison, Wisc.: University of Wisconsin Press, 1989), p. 21.

34. Nineteenth-century pedagogy was first analyzed in some detail in Barbara J. Finkelstein, "Governing the Young: Teacher Behavior in American Primary Schools, 1820-1880." Unpublished doctoral dissertation, Teachers College, Columbia University, 1970. An excellent discussion of teaching methodology in the late 1800s is supplied in Larry Cuban, *How Teachers Taught: Constancy and Change in American Classrooms, 1890-1980* (New York: Longman, 1984)

35. Charles Harper's celebratory *A Century of Teacher Education* affords an obvious case in point.

36. Quoted in Harper, p. 15; and also cited in Henry Barnard, *Normal Schools and Other Institutions, Agencies, and Means Designed for the Professional Education of Teachers* (Hartford, Conn.: Case, Tiffany and Company, 1851), p. 41.

37. Quoted in Robert Ulich, *A Sequence of Educational Influences* (Cambridge, Mass.: Harvard University Press, 1935), pp. 53-54. See John Albree, *Charles Brooks and His Work for Normal Schools* (Medford, Mass.: J. C. Miller, 1907); and Henry Barnard, "Proceedings of an Educational Convention in Plymouth County in 1838," in Barnard, *Normal Schools* (Hartford, Conn.: Case, Tiffany and Company, 1850), pp. 151-157.

38. Quoted in Wickersham, p. 220.

39. Consult James G. Carter, *Letters to the Hon. William Prescott on the Free Schools of New England, with Remarks on the Principles of Instruction* (Boston: Cummings, Hilliard, 1824); and Carter, "Outline of an Institution for the Education of Teachers," reprinted in *American Journal of Education* 16 (1866): 77-79; and in Carter's *Essays Upon Popular Education* (Boston: Bowles and Dearborn, 1826), p. 46.

40. Quoted in Harper, pp. 21-22.

41. The committee's text is cited in Harper, pp. 35-36.

42. Paul H. Mattingly, *The Classless Profession: American Schoolmen in the Nineteenth Century* (New York: New York University Press, 1975), pp. 62-63.

43. Samuel N. Sweet, *Teachers' Institutes* (Utica, NY: H. H. Hawley and Company, 1848), pp. 48ff.; and Samuel P. Bates, *Method of Teachers' Institutes and the Theory of Education* (New York: A. S. Barnes and Burr, 1864), pp. 53-54.

44. Mason S. Stone, "The First Normal School in America," *Teachers College Record* 23 (1923): 263-272; and Raymond B. Culver, *Horace Mann and Religion in the Massachusetts Schools* (New Haven, Conn.: Yale University Press, 1929), pp. 111-126.

45. A primary source for the details of the Lexington school in its earliest years is Arthur O. Norton, ed., *The First State Normal School in America: The Journals of Cyrus Peirce and Mary Swift* (Cambridge, Mass.: Harvard University Press, 1926).

46. Quoted in Harper, p. 34.

47. Consult Benjamin Frazier, "History of the Professional Education of Teachers in the United States," *National Survey of the Education of Teachers* (Washington, D.C.: U.S. Office of Education Bulletin 1933, No. 10, Vol. 5, Part I, 1935), pp. 12, 52ff.

48. Herbst, p. 108.

49. Note the discussion in Joel Spring, *The American School, 1642-1993,* 3rd ed. (New York: McGraw-Hill, 1994), p. 273.

50. Cited in Norton, pp. 67-68.

51. Quoted in Harper, p. 109.

52. Horace Mann, "Report for 1839," *Annual Reports of the Secretary of the Board of Education* (Boston: Rand and Avery, 1868), p. 60.

53. Richard Edwards, "Normal Schools in the United States," *National Education Association, Lectures and Proceedings* (Harrisburg, PA: NEA, 1865), pp. 277-282; reproduced in Merle Borrowman, *Teacher Education in America, A Documentary History* (New York: Teachers College, Columbia University, 1956), pp. 77-78.

54. S. S. Parr, "The Normal-School Problem, " *National Education Association, Addresses and Proceedings* (Topeka: Kansas Publishing House, 1888): pp. 467-469. See also Edgar R. Randolph, *The Professional Treatment of Subject-Matter* (Baltimore: Warwick and York, 1924), p. 204.

55. Cited in Monroe, p. 78.

56. Quoted in Alpheus Crosby, "The Proper Sphere and Work of the American Normal School," in *American Normal Schools, Their Theory, Their Workings, and Their Results, as Embodied in the Proceedings of the First Annual Convention of the American Normal School Association* (New York: A. S. Barnes and Burr, 1860), p. 24.

57. Cited in Herbst, p. 85.

58. See William H. Payne, *Contribution to the Science of Education* (New York: Harper and Brothers, 1887), pp. 261-262; and H. S. Tarbell, "Report of the Sub-Committee on the Training of Teachers," *National Education Association, Addresses and Proceedings* (St. Paul: Pioneer Press, 1895), p. 238.

59. Thomas J. Morgan, *What Is the True Function of a Normal School?* (Boston: Willard Small, 1886), pp. 27-28.

60. Herbst, p. 140. See William F. Phelps, "Normal Schools, Their Organization and Course of Study," *National Education Association, Addresses and Proceedings* (Winona, Minn.: National Education Association, 1866), pp. 131-139.

61. Butts and Cremin, p. 401. See, for example, "Report of the Committee on 'The System of Normal Training Schools Best Adapted to the Wants of Our People,'" *National Education Association, Addresses and Proceedings* (Peoria: N.C. Nason, 1872), pp. 28-38.

62. Cited in Borrowman, pp. 102-103.

63. Quoted in Butts and Cremin, pp. 401-402.

64. Harper, p. 113; Spring, p. 273; and Cremin, "The Heritage of American Teacher Education," p. 167.

65. See Charles A. Harper, *Development of the Teachers College in the United States* (Bloomington, Ill.: McKnight and McKnight, 1935), for a detailed discussion of the conversion of normal schools into full-blown teachers' colleges.

66. See Otto Walton Snarr, *The Education of Teachers in the Middle States: An Historical Study of the Professional Education of Public School Teachers as a State Function* (Chicago: University of Chicago Press, 1945), pp. 43-95.

67. Walter L. Hervey, "The Function of a Teachers' Training College," *National Education Association, Addresses and Proceedings* (Astor Place, N.Y.: J. J. Little & Company, 1891), p. 736.

68. Burke A. Hinsdale, "The Teacher's Academical and Professional Preparation," *National Education Association, Addresses and Proceedings* (Astor Place, N.Y.: J.J. Little & Company, 1891), p. 717.

69.   Burke A. Hinsdale, "Pedagogical Chairs in Colleges and Universities," *National Education Association Journal of Addresses and Proceedings* (Topeka: Kansas Publishing House, 1889), pp. 560-564.

70.   Charles K. Adams, "The Teaching of Pedagogy in Colleges and Universities," *New England Association of Colleges and Preparatory Schools, Addresses and Proceedings of the Third Annual Meeting* (Bedford, Mass: NEACPS, 1888), pp. 17-29. (Hereafter *New England Association.*)

71.   Ibid., pp. 26-29.

72.   Refer to J. B. Sewall, "The Duty of the Colleges to Make Provision for the Training of Teachers for Secondary Schools," *New England Association,* pp. 22-27.

73.   Quoted in Elsbree, p. 320.

74.   Quoted in Tyack, p. 416.

75.   Elsbree, pp. 332-333.

76.   Quoted in Harper, *A Century of Teacher Education,* pp. 113-114.

77.   Arthur G. Powell and Theodore Sizer, "Changing Conceptions of the Professor of Education," in James Cornelius, ed., *To Be a Phoenix: The Education Professorate* (Bloomington, Ind.: Phi Delta Kappa, 1969), p. 61.

78.   James Carter, "On the Development of the Intellectual Faculties and on the Teaching of Geography," quoted in James R. Robarts, "The Quest for a Science of Education in the Nineteenth Century," *History of Education Quarterly* 8 (Winter 1968): 431.

79.   Edwards, pp. 277-282.

CHAPTER 2

1.   See *Report of the Commissioner of Education for the Year 1895-96,* Vol. 1 (Washington, D.C.: U.S. Government Printing Office, 1897), pp. x-xiv; Nicholas M. Butler, *Education in the United States* (New York: American Book Company, 1910), pp. 376-377; U.S. Office of Education, *Biennial Survey of Education, 1928-1930* (Washington, D.C.: U.S. Office of Education Bulletin, 1931, No. 20, 1932), pp. 5, 8, 40; Benjamin W. Frazier, "History of the Professional Education of Teachers in the United States," *National Survey of the Education of Teachers,* Vol. 5, Part I (Washington, D.C.: U.S. Office of Education Bulletin, 1933, No. 10, 1935), pp. 42-59; and Walter S. Monroe, *Teaching-Learning Theory and Teacher Education 1890 to 1950* (Urbana, Ill.: University of Illinois Press, 1952), p. 260.

2.   Edward S. Evenden, *National Survey of the Education of Teachers: Summary and Evaluation* (Washington, D.C.: U.S. Office of Education Bulletin No. 10, Vol. 6, 1933), pp. 37, 39, 72. See also David B. Tyack, *Turning Points in American Educational History* (Waltham, Mass.: Blaisdell Publishing, 1967), pp 412, 417; and "The 1953 Teacher Supply and Demand Report," *Journal of Teacher Education* 4 (March 1953): 3-46.

3. Benjamin W. Frazier, *Development of State Programs of Certification of Teachers* (Washington, D.C.: U.S. Office of Education, Bulletin No. 12, 1938), p. 73.

4. Willard S. Elsbree, *The American Teacher, Evolution of a Profession in a Democracy* (New York: American Book Company, 1939), pp. 337, 343.

5. R. Freeman Butts and Lawrence A. Cremin, *A History of Education in American Culture* (New York: Holt, Rinehart and Winston, 1953), p. 606.

6. Cited in Elsbree, p. 355.

7. Tyack, p. 418.

8. Elsbree, p. 337.

9. Joel Spring, *The American School 1642-1933,* 3rd ed. (New York: McGraw-Hill, 1994), p. 273.

10. H. H. Seerley, "Defects in the Normal Schools that are Responsible for the Opposition and Criticism Urged Against Them in Many Parts of the United States," *National Education Association, Addresses and Proceedings* (Chicago: University of Chicago Press, 1902), p. 542.

11. Charles A. McMurry, *Conflicting Principles in Teaching* (Boston: Houghton Mifflin, 1914), p. 247.

12. Charles A. Harper, *A Century of Public Teacher Education* (Washington, D.C.: American Association of Teachers Colleges, National Education Association, 1939), p. 138.

13. For a more detailed account, consult Jessie M. Pangburn, *The Evolution of the American Teachers College* (New York: Bureau of Publications, Teachers College, Columbia University, 1932).

14. Monroe, p. 294.

15. Butts and Cremin, p. 604; Spring, p. 273.

16. Elsbree, pp. 326-328.

17. James E. Russell, "The Training of Teachers for Secondary Schools," *National Education Association, Addresses and Proceedings* (Chicago: University of Chicago Press, 1901), pp. 636-641. See also Charles A. Harper, *Development of the Teachers College in the United States* (Bloomington, Ill.: McKnight and McKnight, 1935), p. 313.

18. A dated but still useful account of how four-year colleges were evolving is supplied in R. Freeman Butts, *The College Charts Its Course: Historic Conceptions and Current Proposals* (New York: McGraw-Hill, 1939). The background to the emergence of teacher-training institutions in the Midwest is given in Otto Walton Snarr, *The Education of Teachers in the Middle States: An Historical Study of the Professional Education of Public School Teachers as a State Function* (Chicago: University of Chicago Press, 1945), pp. 43-95.

19. Arthur Bestor, "Liberal Education and a Liberal Nation," *American Scholar* 21 (Spring, 1952): 139-149.

20. Alfred L. Hall-Quest, *Professional Secondary Education in Teachers Colleges* (New York: Teachers College, Columbia University, 1925), pp. 65-66, 111.

21. See Warren C. Lovinger, *General Education Teachers Colleges* (Oneonta, N.Y.: American Association of Colleges for Teacher Education, 1948).

22. Elsbree, p. 331.

23. A. Ross Hill, "Should Chairs of Pedagogy Attached to College Departments of Universities Be Developed into Professional Colleges for the Training of Teachers Co-ordinate with Those of Law, Medicine, and Engineering, or Should They be Abolished?" *National Education Association, Addresses and Proceedings* (Chicago: University of Chicago Press, 1905), pp. 512-515.

24. Monroe, pp. 325-326. Teachers College at Columbia University had been founded in 1887 but was not incorporated within the university system until 1898. Thereafter it expanded rather quickly into a graduate professional school. See James E. Russell, *Founding Teachers College* (New York: Bureau of Publications, Teachers College, Columbia University, 1937); and Walter L. Hervey, "Historical Sketch of Teachers College from Its Foundation to 1897," *Teachers College Record* 1 (January 1900): 12-34.

25. Refer to W. A. Luckey, *The Professional Training of Secondary Teachers in the United States* (New York: Macmillan, 1903), pp. 62, 101.

26. Elsbree, p. 331.

27. W. F. Sutton, "The Organization of the Department of Education in Relation to Other Departments in Colleges and Universities," *Journal of Pedagogy* 19 (December 1906-March 1907): 81-130.

28. Jurgen Herbst, *And Sadly Teach: Teacher Education and Professionalization in American Culture* (Madison, Wisc.: University of Wisconsin Press, 1989), pp. 161, 187.

29. Jerome Allen, "Presidential Address," *National Education Association, Addresses and Proceedings* (Winona, Minn.: National Education Association, 1881), p. 199. The exposition here is adapted from James R. Robarts, "The Quest for a Science of Education in the Nineteenth Century," *History of Education Quarterly* 8 (Winter 1968): 431-446.

30. James Donaldson, "The Science of Education," *American Journal of Education* 26 (1876): 485-487.

31. See, for example, Francis B. Palmer, *The Science of Education* (New York: Van Antwerp, Bragg and Company, 1887).

32. Quoted in Merle L. Borrowman, *The Liberal and Technical in Teacher Education, A Historical Survey of American Thought* (New York: Bureau of Publications, Teachers College, Columbia University, 1956), pp. 25-26.

33. Thomas J. Morgan, *What Is the True Function of a Normal School?* (Boston: Willard Small, 1886), p. 14.

34. F. A. P. Barnard, *Annual Report of the President of Columbia College, Made to the Board of Trustees, June 6, 1881* (New York: Columbia College, 1881), p. 55.

35. See Charles DeGarmo, *Herbart and the Herbartians* (New York: Charles Scribner's Sons, 1896); Gabriel Compayré, *Herbart and Education by Instruction* (New York: Thomas Y. Crowell, 1907); Percival R. Cole, *Herbart and Froebel, An Attempt at Synthesis* (New York: Teachers College, Columbia University, 1907); and Harold B. Dunkel, *Herbart and Herbartianism: An Educational Ghost Story* (Chicago: University of Chicago Press, 1970).

36. See C. C. Rounds, "Attacks on Normal Schools," *National Education Association Addresses and Proceedings* (Boston: J.E. Farwell and Company, 1884),

pp. 159-160; Thomas M. Balliet, "The Study of Pedagogics," *Education* 14 (October, 1893): 65; Edward W. Scriptures, "Education as a Science," *Pedagogical Seminary* 2 (1892): 112; and "Report of the Committee of Pedagogics to the National Council of Education," *National Education Association, Addresses and Proceedings* (1884), pp. 42-43.

37. Emerson D. White, *Elements of Pedagogy* (New York: American Book Company, 1886), pp. 10-11.

38. In J. F. K. Rosenkranz, *The Philosophy of Education,* Anna C. Brackett trans. (New York: D. Appleton and Company, 1886), pp. 1-2.

39. Richard G. Boone, "The Teacher as an Expert," *National Education Association, Addresses and Proceedings* (St. Paul, Minn.: Pioneer Press, 1894), p. 897.

40. Josiah Royce, "Is There a Science of Education?" *Educational Review* 1 (January, 1891): 15-25.

41. William James, *Talks to Teachers on Psychology: And to Students on Some of Life's Ideals* (New York: Henry Holt and Company, 1923), p. 7.

42. John Dewey, "The Relation of Theory to Practice in Education," in Charles A. McMurry, ed., National Society for the Scientific Study of Education, *The Relation of Theory to Practice in the Education of Teachers, Third Yearbook,* Part I (Bloomington, Ill.: Public School Publishing, 1904), pp. 9, 14.

43. Ibid., pp. 9-10.

44. Edward L. Thorndike, *Educational Psychology,* rev. ed. (New York: Bureau of Publications, Teachers College, Columbia University, 1910), p. 135.

45. See Frank N. Freeman, "Contribution of Science to Education," *School and Society* 30 (July 27, 1929): 209.

46. See Raymond E. Callahan, *Education and the Cult of Efficiency* (Chicago: University of Chicago Press, 1962); and Thomas James, *The New Cult of Efficiency and Education* (Pittsburgh: University of Pittsburgh Press, 1969).

47. Herbst, p. 169. See Wesley E. Peik, *The Professional Education of High School Teachers* (Minneapolis: University of Minnesota Press, 1930); David Snedden, *Sociological Determination of Objectives in Education* (Philadelphia: J. B. Lippincott, 1921); and Charles C. Peters, *Objectives and Procedures in Civic Education* (New York: Longmans, Green and Company, 1930).

48. W. W. Charters and Douglas Waples, *The Commonwealth Teacher-Training Study* (Chicago: University of Chicago Press, 1928).

49. Consult Robert N. Bush, "Teacher Education Reform: Lessons from the Past Half Century," *Journal of Teacher Education* 38 (May-June, 1987): 13-14.

50. See U.S. Office of Education, *National Survey of the Education of Teachers,* 6 vols. (Washington, D.C.: U.S. Office of Education/U. S. Government Printing Office, 1933).

51. As just one illustration, refer to W. M. Aiken, *The Story of the Eight-Year Study* (New York: Harper, 1942).

52. George S. Counts, "Break the Teacher Training Lockstep," *Social Frontier* 1 (June 1935): 6-7.

53. Mary Anne Raywid, *The Axe-Grinders, Critics of our Public Schools* (New York: Macmillan, 1962), pp. 1, 2.

54. Mortimer Smith, *And Madly Teach* (Chicago: H. Regnery, 1949), p. 7.

55. See Albert Lynd, *Quackery in the Public Schools* (New York: Greenwood, 1977); and Mortimer Smith, *The Diminished Mind: A Study of Planned Mediocrity in Our Public Schools* (New York: Greenwood, 1977); and Paul Woodring, *Let's Talk Sense About Our Schools* (New York: McGraw-Hill, 1953).

56. John Keats, "Are the Public Schools Doing Their Job?" *Saturday Evening Post* 230 (September 21, 1957), reproduced in C. Winfield Scott et al., *The Great Debate, Our Schools in Crisis* (Englewood Cliffs, N.J.: Prentice-Hall, 1959), p. 8.

57. Arthur E. Bestor, *Educational Wastelands, The Retreat from Learning in Our Public Schools* (Urbana, Ill.: University of Illinois Press, 1953); and Bestor, *The Restoration of Learning* (New York: Alfred A. Knopf, 1955).

58. Bestor, *Educational Wastelands*, p. 131.

59. Lynd, quoting from Smith's *And Madly Teach*, p. 99.

60. Agnes Snyder, "Conflicting Points of View and Challenges in the Education of Teachers," *Journal of Teacher Education* 3 (December 1952): 246. A representative sample of the controversy surrounding teacher education in the late 1940s and early 1950s is reflected in American Council on Education, Commission on Teacher Education, *The Improvement of Teacher Education: A Final Report by the Commission on Teacher Education* (Washington, D.C.: American Council on Education, 1949); Warren Lovinger, *General Education in the Teachers Colleges* (Oneonta, N.Y.: American Association of Colleges for Teacher Education, 1947); Van Cleve Morris, "The Education of Secondary School Teachers in the Liberal Arts Colleges," *Association of American Colleges Bulletin* 36 (December 1950): 511-528; Francis Keppel, "Contemporary Issues in the Education of Teachers," *Journal of Teacher Education* 3 (December 1952): 249-255; W. Earl Armstrong, "Current Issues in the Preparation of Teachers for the Elementary and Secondary Schools," *Current Issues in Higher Education, National Conference on Higher Education 1950* (Washington, D.C.: National Education Association, 1950); Charles H. Judd, "Should University Schools of Education Cease to Exist?" *School and Society* 62 (September 1, 1945): 141-142; Frederick E. Bolton, "What to Do About University Schools of Education," *School and Society* 62 (December 29, 1945): 432-433; E. Graham Pogue, "Improving Undergraduate Programs of Teacher Education," *Addresses on Current Issues in Higher Education, National Conference on Higher Education* (Washington, D.C.: National Education Association, 1951): 177-182.

61. Quoted in Lynd, p. 106.

62. Bestor, *Educational Wastelands*, p. 137.

63. Ibid., pp. 121, 137, 138, 142.

64. Ibid., pp. 142, 147.

65. Notable contributions to the literature on teacher education reform of the period include James C. Stone, ed., *Breakthrough in Teacher Education* (San Francisco: Jossey-Bass, 1968); Elmer Smith, *Teacher Education: A Reappraisal* (New York: Harper & Row, 1962); Margaret Lindsey, *New Horizons for the Teaching Profession* (Washington, D.C.: Commission on Teacher Education and Professional Standards, National Education Association, 1961); and B. O.

Smith et al., *Teachers for the Real World* (Washington, D.C.: NDEA National Institute/American Association of Colleges for Teacher Education, 1969).

66. Cited in G. K. Hodenfield and T. M. Stinnett, *The Education of Teachers, Conflict and Consensus* (Englewood Cliffs, N.J.: Prentice-Hall, 1961), pp. 31-32.
67. Ibid., p. 58.
68. Ibid., p. 45.
69. Ibid., p. 65.
70. Ibid., p. 37.
71. William Chandler Bagley, *Education and Emergent Man* (New York: Thomas Nelson, 1934), p. 192.
72. Isaac L. Kandel, *American Education in the Twentieth Century* (Cambridge, Mass.: Harvard University Press, 1957), p. 95.
73. James D. Koerner, *The Miseducation of American Teachers* (Boston: Houghton Mifflin, 1963), pp. 3-4.
74. Ibid., pp. 29, 31.
75. Ibid., p. 32.
76. Ibid., pp. 21, 34, 56, 156.
77. Ibid., pp. 18-19.
78. Ibid., pp. 120-128.
79. Ibid., pp. 156-157.
80. Ibid., pp. 204-205, 207, 212.
81. Ibid., p. 268.
82. James Bryant Conant, *The Education of American Teachers* (New York: McGraw-Hill, 1963).
83. Ibid., p. 13.
84. Ibid., pp 26-27, 142.
85. Ibid., p. 98.
86. Ibid., pp. 159, 161.
87. Ibid., p. 172.
88. Ibid., pp. 54, 56.
89. Stone, pp. 3-5.
90. Ibid., p. 6.
91. See Merle L. Borrowman, "Liberal Education and the Professional Preparation of Teachers," in Borrowman, ed., *Teacher Education in America* (New York: Teachers College Press, 1965).
92. Charles Silberman, *Crisis in the Classroom* (New York: Random House, 1970), p. 375.
93. National Education Association, *Teacher Supply and Demand in Public Schools, 1968* (Washington, D.C.: NEA Research Report 1969-R4); U.S. Office of Education, *Education in the Seventies* (Washington, D.C.: U.S. Department of Health, Education and Welfare Planning Paper 68-1, 1968); and American Association of Colleges for Teacher Education, *Teacher Productivity—1967* (Washington, D.C.: AACTE, 1968).
94. Silberman, p. 413.

95. Paul Woodring, "The Development of Teacher Education," in Kevin Ryan, ed., *Teacher Education, Seventy-fourth Yearbook of the National Society for the Study of Education,* part II (Chicago: University of Chicago Press, 1975), pp. 1-24. See also Seymour Sarason et al., eds., *The Preparation of Teachers* (New York: John Wiley & Sons, 1962).

96. Consult the listing of reform proposals supplied in Donald R. Cruickshank, *Models for the Preparation of America's Teachers* (Bloomington, Ind.: Phi Delta Kappa Educational Foundation, 1985). See H. LaGrone, *A Proposal for the Revision of the Preservice Professional Component of Teacher Education* (Washington, D.C.: American Association of Colleges for Teacher Education, 1964; Smith et al., eds., *Teachers for the Real World*; R. Travers and J. Dillon, *The Making of a Teacher* (New York: Macmillan, 1975); AACTE Committee on Performance-Based Teacher Education, *Achieving the Potential of Performance-Based Teacher Education: Recommendations* (Washington, D.C.: AACTE, 1974); Robert Howsam et al., eds., *Educating a Profession* (Washington, D.C.: AACTE, 1976); Dale Scannell, *Educating a Profession: Profile of a Beginning Teacher* (Washington, D. C.: American Association of Colleges for Teacher Education, 1983); Carnegie Commission on Education and the Economy, *Report of the Task Force on Teaching as a Profession* (Princeton, N.J.: Carnegie Commission for the Advancement of Teaching, 1986).

97. C. Denham and A. Lieberman, *Time to Learn* (Sacramento, Calif.: California Commission for Teacher Preparation and Licensing/National Institute of Education, 1980).

98. See, for example, Bruce Joyce and Marsha Weil, eds., *Perspectives for Reform in Teacher Education* (Englewood Cliffs, N.J.: Prentice-Hall, 1972).

99. Consult W. Warren Kallenbach and Meredith D. Gall, "Microteaching Versus Conventional Methods in Training Elementary Intern Teachers," *Journal of Educational Research* 63 (November, 1969): 136-141; and Willis D. Copeland, "The Relationship Between Microteaching and Student Teacher Classroom Performance," *Journal of Educational Research* 68 (April 1975): 289-293.

100. Walter R. Borg, *Moving Toward Effective Teacher Education—One Man's Perspective* (Logan, Utah: Utah State University, 1975), pp. 2, 4, 5-6.

101. See Charles E. Johnson, "Competency-Based and Traditional Education Practices Compared," *Journal of Teacher Education* 26 (Winter 1974): 355-356; Margaret Lindsey, "Performance-based Teacher Education: Examination of a Slogan," *Journal of Teacher Education* 24 (Fall 1973): 180-186; and Benjamin Rosner, ed., *The Power of Competency-Based Teacher Education, Report of the Committee on National Program Priorities in Teacher Education* (Boston: Allyn and Bacon, 1972).

102. Note the discussion in Henry J. Hermanowicz, "Teacher Education: A Retrospective Look at the Future," *Journal of Teacher Education* 29 (July-August 1978): 10-14.

103. See Leon L. Munson, "Teaching Centers: A Step Backwards," *Journal of Teacher Education* 22 (Winter 1971): 487-488; Daniel L. Merritt and Evelyn Bell, "The Teaching Education Center Is Alive and Well," *Journal of Teacher Education* 23 (Summer 1972): 152-154; J. Michael Crosby, "A Teacher Looks

at Teaching Centers and Educational Reform," *Journal of Teacher Education* 25 (Spring 1974): 31-36; and Teachers' Field Task Force on the Improvement and Reform of American Education, *Inside Out* (Washington, D.C.: U.S. Office of Education, 1974).

104. For example, consult Edward R. Ducharme, "Liberal Education and Teacher Education: Two Forces in Search of Fusion," in Martin Haberman and Julie M. Backus, *Advances in Teacher Education,* vol. 3 (Norwood, N.J.: Ablex, 1987), pp. 250-267.

105. Peter F. Carbone, Jr., "Liberal Education and Teacher Preparation, " *Journal of Teacher Education* 31 (May-June 1980): 13-17.

106. Ibid., p. 16.

107. Paul Shaker and Walter Ullrich, "Reconceptualizing the Debate Over the General Education of Teachers," *Journal of Teacher Education* 38 (January-February 1987): 11-12.

108. The point is made in the Introduction to Joseph L. DeVitis and Peter A. Sola, eds., *Building Bridges for Educational Reform* (Ames, Iowa: Iowa State University Press, 1989; the statistic on percentage of time devoted to liberal arts courses appeared in Carnegie Commission on Higher Education, *Continuity and Discontinuity: Higher Education and the Schools* (New York: McGraw-Hill, 1973), p. 90.

109. Christopher Jencks and David Riesman, *The Academic Revolution* (Garden City, N.Y.: Doubleday, 1969), p. 235.

110. Richard Mitchell, *The Graves of Academe* (Boston: Little, Brown and Company, 1981), pp. viii, 10, 120.

111. Quoted in Warren, p. 5.

112. Cited in B. R. Clark, *The Academic Life: Small Worlds, Different Worlds* (Princeton, N.J.: Carnegie Foundation for the Advancement of Teaching, 1987), p. 167. See also Barbara G. Burch, "Perceptions of the Role and Scholarly Reputation of the Education Professoriate," in Clark, pp. 87-104; F. F. Fuller and O. H. Brown, "Becoming a Teacher," in Kevin Ryan, ed., *Teacher Education, The Seventy-Fourth Yearbook of the National Society for the Study of Education Part II* (Chicago: University of Chicago Press, 1975) p. 29; and Madhu Suri Prakash, "Reforming the Teaching of Teachers: Trends, Contradictions and Challenges," *Teachers College Record* 88 (Winter 1986): 217-240.

113. Rita Kramer, *Ed School Follies, The Mis-education of America's Teachers* (New York: Free Press, 1991), p. 211.

114. Ibid., pp. 212-213.

115. Ibid., pp. 214, 216-217.

116. Quoted in Linda Tafel and Judith Christensen, "Teacher Education in the 1990s: Looking Ahead While Learning From the Past," *Action in Teacher Education* 10 (Fall 1988): 1.

117. Marcia J. Leith, "We've Heard This Song . . . Or Have We?" *Journal of Teacher Education* 38 (May-June 1987): 20-25.

118. B. O. Smith, "Pedagogical Education: How About Reform?" *Phi Delta Kappan* 62 (October 1980): 89.

119. Richard Wisniewski, "Militancy or Commitment," *Educational Leadership* 27 (March 1970): 502.

120. W. Drummond and T. Andrews, "The Influence of Federal and State Governments on Teacher Education," *Phi Delta Kappan* 62 (October 1980): 87-93.

121. Seymour B. Sarason, *The Case For Change, Rethinking the Preparation of Educators* (San Francisco: Jossey-Bass, 1993), pp. 142-143.

122. Robert N. Bush, "Teacher Education Reform: Lessons from the Past Half Century," *Journal of Teacher Education* 38 (May-June 1987), p. 15.

123. Leith, p. 21.

124. Frank B. Murray, "Teacher Education," *Change* 18 (September-October 1986): 18. See also Lynn L. Weldon, "Is Teacher Education an Illusion?" *Journal of Teacher Education* 19 (Summer 1968): 193-196; Margaret Lindsey, "Teacher Education: Reflections," *Journal of Teacher Education* 29 (July-August 1978): 5-9; and Kenneth R. Howey and Nancy L. Zimpher, "The Current Debate on Teacher Preparation," *Journal of Teacher Education* 37 (September-October 1986): 41-49.

125. Holmes Group, *Tomorrow's Schools of Education* (East Lansing, Mich.: Holmes Group, 1995), p. 237.

CHAPTER 3

1. David F. Labaree, "An Unlovely Legacy: The Disabling Impact of the Market on American Teacher Education," *Phi Delta Kappan* 75 (April 1994): 591. See also Kenneth R. Howey and Nancy L. Zimpher, "The Current Debate on Teacher Preparation," *Journal of Teacher Education* 37 (September-October 1986): 41-49.

2. Labaree, p. 592.

3. Ibid., p. 593.

4. Ibid., p. 593.

5. See David F. Labaree, *The Making of an American High School: The Credentials Market and the Central High School of Philadelphia, 1838-1939* (New Haven, Conn.: Yale University Press, 1988); and Labaree, "From Comprehensive High School to Community College: Politics, Markets, and the Evolution of Educational Opportunity," in Ronald G. Corwin, ed., *Research in Sociology of Education and Socialization,* vol. 9 (Greenwich, Conn.: JAI Press, 1990), pp. 203-240.

6. Labaree, "An Unlovely Legacy," p. 595.

7. See Merle Borrowman, "Liberal Education and the Professional Preparation of Teachers," in Borrowman, ed., *Teacher Education in America: A Documentary History* (New York: Teachers College Press, 1965), p. 1. References to the liberal arts tradition within the context of teacher education appear throughout Borrowman, *The Liberal and Technical in Teacher Education: A Historical Survey of American Thought* (New York: Bureau of Publications, Teachers College, Columbia University, 1956); in Lawrence A. Cremin, "The Heritage

of American Teacher Education," *Journal of Teacher Education* 4 (June 1953): 163-164; in G. Clifford and J. Guthrie, *Ed School: A Brief for Professional Education* (Chicago: University of Chicago Press, 1988); and in Bruce Kimball, *Orators and Philosophers* (New York: Teachers College Press, 1986). The discussion is adapted after the treatment supplied in Sharon Feiman-Nemser, "Teacher Preparation: Structural and Conceptual Alternatives," in W. Robert Houston, Martin Haberman, and John Sikula, eds., *Handbook of Research on Teacher Education* (New York: Macmillan, 1990), p. 214.

8. Feiman-Nemser, p. 214.

9. A helpful summary is given in Wayne J. Urban, "Historical Studies of Teacher Education," in Houston, Haberman, and Sikula, eds., pp. 60-63.

10. Arthur G. Powell, *The Uncertain Profession: Harvard and the Search for Educational Authority* (Cambridge, Mass.: Harvard University Press, 1980), p. 159.

11. See Urban, pp. 63-64; and Feiman-Nemser, p. 215.

12. Labaree, "An Unlovely Legacy," p. 595. See also Paul Woodring, *New Directions in Teacher Education* (New York: Fund for the Advancement of Education, 1957), passim; and Walter Doyle, "Themes in Teacher Education Research," in Houston, Haberman, and Sikula, eds., pp. 5-6. Note also Labaree, "The Trouble with Ed Schools," *Educational Foundations* 10 (Summer 1996), pp. 27-45.

13. See Raymond E. Callahan, *Education and the Cult of Efficiency: A Study of the Social Forces That Have Shaped the Administration of the Public Schools* (Chicago: University of Chicago Press, 1962).

14. See Lawrence A. Cremin, *The Education of the Educating Professions* (19th Charles W. Hunt Lecture) (Washington, D.C.: American Association of Colleges for Teacher Education, 1978). The point is registered in Feiman-Nemser, p. 216.

15. Figures cited are drawn from surveys reported in Mary M. Kluender, "Teacher Education Programs in the 1980s: Some Selected Characteristics," *Journal of Teacher Education* 35 (July-August 1984): 34-35.

16. Refer to the findings and discussions reported in Robert A. Roth, "The Status of the Profession: Selected Characteristics and Criticisms of Teacher Education and Teaching," *Teacher Educator* 19 (Autumn 1983): 3; and in Kluender, p. 34. But note also Office of Educational Research and Improvement, *The Condition of Education 1995* (Washington, D.C.: National Center for Education Statistics, U.S. Department of Education, 1995).

17. See W. Timothy Weaver, "In Search of Quality: The Need for Talent in Teaching," *Phi Delta Kappan* 61 (September 1979): 29-32, 46; and the profile given in Weaver, "The Talent Pool in Teacher Education," *Journal of Teacher Education* 32 (May-June 1981): 53-55. Consult also Weaver, *The Tragedy of the Commons: The Effects of Supply and Demand on the Education Talent Pool* (Washington, D.C.: ERIC Document Reproduction Service, No. ED 204-261, 1981); and Weaver, *America's Teacher Quality Problem: Alternatives for Reform* (New York: Praeger, 1983).

18. Office of Educational Research and Improvement, *The Condition of Education 1982* (Washington, D.C.: National Center for Education Statistics, U.S. Department of Education, 1982).

19. Willis D. Hawley, "United States," in Howard B. Leavitt, ed., *Issues and Problems in Teacher Education, An International Handbook* (Westport, Conn.: Greenwood Press, 1992), p. 253.

20. Ibid., pp. 253-254.

21. Office of Educational Research and Improvement, *The Pocket Condition of Education 1995* (Washington, D.C.: National Center for Education Statistics, U.S. Department of Education, 1995), p. 14.

22. The point is taken from Judith E. Lanier and Judith W. Little, "Research on Teacher Education," in Merlin C. Wittrock, ed., *Handbook of Research on Teaching,* 3rd ed. (New York: Macmillan, 1986), p. 539.

23. Emily Feistritzer, *The Condition of Teaching: A State by State Analysis* (Princeton, N.J.: Carnegie Foundation for the Advancement of Teaching, 1983), p. 112.

24. Lanier and Little, pp. 539-540.

25. Frank B. Murray, "Teacher Education," *Change* 18 (September-October 1986): 20. See also Lanier and Little, p. 539.

26. Office of Educational Research and Improvement, see #16; (Washington, D.C.: National Center for Education Statistics, U.S. Department of Education, 1982); A. L. Valdes, *A Nationwide Survey on the Status of Teacher Competency Programs in the States* (Dover, Del.: Department of Public Instruction, 1982); Weaver, "In Search of Quality"; Roth, p. 3; Hawley, pp. 254-255.

27. The preceding discussion borrows from that supplied in Murray, p. 25.

28. Ibid., p. 25.

29. Willis D. Hawley, p. 255.

30. See Howey and Zimpher, p. 42.

31. Carnegie Foundation for the Advancement of Teaching, *Missions of the College Curriculum* (San Francisco: Jossey-Bass, 1977), p. 11.

32. Christopher J. Lucas, *American Higher Education, A History* (New York: St. Martin's Press, 1994), p. 268.

33. Examples of diagnoses include William J. Bennett, *To Reclaim a Legacy: A Report on the Humanities in Higher Education* (Washington, D.C.: National Endowment for the Humanities, 1984); Arthur Levine, *Handbook on Undergraduate Curriculum* (San Francisco: Jossey-Bass, 1978); Gary Miller, *The Meaning of General Education* (New York: Teachers College Press, 1988); Study Group on the Conditions of Excellence in American Higher Education, *Involvement in Learning: Realizing the Potential of American Higher Education* (Washington, D.C.: National Institute of Education, 1984); Lynne Cheney, *50 Hours: A Core Curriculum for College Students* (Washington, D.C.: National Endowment for the Humanities, 1989); E. D. Hirsch, Jr., *Cultural Literacy: What Every American Needs to Know* (New York: Random House, 1987); Allan Bloom, *The Closing of the American Mind: How Higher Education Has Failed Democracy and Impoverished the Souls of Today's Students* (New York: Simon and Schuster, 1987); Association of American Colleges,

Integrity in the College Curriculum (Washington, D.C.: Association of American Colleges, 1985), pp. 23-24, 27-32; Association of American Colleges, *New Vitality in General Education* (Washington, D.C.: Association of American Colleges, 1988); Association of American Colleges, *The Challenge of Connecting Learning* (Washington, D.C.: Association of American Colleges, 1990); C. Wegener, *Liberal Education and the Modern University* (Chicago: University of Chicago Press, 1978); Michael Simpson, "The Case for the Liberal Arts," *Liberal Education* 66 (Fall 1980): 315-319; David G. Winter et al., *A New Case for the Liberal Arts* (San Francisco: Jossey-Bass, 1981); Paul L. Dressel, "Liberal Education: Developing the Characteristics of a Liberally Educated Person," *Liberal Education* 65 (Fall 1979): 313-322; Richard A. Fredland, "Beyond Bounded Education," *Change* 13 (September 1981): 37; Derek Bok, *Higher Learning* (Cambridge, Mass.: Harvard University Press, 1986), p. 40; Linda Ray Pratt, "Liberal Education and the Idea of the Postmodern University," *Academe* (November-December 1994): 49; and Jan H. Blits, "The Search for Ends: Liberal Education and the Modern University," in Blits, ed., *The American University, Problems, Prospects and Trends* (Buffalo, N.Y.: Prometheus, 1985).

34. Robert Paul Wolff, *The Ideal of the University* (Boston: Beacon Press, 1969); Brand Blanshard, *The Uses of a Liberal Education* (LaSalle, Ill.: Open Court, 1973); Christopher Jencks and David Riesman, *The Academic Revolution* (Chicago: University of Chicago Press, 1968, 1977).

35. Quoted in Kenneth R. R. Gros Louis, "General Education: Rethinking the Assumptions," *Change* 13 (September 1981): 34.

36. Ibid, p. 35.

37. Jerry Gaff, "Reconstituting General Education: Lessons from Project GEM," *Change* 13 (September 1981): 53. See also Gaff, "General Education for a Contemporary Context," in *New Models for General Education, Current Issues in Higher Education No. 4* (Washington, D.C.: American Association for Higher Education, 1980), pp. 1-5.

38. Theodore D. Lockwood, "A Skeptical Look at the General Education Movement," *Forum for Liberal Education* (November 1978): 1-2.

39. Paul Woodring, *The Higher Learning in America: A Reassessment* (New York: McGraw-Hill, 1968), p. 201.

40. Blits, p. 93.

41. David S. Saxon, "Science and Liberal Education: What Lies Ahead," in Blits, p. 16.

42. Quoted by Martin Kaplan, "The Wrong Solution to the Right Problem," in James W. Hall, ed., *In Opposition to Core Curriculum, Alternative Models for Undergraduate Education* (Westport, Conn.: Greenwood Press, 1982), p. 187.

43. Ibid., p. 187.

44. William D. Schaefer, *Education Without Compromise, From Chaos to Coherence in Higher Education* (San Francisco: Jossey-Bass, 1990), pp. xii, 23-25, 123-124

45. Murray, p. 20. "We could not find any evidence," one group of educational researchers has noted, "that would provide support for the idea that a broad

liberal arts education promotes the development of the values, analytical skills, love of learning, or other personal and intellectual characteristics one might reasonably attribute to teachers who care about their students and understand what it takes to facilitate learning." They add, however, "The absence of evidence that greater emphasis on the liberal arts in the education of prospective teacher would result in greater teacher effectiveness does not, of course, prove that such changes are undesirable." See Carolyn M. Evertson, Willis D. Hawley, and Marilyn Zlotnik, "Making a Difference in Educational Quality Through Teacher Education," *Journal of Teacher Education* 36 (May-June 1985): 6.

46.   James B. Conant, *The Education of American Teachers* (New York: McGraw-Hill, 1963), p. 106.

47.   N. L. Gage, "What Do We Know About Teaching Effectiveness?" *Phi Delta Kappan* 66 (October 1984): 92. See also Hawley, pp. 256-257. For a fuller discussion of relevant research findings, consult Patrick Ferguson and Sid T. Womack, "The Impact of Subject Matter and Education Coursework on Teaching Performance," *Journal of Teacher Education* 44 (January-February 1993): 55-70.

48.   Martin Haberman, "Twenty-Three Reasons Universities Can't Educate Teachers," *Journal of Teacher Education* 22 (Summer 1971): 134.

49.   Evertson, Hawley, and Zlotnik, p. 5.

50.   Doyle, p. 7.

51.   Gage, 91.

52.   Richard D. Hansgen, "Can Education Become a Science?" *Phi Delta Kappan* 72 (May 1991): 694.

53.   Holmes Group, *Tomorrow's Schools* (East Lansing, Mich.: Holmes Group, 1990), p. 77.

54.   Richard L. Turner, "An Overview of Research in Teacher Education," in Kevin Ryan, ed., *Teacher Education, The Seventy-fourth Yearbook of the National Society for the Study of Education,* Part II (Chicago: University of Chicago Press, 1975), p. 107.

55.   Donald Warren, "Learning from Experience: History and Teacher Education," *Educational Researcher* 14 (December 1985): 5.

56.   Lanier and Little, pp. 552, 558. See also Jane A. Stallings, "Implications from the Research on Teaching for Teacher Preparation," in R. L. Egbert and Mary M. Kluender, eds., *Using Research to Improve Teacher Education* (Washington, D.C.: National Institute of Education, U.S. Department of Education, 1984), pp. 127-145; Pamela L. Grossman, "Learning to Teach Without Teacher Preparation," *Teachers College Record* 91 (Winter 1989): 191-208; Manuel J. Justiz, "Improving Teacher Education Through Research," *Journal of Teacher Education* 35 (July-August 1984): 3; Ralph W. Tyler, "What We've Learned From Past Studies of Teacher Education," *Phi Delta Kappan* 66 (June 1985): 682-684; and Kathryn F. Cochran et al., "Pedagogical Content Knowing: An Integrative Model for Teacher Preparation," *Journal of Teacher Education* 44 (September-October 1993): 263-272.

57.   Lois Thies-Sprinthall and Norman A. Sprinthall, "Preservice Teachers as Adult Learners: A New Framework for Teacher Education," in Martin Haberman and

Julie M. Backus, eds., *Advances in Teacher Education,* Vol. 3 (Norwood, N.J.: Ablex, 1987), pp. 37-38

58. Doyle, p. 11.

59. Ibid., pp. 11-12.

60. Jere Brophy and Thomas L. Good, "Teacher Behavior and Student Achievement," in Wittrock, p. 370. See also Thomas L. Good, "Building the Knowledge Base of Teaching," in David D. Dill et al., eds., *What Teachers Need to Know: The Knowledge, Skills and Values Essential to Good Teaching* (San Francisco: Jossey-Bass, 1990), pp. 17-74.

61. Gage, pp. 89, 91.

62. Murray, p. 23.

63. David C. Berliner, "Making the Right Changes in Preservice Teacher Education," *Phi Delta Kappan* 66 (October 1984): 94, 96. Note also the discussions in Jeffrey Gorrell et al., "Using Lasswell's Decision Seminars to Assure Appropriate Knowledge Base in Teacher Education Programs," *Journal of Teacher Education* 44 (May-June 1993): 183-189; James D. Greenberg, "The Case for Teacher Education: Open and Shut," *Journal of Teacher Education* 34 (July-August 1983): 2-5; Carol Strawderman and Pamela Lindsey, "Keeping Up with the Times: Reform in Teacher Education," *Journal of Teacher Education* 46 (March-April 1995): 95-100; Helen Harrington, "Teaching and Knowing," *Journal of Teacher Education* 45 (May-June 1994) 190-198; and Linda Tafel and Judith Christensen, "Teacher Education in the 1990's: Looking Ahead While Learning from the Past," *Action in Teacher Education* 10 (Fall 1988): 1-6.

64. Lanier and Little, p. 552. See also contributors' analyses in Frank B. Murray, *The Teacher Educator's Handbook, Building a Knowledge Base for the Preparation of Teachers* (San Francisco: Jossey-Bass, 1996), Parts One and Three.

65. Illustrative studies, none of them recent, include John Beery, *Professional Preparation and Effectiveness of Beginning Teachers* (Coral Gables, Fla.: University of Miami, ERIC Document Reproduction Service No. ED 052-156, 1960); J. Bledsoe et al., *Comparison Between Selected Characteristics and Performance of Provisionally and Professionally Certified Beginning Teachers in Georgia* (Athens, Ga.: University of Georgia, ERIC Documentation Center No. ED 015-553, 1967); Patrick O. Copley, *A Study of the Effect of Professional Education Courses on Beginning Teachers* (Springfield, Mo: Southwest Missouri State University, ERIC Document Reproduction Service No. ED 098-147, 1975); and Patricia D. Murphy, *Teaching Strategies Exhibited by First-Year Teachers* (Fargo, N.D.: North Dakota State University, ERIC Documentation Service No. ED 1068-452, 1972).

66. Evertson, Hawley, and Zlotnik, p. 4.

67. Ibid., p. 3.

68. Edgar Stones, "Reform in Teacher Education: The Power and the Pedagogy," *Journal of Teacher Education* 45 (September-October 1994): 311.

69. Ibid., p. 312.

70. Kathy Carter and Walter Doyle, "Preconceptions in Learning to Teach," *Educational Forum* 59 (Winter 1995): 186-195. Illustrations of a phenomenological

approach to teaching and to teacher education include F. M. Connelly and D. J. Clandinin, "Personal Practical Knowledge and the Modes of Knowing: Relevance for Teaching and Learning," in E. Eisner, ed., *Learning and Teaching the Ways of Knowing, Eighty-fourth Yearbook of the National Society for the Study of Education,* Part 2 (Chicago: University of Chicago Press, 1985), pp. 174-198; J. G. Knowles, "Models for Understanding Preservice and Beginning Teachers' Biographies: Illustrations from Case Studies," in I. F. Goodson, ed., *Studying Teachers' Lives* (New York: Teachers College Press, Columbia University, 1992); and A. R. McAninch, *Teacher Thinking and the Case Method* (New York: Teachers College, Columbia University, 1993).

71. Gage, p. 88.

72. Doyle, "Themes in Teacher Education Research," p. 13.

73. An excellent discussion, set in the context of a consideration of research paradigms in education, is offered by N. L. Gage, "The Paradigm Wars and Their Aftermath: A 'Historical' Sketch of Research on Teaching since 1989," *Teachers College Record* 91 (Winter 1989): 135-150.

74. Greenberg, pp. 2-5.

75. Helpful discussions are given in Peter McDermott et al., "The Influence of Classroom Practica Experiences on Student Teachers' Thoughts About Teaching," *Journal of Teacher Education* 46 (May-June 1995): 184-191; Edward J. Meade, Jr., "Reshaping the Clinical Phase of Teacher Preparation," *Phi Delta Kappan* 72 (May 1991): 666-669; and Sue Johnston, "Experience Is the Best Teacher; Or Is It? An Analysis of the Role of Experience in Learning," *Journal of Teacher Education* 45 (May-June 1994): 199-208.

76. The point is adapted and expanded from an argument originally presented in Landon E. Beyer and Kenneth M. Zeichner, "Teacher Training and Educational Foundations: A Plea for Discontent," *Journal of Teacher Education* 33 (May-June 1982): 19.

77. McDermott et al., p. 184.

78. Evertson, Hawley, and Zlotnik, p. 8.

79. Hawley, p. 260.

80. Robert N. Bush, "Teacher Education Reform: Lessons from the Past Half Century," *Journal of Teacher Education* 38 (May-June 1987): 15.

81. Joseph L. DeVitis and Peter A. Sola, eds., *Building Bridges for Educational Reform* (Ames, Iowa: University of Iowa Press, 1989), p. 13.

82. Lawrence A. Cremin, *American Education, The Metropolitan Experience 1876-1980* (New York: Harper & Row, 1988), pp. 497-502.

83. See Robert Howsam et al., *Educating a Profession* (Washington, D.C.: American Association of Colleges for Teacher Education, 1976), p. i; Amitai Etzioni, ed., *The Semi-Professions and Their Organization: Teachers, Nurses, Social Workers* (New York: Free Press, 1969); Thomas Popkewitz, *A Political Sociology of Educational Reform: Power/Knowledge in Teaching, Teacher Education, and Research* (New York: Teachers College, Columbia University, 1991); Paul Mattingly, "Workplace Autonomy and the Reforming of Teacher Education," in Thomas Popkewitz, ed., *Critical Studies in Teacher Education: Its Folklore, Theory and Practice* (London: Falmer Press, 1987), pp. 36-56; Mary

McCaslin and Thomas Good, "Compliant Cognition: The Misalliance of Management and Instructional Goals in Current School Reform," *Educational Researcher* 21 (1992): 4-17; and Thomas Popkewitz, "Professionalization in Teaching and Teacher Education: Some Notes On Its History, Ideology, and Potential," *Teaching and Teacher Education* 10 (January 1994): 1-14.

84. See B. Bledstein, *The Culture of Professionalism* (New York: W. W. Norton, 1976); and Myron Lieberman, *Education as a Profession* (Englewood Cliffs, N.J.: Prentice-Hall, 1956).

85. Doyle, "Teacher Education as a Field of Inquiry," p. 8.

86. Lieberman, p. 509.

CHAPTER 4

1. See Elizabeth Boyter, "A Study of Five-Year Programs," *Journal of Teacher Education* 5 (September 1954): 194-197.

2. Lowell Horton, "Teacher Education: By Design or Crisis?" *Journal of Teacher Education* 22 (Fall 1971): 265.

3. Mei Jiun Wong and Russell T. Osguthorpe, "The Continuing Domination of the Four-Year Teacher Education Program: A National Survey," *Journal of Teacher Education* 44 (January-February 1993): 64-70.

4. Hendrik D. Gideonse, "The Necessary Revolution in Teacher Education," *Phi Delta Kappan* 64 (September 1982): 15.

5. Ibid., p. 15.

6. Ibid., p. 18.

7. David L. Clark, "Better Teachers for the Year 2000: A Proposal for the Structural Reform of Teacher Education," *Phi Delta Kappan* 66 (October 1984): 117.

8. Ibid., p. 117.

9. Donna Kerr, "Teaching Competence and Teacher Education in the United States," in Lee Shulman and Gary Sykes, eds., *Handbook of Teaching and Policy* (New York: Longman, 1983), p. 139.

10. Clark, p. 117.

11. Ibid., p. 120.

12. Dale P. Scannell, "Extending Teacher Preparation Programs," in Arnold M. Gallegos, ed., *Improving Teacher Education, New Directions for Teaching and Learning, No. 27* (San Francisco: Jossey-Bass, 1986), p. 17.

13. Ibid., p. 25.

14. Pauline B. Gough, "On Specialized Preparation for Elementary Teachers," *Journal of Teacher Education* 33 (November-December 1982): 41.

15. Scannell, p. 18.

16. See Arnold M. Gallegos, "The Dilemma of Extended/Five-Year Programs," *Journal of Teacher Education* 32 (January-February 1981): 4-6; E. C. Galambos, *Teacher Preparation: The Anatomy of a College Degree* (Atlanta, Ga.: Southern Regional Education Board, 1985); and American Association of

Colleges for Teacher Education, *Educating a Profession: Extended Programs for Teacher Education* (Washington, D.C.: American Association of Colleges for Teacher Education, 1976). Note also Jeffrey B. Dunbar, "Moving to a Five-Year Teacher Preparation Program: The Perspective of Experience," *Journal of Teacher Education* 32 (January-February 1981): 13-15.

17. Gallegos, p. 6.

18. Ibid., p. 6. See June A. Gordon, "Why Students of Color Are Not Entering Teaching: Reflections from Minority Teachers," *Journal of Teacher Education* 45 (November-December 1994): 346-353; Stafford Hood and Laurence Parker, "Minority Students Informing the Faculty: Implications for Racial Diversity and the Future of Teacher Education," *Journal of Teacher Education* 45 (May-June 1994): 164-171; Cynthia B. Dillard, "Critical Pedagogy, Ethnicity, and Empowerment in Recruiting Teachers of Color," *Journal of Teacher Education* 45 (January-February 1994): 9-17.

19. Frederick R. Cyphert and Kevin A. Ryan, "Extending Initial Teacher Preparation: Some Issues and Answers," *Action in Teacher Education* 6 (Winter 1984-85): 69.

20. Willis D. Hawley, "The Risks and Inadequacy of Extended Programs," in Galambos, *Improving Teacher Education,* p. 27.

21. Ibid., p. 27. See also Hawley, "United States," in Howard B. Leavitt, ed., *Issues and Problems in Teacher Education, An International Handbook* (Westport, Conn.: Greenwood Press, 1992), pp. 251-277.

22. Hawley, "United States," p. 265.

23. Hawley, "The Risks and Inadequacy of Extended Programs," pp. 32-33.

24. Ibid., pp. 34-35.

25. Note the brief discussion in Judith Lanier and Judith Little, "Research on Teacher Education," in Merlin C. Wittrock, ed., *Handbook of Research on Teaching,* 3rd ed. (New York: Macmillan, 1986), p. 217. See also David F. Labaree, "An Unlovely Legacy: The Disabling Impact of the Market on American Teacher Education," *Phi Delta Kappan* 75 (April 1994): 591; and the analysis in Kenneth R. Howey and Nancy L. Zimpher, "The Current Debate on Teacher Preparation," *Journal of Teacher Education* 37 (September-October 1986): 41-49. Of particular importance was the appearance of a nationally circulated study urging the retention of four-year programs: see J. S. Johnston et al., *Those Who Can: Undergraduate Programs to Prepare Arts and Sciences Majors for Teaching* (Washington, D.C.: Association for American Colleges, 1989.

26. Task Force on Teaching as a Profession, *A Nation Prepared: Teachers for the 21st Century* (New York: Carnegie Forum on Education and the Economy, 1985).

27. National Commission for Excellence in Teacher Education, *A Call for Change in Teacher Education* (Washington, D.C.: American Association of Colleges for Teacher Education, 1985).

28. Southern Regional Education Board, *Improving Teacher Education: An Agenda for Higher Education and the Schools* (Atlanta, Ga.: Southern Regional Education Board, 1985).

29. The evolution of the Holmes Group is traced in Barbara Schneider and Stafford Hood, "Pathways to Institutional Change: From the Deans' Network to the Holmes Group," in Kathryn Borman and Nancy P. Greenman, eds., *Changing American Education: Recapturing the Past or Inventing the Future?* (Albany, N.Y.: State University of New York Press, 1994), pp. 107-132.

30. Holmes Group, *Goals for Educating Teachers as Professionals: An Interim Report* (draft document, 1985); Holmes Group, *Tomorrow's Teachers* (East Lansing, Mich.: Holmes Group, 1986); Holmes Group, *Tomorrow's Schools: Principles for the Design of Professional Development Schools* (East Lansing, Mich.: Holmes Group, 1990); and Holmes Group, *Tomorrow's Schools of Education* (East Lansing, Mich.: Holmes Group, 1995)

31. Holmes Group, *Tomorrow's Teachers*, p. 4.

32. The concept of professional development schools spawned an enormous literature. For illustrative commentaries, see D. Thompson Manning, "Historical Lessons for Teacher Education," *Journal of Teacher Education* 38 (December 1987): 20-24; Pamela J. Farris and Betsy J. Smith, "Professional Development Schools: Teacher Education's Last Hurrah?" *Contemporary Education* 64 (Summer 1993): 261-262; Paul N. Dixon and Richard E. Ishler, "Professional Development Schools: Stages in Collaboration," *Journal of Teacher Education* 43 (January-February 1992): 28-34; Nancy Winitzky et al., "Great Expectations: Emergent Professional Development Schools," *Journal of Teacher Education* 43 (January-February 1992): 3-18; Charles W. Smith, "Laboratory Schools/Professional Development Schools: Are They, Can They Be One and the Same?" *National Association of Laboratory Schools Journal* 16 (Fall 1991): 8-17; and Frank Brainard, *Professional Development Schools: Status as of 1989, Occasional Paper No. 9* (Seattle, Wash.: Center for Educational Renewal, 1989).

33. See Ann Bradley, "Report's Delay Underscores Holmes's Struggles," *Education Week* 13 (February 9, 1994): 1, 8; and Julie L. Nicklin, "Education-School Group Issues Scathing, Self-Critical Review," *Chronicle of Higher Education* 41 (February 3, 1995): A17.

34. Task Force on Teaching as a Profession, *A Nation Prepared*, pp. 67, 76, 78; and Holmes Group, *Tomorrow's Teachers*, p. 19.

35. See John Sikula, "National Commission Reports of the 1980s," in Robert Houston et al., eds., *Handbook of Research on Teacher Education* (New York: Macmillan, 1990): 78-81; Vernon L. Clark, "Teacher Education at Historically Black Institutions in the Aftermath of the Holmes/Carnegie Reports," *Planning and Changing* 18 (Summer 1987): 74-79; Edward R. Ducharme, "The Professors and the Reports: A Time to Act," *Journal of Teacher Education* 37 (September-October 1986): 51-56; Julius G. Goldberg, *No More Teacher Traps—Neither in the Name of Holmes Nor Carnegie* (New York: Vantage Press, 1987); Joslyn Green, *The Next Wave: A Synopsis of Recent Education Reform Reports* (Denver, Col.: Education Commission of the States, 1987); Robert L. Hample, "The Political Side of Reform: Are Conflicts, Power Struggles Likely to Occur?" *NASSP Bulletin* 70 (December 1986): 55-64; Robert L. Jacobson, "Carnegie School-Reform Goals Hailed; Achieving Them

Called 'Tall Order,'" *Chronicle of Higher Education* 32 (May 28, 1986): 1, 23; Carl Kaestle, "Education Reform and the Swinging Pendulum," *Phi Delta Kappan* 66 (February 1985): 422-423; Courtney Leatherman, "Reforms in Education of Schoolteachers Face Tough New Challenges," *Chronicle of Higher Education* 34 (April 20, 1988): A1, A30; Malcolm G. Scully, "Study Finds Colleges Torn by Divisions, Confused Over Roles," *Chronicle of Higher Education* 33 (November 5, 1986): 1, 16-23; Albert Shanker, "The Carnegie Report: An Endorsement for Teacher Education," *Change* 18 (September-October 1986): 8-9; John P. Sikula, "Commentary on Reform: Implications for the Education Profession," *Teacher Education Quarterly* 14 (Winter 1987): 52-59; Alan R. Tom, *How Should Teachers Be Educated? An Assessment of Three Reform Reports,* Fastback No. 255 (Bloomington, Ind.: Phi Delta Kappa Educational Foundation, 1987; Sam P. Wiggins, "Revolution in the Teaching Profession: A Comparative Review of Two Reform Reports," *Educational Leadership* 44 (October 1986): 56-59; David F. Labaree, "Doing Good, Doing Science: The Holmes Group Reports and the Rhetoric of Educational Reform," *Teachers College Record* 93 (Summer 1992): 628-641; James W. Fraser, "Preparing Teachers for Democratic Schools: The Holmes and Carnegie Reports Five Years Later—A Critical Reflection," *Teachers College Record* 94 (Fall 1992): 7-40; Kay S. Bull and Adrienne E. Hyle, "Five Year Teacher Education Programs: Potential Impact on Training Teachers for Rural Schools," *Journal of Rural and Small Schools* 4 (Winter 1990): 20-26; and Linda S. Guest, *Improving Teacher Preparation: What the Reform Reports Recommend* (Denver, Col.: Education Commission of the States, 1993).

36. See "State-College Deans Rap Holmes Report as a 'Source of Conflict,'" *Education Week* 5 (1986): 7.

37. Schneider and Hood, p. 128.

38. Ibid., p. 128.

39. Holmes Group, *Goals for Educating Teachers as Professionals,* (1985), pp. 49, 52.

40. Holmes Group, *Tomorrow's Teachers,* pp. 49, 50, 52.

41. William R. Johnson, "Empowering Practitioners: Holmes, Carnegie, and the Lessons of History," *History of Education Quarterly* 27 (Summer, 1987): 228.

42. Holmes Group, *Tomorrow's Teachers,* p. 52.

43. Johnston, p. 228. A relevant discussion is given in Anne Reynolds, "The Knowledge Base for Beginning Teachers: Education Professionals' Expectations versus Research Findings on Learning to Teach," *Elementary School Journal* 95 (January 1995): 199-221.

44. Alan Tom, *The Case for Maintaining Teacher Education at the Undergraduate Level* (St. Louis, Mo.: Washington University, Coalition of Teacher Education Programs, 1986), p. 31

45. Quoted in Howey and Zimpher, p. 42.

46. Michael W. Andrew, "Differences Between Graduates of 4-Year and 5-Year Teacher Preparation Programs," *Journal of Teacher Education* 41 (March-April 1990): 45-51.

47. Reported and summarized in David G. Armstrong, Lynn Burlbaw, and Connie Batten, "Extended Teacher-Preparation Programs: What the Literature Tells Us." Paper presented at the annual meeting of the Association of Teacher Educators, New Orleans, February, 1991, pp. 9-19.

48. Howey and Zimpher, p. 48.

49. Kenneth R. Howey, "Research about Teacher Education: Programs of Teacher Preparation," *Journal of Teacher Education* 40 (November-December 1989): 23-26. See also Howey and Zimpher, *Profiles of Preservice Teacher Education: Inquiry Into the Nature of Programs* (Albany, N.Y.: State University of New York Press, 1989).

50. Wong and Osguthorpe, p. 64.

51. American Association of Colleges for Teacher Education, *RATE V: Teaching Teachers: Facts and Figures* (Washington, D.C.: American Association of Colleges for Teacher Education, 1991).

52. David L. Clark and Terry A. Astuto, "Redirecting Reform, Challenges to Popular Assumptions About Teachers and Students," *Phi Delta Kappan* 75 (March 1994): 513, 517. See also Clark et al., *Challenging the Assumptions That Control Change in Education* (Bloomington, Ind.: Phi Delta Kappa, 1994).

53. Clark and Astuto, p. 517. Note the useful discussions provided by Ellen C. Lagemann, "The Complexity of Educational Change," *Teachers College Record* 96 (Fall 1994): 1-7; and Lagemann, "Reinventing the Teacher's Role," *Teachers College Record* 95 (Fall 1995): 1-7.

54. Landon E. Beyer, "Reconceptualizing Teacher Preparation Institutions and Ideologies," *Journal of Teacher Education* 40 (January-February 1989): 22-226.

55. Martin Haberman, "Twenty-Three Reasons Universities Can't Educate Teachers," *Journal of Teacher Education* 22 (Summer 1971): 136.

56. James R. Delisle, "An Ed School Is No Place for a Teacher," *Education Week* (March 25, 1992): 1. See also Martin Anderson, *Imposters in the Temple: American Intellectuals are Destroying Our Universities and Cheating Our Students* (New York: Simon and Schuster, 1992).

57. Haberman, pp. 135, 136, 137.

58. Ibid., p. 134.

59. Ibid., p. 134.

60. Douglas J. Simpson, "Professional Development Schools, Prescriptions and Proscriptions: A Fictitious Letter to Evangelina Ramirez," *Journal of Teacher Education* 45 (September-October 1995): 253, 254. See also Nancy Green et al., "Spanning Cultures: Teachers and Professors in Professional Development Schools," *Action in Teacher Education* 15 (Summer 1993): 18-24.

61. Lee Teitel, "Can School-University Partnerships Lead to the Simultaneous Renewal of Schools and Teacher Education?" *Journal of Teacher Education* 45 (September-October 1994): 245-252. Even stronger is a judgment offered by Warren Corbin: "The belief that universities and public schools are both in the 'education business' leads to the superficial and erroneous conclusion that the purposes and needs of both are identical," he observed. "Their purposes and needs are no more identical than those of a peanut vendor in the street and

General Motors, even though it could be said that both the vendor and G.M. are in the sales business." See Corbin, "Universities Should Get Out of the Business of Teaching Teachers," *Chronicle of Higher Education* 29 (January 23, 1985): 88.

62. Quoted in Walter Doyle, "Themes in Teacher Education Research," in Houston, p. 7. Also consult Thomas Sowell, *Inside American Education, The Decline, the Deception, the Dogma* (New York: Free Press, 1993), p. 23.

63. Doyle, p. 7.

64. Ibid., p. 7.

65. Madeleine R. Grumet, "Generations: Reconceptualist Curriculum Theory and Teacher Education," *Journal of Teacher Education* 40 (January-February 1989): 13-17

66. Elizabeth Hunter, "A Collaborative, Connected, Completely Organic, All-Natural Teacher Education Program," *Journal of Teacher Education* 31 (July-August 1980): 9.

67. Ibid., pp. 7-8.

68. Ibid., p. 10.

69. Judy Swanson, "Systemic Reform in The Professionalism of Educators," *Phi Delta Kappan* 77 (September 1995): 36-39.

70. Ibid., p. 39. See also Michael G. Fullan, "Coordinating School and District Development in Restructuring," in Joseph Murphy and Philip Hallinger, eds., *Restructuring Schooling: Learning from Ongoing Efforts* (Thousand Oaks, Calif.: Corwin Press, 1993); Mary Alice Barksdale-Ladd, "Teacher Empowerment and Literacy Instruction in Three Professional Development Schools," *Journal of Teacher Education* 45 (March-April 1994): 104-111; Pamela C. Boyd, "Professional School Reform and Public School Renewal: Portrait of a Partnership," *Journal of Teacher Education* 45 (March-April 1994): 132-139; Gary Sykes, "Fostering Teacher Professionalism in Schools," in Richard Elmore et al., *Restructuring Schools: The Next Generation of Reform* (San Francisco: Jossey-Bass, 1990); and Seymour Sarason, *The Case for Change: Rethinking the Preparation of Educators* (San Francisco: Jossey-Bass, 1993).

71. Robert A. Roth, "The University Can't Train Teachers? Transformation of a Profession," *Journal of Teacher Education* 45 (September-October 1994): 261. See also Roth, "Alternate and Alternative Certification: Purposes, Assumptions, Implications," *Action in Teacher Education* 8 (Summer 1986): 1-6; Roth, "Emergency Certificates, Misassignment of Teachers, and Other Dirty Little Secrets, " *Phi Delta Kappan* 67 (June 1986): 725-727; Roth, "The Teacher Education Profession: An Endangered Species," *Phi Delta Kappan* 71 (December 1989): 319-323; and Roth, "Dichotomous Paradigms for Teacher Education: The Rise or Fall of the Empire," *Action in Teacher Education* 4 (Spring 1992): 1-9.

72. Emily C. Feistritzer and David T. Chester, *Alternative Teacher Certification: A State by State Analysis* (Washington, D.C.: National Center for Education Information, 1992); Feistritzer, *Who Wants to Teach?* (Washington, D.C.: National Center for Education Information, 1992); National Association of State Directors of Teacher Education and Certification, *Manual on Certification*

and Preparation of Educational Personnel in the United States (Dubuque, Iowa: NASDTEC, 1992); and American Association of Colleges for Teacher Education, *Teacher Education Policy in the States: A 50-State Survey of Legislative and Administrative Actions* (Washington, D.C.: AACTE, 1990).

73. Nancy E. Adelman, *An Exploratory Study of Teacher Alternative Certification and Retraining Programs* (Washington, D.C.: Policy Studies Associates, 1986); Neil B. Carey et al., *Recruiting Mathematics and Science Teachers Through Nontraditional Programs: A Survey* (Santa Monica, Calif.: Center for the Study of the Teaching Profession, RAND Corporation, 1988); Martin Haberman, "Alternative Teacher Certification Programs," *Action in Teacher Education* 8 (Summer 1986): 15; Linda Darling-Hammond, "Teaching and Knowledge Policy Issues Posed by Alternate Certification for Teachers," *Peabody Journal of Education* 67 (Spring 1990): 123-154; Vicky Dill and Delia Stafford, "School-Based Teacher Education," *Phi Delta Kappan* 75 (April 1994): 620-623. Especially helpful in its discussion of one type of alternative program is Kate Hawkey, "Learning from Peers: The Experience of Student Teachers in School-Based Teacher Education," *Journal of Teacher Education* 46 (May-June 1995): 175-183.

74. Specific findings are summarized and discussed in Darling-Hammond, pp. 130-132; and in Edith Guyton, Marian C. Fox, and Kathy A. Sisk, "Comparison of Teaching Attitudes, Teacher Efficacy, and Teacher Performance of First Year Teachers Prepared by Alternative and Traditional Teacher Education Programs," *Action in Teacher Education* 13 (Summer 1991); and Julie Meltzer, Myron Trang, and Betty Bailey, "Clinical Cycles: A Productive Tool for Teacher Education," *Phi Delta Kappan* 75 (April 1994): 612-619.

75. Roth, "The University Can't Train Teachers?", pp. 266-267.

76. Ibid., p. 267.

77. John I. Goodlad, Roger Soden, and Kenneth A. Sirotnik, eds., *Places Where Teachers Are Taught* (San Francisco: Jossey-Bass, 1990), p. xi. See also Goodlad, "Better Teachers for Our Nation's Schools," *Phi Delta Kappan* 72 (November 1990): 185-194; and Goodlad, "A Study of the Education of Educators: One Year Later," *Phi Delta Kappan* 73 (December 1991): 311-316.

78. Goodlad, *Teachers for Our Nation's Schools* (San Francisco: Jossey-Bass, 1990); Goodlad, *The Moral Dimensions of Teaching* (San Francisco: Jossey-Bass, 1990); and Goodlad, Soden, and Sirotnik, eds. *Places Where Teachers Are Taught* (San Francisco: Jossey-Bass, 1990).

79. Goodlad, "Better Teachers for Our Nation's Schools," p. 186.

80. Ibid., p. 187.

81. Ibid., p. 188.

82. Ibid., p. 188.

83. Ibid., pp. 191-192.

84. See Kenneth A. Sirotnik and John I. Goodlad, eds., *School-University Partnerships in Action* (New York: Teachers College Press, Columnbia University, 1988); and Sirotnik, "The School as the Center of Change," in Thomas J. Sergiovanni and John H. Moore, eds., *Schooling for Tomorrow: Directing Reform to Issues That Count* (Newton, Mass.: Allyn and Bacon, 1989).

85. Goodlad, "Better Teachers for Our Nation's Schools," p. 185. Apropos is the following comment by Martin Haberman: "Nothing [education professors] offer future teachers—whether skills, values, or theory—can withstand what they learn on the job as practitioners. If preservice preparation should prove more powerful than the situational press, the teacher would probably be fired. If, on the other hand, there were complete harmony between preparation and practice, then the preservice would be an overexpensive waste, since teachers learn more and faster on the job." See Haberman, "Twenty-Three Reasons Universities Can't Educate Teachers," p. 137.

86. Chester E. Finn, Jr., "An Insider Grades Education Schools," *Christian Science Monitor* (December 3, 1990): 15. For other early reactions to the Goodlad study, consult Joseph Shenker's review of *Teachers for Our Nation's Schools,* in *Teachers College Record* 93 (Summer 1992): 733-737; John O'Neil's discussion of the same work in *Educational Leadership* 48 (April 1991): 88; the review of *Teachers for Our Nation's Schools* and of *Places Where Teachers Are Taught* offered by Wayne J. Urban in *Educational Studies* 22 (Winter 1991): 538-544; and a review of the same two volumes by Joseph T. Durham in *Journal of Negro Education* 60 (Summer 1991): 486-488.

87. Quoted in Laurel Shaper Walters, "Straight Talk on Teacher Training," *Christian Science Monitor* (December 3, 1990): 15.

88. Goodlad, "A Study of the Education of Educators," pp. 313, 316.

89. Wendy Kopp, "Teach for America: Moving Beyond the Debate," *Educational Forum* 58 (Winter 1994): 187-192; and see Michael Shapiro, *Who Will Teach for America?* Washington, D.C.: Farragut, 1993).

90. Jonathan Schorr, "Class Action, What Clinton's National Service Program Could Learn from 'Teach for America,'" *Phi Delta Kappan* 75 (December 1995): 315-318.

91. Corbin, p. 88.

92. *A Call for Change in Teacher Education,* p. 15.

93. Ibid., p. 15.

94. For a more extensive analysis, consult Madhu Suri Prakash, "Reforming the Teaching of Teachers: Trends, Contradictions, and Challenges," *Teachers College Record* 88 (Winter 1986): 217-240.

CHAPTER 5

1. Refer to David L. Clark and Robert F. McNergney, "Governance of Teacher Education," in Robert Houston et al., eds., *Handbook of Research on Teacher Education* (New York: Macmillan, 1990), pp. 101-118.

2. Descriptive data on state certification standards are drawn from John Tryneski, ed., *Requirements for Certification of Teachers, Counselors, Librarians, Administrators,* 60th ed., 1995-96 (Chicago: University of Chicago Press, 1995), as revised and updated by reference to documents supplied by each of the 50 states.

3. Compare the outlines supplied in Tryneski with the profiles given in Arthur E. Wise and Linda Darling-Hammond, *Licensing Teachers: Design for a Teaching Profession* (Santa Monica, Calif.: RAND Corporation, 1987). Relevant discussions of state rules and regulations appear in Lawrence M. Rudner and Thomas E. Eissenberg, *State Testing of Teachers: The 1989 Report* (Washington, D.C.: American Institutes for Research, 1989); in Leonard Kaplan, "Teacher Certification: Collaborative Reform," *Educational Forum* 58 (Winter 1994): 168-172; in Robert A. Roth and Chris Pipho, "Teacher Education Standards," in Houston et al., eds., pp. 119-135; and in Association of Teacher Educators Commission on Quality Standards and Enhancement of Teacher Education, *Mission Statement* (Reston, Va.: Association of Teacher Educators, 1993).

4. See Arthur E. Wise, "The Coming Revolution in Teacher Licensure: Redefining Teacher Preparation," *Action in Teacher Education* 16 (Summer 1994): 1.

5. Note the commentary in Richard J. Murnane, "The Case for Performance-Based Licensing," *Phi Delta Kappan* 73 (October 1991): 137.

6. Wise, pp. 1, 3.

7. Ibid., p. 3.

8. Clark and McNergney, p. 110.

9. Walter Haney, George Madaus, and Amelia Kreitzer, "Charms Talismanic: Testing Teachers for the Improvement of American Education," *Review of Research in Education* 14 (1987): 199.

10. Murnane, p. 139. See also Murnane et al., *Who Will Teach? Policies That Matter* (Cambridge, Mass.: Harvard University Press, 1991).

11. Murnance, "The Case for Performance-Based Licensing," p. 142.

12. Roth and Pipho, pp. 120-121. See Carolyn M. Evertson, Willis D. Hawley, and Marilyn Zlotnik, "Making a Difference in Educational Quality Through Teacher Education," *Journal of Teacher Education* 36 (May-June 1985): 2-12; Willis Hawley, *Directions of Teacher Education in the United States* (Paris: Organization for Economic and Community Development, 1989); and Hawley, *Notes on the Redesign of Teacher Education* (Denver, Col.: Education Commission of the States, 1986).

13. Roth and Pipho, p. 120.

14. The specific context for his remarks involved issues having to do with relations between NCATE and the American Association of Colleges for Teacher Education (AACTE). See Gary D. Fenstermacher, "Controlling Quality and Creating Community: Separate Purposes for Separate Organizations," *Journal of Teacher Education* 45 (November-December 1994): 329-336.

15. Ibid., p. 330.

16. Consult Timothy M. Stinnett, "The Accreditation of Institutions for Teacher Preparation." Unpublished doctoral dissertation, University of Texas, Austin, 1951); George R. Overby, "A Critical Review of Selected Issues Involved in the Establishment and Functioning of the National Council for Accreditation of Teacher Education from Its Origin Through 1965." Unpublished doctoral dissertation, Florida State University, 1966; John R. Mayor and Willis G. Swartz, *Accreditation in Teacher Education: Its Influence on Higher Education* (Washington, D.C.: National Commission on Accrediting, 1965); Chris W.

Wheeler, *NCATE: Does It Matter?* (East Lansing, Mich.: Institute for Research on Teaching, Michigan State University, 1980); and Richard Roames, "Acccreditation in Teacher Education: A History of the Development of Standards Utilized by the National Council for Accreditation of Teacher Education." Unpublished doctoral dissertation, University of Akron, 1987.

17. See Benjamin W. Frazer et al., "Establishment and Growth of Normal Schools and Departments in Colleges and Universities from 1839 to 1865," *National Survey of the Education of Teachers,* Vol. 5 (Washington, D.C.: U.S. Government Printing Office, Office of Education Bulletin 1933, No. 10, 1935), Chapter 2, pp. 10-23.

18. "Report of the Committee on Normal Schools," *National Education Association, Proceedings and Addresses of the Thirty-Eighth Annual Meeting* (Washington, D.C.: National Education Association, 1899), pp. 836-837.

19. Benjamin W. Maxwell, "Report of Committee on American Teachers Colleges," *National Education Association, Addresses and Proceedings of the Sixty-First Annual Meeting* (Washington, D.C.: National Education Association, 1923), pp. 483-484.

20. National Education Association, "Conference on Accrediting," *Minutes of the Conference on Accrediting* (Washington, D.C.: National Education Association, April 27-29, 1951).

21. National Council for Accreditation of Teacher Education, *Standards, Procedures, and Policies for the Accreditation of Professional Education Units* (Washington, D.C.: NCATE, 1995), pp. 1, 3. See also National Council for Accreditation of Teacher Education, *Teacher Preparation, A Guide to Colleges and Universities, 1994-95* (Washington, D.C.: NCATE, 1994-95).

22. Figures cited are taken from an NCATE fact sheet derived from statistics supplied in National Association of State Directors of Teacher Education and Certification, *Manual on Certification, 1994-1995* (Washington, D.C.: NASDTEC, 1994).

23. National Council for Accreditation of Teacher Education, *Standards, Procedures, and Policies,* pp. 16-17.

24. Ibid., pp. 17-18.

25. Ibid., p. 12; Wise, "The Coming Revolution," p. 9; and Harry D. Gideonse et al., *Capturing the Vision: Reflections of NCATE's Redesign Five Years After* (Washington, D.C.: American Association of Colleges for Teacher Education, 1991).

26. Examples include National Science Teachers Association, *NSTA Standards for Science Teacher Preparation* (Arlington, Va.: National Science Teachers Association, 1992); National Academy of Early Childhood Programs, *Accreditation Criteria and Procedures of the National Academy of Early Childhood Programs* (Washington, D.C.: Washington, D.C.: NAEYC, n.d.); and Association for Childhood Education International, *Elementary Education Curriculum Folio Guidelines for the NCATE Review Process, Basic Preparation* (Wheaton, Md.: ACEI, n.d.).

27. National Board for Professional Teaching Standards, *Toward High and Rigorous Standards for the Teaching Profession: Initial Policies and Perspectives of*

the National Board for Professional Teaching Standards (Detroit, Mich.: National Board for Professional Teaching Standards, 1989).

28. Ibid., pp. 2, 5, 6.

29. Ibid., pp. 13-14.

30. American Federation of Teachers, "Creating a Profession of Teaching: The Role of National Board Certification," *American Educator* 14 (Summer 1990): 8-21, 40-45.

31. Wise, "The Coming Revolution," p. 11.

32. M. Jean Miller and Linda Darling-Hammond, *Model Standards for Beginning Teacher Licensing and Development: A Resource for State Dialogue* (Washington, D.C.: Interstate New Teacher Assessment and Support Consortium/Council of Chief State School Officers, n.d.), p. 3.

33. Ibid., p. 5.

34. Refer to Interstate New Teacher Assessment and Support Consortium, *Next Steps: Moving Toward Performance-Based Licensing in Teaching* (Washington, D.C.: Council of Chief State School Officers, 1994); and Interstate New Teacher Assessment and Support Consortium, *Assessment Development for Teacher Licensing: The Portfolio Project* (Washington, D.C.: Council of Chief State School Officers, 1994).

35. See National Council for Accreditation of Teacher Education, *Standards, Procedures, and Policies,* pp. 17-18.

36. National Council for Accreditation of Teacher Education, *An Introduction to the New Professional Teacher Project* (Washington, D.C.: NCATE, n.d.), p. 1.

37. National Council for Accreditation of Teacher Education, *A Vision of the Future: The New Professional Teacher Project* (Washington, D.C.: NCATE, n.d.), p. 1.

38. Ibid., p. 1-2.

39. Ibid., pp. 1-2.

40. National Council for Accreditation of Teacher Education, *Teacher Preparation: A Continuum, The New Professional Teacher Project* (Washington, D.C.: NCATE, n.d.), pp. 1-2, See Arthur E. Wise, "Professionalization and Standards: A Unified System of Quality Assurance," *Education Week* (June 1, 1994): 48; and Arthur E. Wise and Jane Leibbrand, "Accreditation and the Creation of a Profession of Teaching," *Phi Delta Kappan* 75 (October 1993): 133-157.

41. National Board for Professional Teaching Standards, *Toward High and Rigorous Standards for the Teaching Profession,* pp. 9, 13.

42. National Council for Accreditation of Teacher Education, *Standards, Procedures, and Policies,* pp. 15-16.

43. Fenstermacher, p. 331.

44. See Gary D. Fenstermacher, "The Knower and the Known: The Nature of Knowledge in Research on Teaching," in Linda Darling-Hammond, ed., *Review of Research in Education* 20 (1994): 3-56; D. Jean Clandinin et al., *Learning to Teach, Teaching to Learn* (New York: Teachers College Press, 1993); Freema L. Elbaz, "Research on Teacher's Knowledge: The Evolution of a Discourse," *Journal of Curriculum Studies* 23 (January-February 1991): 1-19;

D. A. Schön, *The Reflective Turn: Case Studies in and on Educational Practice* (New York: Teachers College Press, 1991).

45. Fenstermacher, "Controlling Quality and Creating Community," p. 331.

46. See John Goodlad et al., *The Moral Dimensions of Teaching* (San Francisco: Jossey-Bass, 1990); Hugh Sockett, *The Moral Base for Teacher Professionalism* (New York: Teachers College Press, 1993); and Kenneth A. Strike and P. Lance Ternasky, eds., *Ethics for Professionals in Education* (New York: Teachers College Press, 1993).

47. Fenstermacher, "Controlling Quality and Creating Community," p. 331.

48. David A. Labaree, "Power, Knowledge, and the Rationalization of Teaching: A Genealogy of the Movement to Professionalize Teaching," *Harvard Educational Review* 62 (1992): 148.

49. Ibid., p. 149; and see M. Bruce King, "Locking Ourselves In: National Standards for the Teaching Profession," *Teaching and Teacher Education* 10 (1994): 95.

50. Labaree, p. 149. On the other hand, the argument does seem to be circular, since nobody claims that the professional autonomy accorded physicians is somehow "antidemocratic." The relevant issue with respect to teaching, once again, hinges on whether there exists a special expertise possessed only by teachers and not readily intelligible or accessible to the public at large.

51. King, pp. 103, 102.

52. Ibid., p. 104.

53. Fenstermacher, "Controlling Quality and Creating Community," p. 332.

54. Ibid., p. 333.

55. Miller and Darling-Hammond, *Model Standards for Beginning Teacher Licensing and Development,* p. 3.

56. National Council for Accreditation of Teacher Education, *Standards, Procedures, and Policies,* p. 18.

57. Ibid., p. 18.

58. Ibid., p. 19.

59. Ibid., p. 19.

60. Office of Teacher Education and Certification, *Guiding and Assessing Teacher Effectiveness: A Handbook for Kentucky Internship Program Participants* (Lexington, Ky.: Office of Teacher Education and Certification, Education Professional Standards Board, June, 1995), p. 89.

61. Baird W. Whitlock, *Educational Myths I Have Known and Loved* (New York: Schocken Books, 1986), p. 113.

62. Eva C. Galambos, *Teacher Preparation: The Anatomy of a College Degree* (Atlanta, Ga.: Southern Regional Education Board, 1985), 13-14, 21.

63. Ibid., pp. 23, 29.

64. Frederic Mitchell and Michael Schwinden, *Profiles of the Education of Teachers* (Flagstaff, Ariz.: Northern Arizona State University, 1984), p. 4.

65. Cited in Thomas Toch, *In the Name of Excellence, The Struggle to Reform the Nation's Schools, Why It's Failing, and What Should Be Done* (New York: Oxford University Press, 1991), p. 294.

66. Oklahoma State Department of Education, *Teacher Education and Certification, Guidelines and Procedures Handbook* (Oklahoma City: Oklahoma State Department of Education, 1995), p. 22.

67. Kansas State Board of Education, *Certification and Teacher Education Regulations* (Topeka: Certification Section, Kansas State Board of Education, 1995), p. 33.

68. Toch, p. 157.

69. Ibid., p. 163.

70. Ibid., p. 164.

CHAPTER 6

1. Virginia Richardson, "The Case for Formal Research and Practical Inquiry in Teacher Education," in Frank R. Murray, ed., *The Teacher Educator's Handbook: Building a Knowledge Base for the Preparation of Teachers* (San Francisco: Jossey-Bass, 1996), p. 721; and Peter Scales, "How Teachers and Education Deans Rate the Quality of Teacher Preparation for the Middle Grades," *Journal of Teacher Education* 44 (November-December 1993): 378-383.

2. Dorothy H. Mayne, "Recommendations from Teachers in Small Rural High Schools for Modification of the Teacher Training Program of the University of Alaska: A Survey." Unpublished master's thesis, University of Alaska, 1980.

3. David Lillie et al., "Evaluation of Teacher Training: The Master of Education Program in Special Education at the University of North Carolina at Chapel Hill," *Teacher Education and Special Education* 9 (Summer 1986): 128-135.

4. Robert J. Drummond, *Beginning Teachers: What They Have to Say About Their Performance and Preparation* (Washington, D.C.: Educational Resources Information Center, ERIC: MF01/PC02, 1991).

5. Martina Wamboldt et al., *1992 Survey of First- and Third-Year Teachers and Their Supervisors* (Denver, CO: Colorado State Department of Education, Planning and Evaluation Unit, 1993).

6. Don Holste and Don Matthews, *Survey of 1991 Teacher Education Graduates Conducted in May 1992* (Champaign, IL: Council on Teacher Education, College of Education, University of Illinois, 1993).

7. John E. McEneaney and E. Marcia Sheridan, *Evaluating the Effectiveness of an Undergraduate Teacher Education Program* (Washington, D.C.: Educational Resources Information Center, ERIC: MF01/PC01, 1993).

8. Patricia D. Murphy, *Follow-Up Studies in Program Evaluation* (Washington, D.C.: Educational Resources Information Center, ERIC: MF01/PC01, 1992).

9. Kawanna J. Simpson and Rosetta F. Sandidge, *Determining the Success of Teacher Preparation by Assessing What Teacher Education Graduates Know and Are Able to Do* (Washington, D.C.: Educational Resources Information Center, ERIC: MF01/PC01, 1994).

10. Beverly Cabello and Janice Eckmier, "Looking Back: Teachers' Reflections on an Innovative Teacher Preparation Program," *Action in Teacher Education* 17 (Fall 1995): 33-42.

11. B. E. J. Housego, "A Comparative Study of Student Teachers' Feelings of Preparedness to Teach," *Alberta Journal of Educational Research* 36 (September 1990): 223-239; Michael D. Andrew and Richard L. Schwab, "Has Reform in Teacher Education Influenced Teacher Performance? An Outcome Assessment of Graduates of an Eleven-University Consortium," *Action in Teacher Education* 17 (Fall 1995): 43-53; and Madeline Hurster and Marilyn Schima, "Students' Perceptions of Coverage of Health Education Competencies by Their Professional Preparation Programs," *Journal of Health Education* 25 (November-December 1994): 362-368.

12. B. E. J. Housego, "How Prepared Were You to Teach? Beginning Teachers Assess Their Preparedness," *Alberta Journal of Educational Research* 40 (September 1994): 355-373.

13. Thomas D. Purcell and Berniece B. Seifert, "A Tri-State Survey of Student Teachers," *College Student Journal* 16 (Spring 1982): 27-29; Edward Holdaway et al., "The Value of an Internship Program for Beginning Teachers," *Educational Evaluation and Policy Analysis* 16 (Summer 1994): 205-221.

14. James E. Renney and Victor L. Dupuis, *An Analysis of the Perceived Needs and Proficiencies of Preservice Teachers for Program Evaluation* (Washington, D.C.: Educational Resources Information Center, ERIC: MF01/PC01, 1983).

15. Leslie Huling and Gene E. Hall, "Factors to Be Considered in the Preparation of Secondary School Teachers," *Journal of Teacher Education* 33 (January-February 1982): 7-12.

16. Frances O'Connell Rust, "The First Year of Teaching: It's Not What They Expected," *Teaching and Teacher Education* 10 (March 1994): 205-217.

17. Robert P. Craig, "Reflection and Imagination: A Wholistic Approach to Teacher Education," *Teacher Education Quarterly* 21 (Summer 1994): 39-46.

18. Judy Reinhartz and Don M. Beach, "The Principal: A Vital Component in Assessing Teacher Education Programs," *NASSP Bulletin* 66 (October 1982): 68-70.

19. Kenneth D. Peterson, "Teacher Education Program Evaluation Through an Institutional Board Review of Graduates," *Journal of Research and Development in Education* 22 (Summer 1989): 14-20.

20. Edwin G. Ralph, "On Assembling the Pieces: What Do Retired Educators Tell Us?" *Action in Teacher Education* 16 (Summer 1994): 62-72.

21. M. Rosenfeld and R. J. Tannenbaum, *Identification of a Core of Important Enabling Skills for the NTE Successor Stage I Examination,* Research Report No. 91-37 (Princeton, NJ: Educational Testing Service, 1991).

22. Anne Reynolds, R. J. Tannenbaum, and M. Rosenfeld., *Beginning Teacher Knowledge of Education in the Elementary School: A National Survey,* Research Report No. 92-71 (Princeton, NJ: Educational Testing Service, 1992).

23. Anne Reynolds, R. J. Tannenbaum, and M. Rosenfeld, *Beginning Teacher Knowledge of General Principles of Teaching and Learning: A National*

Survey, Research Report No. 92-60 (Princeton, NJ: Educational Testing Service, 1992).

24. M. Rosenfeld, A. Reynolds, and P. Bukatko, *The Professional Functions of Elementary School Teachers,* Research Report No. 92-53 (Princeton, NJ: Educational Testing Service, 1992).

25. Anne Reynolds, "The Knowledge Base for Beginning Teachers: Education Professionals' Expectations versus Research Findings on Learning to Teach," *Elementary School Journal* 95 (January 1995): 199-221.

26. Ibid., pp. 200-201.

27. National Council for Accreditation of Teacher Education, *NCATE Standards, Procedures, and Policies for the Accreditation of Professional Education Units* (Washington, D.C.: NCATE, 1990), p. 48. Subsequent to the initiation of the study, in 1995 NCATE issued a revised set of standards.

28. National Center for Educational Statistics, *Schools and Staffing Survey, 1990-91* (Washington, D.C.: U.S. Department of Education, 1992), p. 77.

29. Ibid., p. 77.

30. National Center for Educational Statistics, *Digest of Educational Statistics 1994* (Washington, D.C.: U.S. Department of Education, 1994). See also Office of Education Research and Improvement, *America's Teachers: Profile of a Profession* (Washington, D.C.: U.S. Department of Education, 1993).

31. National Center for Educational Statistics, *Schools and Staffing Survey, 1990-91,* p. 77.

CHAPTER 7

1. Frank B. Murray, "Beyond Natural Teaching: The Case For Professional Education," in Frank B. Murray, ed., *The Teacher Educator's Handbook: Building a Knowledge Base for the Preparation of Teachers* (San Francisco: Jossey-Bass, 1996), p.3.

2. Reported in the *San Francisco Chronicle* (July 15, 1986), p. 12; and cited in Pamela L. Grossman, "Learning to Teach without Teacher Education," *Teachers College Record* 91 (Winter 1989): 191.

3. Jack L. Nelson, Stuart B. Palonsky, and Kenneth Carlson, *Critical Issues in Education* (New York: McGraw-Hill, 1990), p. 233.

4. Note the helpful discussion offered by Edmund W. Gordon, "Culture and the Sciences of Pedagogy," *Teachers College Record* 97 (Fall 1995): 32-46; and by Robert Donmoyer, "The Concept of a Knowledge Base," in Murray, pp. 92-119. See also M. C. Reynolds, ed., *Knowledge Base for the Beginning Teacher* (Elmsford, N.Y.: Pergamon Press, 1989).

5. William D. Schaefer, *Education Without Compromise, From Chaos to Coherence in Higher Education* (San Francisco, Cal.: Jossey-Bass, 1990), p. 10.

6. Nelson, Palonksy, and Carlson, pp. 236-237.

7. Schaefer, pp. 19-20.

8.   Richard Arends and Nancy Winitzky, with Arlene Ackerman Burek, "Program Structures and Learning to Teach," in Murray, pp. 531-532.

9.   Ibid., pp. 533-534.

10. B. O. Smith, *A Design for a School of Pedagogy* (Washington, D.C.: U.S. Office of Education, 1980).

11. See Grossman, pp. 191-208; Carol Strawderman and Pamela Lindsey, "Keeping Up with the Times: Reform in Teacher Education," *Journal of Teacher Education* 46 (March-April 1995): 95-100; and Ellen C. Lagemann, "Reinventing the Teacher's Role," *Teachers College Record* 95 (Fall 1993): 1-7.

12. The argument is summarized and adapted from Nelson, Palonsky, and Carlson, pp. 236-240.

13. Ibid., p. 238.

14. Lagemann, p. 1.

15. Nelson, Palonsky, and Carlson, p. 234.

16. Lee S. Shulman, "Those Who Understand: Knowledge Growth in Teaching," *Educational Researcher* 15 (February 1986): 9; and Schulman, "Knowledge and Teaching: Foundations of the New Reform," *Harvard Educational Review* 57 (February 1987): 1-22. Note also the discussion in Kathryn F. Cochran, James A. DeRuiter, and Richard A. King, "Pedagogical Content Knowledge: An Integrative Model for Teacher Preparation," *Journal of Teacher Education* 44 (September-October 1993): 263-272.

17. The point is registered by Nelson, Palonsky, and Carlson, pp. 235-236.

18. Note, for example, the scope of content coverage supplied in Anita E. Woolfolk, *Educational Psychology,* 6th ed. (Needham Heights, Mass.: Allyn and Bacon, 1995); Thomas L. Good and Jere Brophy, *Contemporary Educational Psychology,* 5th ed. (White Plains, N.Y.: Longman, 1995); and Ernest T. Goetz, Patricia A. Alexander, and Michael J. Ash, *Educational Psychology, A Classroom Perspective* (New York: Macmillan, 1992), among many others.

19. See Elden R. Barrett and Susan Davis, "Perceptions of Beginning Teachers' Inservice Needs in Classroom Management," *Teacher Education and Practice* 11 (Spring/Summer 1995): pp. 22-27. Consult also Catherine H. Randolph and Carolyn M. Evertson, "Images of Management for Learner-Centered Classrooms," *Action in Teacher Education* 16 (Spring, 1994): 55-63;

20. Cameron White, "Making Classroom Management Approaches in Teacher Education Relevant," *Teacher Education and Practice* 11 (Spring/Summer 1995): 16. Note the useful discussion in Carol S. Weinstein et al., "Protector or Prison Guard? Using Metaphors and Media to Explore Student Teachers' Thinking about Classroom Management," *Action in Teacher Education* 16 (Spring 1994): 41-54; H. and in James McLaughlin, "From Negation to Negotiation: Moving Away from the Management Metaphor," *Action in Teacher Education* 16 (Spring 1994): 75-84.

21. An example of a useful resource for the curricular portion of this instructional area is George J. Posner and Alan N. Rudnitsky, *Course Design: A Guide to Curriculum Development for Teachers,* 3rd ed. (New York: Longman, 1986). See also Ellen L. Kronowitz, *Beyond Student Teaching* (New York: Longman, 1992).

22. Adapted in part from Council for Exceptional Children, *CEC Standards for Professional Practice* (Reston, Va.: Council for Exceptional Children, 1994), pp. 2-5, 7-13; and from Council for Exceptional Children, *CEC Policy Manual* (Reston, Va.: Council for Exceptional Children, 1993), Section 3, Part 2, pp. 4-7.

23. See Robert Heinich, Michael Molenda, and James D. Russell, *Instructional Media and the New Technologies of Instruction,* 5th ed. (New York: Macmillan, 1996).

INDEX